Praise for *Life is* ⊾

Judith has confidence in her own words ɑ
pages.

—Kelly Hess, author of *Block Myst trilogy.*

Judith has done an outstanding job on these pages. She puts things in perspective with her positive philosophy. The messages are wonderfully written, well thought-out, well organized, comfortably and delightfully inspirational. Among the best I've read.

—Syl Bestwick, author of *In the Shadow of The Bell Tower*

These pages are better than good! If Judy's purpose is to make you think, she has suc-ceeded. If it is to make the reader aware of themselves and how complicated they make life, she has succeeded.

—Alice Fried, author of Outside Child, and *Menopause Sisterhood and Tennis*

Simply wise and well-stated. Up-beat, feels good to read, and makes me think. Wisdom laced with common sense.

—Scotti Butler, author of *Tales From a Life Well Lived*

Judith's writing is beautifully expressed as are her inspiring ideas. Thought-provok-ing, and good old-fashioned advice!

—Carol Morrison, author of *Nellie Estelle*

Judith's words are uplifting, and I wonder how she has reached this place to stay so positive and to help people.

—Joan Coulson, author of *Always for Judy:*
Witness to the Joy and Genius of Judy Garland

I definitely need messages about focusing on the good things in life. Thanks for thought-provoking, interesting messages.

—Lauren Filarsky, author of *In the Misty Moonlight* and *Emma and Starfire*

I love these pages and look forward to more as I read them.

—Laurie Rowlinson-Evans, author of *The Mountain Shadows series*

Excellent! Thought-provoking.

— Lori Jo Dickenson, author of *Passion Poems*

LIFE

IS

SIMPLE

if we let it be

*Daily Inspiration
for Living Simply*

JUDITH JORDAN

indiepen

A Vedere Press Company

Life is Simple: If We Let It Be
Copyright © 2019 by Judith Jordan

Printed in the United States of America

First Printing 2019

ISBN: 978-0-9862113-2-4

INTRODUCTION

So many of us make life so much more difficult than it needs to be. We obsess over things that have gone wrong in the past. We worry about things that might go wrong in the future. We work hard to control every situation that comes along in the present. But all this is wasted energy. When we relax and move into life as it comes, taking the time to make wise choices and think about consequences, life becomes simpler, more peaceful, and more rewarding.

On the following pages you'll find a message for each day of the year that can motivate you to simplify your life and to enjoy the journey. Some of the stories you'll read are from personal experience, and some from experiences of people I know first-hand (although I've changed some names to protect privacy). I've been inspired by things I've read, quotes by wise people, awareness of my surroundings, and even from the comics. And much of it simply comes from deep within my soul.

As you read, I hope you will come to know that as you walk this path of life, you don't walk alone. There is a Higher Power that walks with you as you follow your destiny. Although there are occasional references to spirituality or religion, I have been careful not to advocate for any particular belief. Whether you adhere to a certain faith tradition, or to none, the messages are unspecific enough that there is something in them for just about everybody. And, because you've been led to pick up this book, they are for *you*.

While reading these daily thoughts, you will be the only one getting the meaning they convey for you because you'll be reading through the lens of your own unique perception and guidance.

You will gain comfort from the agreement of what you read, or you will be stimulated by your disagreement, driving you to find your own truth. Either way, you will agree that life doesn't have to be overly complicated. By our own thoughts and actions, life can be more livable if we get out of our own way and let life be simple.

Life *is* simple if we let it be. Sure, stuff happens, but it's not what happens that defines us, it's how we respond to what happens.

This book is a compilation of messages that I hope will inspire you to live in the moment with an open mind and an open heart and to look at the world in a positive light, choosing to see the good in all situations.

We all make some mistakes along the way, but we find we can learn from our mistakes, and from the mistakes of others, and that we can make choices that benefit both ourselves and those around us. Mistakes are our teachers.

If you start your day with this book, you'll carry the positive thoughts with you throughout the day, remembering to live simply. If you choose to read it at the end of your day, you will hold the messages in your mind as you sleep and rest easy knowing you don't have to struggle through the next day.

Thank you for picking up this book, I sincerely hope it serves to make your life simpler.

Judith Jordan

This book covers one calendar year, but you can start it on any day.
Then, at the end of the year, you can go back and start it again.
The messages will have a different meaning for you
each time you read them because you will be
in a different place in consciousness.

NEW LIGHT

People find many ways to usher in a new year. Some like to imbibe a little too much at a New Year's Eve party, then begin the new year regretting it. Others have a ritual, like dinner at a favorite restaurant, then dancing into the wee hours of the new year. Many enjoy seeing the ball drop at Times Square in New York City. Still others like to set off fireworks to make sure their neighbors are awake at midnight. There are countless inventive ways to celebrate, but none of them can top what the director of the museum in my home town, along with her daughter, did to ring out the old and bring in the new.

Both women are avid hikers and are no strangers to the High Sierra grandeur and its challenging trails. Early in the day on New Year's Eve, this duo set out to reach an overlook cliff on El Capitan in Yosemite National Park. They hiked several miles up the mountain to reach their destination, got to the overlook about an hour before sunset, made camp, then waited for the sun to go down. With an unobstructed view, they watched the last light of the passing year fade away. In the morning, they threw off their sleeping bags, and turned around to see the first light of the new year rising in the east.

They came down from the mountain on New Year's Day, reeling from a perspective that's infinitely better than watching any ball drop or suffering from a hangover. Their experience alone, was a celebration, and inspired me to poetry:

It was cold and clear on that New Year's Eve,
Where we'd climbed with all our stuff.
High above the valley floor,
We sat upon the bluff.

The sun went down with fiery light.
The last sunset of the year.
Then we snuggled warmly in our bags,
Holding that sight dear.

Stirring early at first light,
Here came the rising sun.
We saw what we had come to see;
A new year had begun.

RESOLUTIONS

If you don't make New Year's resolutions because you pretty much know you won't keep them, try to make daily, or even hourly resolutions or goals. Things change throughout every day, and if you've established a set goal for the day, something unexpected may enter your life to alter the plans you've made.

One day, as I was getting ready to wash my car, a good friend came by on his way to the marina to check out boats for sale and asked if I wanted to ride along. I did want to, and there went my resolve to wash the car. I had a great day in the sun, by the water!

Although we can't be so irresponsible that we leave critical things undone, life can be more fun if we're open to spontaneity. There's no need to feel rushed to accomplish every little thing we think we *have* to do. There's time enough to get it all done. I've taken on projects that are very time consuming and left other things—like laundry and dirty dishes—undone until my project was finished, or at a good stopping place. The laundry and dishes were still there waiting for me when I could happily turn my full attention to them without feeling rushed.

I've learned that time is illusion—we made it up. Without time as a constraint, we get to choose to be happy doing what we *want* to do rather than feeling pressured about what we *should* be doing because we've made some mighty resolution. Only *you* can make *you* happy, and God's will for all of us is perfect happiness

Making hard fast New Year's resolutions implies there is imperfection in our life, so here's an idea . . . instead of resolving to go to the gym three times a week, eat more nutritiously, clean out the garage, or whatever we feel we need to do better than we've been doing, we can resolve to celebrate the ways in which we are *magnificent*. We can still go to the gym, eat well, or clean the garage, but we can simply do these things because we want to get healthier or put the car into shelter, not because we've *resolved* to do them. We can do them on our own time schedule without feeling guilty about breaking a resolution.

You may have different priorities than the gym, food, or garage—you can fill in the blanks for yourself. You won't be doing these things out of obligation because you've made that resolution, though, you'll be doing them because it will make you *feel* better about yourself. We can all live the message of that old song, *Don't Worry, Be Happy.*

IT'S THE PEOPLE

The New Year isn't just about resolutions. It might be a time to take stock of what's going on in our life, what's working and what isn't.

Take a look at your work situation. Do you love your job? Are you getting the promotions you deserve? Is your salary enough to allow you to live comfortably? If your answer to any of these questions is *No* then you might be thinking about making a change. If so, you'll need to update your résumé. The beginning of every New Year is a good time to update your résumé, so you're always résumé-ready. Doing this update doesn't mean you have to change jobs, but keeping up on your capabilities and talents can help you know where you want to be professionally.

You can start by focusing on the good stuff. What have you accomplished? What are you most proud of? Now, use this in your updated résumé. When that's done, focus on some specific goals for the New Year—small goals and big ones. A small goal might be that you want to get some additional experience or learn a new skill, and that could mean picking up new projects in your current position. A big goal might be, "I want to get away from this place and do something different." That's when we develop an action plan.

The number one focus now will be on people, because people hire people. The more people we can connect with about the goal we've determined, the better the chance of actually accomplishing that goal. To turn our goals into action, we need to remember, it's all about people. In this age of internet "send me your résumé" job searches, connecting with the people who can help us get what we want is becoming more complicated. But don't be dismayed. When we've identified what companies could use someone with our skills, we can use the internet to find names of those who do the hiring. When we've done that, we can call to make appointments with those specific people. If the watchdogs on the phone aren't accommodating, we can go to the place of business and ask to see that person. Turning someone away in person is harder than not taking their phone call.

It's a people game. The more people you can actually connect with, the more likely you are to be successful in your search. And you may actually find yourself having to decide which great job to take. If you're looking for a new job, remember, *it's the people!* (And, don't quit your present job until you've found a new one.)

JUST FOR TODAY

In the early 1900's, Frank Crane was a writer for the Boston Globe. His column *Dr. Crane Says* carried some positive messages. I was inspired by the ten ways he listed to improve one's life . . . Just for a Day.

1. Just for Today, I will try to live through this day only, and not tackle all life's problems at once. I can do some things for twelve hours that would appall me if I felt I had to keep them up for a lifetime.
2. Just for Today, I will be happy. What Abe Lincoln said is true, "Most folks are about as happy as they make up their minds to be." Happiness comes from within, it's not a matter of externals.
3. Just for Today, I will adjust myself to what is, and not try to adjust everything to my own desires. I will not try to regulate, change, or improve anyone but myself.
4. Just for Today, I will take care of my body. I will exercise it, care for it, and nourish it. I will not abuse it nor neglect it, so that it will be a perfect machine for my will.
5. Just for Today, I will improve my mind. I will learn something useful. I will read something that requires effort, thought, and concentration.
6. Just for Today, I will do somebody a good turn and not get found out. If anybody knows about it, it won't count.
7. Just for Today, I will do two things I don't want to do, just for exercise.
8. Just for Today, I will be agreeable. I will talk in a well-modulated voice, be courteous and considerate. I will be liberal with flattery and criticize not one bit, nor find fault with anything.
9. Just for Today, I will have a quiet half-hour all by myself, and relax. During this time, I will think of God so as to get a little more perspective to my life.
10. Just for Today, I will be unafraid to enjoy what is beautiful, and believe that what I give to the world, the world gives to me.

Truly, words to live by. Let's see if we can make this new year a little better by remembering Frank Crane's words, and living them today, tomorrow, and all the days to come.

COUNT TO TEN

When you were a kid, and you were angry about something, your mother probably told you to settle down and count to ten. I know mine did. When my sister wouldn't let me have the thing she was playing with, or I didn't get to watch the TV program I wanted to, or was upset or disappointed over myriad other maddening things that came up in my life, I would get angry and lash out at the offending party. But as I got older, I learned to stop my angry tirade and slowly count to ten (Mother's advice). I found that if I took a good look at whatever was upsetting or disappointing me, it usually didn't seem so important, and I felt better when I cooled off. In a calmer state, I could then try negotiating for what I wanted. Sometimes the negotiation worked, sometimes it didn't, but I learned that anger definitely didn't get me what I wanted. This lesson has served me well throughout my life, only now I just stop and take three deep breaths to calm myself instead of actually counting to ten.

It's been said, "The greatest remedy for anger is delay." But we've also heard, "Strike while the iron is hot." I think we're talking about two different things here. Yes, if there is immediate action to be taken in a circumstance, to correct an error or to save a situation, we do need to act. But if the situation induces anger in us, we're better off delaying action until we are certain the action is appropriate and coming from a place of reason and not from knee-jerk reaction.

We are never upset for the reason we think. There is usually an underlying cause for our negative emotions, a reason that has nothing to do with what we are demonstrating anger about. Delaying action gives us a chance to really look at why we're angry or upset, and in so doing we can respond to the situation at hand in a peaceful manner, not exacerbating the situation unnecessarily.

A Course in Miracles tells us that any action not coming from a place of love is a *call for love*. Very often the person who makes us angry is in an emotional position he doesn't quite know how to deal with so, to make himself feel better, he lashes out at us. But we don't have to buy into the fight. We can stop the aggression by delaying our response—by hearing our Mother's voice telling us to count to ten.

INTENTION

Ask yourself this: "What is my intention?" Intention can be a desire to do good and be helpful, or it can be misguided, used to boost egos or even to cause harm. If we're helping out at a local church or agency that provides meals for the disadvantaged community, and we're doing it from a place of love and it warms our hearts to see these people getting at least one good hot meal a week, then we are living from good intention. But if we're doing it to appear virtuous in the eyes of others or because we want to be seen as a really nice guy, that might be misguided intention.

Our good is not measured by the busy lifestyle we lead or by how great we tell people we are or how much money we have or what kind of car we drive. Our good is measured by what's in our hearts. The great truth is that if we don't live from our hearts, we don't live at all. And we can tell when we're living from our hearts by asking ourselves this simple question: "What is my intention?" If our heart is open, and our intention is to serve, to love, and to benefit all involved, then we know our intention is well placed. We will feel a peace, and we will know we're making good decisions and taking right action.

Intention without action, though, doesn't work. If we tell someone we'll do something with or for them, we've announced our intention. But if we don't follow through on our promise, our true intention must have been to fail them and let them down.

A woman I worked with a long time ago had such a need to be looked upon favorably by her clients that she would make mistakes on purpose, or withhold information on purpose, then come back later, after they had been perplexed by the problem, correct the mistakes and provide good information so she looked like the hero. Her clients saw her as a problem solver, not realizing that she had actually caused the problem. Her intention was simply to make them think she was helpful and on top of things. This was clearly misguided intention.

If we can remember every day, in every situation, to take a look at our intention, to know that our goal is to foster love, help, or care, we'll know that we're living from right intention.

YOU ARE ENOUGH

When was the last time you cooked a gourmet meal just for yourself? When was the last time you took yourself, all alone, to a movie, a concert, a play, or out to dinner? When was the last time you bought flowers for yourself? You might be scratching your head, thinking, "Why would I waste all that effort and money just for myself?" Now ask yourself, "Who is the most important person in my life; who will always be with me, no matter what?" The answer to this last question is, of course, you! You are the only person who is always, and will always be, with you. And, you are enough.

I had a friend who decorated her home for Christmas every year, but she never turned on the tree lights unless someone was coming over because she felt it would be wasting electricity. It's as though she didn't think she was worthy of the beauty of the lights for herself. Although I am an energy saver—I turn off lights when I leave a room and put on a sweater rather than turning up the heat—I do turn on my Christmas tree lights, just for me. I also bring flowers into my home because I love to see them and because I deserve the beauty for myself, even if I'm not sharing it with someone else.

Sharing experiences is a wonderful thing but pleasing ourselves is equally wonderful. Somehow, we feel it's our duty to take care of someone, and what more deserving someone is there than yourself?

Too many people believe they need some kind of reason to experience goodness and joy, but the truth is that life itself is reason enough to celebrate. We have the power to create the life we want. If we want to take a walk in nature, we can do that. If we want to buy new towels, we can do that. If we want to cook a great dinner, or write a book, or plant a garden, we can do that. Making ourselves happy is reason enough to have a beautiful experience. And when we're happy, it follows that those around us are also happy. Happy is contagious.

Our reality is of our own making. What we believe about something is what it will be for us. If we believe that we need more people, money, or things to make us happy we will keep waiting to be happy until we can have all that. But if we believe we can be happy just because we want to be happy, we can find happiness in the small moments and allow these moments to grow.

I will continue to turn on my Christmas tree lights and bring flowers into my home, just for me. I will continue to choose happiness because I'm worth it. And so are you.

LEMONADE

Have you ever had what you considered a really bad experience then discovered that it had set you up for really good experiences? Consider the story of Joseph in the Bible. His brothers were so jealous of their father's attention to him that they threw him into a pit, leaving him to die. But when travelers found Joseph and took him to Egypt, he was elevated to a high position. When a famine came to Joseph's homeland, his brothers went to Egypt to ask for food and were sent to see the brother they thought had died. They begged Joseph for forgiveness but he said forgiveness was not necessary, that what they had done with evil intent, God had intended for good.

When life hands us challenges we think we can't handle, instead of thinking, "How will I ever get through this?" we can ask, "How can I use this experience for good?" When I left my emotionally abusive husband, with a very low opinion of myself, a complete lack of self-worth, and no job, I couldn't just curl up and feel sorry for myself, I had three small children to provide for. Through the pain and confusion of the situation, I had to pull up on my boot straps and keep going. My first action was to find a job which, to my surprise, I did very quickly. Since my self-esteem had been so damaged, I was quite frankly stunned when I was hired immediately, at my first interview, for a really fun job with L.A. Airways, a helicopter commuter service. I was able to support my family and had the opportunity to do some travelling (for free) through the company's contacts with the major airlines. I am actually grateful to my ex-husband, because if I'd stayed in the marriage that was holding me back, I surely wouldn't have discovered my own worth and ability, nor would I have grown into the confident person I am today.

I'm not saying that I've never had any more bad experiences, but I've learned that bad doesn't have to mean forever. And even good doesn't mean forever either. Life is full of ups and downs. I know now, though, that when I have challenges and things look bleak, I can keep my chin up, knowing that everything I experience in life sets me up for new and better life experiences.

We aren't victims of a cruel world. We are victors in our own world. As we grow in strength and in spirit, we can make something good out of just about anything that comes our way. We can make lemonade out of the lemons that drop into our lives.

SUPPORT YOUR VISION

Inspired by the book *Shoeless Joe,* Phil Robinson began writing the script for the movie *Field of Dreams.* He brought the idea to 20th Century Fox and the concept was dismissed as being too esoteric and noncommercial. Robinson was not deterred, however, and continued writing. He later submitted the script to Universal Studios where it was met with interest and accepted for production. The movie went on to be one of the top money-making films of the era.

Jonathan Livingston Seagull was rejected by several publishers before coming to the attention of Eleanor Friede at Macmillan, who convinced the company to buy it, and paid Richard Bach a $2,000 advance. Within two years of publication, over a million copies were in print and the book had reached number one on the New York Times Best Sellers list. A year later, it was at the top of Publishers Weekly's best-selling books in the U.S. and is now listed as one of Fifty Timeless Spiritual Classics. Richard Bach kept writing!

The script for *Forrest Gump* was pitched for nine years before Paramount finally accepted it. During shooting, the studio found they were going way over budget and wanted to cut out important scenes. Tom Hanks and two others were told that if they wanted these scenes in the movie, they would have to invest two million of their own dollars. They agreed, the movie was completed with all the scenes and became the third highest-grossing film of all time. Tom Hanks ultimately made a multi-million dollar return on his investment.

These stories confirm that when someone is committed to a project, believe in themselves, put their whole heart and soul into it, and stay true to their vision, they can be successful. And so can we! Our project doesn't have to be as grand as making a movie or writing best-selling book, it can simply be raising a family, pursuing a hobby, learning a new language, or travelling to places we've longed to see.

If we give one-hundred percent, hold to our dreams, keep going, don't settle for less that we deserve, and never forget our own value and our own worth, our vision *can* become a reality. When we live what we believe, and refuse to settle, we will be richly rewarded.

Remember, though, rewards don't always have to be monetary. The feeling of accomplishment and peace of mind might be the greatest reward any of us can receive.

WINTER WONDERLAND

Sometimes cold winter days leave us feeling blue, cabin fever sets in, and we long for the great outdoors. If you live in a snowy climate, it's probably necessary that you get outside to shovel sidewalks and driveways or to dig your car out of the snow, and you might not look forward to these outings. Another, more pleasant, outing could be to bundle up in your warmest clothes and go out for a walk. If you're just doing chores, you might be missing something, but if you get out, just to get out, you can look around and appreciate the beauty of nature; the snow resting on branches of trees, the beauty reflected in icicles dripping from eaves, the critters romping in the soft snow. Even when you do go out to clear walkways, instead of grumbling about the work, look around, take in the beauty; it will lift your spirits.

I lived in northern British Columbia for a few years and when I went out to split wood for the fire or go to the outhouse (yes, there was an outhouse!), I was always amazed at the winter wonderland surrounding me. I breathed the cold air into my lungs and felt invigorated. I sometimes followed deer tracks in the snow, hoping to catch a glimpse of a lovely doe or a beautifully-antlered buck.

I live in California now, and have to drive several hours to find snow, but I still get out on cold mornings, my breath coming out in puffs of white, to walk in nature. Nature is the great equalizer. It can restore balance to your life. And the best part is—it's always there! Even if you live in the cement jungle of a big city, there is usually a park nearby in which to walk, jog, bike, or simply sit and relax. And there's ever-changing beauty all around, so each outing is a little different from the last.

We are always open to choose an aspect of nature that feeds our soul. It doesn't have to be big or far away. It can be as simple as a garden in our own back yard or tending to potted plants on our patio. If we get outside, even small doses of nature can restore a sense of wonder at this beautiful planet we inhabit.

Cabin fever is not a necessary part of winter. We don't have to stay cooped up inside waiting for spring. Whenever we can, wherever we are, we can get out in nature. Nature will heal the blues and will renew our soul. Nature and natural beauty are God's gifts to us. Let's make sure we make the most of what's been given us to enjoy.

SIZZLE WITH ZEAL

I recently had a conversation with an acquaintance whose subject matter held little or no interest for me, but he was so enthusiastic about what he was talking about, it piqued my interest. I found myself asking questions, and by the end of our conversation, I felt I had been exposed to something intriguing. Even though what this fellow had to say was a far cry from anything I thought I'd ever care about, his passion for the subject was so great that I became absorbed with the subject matter. I listened, paid attention, actually learned something, and found myself relaying the information to a friend later on. That's how contagious enthusiasm can be.

I worked, for a time, selling advertising for a small publication. I was so enthusiastic about what I was doing that many of my customers asked if I owned the business. They couldn't understand how someone could have such passion for their job unless they stood to benefit on an ownership level. The truth is, I was just doing what I was there to do to the best of my ability, and I was having fun doing it. This is a good example of the fact that it's not the words we impart that hold the meaning, it's the energy with which the words are conveyed that carries the most meaning. When our passion comes through, others are inspired.

You could try a little experiment, if you'd like. Take note of those people you come in contact with throughout the day and pay attention to the passion and enthusiasm they are exuding. Also notice those who don't appear to radiate excitement. I think you'll find yourself gravitating toward the people who are the most enthusiastic. It just feels better to be around others from whom you feel intensity and excitement than those who just kind of ho-hum through their day, not really feeling passionate about anything. Then give attention to how much passion *you* are showing and see if you can inspire others with your enthusiasm.

Charles Fillmore, co-founder of the Unity Church, remained so hooked on life that he is quoted, in his 94th year, as saying, "I fairly sizzle with zeal and enthusiasm." One of the things that I've been saying for as long as I can remember is, "If I can't have fun doing something, I just don't do it." I will continue to engage in life, and to let my enthusiasm spring forth, and you can do the same.

CELL PHONE MANIA

People these days appear to be missing out on some interesting aspects of life as they get lost in their cell phones. We see people walking together, each talking on the phone or texting. They may be communicating, but it's probably not with the person alongside them. Too often we see people together at a restaurant, lost in their cell phones, texting or checking email or whatever it is that is holding their attention. Why is their interest not in the person sitting across the table? Why, when a text comes through, do people suddenly ignore the people they're with to whip out their phones? I don't mean to be knocking the use of cell phones, our lives have, in many ways, become easier by having them. Actually, I don't know why they are even called *phones* anymore, they're used for so much more. Maybe they should be called communication devices. But it seems to me that when we are preoccupied with our device, we are missing out on important person-to-person connections. I, for one, like to see the expressions on my friends' faces when I tell them some great news or relate an interesting story. I like to feel a joining with the people I'm with, to share experiences, and talk about those experiences face-to-face.

I can't help wondering if one day, communication devices will take the place of human interaction. I wonder if the down-turned head is going to become the new shape of the human body. I wonder if future generations will have longer thumbs in order to text more easily. Silly thoughts, I know, but I also wonder if we have become a generation of escapists. Are we hiding behind our phones so that we don't have to face people and situations we don't want to deal with? It's as though people are so tied to their devices that they miss out on what's actually going on around them.

And being totally absorbed in our devices can also be a danger. Almost every day I see someone narrowly escape being hit by a car, or physically walking into another person, or a tree, while texting. And what about traffic accidents caused by people talking or texting while driving?

Just for today, let's try using our communication devices for the good they were meant, and putting them away when we have the opportunity to interact on a personal level. Let's try looking people in the eye when we talk with them and appreciate who they are and what they have to offer. Let's see how that feels.

BETWEEN SUCCESSES

People tend to measure their lives by successes and failures. If we have a goal, or even a desire, for our life to look a certain way, and it does, we call that success. If our life doesn't measure up to those goals or desires, we might call that failure. But nothing is ever totally a failure, nor, sadly, is everything ever successful in every way. It's been said that the only time we fail is the last time we try. When we give up and believe we *can't* is when we feel we've failed. I've stopped using the word *can't*, because I believe I *can*.

Failure can be a positive thing. It keeps us on our toes. We don't need to throw in the towel as soon as the waters get choppy, nor do we need to keep striving to make something work when it's clearly not working. If everything were perfect, we might be so complacent that we miss out on opportunities for learning and personal growth. What we've named *failure* is simply a learning process. We are constantly learning what works and what doesn't work. When we're open to these lessons, what so many of us see as failure is just a temporary set-back, and we can look deep inside ourselves for the strength to move on to our next success. It doesn't even have to be a huge success. Friendships are some of life's greatest successes.

Sir Winston Churchill defined success as "The ability to go from one failure to another with no loss of enthusiasm." I've had many successes in my life, and I've had some failures. I've chosen not to wallow in the failures or to lament that it's just my lot in life. I've had relationships that ended (not failed) because one of us simply outgrew the other or the hard work of trying to make it work didn't work. It hurt sometimes, and there were tears, but through it all, I never forgot that God's will for me is perfect happiness, and I choose to let God's will be done. I've owned businesses that fed me both emotionally and monetarily that have ended (not failed) either by my choice to sell or close the business. I've also been out of work for periods of time. I've said of those times that I am *between successes*, because new successes always come.

Failure isn't permanent, it's a stepping stone to success. If you can keep an open mind and an open heart, and don't stop when you're behind, the next stone you step on can be the gateway to a new success.

DON'T LIVE TO LABELS

Everything in life seems to have a label. We label some things as good, and we label other things as bad. But the labels that affect our life the most are the labels we put on our self, on what we believe about our self. These labels are what create our *self-perception*. Unfortunately, sometimes that perception is negative. We have an on-going inner dialogue, and if we can change the labels we give ourselves we can change that dialogue. We can learn to see ourselves in a different, more positive way.

There is a term in psychology called *Iatrogenic Labeling*, which is beneficially motivated but can have destructive effects. The label can create more damage than what that label describes. For example, if parents see their child as a slow learner and this information is relayed to his teacher, thinking it will help the teacher understand him better, the teacher might expect to see the child falling behind and may treat him differently, thereby labeling the child "slow." As a result, the child might not be exposed to the learning opportunities that would challenge him to work to his full potential. The parents felt this information would protect the child, but the ultimate result was damaging.

Whatever label we put on ourselves—and, trust me, we all give ourselves labels—is what we believe about ourselves, and it's what we become because, of course, we want to be right! A person who refers to a chronic ailment as "my" ailment has taken ownership of it, identifies with it, and it becomes a part of who he is. If someone else with that same ailment considers it simply something he lives with and doesn't identify it as a part of him, it doesn't become a label. We've all known people with severe disabilities who are happy, outgoing, and able to accomplish what they need to do. That's because they haven't labeled themselves as disabled. They have simply adjusted and haven't accepted the label a warped society might put on them.

Don't live to any self-defeating labels. Step into life believing you are the best you can be, and don't accept anything less. If labels have held you back, change any negative inner dialog to a self-perception that is true to what you really are—a beautiful child of God. You can then wear a label of self-love, and you'll see how much better you'll feel, not only about yourself, but about everyone and everything around you.

HO'OPONOPONO

Are you in a situation that you feel you cannot change or correct and you'd like to overcome that feeling? If so, read on. Doctor Ihaleakala Hew Len, a psychologist who is best known for his use of the ancient Hawaiian healing technique *ho'oponopono*, was assigned to a ward for the criminally insane in a mental hospital, where he quickly learned that what was being done for these patients clearly was not working. And he knew what he had to do. Dr. Hew Len sat in his office every day, and without actually meeting with the patients, brought each one to mind individually, and invoked the practice of *ho'oponopono*. The energy of his belief in his words was felt by the patients, and over time, violence in the ward decreased, patients improved markedly, and the ward was ultimately shut down.

Just as it works for Dr. Hew Len, *ho'oponopono* can work in our own life, for our own benefit. It's a simple but profound tool that will open our hearts to positive feelings of love and gratitude. The word means, "Restoring balance and harmony," or "To make (ho'o) right (pono) right (pono)." It is performed by meditating on the words, *I'm sorry. Please forgive me. I love you. Thank you.* and can significantly change situations by shifting our thoughts about them. One of the principles of *ho'oponopono* is to accept full responsibility for the world we see as a creation of our own thoughts and beliefs. The world we see is an illusion and when we can get past any negativity in the illusion, we can keep our minds positive and peaceful. We can use the practice of *ho'oponopono* to reduce stress, heal relationships, and to forgive.

Ho'oponopono can be used during the tough times when someone has upset or hurt us. Teachers of the practice call this "cleaning." We can clean our self of our own negative feelings and permanently erase from our memory or consciousness any negativity that is keeping us from peace. By sending love and forgiveness to the person who hurt or upset us, we will also be gaining forgiveness for our self. Through this practice, we can learn to face situations without anger or stress.

Saying, *I'm sorry. Please forgive me.* allows our heart to open to forgiveness of self and others. *I love you.* can mean love for our self or another. *Thank you.* expresses gratitude for the relief that comes from the positive practice of *ho'oponopono*.

FIND YOUR PASSION

Every once in a while, we encounter someone who inspires us. I met someone like that recently. A group of my yoga students took me to lunch and when the waitress asked if this was some sort of celebration, they said they were celebrating their yoga teacher, to which she replied, "I just love yoga." She seemed inspired by this table-full of people who were all practicing yoga.

As we talked, I was equally inspired by *her* story. Her children were grown, and she had been feeling a void in her life. One day her mother asked, "What is your passion?" Still feeling undecided, she spent a day at the beach where a number of young children were building a sandcastle. She watched them for awhile, was led to join them, and in playing with those children, felt a moment of clarity. She knew then that working with young children, teaching them, inspiring them, and helping to form their lives, was what made her heart sing. She'd found her passion! She decided then and there what her future would look like, enrolled in classes in early childhood development, took the necessary steps to obtain a license, and was, at the time we met, waitressing while in the process of opening a pre-school. She is now happily feeding her passion and, in so doing, providing an important service for the families in her community.

One of my good friends spent more than 25 years working at a job she didn't enjoy but stayed with for the retirement benefits the company offered. During an economic downturn, with company downsizing, she was let go. She was devastated but began looking for work she had a passion for rather than working for some future benefits. She is a very friendly, always up-beat person who genuinely loves people, and now works at a big-box store serving samples of the good food they offer. She is so popular that people return to the store just to interact with her. And because she's so passionate about what she's doing, the business also benefits.

We can learn from these stories. If you're feeling a void in your life and aren't fulfilled, look deep within yourself and ask, what is my passion? Then follow that passion! When we're passionate about what we're doing, not only is our life simpler and more pleasant, we're also helping others. Passion is contagious. It reaches out and touches the world in ways even beyond our own awareness.

SAY AH!

We've all had doctors tell us to open our mouth wide and say "Ah." We also say *ahhh* as a sigh of relief when we come into the warmth after being out in the cold, or cooling off on a hot day. Coming home after a hard day's work, we may fall into our favorite chair and breathe *ahhh*, feeling a deep relaxation. And after enjoying a good meal, *ahhh* is that good feeling of satisfaction.

Ah can also be associated with spiritual inspiration. It's the sound in the names of many spiritual masters, chants, songs, and uplifting words: G*a*d, Y*a*hweh, Buddh*a*, Jehov*a*h, Krishn*a*, Moh*a*mmed, Sh*a*lom, *Au*m, H*a*llelu-j*a*h, *A*men, *A*loha, N*a*masté, and even in what we may call our loving parents, M*a*ma and P*a*pa.

Ah is also used to indicate a trigger in our minds, as in, "*Ah*, yes, now I remember." Other times we are moved to say *ah* is when we see a litter of kittens or puppies "*Ahhh*, aren't they adorable." Or when we wake up in the morning and say *ahhh* with a good stretch

I have 18 grandchildren and great-grandchildren, and love to have them visit, but sometimes their energy and exuberance is so high that when they leave, I breathe an *ahhh,* which is really a mixture of relief and feelings of such deep love for them it brings me to tears.

Sometimes the real reason for saying *ahhh*, is more mechanical. When we drink a glass of water, we tend to take a deep breath before drinking then hold that breath as we drink, releasing an *ahhh* sound as we exhale when we finish. And when lowering ourselves into a bath that may be a little too hot, the anticipation of the heat causes us to hold our breath, and when that anticipation is over, we react with a nice, soothing *ahhh*.

These mechanics may be true, but I prefer to think of *ahhh* sounds as emotional. I find it feels good to express pleasure, comfort, relief, release, adoration, amazement, joy, surprise, and other gratifying feelings with the sound of *ahhh*. If we allow ourselves to get caught up in the perceived complexities of life, we forget to be open to the simple good that surrounds us. When we can appreciate that goodness, we find our moments of *ahhh* come more frequently. Say *Ahhh!*

HOW MANY BOOKS?

I'm looking at my bookshelves. They take up a whole wall and are filled with books. There are books of fiction, I can see about eight different Bibles, and there is shelf after shelf of books on different religious traditions, spirituality, psychology, positive thinking, and how to better your life. There are books written by people whose lives have been altered by prayer, meditation, and inspiration from revered spiritual teachers. I've read many of these books, but there are others I haven't gotten around to yet. There are also shelves of children's books that my great-grandchildren love to read and that I love reading to them.

I remember my mother being an avid reader as I was growing up. She mostly read magazines. She liked the recipes, the decorating tips, and the stories about real people, but she liked the fictional short stories the best. In fact, she tried her hand at writing and submitting stories to these magazines, and a few were even published.

I don't remember seeing a lot of books in our house, but one book I do remember is the one that caught my eye just now, on my own bookshelf. It belonged to my mother, and she read it a lot. The title of the book is *Keys to Happiness*. I took the book down from the shelf and thumbed through it. My family wasn't religious, we never went to church, but my mother had a spirituality that even she couldn't have named, and that I came to realize only as I cared for her in her final years, and even after her death.

Keys to Happiness is a compilation of uplifting articles taken from Reader's Digest, which was one of her favorite magazines. The articles are by and about regular every-day people with titles like: *There is Magic in a Word of Praise, Journey Beyond Fear, Don't Sell Yourself Short,* and *I'd Pick More Daisies.* There is so much wisdom in this little book, and I believe my mother thoroughly digested that wisdom as she read. The book is old, its pages are dog-eared, and some have even come loose from the binding. This was my first clue that she used it a lot and took the messages to heart.

If I were to count the self-help and spiritual books on my shelves, the number would be staggering, and I'm still trying to figure life out. My mother had one book, she lived life from the knowledge that book imparted to her, and she lived a long, full, peaceful, and simple life full of love.

BROTHERHOOD

Do you know someone whose life, actions, and attitudes are so different from yours that it makes you wonder how they live with themselves? You may be, like me, on a spiritual path that leads you to spiritually based books, to attend seminars and retreats, to study the Bible and other religious or spiritual texts, and to find the positive aspects of situations, other people, and your own life. The person you find different may be someone whose negative attitude leads them to be defensive, to find fault with everyone and everything, to complain bitterly, and to feel like they are a victim of this world. And this person most likely doesn't understand why you are like you are.

Just as you and I are receiving a payoff for the work we're doing, they, too, are getting a payoff that they enjoy. They have probably found others who think like they do, and together they can complain about the world and everything in it. It's like a negative brotherhood, and unfortunately, there are too many of these brotherhoods in our world. But, happily, there are just as many positive, up-beat brotherhoods.

We are all on a complicated journey through life. We are all evolving. We do this in our own way, at our own pace, and we need to let those who think, feel, and act different from us make the journey in their own way. They need to master their life just as we need to master ours. Our paths to mastery are just different.

We may think that if we try hard enough, our positive attitudes will help change these negatively inclined people, but in most cases, it won't. In fact, their negativity is more likely to rub off on us, and their defensiveness can cause us to also be defensive. We have no control over what another person does or thinks, or how they act. The only person we can control is ourself. If we can stay on our path, mastering our life lessons from where we are, allowing others to master theirs from where they are, we can be true to our own beliefs. We can all grow at our own rate and in our own time. We can love and bless this "different" person. Just as we pay attention to, and stay in touch with, what brings *us* joy, they will figure out their own next step.

We're all here to learn, to grow, and to remember who we really are—perfect children of God. Some people have forgotten this, but left alone to find their way, the truth will eventually dawn on them, and they will find the joy that we feel on our chosen path.

THE HOKEY POKEY

On the wall over my computer I have a quote. There are actually dozens of quotes on the wall over my computer, but the one I'm thinking about says *What if the Hokey Pokey IS what it's all about?*

What if nothing in life is any more important, pressing, or worrisome than a silly song and dance? What if we can laugh in the face of adversity? I think we can. We really don't have to allow ourselves to become upset over anything. If we put too much importance on our troubles, it can tear us apart emotionally. This is not to say we should never show emotion. Emotion is a good thing, it allows us to express what we're feeling: When we're sad, we can cry. If something frightens us, we can scream. If someone lets us down, we can feel disappointment. But, holding on to negative emotions for too long can hurt us physically as well as spiritually. Sometimes we read too much into perceived problems or certain circumstances. And much of the time, it's because we don't understand why things happen the way they do. When people leave us or mistreat us, it's usually because they are living their life script, and perhaps the hurt we feel is part of our script. We need to remember that there is some good in every situation. We can do what we can to right a wrong, or we can accept what is and move on.

How well do you remember the girl who turned down your invitation to the prom in high school? How well do you remember the shoes you really wanted when you were young, that your parents said weren't practical? Do you remember how devastated you were? Those things may have felt insurmountable at the time, but you got over them a long time ago. Troubles have a way of sinking into the background if you let them, and bad things have a way of working themselves out.

When we feel like our life is broken, we might do well to remember the Hokey Pokey and take a few minutes to put our right foot in, put our right foot out, put our right foot in and shake it all about, followed by our left foot, our right hand, our left hand, and any other body part we choose. As we shake it all about, we'll be symbolically shaking off what it is that's bothering us. When we turn our self around, we'll be turning away from our troubles, leaving them behind. Maybe there *is* more truth to the Hokey Pokey being what it's all about than we realize.

LIFE'S ROLLERCOASTER

Rare is the person whose road of life doesn't have any bumps, a person who has or gets everything they want or need, and who doesn't endure major setbacks. I knew someone who, for a long time, I believed to be that rare person. She was spoiled as a child, never denied anything she wanted, was always first to have the latest fashion trend, got a new car for graduation, and after marrying, was pampered by her husband. I liked this person, she was a good friend, but needless to say, I was a bit envious. As we travelled through life, however, her road began to have some little bumps. She missed job opportunities, her marriage ended in divorce, and because she was so used to having things go her way, she was ill-equipped to maneuver over and past these bumps. In her state of confusion, she became angry, depressed and lost confidence. I lost contact with this friend several years ago, but not before I learned that the bumps in my own life were making me stronger, and that her formerly perfect life was not so enviable after all. Life's bumps are our teachers, and we are learning life lessons all the time.

Happiness is a choice, and *perfect* doesn't necessarily make life any happier. The bumps in our road, our ups and downs, are all blessings. What we think might be a life-long disappointment or condition, can actually make us stronger. When there are bumps on our journey, we can play with them. We can think of them as the rollercoaster of life. We go up, up, up, then suddenly drop, then we go up, up, up again and the next big drop doesn't scare us as much because we know we will be going up again, that the ride will finally even out, and we will have enjoyed the whole experience.

No one has a life that is perfect in every way, and whatever we don't let stop us will make us stronger. We don't need to envy the person we think has everything going for them, because they don't. And the more bumps in our road, the more well-rounded our own life will be. Bumps have a funny way of turning into stepping stones.

MY MOTHER

My mother spent her life helping others and making lives better. She was generous with her time, her love, and her service. Her family was the bright light in her existence, and it was hard for her to leave this life. She felt we still needed her to take care of us. She finally let go in her ninety-second year. Today is my mother's birthday.

My mother was a strong woman. Strong in body, in mind, and in determination. She was the driving force behind everything she did. In organizations, she was the leader or the president. In family matters, she was the organizer. People *relied* on her leadership. As her spirit lives on, she is likely still organizing and leading, and maybe God is letting her manage some things in Heaven.

My mother spent her lifetime in community service. She never thought of this work as charity, she simply made things happen to help and bring joy to others. She was a catalyst in shaping new programs to benefit children through PTA work, serving on boards from elementary school through national levels, and was awarded an honorary college degree in recognition of her work for the schools. She worked with service clubs, spearheading fund-raising events for charities. Even in her last years, she sewed lap-robes for hospital patients.

My mother had some idiosyncrasies. I called them "analities" because she was anal about many details. She set the table perfectly for *every* meal, with knives, forks, and spoons, all in their correct places, with plates under bowls for cereal, soup, or dessert, and she always used cups *and* saucers. Towels were folded and stacked with alternating colors, appliance cords were in toilet paper tubes to keep her kitchen counters neat, tops of canned goods were washed and dated so the oldest ones would be used first. And she was the consummate hostess, even in her final months, making sure visiting nurses and physical therapists were comfortable in our home.

I brought my parents to my home for their last years. I took care of them and was truly blessed by the experience. I inherited my mother's strength, more by osmosis than by training, and we clashed at times, but through it all, we each gained a new respect for the other. We both learned some hard lessons and made great strides in spiritual growth. God, in His Infinite Wisdom, allowed us to be together for these years to become teachers to one another. Sometimes, even now, if I find myself doing some idiosyncratic thing, instead of saying, "My God, I'm just like my mother." I say, "*Thank God*, I'm just like my mother."

TALK OUT LOUD

Do you talk to yourself? Do you talk *out loud* to yourself? I'll bet many of you are answering "yes" to the first question and "no" to the second. These would have been my answers a while back. I live alone now, so much of the time there's been no one around to talk to, but I still had a great many thoughts. I would talk to myself about those thoughts . . . but I would do it in a whisper. I would even sing in my head, without making a sound. It seemed kind of silly, though, to be whispering and singing without sound, so I asked myself, "What's the matter with me? Why do I hold back expressing myself just because there's no one else to hear? *I'm* here, and I am enough of an audience to listen to what I'm saying about what I'm thinking and feeling!"

My son Steve talks out loud to himself all the time (or maybe he's talking to his dog). And he sings, and he makes motor noises and shifting noises and screeching brake noises when he drives. And he cheers out loud—very loud—when he watches sports on television, while I mostly just clap when touchdowns, runs, goals, and baskets are made by my favorite teams. I think Steve has more fun than I do. I've learned from him that talking, singing, cheering, and making funny sounds makes me feel good! I've changed my mind about talking out loud to myself. I do it now. I do it a lot.

When I've asked other people about talking out loud to themselves, some say it makes them feel self-conscious. Self-consciousness comes from a fear of being judged. But when we're alone, who is there to judge? Only ourselves. And why should we judge ourselves for expressing ourselves? If someone shows up and hears us talking to ourselves, who cares!? They might just be interested enough in what they hear that they join in the conversation and engage in what we are talking to ourself about.

I've always said that when I'm alone, I'm in good company. And so are you! When we talk to ourselves, we're talking to someone who wants to hear what we have to say. I've found that verbalizing thoughts brings more attention to them. Questions find answers, perceived problems are worked out, I remain conscious throughout the day, and life becomes simpler.

Let's talk out loud, sing out loud, cheer out loud, pay attention to what we say to ourself. And, don't forget to laugh . . . out loud. At yourself. At what you say and what you do. You may just find that some of the best conversations you have are with yourself.

IGNORANCE IS BLISS

Henry Ford once said, "Think you can or think you can't, either way you'll be right." Our minds are so powerful that what we *think* we are becomes *what* we are. We came into this world perfect, as God created us. Then as we grew, we became indoctrinated into the beliefs of others. We forgot our perfection, and our perceptions changed. We listened to parents, teachers, ministers, and others we looked up to, who told us what we can and cannot accomplish, how we must and must not think and act, and much of this indoctrination changed our beliefs about ourselves.

When I first started in Real Estate it was late in October. I was fresh out of Real Estate school and gung-ho to get started in my new profession. I took all the floor time I could get. I got clients, I researched properties, I showed properties, I wrote contracts, and by the end of the year I had five escrows open plus one that had already closed. Several of the long-time agents at the firm registered their surprise at my doing so well, having started so late in the year. Their experience was that nobody buys a home at the end of the year, they're too busy with the holidays to make big life changes. No one told me this ahead of time, so I was working from a place of ignorance. I didn't know I *couldn't* sell property late in the year, so I just pushed forward and *did* it.

The lesson here is to not ever let anyone tell us that something we've set our mind to can't be done. If we believe in ourself, and we believe we can, then we will. But if we let someone tell us, or we tell ourselves, that we can't, then we won't. Everything that has ever been done—the invention of the wheel, the light bulb, the automobile, the airplane—at one time had never been done. If someone had told the cavemen that a wheel was a stupid idea, we would all still be walking everywhere. If someone had told Henry Ford that a horseless carriage was a bad plan, we wouldn't have the cars we now drive. If someone had told Thomas Edison that the light bulb couldn't be done, and he believed them, we would still be living in the dark. If someone had told the Wright Brothers that a flying machine was impossible, we wouldn't be earning frequent flyer miles with every trip we take. These forward-thinking inventors didn't know that what they were doing was impossible, so they carried on, which proves that sometimes, ignorance *is* bliss.

GET OUT OF THE MAZE

You've heard about the mouse in the lab that repeatedly made its way through a complicated maze to get to the treat that was waiting at the end. When the scientists who were conducting this experiment stopped putting the treat out, the mouse, for a short while, continued making its way through the maze hoping for that tasty morsel. After not finding a reward after several tries, the mouse stopped forging the maze because it wasn't worth the trip without the treat.

Sometimes we aren't as smart as that mouse and we keep doing the same thing over and over thinking it will get better, or easier. We stay in jobs we dislike. We stay in relationships that no longer bring us joy or may actually be destructive. We keep going to the church of our childhood after it no longer feeds our spirit. We keep doing things that someone else thinks we should do that we really don't want to do. We keep doing these things and more, when we could, like the mouse, simply stop facing that complicated maze and relax into our good. Albert Einstein described the definition of insanity as "Doing the same thing over and over again and expecting a different result."

When the circumstances of our lives become uncomfortable, or even unbearable, we don't have to keep running through a virtual maze in hopes of finding happiness. We can simplify our lives by opening up to the fact that the treat we once enjoyed is no longer there. We can take steps to change our circumstances, or we can change our minds about those circumstances. We can look at our lives with a different perspective. Wayne Dyer says, "When we change the way we look at things, things change the way they look." If we're feeling unfulfilled, not living to our full potential, feeling bitter, victimized, or just generally unhappy, we have a choice. We can either leave the job, relationship, or situation that doesn't feel right, or we can look at it in a new and different way.

The maze was still there in the lab, enticing the mouse, but when it was no longer rewarding to wend its way through, the mouse changed its mind. It didn't need to keep feeling the frustration of not finding a reward. When we change our minds about what's going on in our lives that we don't feel good about, we can see these things in a different light, we can create a new perspective. We see the world not as *it* is, but as *we* are. Let's look at the world in a positive light and see the change that makes in our lives.

MORE LIKE YOU

Do you ever think, "I wish I could be more like (fill in the blank)?" We all have people that we admire and look up to—educators, business leaders, sports figures, accomplished doctors and scientists, even some of our own contemporaries—and that's okay. These people deserve to be respected for their accomplishments, and we can learn from them. But, like these sometimes-famous people, we deserve to be loved, respected, and admired for who and what we are. And the most important person to hold us in high esteem is ourselves. Every person's destiny is unique to themselves. Every soul is born into this world for a purpose. Our purpose is to be the best person we can be, to be our best self.

If we feel like we'd like to be more like someone else, it's pretty likely that that someone else is thinking they'd like to be more like someone they admire. But we were never supposed to be the same. Just as there are no two identical snowflakes, every person on this planet is unique.

We can aspire to accomplish great things. We can get the best education, the best training, and maybe even do work that the people we look up to are doing or have done, but if we work hard to emulate someone else, we've lost our best ally.

Each of us manifests our own good and our own destiny according to our own strengths and abilities. If everyone was a great scientist, inventor, or statesman, there would be no one to build our buildings, our roads, and our homes. There would be no one to drive the bus that takes our children to school every day. There would be no one to plant trees, bushes, and flowers in our parks. There wouldn't even be anyone to haul away our rubbish in that big truck that our children like to run out to watch on trash day. When we pay attention to our worth, our inclinations, our desires, our abilities, we will form a vision of how we'd like to see our self. Honor that vision!

You are not like someone else because you were not meant to be. You were meant to be your own best self, and if you are true to yourself you will fulfill your destiny, and you will serve your fellow man in the process. And, think about this: right now, there may be someone out there, someone you know, or someone you don't know, who is thinking, "I wish I could be more like (fill in *your* name here)."

SELF / NON-SELF

Sometimes we wonder, *who are we, really?* We each identify our *self* with the vessel of our body: flesh, bone, muscle, organs, a nervous system, a brain. But there's more to us than these physical components. Conditions of life come together resulting in the *experiences* of life. If we were simply form—the body—there would be no way to experience all the sensations that come along to make us who and what we are. We are more than physical form, we are an entity that feels emotion, that differentiates pleasant and unpleasant, that forms perceptions that give rise to thoughts, concepts, and mental habits that we identify with; a mind that tells our body what to do and how to move under certain conditions.

Our *self* is in constant flux, and when we identify solely as a *body*, this flux can become very confusing. This doesn't mean that what we perceive with our body's senses isn't real to us; conditions do come together resulting in the circumstances we experience. These circumstances exit, they just don't exist independently of the conditions that caused them. If the body was just an inert form without the accompanying emotions, perceptions, and thoughts, we wouldn't experience these circumstances. The body, in this way, can be compared to a cup. A cup is simply a vessel. It's what's inside that cup that gives it meaning.

Buddhism teaches that *non-self* is one of the three marks of existence; the others being *suffering* and *impermanence*. The body is impermanent, it gets old, and it finally dies. If we die having identified only with our physical body, we will have missed out on life itself.

Now, while you're alive, be aware; think about all the ways your mind shores up the notion of *self*. Reflect on all the likes and dislikes, all the thoughts and emotions that are there to feed your self-concept, and you'll find there's so much more to *you* than just your body. When you are mindful of each of life's experiences as they arise, you can learn to observe them, to enjoy—or not enjoy—them without grasping or labeling them as *mine*. Just as the body, they, too, are impermanent. Becoming less attached to your body, thinking that's all you are, you will become less self-referential, your awareness will expand, and life will become simpler and more enjoyable. If *self* is your body, then *non-self* is the experiences of your life.

IT'S NOT A LIE

Imagine sitting in a courtroom and hearing different witnesses to an event telling completely different accounts of what they saw. You might think some of them are lying, but they're not, they simply saw the event from different perspectives.

In psychological experiments, a series of random unrelated photos were shown to groups of subjects. Since these photos had no connection to each other, the subjects imagined ways to connect them by believing they'd seen other photos that made the unrelated ones make sense. This process has come to be known as *Rational Closure*. In trying to understand the ability of the human brain to acquire and maintain meaningful perceptions in apparently chaotic situations, psychologists have found that the brain has self-organizing tendencies with respect to visual recognition. In the case of the photo experiment, subjects imagined seeing other photos that fit together instead of just collections of unrelated ones, thus forming a perception that had a reality of its own, independent of its parts. When told that the way they described the meaning of the photos they had seen was not at all like the photos they had actually been shown, they became defensive and argued that the imagined photos had indeed been there.

Like the subjects in this experiment, we all have an idea of reality that fits into our belief system, even if it has nothing to do with actual reality. When we see something in a certain way, we believe it. Differing views of reality don't just happen in experiments and courtrooms, they happen in our life every day. We interpret uncertainty of meaning in a way that works for us. On a personal level we can choose to see situations as supporting our happiness and peace of mind, or we can see them as something that victimizes us, or brings us unrest. We have the power to self-create. We can honor ourselves and our destiny of good by choosing to interpret uncertainty in ways that empower us, that support us rather than limit us, and we can argue for our good and well-being. These beliefs are not lies, they are actually the truth of who and what we are.

Next time you hear someone describe something in a way that doesn't agree with your own perception, just know it's not because they're lying, it's simply that they see a different meaning than you do; a meaning that fits into their belief system, from where they are in consciousness. Actual reality leaves a lot to the imagination, and if you imagine good in your life, that is what you'll see.

ATLAS SHRUGGED

We've all seen pictures and statues of Atlas with the world on his shoulders. But have you noticed that Atlas is bent over and appears to be struggling under that heavy weight? In Homer's *Odyssey*, Atlas is said to personify the quality of endurance, *holding the tall pillars that hold the earth and the sky apart.*

Sometimes you may feel like you're carrying the weight of the world, that you are responsible for keeping the sky and the earth from colliding. You may feel overburdened, and that life is just too hard. But it doesn't have to be. You don't have to control every little aspect of your life and you don't have to carry all the weight.

I have a friend who is a bank manager. He will tell you he has a MBWA degree—*Management By Walking Around.* His job is a very important one but he doesn't allow it to be stressful. Where he sees a need, he follows up, does what he's been trained to do, then walks around some more. And he's one of the happiest, most relaxed, and fun-loving people I know. He is aware that he doesn't have to be Atlas, carrying the whole load.

Through talent, hard work, and wise management, my uncle John became very wealthy and once purchased a house located on a hundred acres of land. The house had been vacant for some time and my children and I spent a lot of time there doing our share of work getting things cleaned up. Behind the house was a swimming pool that had gone unused for years. The decking was brick, and it was covered in mud. One day John took me to the muddy pool deck and told me to "find the bricks." That was my only instruction. He knew he didn't have to be Atlas and carry the burden of that job, so he didn't stand over me giving constant direction, he trusted me to clean the bricks.

Atlas may have personified endurance until it became a mighty weight, but we don't have to. When we feel the weight of the world on our shoulders, we can set that burden down and let other people help us. The universe is on our side. God's will for us is perfect happiness, and it's hard to be happy if we're overburdened. We can quit doing things we really don't want to do, and we don't have to stay in burdensome situations. We can empower others by allow- ing them to use *their* gifts and talents. When we release the burdens that don't belong to us, we can enjoy life more. When we enjoy our life, people will enjoy us and will be there to help shoulder the burden, and life will be simpler.

THE MOVIE OF YOUR LIFE

Have you ever gotten up and walked out in the middle of a movie because you weren't enjoying the show? Maybe it was too gory or violent. Or was it offensive to your psyche or your intelligence? We tend to stay through the whole movie to see if it gets better, and cover our eyes during the gory parts, but we seldom get up and leave.

Sometimes life can be like a bad movie. We could be staying in a job we hate, a relationship that isn't rewarding, or a living situation that doesn't feel comfortable, because we think if we stay it might get better. Sometimes these things do change—or we change the way we look at them. But if in staying, even after repeated attempts to make or see change in a situation, it doesn't get any better, maybe it's time to dig up the gumption to get up and walk out.

I'm not suggesting we walk away when the first little thing goes wrong, I'm only suggesting that when situations become too uncomfortable, or unbearable, we take a good hard look at them to figure out what action we can take, or choice we can make, to turn them into rewarding experiences. We always have a choice, and no one deserves to live a life of pain or total discomfort. If we get up and leave a bad movie, we can go see another one, one that appeals to us, one that we can enjoy.

We are the author of our own life. We write the script, and sometimes the things that bother us the most in the movie of our life are of our own making. Freud philosopher, Albert Camus, wrote, "What is happiness except the simple harmony between a man and the life he leads?" Camus contributed to the rise of the philosophy of *Absurdism*: *Extremely unreasonable or foolish thinking; living in a chaotic universe*. He was devoted to opposing negativity, skepticism, cynicism, and despair while delving into the cause of individual freedom; the absence of restraint on our ability to think and act for ourselves.

When we live our individual freedom, we contribute to the decline of remaining in unreasonable, awkward, or uncomfortable situations. If we don't like the movie, we can find a better one. If we want to see more joy in our world, we can choose again.

As you travel this journey through live, make wise decisions, think for yourself, act accordingly, and live in peace, happiness, and the simple harmony between yourself and the life you lead.

MOVE YOUR FEET

Snoopy is walking down a street and comes to an intersection with a sign that reads, *To cross street push button and wait for walk signal.* He pushes the button and waits, and waits, and waits. Then along comes Charlie Brown who walks past Snoopy into the intersection saying, "You have to move your feet, too!"

Charles Schulz had the ability to impart so much wisdom through the characters in his comic strips. And that wisdom—along with the strip—lives on.

Charlie Brown was right; we *do* have to move our feet. If we just read the directions for doing, or building, or learning something without taking the necessary action to *get it done*, we'll never get anywhere. We won't even be able to cross the street.

I bought a keyboard awhile back, along with a book entitled, *Learn to Play Piano in Six Weeks or Less.* The book has been on the keyboard's music rack since that time and I'm no closer to learning to play piano than I was when I made those purchases. Why? Because that book is not going to magically give me the ability to play piano, I have to take action, I have to move my feet. I have to use the book and follow its direction if I ever want to learn to play piano.

If we really want to get somewhere or realize our vision, we have to move our feet. If we're looking for a new job, for instance, we need to make looking for a job a full-time job because it's not likely that someone will come knocking at our door offering us exactly what we want. If we're looking for a relationship, we have to put our self in places where people gather so we can meet new people. That's why internet dating sites are so popular, and even sometimes successful, feet are moving. When we bring that box home from Ikea, we have to open it and follow the pictures that tell us how to change those pieces into a shelving unit, a dresser, or a chair. Instructions aren't enough on their own, no matter how simple; we have to move our feet! Bills and problems aren't going to go away by ignoring them. We have to take action to pay the bills and to remedy the problems. We have to move our feet!

If you want something in life, don't just wait, and wait, and wait, you have to keep moving your feet. Moving your feet will lead you to where you want to be, and maybe even to something better than you originally planned.

THE BEST AND THE REST

When I was a kid, we had a German shepherd named Butch, and when preparing his dinner, we added leftovers from our own dinner. Very often, it was peas that were left over. This dog didn't like peas, and after he'd finished eating, the peas were left in the bottom of his bowl. I never could figure out how he was able to eat around the peas, but because he knew what he liked and what he didn't, he chose not to deal with what he didn't like and left them behind. This dog knew the spiritual lesson of "Take the Best and Leave the Rest."

Sometimes I think animals are more spiritually aware than most people, they don't spend time on things that don't serve them. If we take care of our animals, they will love us unconditionally, but if we mistreat or ignore them, they might chew up our shoes or pee on our furniture, or they might even take up with a neighbor who treats them better.

It's likely there have been things in our own life that we wouldn't have minded "eating around." In our relationships, for example, if there are factors that we don't like, we can be honest and open with the other person and tell them—kindly and lovingly—what it is that bugs us. Then come choices. That person can thank us for being forthcoming, and perhaps change a bit, or they can get angry. But we have to remember that their anger is about *them*, it's not about *us*. Anger is defense, and defense is attack. We also have another choice. If the thing that annoys us doesn't stop after we've talked about it, we can choose to accept it as part of the person we care about, we can work toward a compromise, or we can walk away, blessing them for the experience we've gained from the connection. There is a nugget of good in every experience, and we can extract that nugget, use it to our benefit in future situations, and leave what we don't feel good about behind. We can release regret, pain, and negative emotions, and accept peace, love, and joy.

Only the best belongs to us, the rest we can let go. We are all teachers to one another, and every person in our life—every teacher—will impart some wisdom we can use. Others might offer ideas or experiences that we don't understand, agree with, or wish to participate in, and we are not required to accept these things that are not in our best interest. Remember, like Butch, we are always free to "Take the Best and Leave the Rest," and to eat around the peas.

KNOWLEDGE AND WISDOM

I'm old enough to remember a time where there were no computers, cell phones, and the myriad technical devices we take for granted today. Even though those various devices were designed to make life easier, at first, I found them to be hard to adapt to.

I was especially computer resistant for a time because I'm someone who has always been curious about what makes things tick. I've been good with mechanical things, can use tools well and easily, and when I've needed something, I've figured out a way to make it, build it, or fix it. But computers were different. I could never make, build, or fix a computer, and I didn't understand why it does what it does and how it works. I felt I had to know the hows and whys before I could venture into a world that was beyond my comprehension.

Then I ran across a quote by Martin H. Fisher, a German-born physician and author, who said, "Knowledge is a process of piling up facts; wisdom lies in their simplification." I meditated on those words and was guided to simply use the computer and take the mental stress out of it. I realized I didn't have to know the inner workings to make the computer work for me, there are people I can call on for help if I need to, people who *do* know the hows and the whys. I only have to turn it on and everything I need is there for me to find and use.

It's that way with much of life. We might be building up knowledge and facts about a lot of things, but we can never know everything about everything. So we turn to wisdom. Wisdom to know that we don't *have* to know everything, that life is simpler when we relax, work with what we know, and accept what we don't know. There are always other people we can go to for help.

There's no need to beat ourselves up for what we can't do, or what we find hard to understand. Sometimes we can get so identified with the search that we don't know when we've found what we're looking for. When we relax into the simplification of what we *do* know and the wisdom we *do* have, and stop trying to figure everything out, life smooths out and we can do what's ours to do, do it well, and have the wisdom to allow life to be simple.

HUGGING

"I need a hug!" How many times have you felt this way and found someone in your life to say it to. Someone to make your day a little better with a little hug?

At the Unity church I attended for more than 20 years, there was a time in the Sunday service when the congregation stood and sang a song called *I Behold the Christ in You.* As we sang, everyone looked around at the people standing near them, making a holy connection. The song was followed by what I call "Huggy Time." It was a beautiful way to connect with people, and at times, became so long that it took someone to remind the congregants to stop hugging and return to their seats so they could get on with the service. The hugs brought a closeness to the group which left everyone feeling better throughout the week to follow.

Hugging is a beautiful thing. We hug our parents, our children, our spouses, our friends, and our pets. A hug is a safe way to express love to one another; and it *feels good.*

I recently ran across a bookmark I had made for those in my *A Course in Miracles* study group that is a wonderful description of hugging. I really don't know its origin, but I'll share it here.

Hugging is healthy: It helps the body's immune system,
it cures depression, it reduces stress, it induces sleep,
it is invigorating, and it has no unpleasant side effects.
Hugging is nothing less than a miracle drug.

Hugging is all natural: It is organic, naturally sweet,
has no pesticides, no artificial ingredients, and is 100% wholesome.

Hugging is practical: There are no moveable parts or
batteries to wear out, no need for periodic checkups,
has low energy consumption and high energy yield.
It is inflation-proof, non-fattening, theft-proof, non-taxable,
non-polluting, has no insurance requirements.
And it is, of course, fully returnable.

Next time you feel a little down and in need of an energy booster, find someone to hug. In my experience, all hugs, both given and received, end with a warm feeling in your heart and a smile on your face.

SYNCHRONICITY

My plumber Eric, who had been employed at a large plumbing company, had done work for me both at my home and at my rental properties. When I had a very large project (completely replacing the entire sewer system at a commercial property), I called on him to do the job. At that time, he and a partner, Jim, were working toward leaving the big company to start their own plumbing business. They had obtained their contractor's license, had new top-of-the-line equipment, and were able to do my big job under their new name and license. It was their first job on their own. The timing of my need and their new start came together through synchronicity—what the dictionary defines as *meaningful coincidence.*

Meanwhile, there was an organization that had 17 fitness centers located around the local area. They had been using the large company that Eric and Jim had been associated with for their plumbing needs, but were looking to make a change. They chose a company from an ad they had come across, and when they called this new company for service, Eric and Jim showed up. It would have been unscrupulous to solicit clients of the big company, so being honest and above-board businessmen, they had not done that. Since the call for service was made to a company the fitness center owners knew nothing about, synchronicity was at play. The fitness center owners were surprised, and pleased, that they'd accidentally come across this new business, and now it is their go-to for plumbing needs. Eric and Jim are on solid ground with this very big client, and through that connection they're getting other jobs. Their business is thriving. Because they had set an intention to build their new business at the same time the fitness center owners were ready to make a change, synchronicity made it happen.

If we want something to happen, the power of intention will synchronize the right people and events to be where we need them, and we can let go and stop worrying about the outcome. If we can surrender the *how* of getting what we desire, the universe will step in and find it for us.

My huge job was a jumping-off place for Eric and Jim, and everything after that was a series of events carefully orchestrated by the universe. Everyone involved was a winner. If you want to win in life, relax, let life be simple, set a firm intention, and allow destiny to take care of the details.

CELEBRATE MIRACLES

How often do we stop to realize and appreciate the wonders of the world? I'm not talking about the Grand Canyon or the Taj Mahal, I'm referring to the miracles we encounter every day of our lives, all the good that surrounds us.

When you get up in the morning, turn on the water in the shower and step into the warm spray, do you give any thought to the technology that brought that refreshing activity to you? I certainly do. While I was living in the wilds of northern British Columbia, we didn't have that indulgence. We had to scoop water out of a dugout in five-gallon buckets, bring it into the house, strain out the pond shrimp and other debris, heat the water on the stove, pour it into a shower bag, and wash with a little spray hose that was attached to the bag. After almost three years of that, I was extremely grateful for my shower when I came back to civilization. I often stayed in it, soaking in the luxury, until the water ran cold.

In this day of technology overload, we might have a problem with our computer and have to make a call for support. Or our cell phone might not work if we wander into a place that doesn't have service or Wi-Fi. When this happens, we might get upset and complain that "nothing ever works right." But if we think about it, these times are infrequent. Most of the time, our computer works well. There are cell towers that our phone magically connects to, passing from one to another wherever we travel. The mystery of Wi-Fi lets us connect to the internet wherever we happen to be. We can even surf the web from an airplane at 35,000 feet above the earth.

There is so much good in our life that we probably don't even think about, it's just there for us at any time. Next time your power goes out in a storm, or the water company has to turn off your service to work on the lines, light candles for illumination and fill buckets so you'll have water to drink or wash with, and give thanks that these conditions are temporary. You can even bring joy into these perceived inconveniences by turning them into adventures for your family.

Today, let's take time to notice all the things that make our life easier, and celebrate them. Let's keep our mind and heart open to the miracle of all the good in our world and feel grateful for it. Our spirits will be lifted and we'll see how, by comparison to those who don't have the convenience of electricity, running water, computers, and cell phones, our life is blessed, and we can let our heart sing with gratitude.

RICH OR CHEAP

There is a cost to cutting corners. When we buy something that is cheap because we don't feel we can afford its expensive counterpart, we think we are saving money, but cheap doesn't always mean a bargain. In the long run, cheap will cost us more because cheap things often break and we have to repair or replace them.

When I was in the business of sub-contracting, there was a bidding process to get jobs. I always bid what I felt my product and services were worth, and I sometimes lost jobs to other sub-contractors whose bids were lower than mine. Those sub-contractors, however, often came back with change orders throughout the job and the final cost to the builder turned out to be more than my original bid. There were several builders with whom I had a great rapport, and for whom I did repeated jobs. These builders learned that it worked to contract with me, even when there were lower bids, because they knew I was honest, that I worked with integrity, that my bids were complete, and there wouldn't be hidden costs. These builders got quality work from me and my employees and were happy to pay the price.

There's a proverb that says, "I'm not rich enough to buy cheap things." This may not sound like the most budget-friendly tip, but it really is the truth. When we're thinking of buying knock-offs of cosmetics, fragrances, or designer labels, there's a point at which economizing starts to turn into wasted money. We really do get what we pay for. The trick is to find top quality at a fair price. Retailers know that when people see items that are expensive, they assume they are the best, but this isn't always the case. Good quality doesn't have to be the most expensive, and buying cheap items, just to save money, often backfires.

This all speaks to our consciousness. If we have a mentality of abundance, we know we deserve the best, and we don't shy away from buying good quality. If we have a mentality of lack, of not enough, we might not feel like we deserve what it is we really want, and we buy something cheaper. Having a lack-mindset will keep us from getting a lot of what would really make us happy.

Hold out for quality, because you're worth it. If you settle for less, it will probably cost you more in the long run, and nobody is rich enough to buy cheap things.

REAR VIEW MIRROR

We all have a past and a future, but the only place we can really live is in the present—this current moment—so we want to make the most of every moment because a moment later that moment becomes the past.

Are you living in the past? Are you dragging a bunch of baggage along with you into the now? It doesn't have to be a long-ago past, it could be yesterday, last week, or a few minutes ago. If so, to simplify your life, let it go! Consider this: When you're driving in your car, and you look in the rear-view mirror, you're seeing what's behind you. That's your past. See how small it is. Now look through the windshield and see how much bigger it is than that little mirror, and see how it's filled with what's before you. Even if the circumstances of your past were not what you might have hoped for, even if you've been wronged, it's in the past. It's in that little mirror. It's behind you. It's somewhere you've been. It isn't where you are now, and it doesn't have to define your future.

We hear a lot about identity theft these days. When we can't let go of a bad past—what's in our rear-view mirror—we are stealing our own identity today. *Today* we are free, we are unlimited, we are as God created us, whole and perfect in every way.

When Michelangelo sculpted the classic statue of David, it is said that he looked at the big piece of stone and saw nothing more than stone. Then the more he looked at it, the more he began to see a future possibility—a magnificent statue—and he chipped away at the stone, clearing away anything that wasn't David.

If your past is keeping you from being your best self, you don't have to recreate who you are, you simply have to clear away what you once were. If you can imagine your past as chunks of stone left lying at the feet of a beautiful statue, you can gather up those chunks and throw them away. Just as Michelangelo discovered David within the stone, you simply need to discover what's within you. Find what it is about your past that no longer serves you and throw it away. Drive away from it, leave it in your rear-view mirror. When all the "junk" is gone, the only thing left is the beauty, potential, and peace that lies before you.

THE WISDOM OF CONTROL

Is there someone in your life who is über-controlling? It could be a parent, a spouse, an employer, a friend, or even a religion. Are *you* so controlling of someone else—an offspring, a spouse, an employee, a friend—that it keeps them from living the easy, spontaneous life that would allow them more joy? Maybe you are so *self*-controlled that you have little adventurous joy in your own life.

There needs to be control in the world and in our society or there'd be no forward movement. We need traffic laws to control safety on our roads and highways. We need rules in our schools to maintain a controlled learning environment. We need laws in our land to keep people from hurting each other. Parents need to control their young children to keep them safe and healthy. But most of all, we need to extend control to ourselves, and part of that control is getting out of our own way.

We are in our own way when we are hesitant or fearful when new opportunities come along. We may find our self thinking," I've never done this before, so I don't think I can." But sometimes if we can release our control button and press the spontaneity button, we'll find we're learning something new and having a good time.

A decent amount of self-control is, of course, necessary. We don't want to go head-long into a dangerous situation just because someone tells us we'd like it. Self-control can keep us safe, and some control of others might keep them safe, as well. But control, laced with wisdom, can guide us to adventures that we might have missed out on otherwise.

Like everything else in life, there is balance in control, and we can learn to use control wisely. We can't let too little control lead us into self-defeating, dangerous, or illegal activities, but we can't let too much control keep us from enjoying life to the fullest. We also can't let our control over others hold them back. As we venture into a new situation, or think through a decision, remember that control combined with wisdom lets us assess a situation, decide if it's a good idea, and let go of any unfounded fear or hesitation that might keep us from going forward in life.

There is wisdom in control, and that wisdom is inside you. Listen to your gut reactions, your emotional feelings. When you can move on using wise control you will simplify your life.

OUT BY THE ROOTS

You've heard people say, "I can forgive, but I'll *never* forget." Perhaps you've said this yourself, or at least thought it. But if you're still carrying the memory of a hurt or a misdeed, you haven't fully forgiven. Forgiveness is a gift you give to yourself. It's easier to forgive another, it's harder to forgive yourself for holding onto the distress you feel for the wrong that's been done. When you keep someone in the prison of your judgment, however, you have to sit at the door of their cell to make sure they don't escape. Now you, as the jailer, are in prison as well. If there is someone you have a hard time forgiving, forgive for your own sake, not theirs. Free yourself from that prison. Forgiving someone may not change their life, but forgiving yourself will indeed change yours.

Forgiving doesn't mean accepting. Forgiving someone for an offence doesn't make that offence okay, and it also doesn't mean we have to be close with the offender. Forgiveness is simply a tool for bringing our own emotions back to a comfort level, and to feel the release and the peace that comes with forgiveness.

Forgiving doesn't have to be face-to-face, either. The person we're forgiving doesn't even have to know we've forgiven them. I once had a boyfriend whose job took him to a far away location. I thought we could maintain a long-distance relationship, but he thought differently. I was hurt and I was angry, then one day I opened my mind to the gift of forgiveness. I forgave him for being a jerk and for leaving me (forgiveness isn't always pretty), and when I did this, I felt a peace that was all consuming, and all the hurt and anger disappeared

Forgiving is like getting the weeds out of our garden. We have to pull them out by the roots. If we just cut off the tops of the weeds, the roots are still alive in the ground to come up again and again. Forgiving *means* forgetting. Getting the misdeeds out of our mind. Getting the weeds out by their roots. When we get to the root of forgiveness and rid ourselves of the thing we're forgiving, it's gone. It can't keep growing in our consciousness. It can't keep us tethered to the memory or the emotions surrounding the memory.

You have forgiveness opportunities every day. Forgiveness is a choice. You do it for yourself. In forgiving, you get the memory of wrongs and misdeeds out of your mind. You get the weeds out by the roots. Clearing away the weeds of hurt leaves you free to live a peaceful, happy, loving, and simple life . . . and for flowers to grow.

DO YOU TALK GOOD?

My grandkids sometimes call me "Gramma Grammar" because I often gently offer a correction when they say things like, "me and him" or "where's it at?" or "how many is there?" or "we had went" or "had took" or use "good" when "well" would be correct. And I bristle when I read the newspaper and see things like, "there is" instead of "there are" when writing about more than one person or thing, or "up until then" (don't need the "up"), or "irregardless" (no such word), and then there's the double negative, "You couldn't hardly see the road for the fog."

I don't mean to be judgmental, I'm certainly not the perfect grammarian myself. I sometimes even make up words. And I love commas. You could say I'm commadicted (there's a made-up word). But please don't judge, just pause a bit when you see a comma as you read these pages, and I'll be happy.

We don't need a degree in language arts to speak or write well, and we don't need to have a vocabulary of two-dollar words, but in this world, like it or not, we are judged by the way we express ourselves. In a court of law, for example, a person on trial might be perceived more positively when using proper grammar. Also, when at a job interview, we will sound smarter, more capable, and make a better impression when we use good grammar.

Every generation seems to pick up a word that they over-use, like, "like." In a job interview, if every other word is "like", like, you probably won't, like, get the, like, job. And it irks me when I attend a lecture or a class and the speaker says "you know" repeatedly. If I knew, I wouldn't be there to learn, would I?

Some grammatical idiosyncrasies are geographical, and some even kind of endearing. Midwesterners tend to say "I seen" instead of "I saw." And our southern friends just love "y'all" and "I'm fixin' to."

The message here is to pay attention to the way we speak and how we express ourselves. It may not be fair, but those who speak well do get farther in life.

"Gramma Grammar" might be annoying at times, but if it helps the next generation to speak better and to express themselves on paper more intelligently, I can take the eye-rolls I get from my grandkids.

KINDNESS

In a *Pickles* cartoon by Brian Crane, Grandpa is imparting wisdom to his little grandson. He says, "Nelson, you're going to meet people in this life who are hard to like, but you should always be kind, even if it isn't always easy. Everyone you meet is fighting a secret battle that you know nothing about." Then, in the last frame, Grandpa reaches around to the back of his shirt and adds, "For instance, I have a scratchy tag on the inside collar of this shirt that is driving me batty!"

It would be nice if a scratchy tag was the worst thing we had to deal with, but the advice Grandpa gave is quite sound. There *are* people in this life that are hard to like, and sometimes it *is* hard to be kind to these people, but, as Grandpa says, we don't know what they are going through. Everyone is indeed fighting some kind of battle, and it's often a battle within themselves. When we know this, it's easier to overlook negative and disruptive behavior, which makes it easier to be kind. We can't fix other people's problems for them, but we can be kind. We can be kind to everyone! All the time!

Have you experienced some event in your life that made you feel disconnected from others? Do you remember how alone you felt? Do you remember how good it felt when someone acted kindly toward you? Kindness is a magic bullet. When kindness becomes our nature, when we are kind just because we are kind, we never know whose life we will touch, or how they will *be* touched.

Kindness doesn't have to be some big, over the top gesture. It can be as simple as a smile, a friendly hello, holding the door open for another, or letting someone with only one or two items go ahead of you at the check-out counter. We can never know what's going on in the mind or in the life of another. Someone we encounter may be facing a challenge and acting in a way that's hard to like, but kindness can sometimes help him see things differently. Kindness can heal.

And, kindness doesn't have to be something we do for someone else. We need to be kind to *ourselves*. Our problems and challenges can seem much more manageable when we treat ourselves with kindness and understanding.

THINGS TO KNOW

There are things to know that can simplify your life. They're not hard things, just everyday actions. No one is perfect, but we can all make our life, or the life of someone else, a little better if we live by these things to know:

1. Everything isn't always about you. Sometimes it's about someone else. Be sure to let other people have their turn.
2. Live with integrity. Be the kind of person that you want to be and give others the freedom to be who they are, without judgment.
3. Help your fellow man. Take a look around and see who has a need you can fill for them.
4. Make good choices. Say yes to things that will make your life better, and no to anything that will make it worse.
5. Be responsible. Clean up after yourself, pay your bills on time, and don't let the sun go down on anger or dirty dishes.
6. Be kind. You can get grease spots out of almost anything with baking soda, but nothing washes away an unkind word.
7. Love your body and take care of it. It's the only body you'll ever have, so do your best to make it last.
8. Surround yourself with beauty. Enjoy flowers on your table, art in your home, music that makes you want to dance, and loving people who lift you up and make you a better person.
9. Do the right thing. The wrong thing might be easier, or even more fun, but in the long run, the right thing is easier to live with.
10. Smile at everyone you see. Smile at old people, at children, and at strangers. It might make them feel better and it will certainly make you feel good.
11. Love and accept yourself. Recognize your beauty, inside and out, and know that you are loved.
12. Express gratitude. Look for things around you to be grateful for. Begin each day by consciously thinking of two or three things that you feel deeply grateful for and give thanks for those things.
13. Make and keep at least one good, longtime friend who knows everything about you and likes you anyway; someone who will always have your back and who you can trust completely.

STOP, LOOK, AND LISTEN

We would all like our lives to be peaceful, stress-free, and simple but, unfortunately, this is not always the case. Even the most spiritually evolved, at times, face conflict and situations that may not be comfortable. With talk of war circling the globe and politicians poking accusations at one another, it's sometimes hard to stay at peace without escaping to the top of a mountain somewhere.

We live in this world, we're involved in this world, and we have to figure out how to exist in this world. Since we see the world through our own perception, we can choose to make troubling times real for us, or not. Love is the only reality, but sometimes our egos get in the way, and ego loves conflict.

If we have become involved in a conflict, we can Stop, Look, and Listen. We might find something of value in the disagreement. Have we done something to make the person we are conflicted with feel the way they do? We can ask ourselves, "What is my role in this?" As we know, there are two sides to every story, and there might be something in our own mind that we can change to make things better. It's easy to find fault in someone else, but we also have to be able to see any error in ourselves, in our own perception, in the way we are seeing the situation.

Buddhist teaching has a word—*Shimpa*—which means an irritant in the mind. This irritant builds a case then throws it out into the world to cause conflict. The Yiddish word, *Yenta*, calls to mind a busy-body or a gossip who sometimes stirs up trouble. We have to be careful not to be affected by Shimpa or Yenta mindsets in others, and to make sure we don't project them ourselves.

When we find ourselves in an altercation or dispute, whoever is the saner at the time sets the tone. *We* can be that saner person. There is never a good reason to attack or to defend. We can learn to yield, knowing that what everyone really wants is peace and love, and the only way to attain this is to be truly helpful. When we can gently discuss a misunderstanding, we can find our own part in it, and we can help the other person discover why he's feeling attacked or wronged. When we Stop, Look, and Listen we'll discover contributing factors to any conflict, then we can usually find a peaceful solution.

A DAY OF LOVE

Today is Valentine's Day; a day of love. This is the day we get really sappy and buy flowers, candy, cards with sweet loving messages, and sometimes lavish gifts for the one we love to show them just how *much* we love them. And, if our partner is equally sappy, we might be the recipient of these loving gestures. People love to love. More weddings take place on this day than on any other day of the year. Love is in the air!

But what if you don't have a special someone in your life? Who do you lavish attention on, and who will shower that affection on you? The answer is easy. You can show love to yourself today. You don't need to feel alone, lonely, separate, or outside of love because you didn't get flowers, or a card, or a gift today, because you are never alone. You are never separate from yourself, and you are never separate from God. God's love shines on you all the time, reminding you that you are loved unconditionally, in every circumstance, no matter what.

This Valentine's Day, we can buy flowers for ourselves. Or give them to a good friend. We can send cards to people we care about. It will brighten their day, which will brighten ours, because when we give love, love comes back to us. We can invite friends over or plan a fun outing with someone who may also be feeling alone. Our love goes far beyond the one person we are in a relationship with. We can love, accept, and show appreciation for anyone today and feel acceptance, appreciation, and love coming back.

Enjoy this day of love. Express love and lavish attention on yourself. Get a massage, buy some new clothes, or a new pair of shoes, or something special for your home. Express love to everyone you encounter with a smile and a cheery hello. Then at the end of the day, take time to really *feel* the love of this day. You will find there's a big smile on your face.

We can be happy for those who do have a special someone to spend this day of love with, but we can also be happy for our own company. Remember, when we are alone, we are in good company. We can let every day be a Day of Love.

ARE YOU A MYSTIC?

There are two kinds of people: Ordinary People, and Mystics. Ordinary People can't really *see* what's happening because they are projecting, and projection makes perception, and perception is what they *choose* to see. A Mystic has vision, is usually more open, has more foresight, and simply sees and accepts what's going on without judgment. Mystics can look at the world and see it as it is, and can let circumstances be what they are.

My good friend, Greg, argued with his son, Alan, over his college major. Alan wanted to study the arts with a mind to becoming a movie producer. Greg felt he should choose a more marketable field in which he could obtain gainful employment after graduation. Alan won out in this dispute, attended a theater college at a prestigious university, and has since directed and produced several short-subject films. Not knowing much about Alan's chosen field of study, Greg had been projecting his own ideas of how this might not work out for his son because it was a long shot. Alan, on the other hand, had foresight. He had a vision of what he wanted to accomplish, saw it happening for him, stuck to his vision, and is doing well. Proof that father doesn't always know best.

All parents have an idea of how their children's lives should be, but we need to recognize that even after we've raised and nurtured them through their young lives, they are going to have their own ideas, their own vision, and their own concept of what their own life will look like. Many parents work hard to direct their children into certain ways of life, and children work just as hard to find their own way. My grandmother wanted my father to become an accountant because he had a brilliant mind for numbers. But he had other ideas. He wanted to work with his hands, his strength, and his ability to lead others. He ultimately spent 40-plus years working for a very large manufacturing firm in a supervisory capacity and led a long, full, and contented life.

We need to let people be who they are, especially as parents. When children are young, it's a parent's job to direct and guide them, and to instill good values, but the time comes when we have to let go and allow them to find their own way.

There is a little Mystic in all of us, and when we let go and allow people and circumstances to be exactly what they are without projecting our own ideas of how they *should* be, we'll find that inherent wisdom and internal guidance will lead to right and perfect outcomes.

IDOLS

Many people have Idols—I don't mean some kind of religious statue or icon—I mean other *people* that they idolize; people they think have greatness beyond what they, themselves, have. These idols could be recording artists, film stars, or sports greats. They could be religious leaders or politicians or anyone with name recognition who is held in high regard. We tend to get excited when we have a brush with the greatness of these idols, but, in truth, these people are no greater than we are, they simply have a different kind of job.

I remember a time when I was a young child and went to church with a little friend and her family. This was a Catholic church, and there happened to be a visiting Bishop in attendance that day. There was an excitement in the air and I observed the parishioners bowing to the Bishop as he strode down the aisle. Some people gently touched his robes, still others fell to their knees and wept. Not having had any religious training or background, my young self was surprised by the reaction of the people. What I saw was a man, a simple man, like all the other men who were there. Yes, he was dressed in robes and wore an interesting looking hat, but I didn't understand all the emotion I was seeing. I don't mean to offend my Catholic friends with this memory. I have since learned more about different religions, of course, and now understand the reverence the people of the church held for the Bishop. But at the time, I was unaware of greatness in anyone, with the possible exception of my mother, father, and two grandmothers whom I idolized.

When we've attended concerts by famous musicians, we've encountered people pushing and shoving to get closer to the stage and to the star. And we pay top dollar for front row seats at sporting events. We want to have that physical brush with greatness.

There *is* something stimulating about being close to or meeting great people, but the truth is that we are around great people every day, everywhere we go, because we are *all* great. *We* are great! Our greatness lives within us. When we look outside ourselves for greatness, when we idolize greatness and seek it in someone famous, we remain on a constant and frustrating quest. But when we recognize it within ourselves, we can share it with a quiet confidence which will help others to find the greatness within themselves.

BIKE CHAIN

My twelve-year-old great-granddaughter texted me a picture of her pant legs rolled up and asked if I'd ever done that. She said it was a new fashion trend. I told her I did that when I was a kid, only it wasn't a fashion statement then, it was to keep my pant legs from getting entangled in my bike chain.

Children are different today. They are growing up and maturing much faster, and learning so much more. When I was twelve, fashion was the farthest thing from my mind. I was too busy riding my bike, playing kick-the-can, and building forts in the tall weeds in the vacant lot across the street.

I've got some great memories of the past, but I'm thoroughly enjoying building memories with my ever-growing family today. Having little ones around keeps me on my toes. When an eight year old can name the capital of every state in the U.S., an eleven year old can teach me everything I need to know about every sport, a three year old can relay, in minute detail, what she saw and learned at the Aquarium, a little nine year old ballerina knows every movement of the Nutcracker by heart, a seven year old can impress an audience with her Irish dancing and, best of all, when they can all teach me something about technology that I don't know, I see the wonderful magnificence of today's children.

An innocent, child-like mind is open to all possibilities, and it is our responsibility, as grown-ups, to allow children to be children, to let them develop their own personalities, and to become who they came here to be. We think we know it all, but we may actually know too much. We've learned too much about limits. If we could look at the world through innocent, child-like eyes, we might not believe those limiting thoughts, we might be less jaded and better able to guide our children to be strong, self-confident, productive adults. When a child displays a strong interest in a unique area, we need to inspire them to develop their gift and to live their dream.

You may be an adult, but it's not too late for you. Look at the world and all it holds for you through the eyes of a child and see its beauty and its possibilities. Be playful but be careful. If your pants get caught in the bike chain of life, pick yourself up, try again, and maintain that child-like "I can do this" wonder. And don't give up on your dream. Dreams are wasted if they remain dreams.

WHAT DO YOU WANT?

What do you want? What do you really, really, want? We all want something. We say we want a beautiful new house, or a deeply loving relationship, or a job that we love so much we jump out of bed in the morning anxious to get to. But, think about this: How would those things that we want so badly make us *feel*? Would the house make us feel secure? Would the relationship make us feel cherished? Would the job give us a sense of self-worth? The reality is that what we want is not a house or a partner or a job. What we are actually seeking is security, love, and self respect. It's the *feelings* that we long for, not the circumstances. If we got all the things we think we want, but not the *feelings* we're seeking, we would still feel dissatisfied.

Those feeling are within us. They don't come from outside sources. We cultivate them where we are. When we crave something, we can stop and take a look within. If we can immerse ourselves in the *feelings* of what our hearts desire, we will also feel the reward we want so badly. When we *feel* secure, loved, and worthy, and are feeling our authentic self, that new house, relationship, or job could manifest before our very eyes.

I know this works because it worked for me. One of the bosses at a place I worked when I was much younger, had a cute little Mercedes Benz SL. At that time, I didn't know that Mercedes Benz was a really special make of car, I just liked the way it looked, and I set my mind to someday having one just like it. Every day, I felt myself driving that car, imagining it with the top down and feeling the breeze on my face. Whenever I saw another one like it, I felt a camaraderie with the person driving. Then one day I saw one for sale and was drawn to take a look. I found the price was right, I was able to sell the car I'd been driving, and the little convertible sports coupe was mine. This is just a small example of manifested feelings. Rather than longing for the car itself, I let the *feeling* of having it wash over me, and the car manifested in my life.

When we recognize how powerful our mind is, how our life can change when we focus on the *feelings* having what we crave would bring, we'll find the manifestations come naturally. What we actually *think* we want could be limiting our good. Something even better might be in store for us when we can really *feel* our good, not just *wish* for it.

RIGHT OR HAPPY

We all want to be happy, and we also want to be right, but sometimes the two don't happen together. There are right-fighters among us who, no matter what, fight for what they think is right, and make everyone else wrong. But nobody, not you and not me, can be right all the time, and being able to admit when we are not right is a positive trait. It's humility and it's integrity.

A recent lesson for me came from a pretty unimportant situation. But no matter how trival, I wanted to be right. My desk calculator quit working. I use that calculator every day and found myself getting miffed every time I started to use it, but couldn't. I had just installed a new ink ribbon, and it worked fine, until it didn't. My son, who can troubleshoot almost anything and make it work, suggested the problem might be with the new ribbon. I had changed the ribbon dozens of times in the past, I knew how to do it, and was adamant that could not be the problem. There had to be something else wrong. My son, sure he could fix the problem, opened up the calculator to see what he could do. He found that the ribbon had come out of its groove and wound itself around the little post the spool sits on. He took the ribbon out, rewound it on the spool, reinstalled it, and everything worked just fine. *A Course in Miracles* asks us if we'd rather be right or be happy. The frustration I'd been feeling was unjustified. I'd been wrong in my insistence that the ribbon couldn't be the problem and was happy that I'd been wrong.

When faced with a problem and feeling anger or frustration, we can take another look. We can try to see the problem in a more positive light, ask ourselves how we could see it differently, and what part we might be playing in worsening the situation. Maybe, just maybe, the way we'd been seeing the problem was wrong. Maybe we could be happy by seeing it differently. Maybe by listening to someone who has a more relaxed approach to the problem, we could find that we don't always have to be right, that being happy is far more important. When we can replace our need to be right with being happy, our life will be simpler.

IT'S NOT MY FAULT

Some people are chronically late for everything and always have an excuse for their tardiness. Others arrive predictably on time or even early, and are well prepared for meetings, classes, presentations, or whatever it is that they're doing. I know people in both these categories and have to admit it's more pleasant to work with the on-timers.

Psychologists say that being late is a need to be noticed. When someone arrives late, there is a bit of disruption. This causes others to notice them and their arrival. It's like a child throwing a tantrum; they get attention. It may not be good attention, but they do get noticed, and that's what late-comers need to feed their hungry ego.

When we're late, the excuses we give are just that—excuses—they're not reasons. The reason is usually that we are not fully committed to being on time. When we have to be someplace at a certain time, there are two kinds of people; those find a way to arrive promptly, and those who find excuses for why they can't get there in a timely manner. Our intention sets the tone of our life. If we intend to be on time, we will be there. If we really don't consider it a priority, it will never happen.

I have a friend who was always twenty to thirty minutes late for everything. Her husband, in an attempt to cure her tardiness, set all the clocks in their house fifteen minutes fast. Now she is only five or ten minutes late.

People laugh at procrastinators, but there's little humor in the frustration their lack of commitment causes others. When someone arrives late to a meeting or a class, it causes a break while this person gets settled and has to be caught up with what they've missed. This results in the whole group, along with the essence of the meeting or the lesson, to be disrupted. If we have to be late, we need to give others the courtesy of simply slipping in and taking our place without using up other people's time and attention by expounding on excuses.

Being late is a choice. We are the source of our experiences. If we choose to be on time, it will happen. If our choice is to drag our feet or put things off, we will continue to be late. When we're late, we might say it's not our fault, and sometimes it may not be. To simplify our life, though, if we say we'll be someplace or meet someone at a certain time—let's be there! When we can commit to being on time, if we make it a priority, we'll find that our life will be simpler.

SOFT AND STRONG

I recently had a conflict with a medical billing company. They sent a statement showing a large amount owing. I called to tell them that my insurance had covered that amount and that I had written verification reflecting that payment. That should have been the end of it, but it wasn't. Several phone calls followed, each from a different representative who, it seemed, had not communicated with the previous agents. I was getting a little frustrated, and in talking with a friend, he suggested I let them know in no uncertain terms of my frustration, and even gave me words—angry words—to relay that to them. I chose another way. Every time I got a call from this company, I calmly told each caller that the bill had been paid by my insurance company. After a few more phone calls they finally got the picture, and the matter was resolved. No one had to get angry, it was a simple misunderstanding, and was easily taken care of—after they started communicating with one another. I could have gotten angry, vented my frustration, and raised my voice asking why they couldn't get this right. This would, however, have invoked anger in them, they would have gotten defensive, and we all would have lost our peace. These were people who were simply doing their job.

When we're confronted with a conflict with a person or business institution, we have a choice. If we express anger, defiance, and resistance, we are inviting the person we're dealing with to match that energy, and they are likely to dig in their heels, refuse to even consider seeing the situation from our point of view, and the conflict could be never ending. But if our energy is calm and reasonable, we will likely meet that person on common ground and resolve the conflict in a mutually supportive manner. Everyone wins.

Most conflicts are born of a person's resistance—yours or someone else's—but you can be the one to remain reasonable, knowing that a calm demeanor will win over anger and defensiveness. Misunderstandings don't have to become mini-wars. They can always be resolved if at least one of the people involved stays soft and yielding. Lao-tzu, in the *Tao te Ching*, says, *Water is soft and yielding, but water will wear away rock, which is rigid and cannot yield . . . What is soft is strong*. You can be both soft and strong to resolve differences, and isn't that infinitely better than being rigid and unyielding and losing your peace?

LIVE TODAY

Nineteenth century philosopher John Henry Newman is quoted as saying, "Fear not that thy life shall come to an end, but rather fear that it shall never have a beginning." As I read that quote, I could relate. When I was younger, there were things I wanted to have or to do but always had the idea that I had to wait until the time was right. Then one day I woke up to the fact that *today* is the best time to have and do what I want! I stopped waiting. I stepped forward in life, took advantage of opportunities, and found ways to have or do what made me happy. A wise person once said, "I refuse to tiptoe through life only to arrive safely at death." That's what I had been doing. I was tiptoeing, living so carefully that I never took chances, and I found that some of what I was waiting for never came about.

I came by this way of careful thinking naturally because it's what I saw as I was growing up. Having lived through the great depression, my parents had the fearful mindset that so many of their generation had, and never took chances. We never went on family vacations because my dad feared spending the money a vacation would cost, in case some emergency should come up that he'd need the money for. After I was grown, and out of the house, my parents did do some travelling. They took driving trips and made sure to pack anything and every-thing they thought they might need. They couldn't risk needing something they didn't have at hand. They were always *ready.* During their 68 years of marriage, they moved only three times, and the last move was to my home where I could care for them. All this is not to say they were wrong in their journey through life. They were happy and they lived the way that was comfortable for them. But I couldn't find the joy I longed for in that careful lifestyle. I wanted to be more spontaneous. I wanted to explore. I didn't want to wait for perfect timing. I wanted to life fully and enjoy every *today.*

You probably know people who lament lives that aren't fulfilled. Don't be one of them! Yesterday is gone, you can't change it. Tomorrow isn't here yet, you don't really know what it will bring. Today is what you have right now! Don't wait for life to begin! Each tomorrow will be too late to enjoy every today. Today is useless to you if you drag the past into it or if you wait for tomorrow to make the most of your life. Life is simpler, more fulfilling and rewarding, if you live *today*—every day.

CAUSE AND EFFECT

A cartoon by Wiley Miller depicts a man standing at the Pearly Gates where a sign is posted stating, *No Religion Beyond This Point*, and the man says, "I always wondered how they could achieve peace and tranquility here for an eternity."

This cartoon brought to mind Walter Starke's telling book *It's All God,* in which he talks about objectivity and subjectivity—cause and effect. To have an effect, there must be a cause. *Cause* is subjective; it is the unseen state of consciousness, it is more internal; while *Effect* is seen in external form. Those who see things from a materialistic standpoint (form or effect) are objective, while those whose approach to life is intuitive, who think in terms of creation (cause), see things more subjectively. Both approaches are valid states of consciousness, but each of us tends to be attuned to one more than the other. When we see things with the body's eyes, we're seeing effect. When we go within and see with the eyes of Spirit, we see cause, or creation. Many religions are objective and worship Idols—statues and other forms they can see—while others seek to find answers subjectively, looking within.

Quantum Physics has proven scientifically that consciousness changes form and that mind-over-matter is not just a superstition, it is a scientific fact. Minds create matter. They've also proved that the illusory division between space and time, energy and matter, spiritual and material is just that, illusory. Doing away with the basic dualism of subject verses object has joined cause and effect. There cannot be matter without underlying spirit. What we *believe* (subjective cause) brings about what we *see* (objective effect).

There are many religions in our culture. Different people believe differently, and all of these people are right because their belief system is what works for them. The unfortunate result of some of these differences is that wars are fought over religion. Instead of accepting the findings of Quantum Physics, which proves there is not a duality, that we are all one creation in spirit, these warring people think they are right, and that everyone else is wrong.

We don't have to wait until we get to the Pearly Gates where religion is banned (as in the cartoon) to see that religion doesn't divide us. We don't need to try to change someone else's beliefs to match our own. If we can open our hearts and minds, let go of religious prejudices, accept all people of all faith traditions, respect them and their beliefs, we can achieve peace and tranquility here and now.

HEAD AND HEART

Many people are searching for their vocational or spiritual path. Some search with their head, others with their heart. The most successful searches, however, are with both head and heart.

If you already excel at a vocation you really enjoy, something you'd do even if you were not paid to do it, there's a passion that comes from your heart as well as an ability that comes from your head. When you can find that perfect balance you know you have found what Buddhism calls *right livelihood,* and you can stop searching.

The same thinking goes into finding your spiritual path: what Buddhism calls *right mindfulness.* When you find you are living with a moment-to-moment presence, manifesting awareness of the workings and content of the mind along with awareness of the body, feeling your truth and knowing its passion, you know you've found your right path, and you can stop searching.

Some people get passionate about one spiritual path or belief system but are drawn away from that path when something else piques their interest. It's good to explore different thought patterns, but they can sometimes be divergent and life can become complicated, not knowing what to believe. Others might engage in one course of study which leads to a certain vocation, then find that path isn't fulfilling, and begin to search for another career path.

Sometimes this happens—both vocationally and spiritually—when other people tell us we're in the wrong place and there is something else we should try. To really find our way, though, we can't let others distract us from our true calling. We must listen to our own voice and feel our own heart. When we let only our head guide us, we'll never be quite satisfied. We might feel no reward, or we could get into something that is not comfortable or may even be dangerous. When only our heart is involved, we can also go into things that feel good at the start but can become uncomfortable or risky.

There's a fine balance between head and heart. When they are in alignment, and we feel clarity of direction along with passion of purpose, we know we've found our path. We can get anywhere we want to go when we engage both head and heart—thinking with our head and feeling with our heart.

LIFE IS FUN, IF WE LET IT BE

For a time, I worked at an emerging city. I was assistant city clerk and the job had many aspects, one of which was taking minutes at city council meetings. The square mileage of this city had been nothing but dairy farms for decades, until developers began purchasing acreage from the dairymen and building tracts of homes. This transition was fast and popular so there were a lot of decisions to be made by the council in a relatively short time, and their meetings often lasted into the wee hours of morning. This was before computers, and I recorded the proceedings by hand, then transcribed my notes the next day. Since it was essential that the details be correctly recorded, the city sent me to school to learn a type of shorthand (which I've unfortunately forgotten most of).

Although the city job was very difficult, I found a way to take the stress out and make it fun. I enjoyed the dairymen who were mostly Scandinavian and who called me *Yoody*. I enjoyed interacting with the planning and building departments, with the councilmen (they *were* all men), and with the developers. I learned a lot that helped me later, when I began to work in real estate.

After I left that job to move to another city, a man was hired to replace me. When he found he couldn't keep up with the work, they hired him an assistant. Since I'd made friends with others in city hall, I talked with them often and was told how these new people constantly complained about how much work they had to do and how hard it was.

My intention had clearly been to do my job well and to enjoy doing it, so that's how it was for me. Sometimes we can change conditions, sometimes we can't, but we can always change our mind about how we feel. If we can adopt an attitude of play, we can make anything fun. I made that challenging job fun. The people who followed me couldn't see past the demands, so failed to see any fun.

Just like the title of this book, *Life is Simple: if we let it be,* life can also be *fun*, if we let it be. I'm not saying we should make light of what's essential, but if we keep a playful attitude, we can even make dealing with frustrating people fun.

Next time you're tempted to complain about something that needs doing, take a minute to see the fun in it. You'll find the job to be simpler and you will probably get it done faster. And, if you find yourself 10,000 feet in the air without a parachute, try to laugh on the way down. (Just kidding)

LET GO AND LET GOD

You may not be religious, but I'm pretty sure you pray because prayer is thought, and we all think.

When I first started attending a Unity church, a wise woman told me that when we pray, we are really talking to our self and that answered prayer is the result of changing our own thinking. We don't pray beseeching God to bring us the new car we want so badly, God is not in the car business. When we ask for that car, we've put our desires out into the universe and the law of attraction takes over. What comes into our lives is what we attract, and if our true belief is that we'll get that car, it will be attracted to us.

We don't need to keep asking God for something over and over. Once we ask, our desire, our wish, our prayer is sent into the universe, and we can relax, let go, and let God. Just as we wouldn't follow a letter we mailed through the whole sorting, travelling, and delivery process, we don't need to follow up with God.

God lives within us and because, internally, we know what's best for us, our prayer will be answered. There's no need to obsess, but we do need to take the necessary action steps to manifest our desire. When we ask God for guidance, and listen to that internal voice, what we desire—or something better—will come to us even if it takes some action on our part. There's an old proverb that says, *Pray to God, but row for the shore.* We might need to stop and take stock now and again, but God will be with us all the way.

We may not call the deity we pray to *God*, but whatever our Higher Power, we pray and then let go. As we listen for answers, we will see our life change. Our prayers will be answered and we'll be taken care of in ways that we couldn't take care of ourselves. We don't have to deny our self food or anything else we need to stay alive, healthy, and happy to have our prayers answered. Once we've prayed sincerely, we can let it go. God hears our prayers and any outcome will be the will of God. God is our source for good.

Prayer is thought. We don't pray to change God's mind, it's our own mind that is changed. Changing our thinking changes our life. So, when we say *Amen*, we know that the God that lives within us has heard our prayer, and we feel a deep peace as we let go, and let God handle the details. Our next prayer will be one of gratitude. The most important prayer we can utter is *Thank you, God.*

LIFE'S TEACHERS

In a discussion group I attended, the subject of Life's Teachers came up. Someone said, "We can learn how to live peacefully and simply and be going along just fine . . . and then we get married!" Most of us laughed at this statement, but others groaned.

People come into our life to be our teachers. Some are often annoying in some ways and they might be critical of us. Our first impulse in these times is to fight back, to defend our self. But we'd see this is not the best way to find the inner peace we long for. When we become defensive of a perceived attack, that defense becomes further attack.

The conversation in our group was centered on spouses, but other teachers might be parents, employers, friends, our children, or even casual acquaintances who pass briefly through our life. When we begin to feel defensive, the wise thing to do is to stay open to what these people are saying because they are often serving as a mirror of the self-critic inside ourselves. Annoyance and criticism can't bother us unless we believe it on some level. When we become defensive it's a pretty sure bet we see what they're saying or doing is alive and well within us.

When we are confident in our own self-worth, seemingly negative comments won't inflame us. If we hold some doubt about our self or our motivations, someone we've attracted into our life will very likely magnify those doubts and voice them. If we don't retaliate, and instead, remain calm and look inside to see if there is any truth in what these teachers are saying, we can rise above the criticism, change our own thinking to overcome those self-doubts, and find an inner peace.

If we think someone in our life is constantly finding fault, we need to thank that critic. What they're saying often matches what our own self-critic believes. We can stop to appreciate what we interpret as criticism. It can help us grow in self-awareness and enhance our self-worth and our confidence.

I'm certainly not suggesting that we tolerate abuse, only that we remember that we all see things through our own perceptual field, and if someone else's perception of us feels like criticism, we can take a good look at it. If we see a kernel of truth, we can take the necessary steps to easily correct our thinking or our actions. But if we find the criticism nasty, completely untrue, or just plain mean, we don't have to defend our self with further attack. We simply need to realize it's not true and then forget it. This helps to keep life simple.

WHAT'S THE HURRY?

I read an article about how the chip technology on credit cards is causing frustration for both customers and merchants because it takes so long for the machine to read the chip.

In our culture, we are encouraged to move fast, drive fast, eat fast, think fast, and do things in a hurry. Even our music is fast and the words to songs often impossible to understand. Unfortunately, our hurry to be in a hurry sometimes leads to chaos or causes us to make mistakes or demonstrate bad judgment. What we think of as speed can actually be wasteful.

When traffic is heavy when we're driving, we can get tense and angry, or we can stay calm and relaxed enjoying the music on the radio and the natural beauty around us. We can even share a smile with other drivers to bring them a little joy and maybe make their day better. We will arrive at our destination unruffled, with a positive attitude. Being tense and worried about being late is not going to get us where we're going any faster, so we might as well enjoy the ride.

I like to keep life simple. When I approach a project or an important decision, I like to take time to think about what I'm doing. In fact, I usually take more time thinking and planning than actually executing a project or acting on a decision. I find that when I rush headlong into something, I end up making mistakes or bad decisions, and have to correct the mistakes or regret the decisions.

There is wisdom in the words, *haste makes waste*. When we're driven by speed, we make mistakes or we break things. When we slow down a little, whatever we're doing still gets done, but we feel relief rather than stress. There's also wisdom in the words, *stop and smell the roses*. If we relax as we go through our day, and literally stop to smell the roses, or enjoy a leisurely cup of tea, we'll find we will accomplish as much as we would have if we'd been tense and in a hurry.

The next time you have to wait those few seconds for the machine to read your card chip, use those seconds to look around, find something pleasant to look at, or share a friendly word with the merchant if you're the customer, or the customer if you're the merchant. Maybe these few seconds won't seem wasted, can be productive, and can make you, or someone else, smile.

LEAP DAY

Every four years, February has an extra day; we call this day Leap Day. It's a time when the Gregorian calendar that we use today catches up with the ancient Julian calendar, giving Leap Years 366 days rather than the normal 365. It does this to synchronize the calendar with the astronomical or solar year, which is the length of time it takes the earth to complete its orbit around the sun. This orbit takes approximately 365 and 1/4 days, is called a Tropical year, and the seasons follow. If we didn't have Leap Years, our calendar would gradually lose time until we were celebrating Christmas in the middle of summer. To catch up, a day is added to the calendar every year that is divisible by four. Since February is our shortest month, it gets that extra day. To get more technical, this extra day makes Leap Year about 11 minutes and 14 seconds longer than a typical year, so to make up for that, every 100 years—every century year—that extra day is taken out, unless the year is divisible by 400, then it isn't. For example, in 1700, 1800, and 1900, there was no Leap Day. That day was "leaped over." In 2000, Leap Day was left in because 2000 is divisible by 400.

Now that I've confused you with this brief science lesson, let's leap to a fun historical fact connected to Leap Day. In the 5th century, St. Brigid convinced St. Patrick to allow a woman to ask a man to marry her on this day. Before that, marriage could only be proposed by a man. If the woman's proposal was turned down, the man had to give her something of value. Maybe this was an ancient form of women's lib.

I like to consider Leap Day as a time for *me*. Most days are spent taking care of the needs of our clients, employers, spouses, children, parents, and others who make demands on us. We think we need to fulfill the needs of others before we can take care of our own needs, and we kind of get lost in the mix. This can cause a bit of resentment, and that's not a comfortable feeling. Just as the calendar is catching up on this day, this could be a symbolic day for you to catch up with yourself. No, you don't have to wait four years for your needs to be met, but if you start with this day, you can begin to take care of yourself every day. If you are true to yourself every day of the year, there won't be a need to catch up every four years, or at all. There is time enough, not just on Leap Day, to do whatever it is that makes your heart sing. This doesn't mean you can turn away from those who require your attention or your care, but you'll be a better caregiver if your own spirit is energized by taking care of yourself.

THE LION & THE LAMB

The old saying goes, "March comes in like a lion and goes out like a lamb." The month starts with stormy weather and ends with blue skies, sunshine, and flowers. Even some *days* are like the lion and the lamb. When we wake up grumpy, everyone around us feels it. As the day goes on and our attitude gets better, we become more peaceful and more pleasant to be around.

The lion and lamb metaphor actually goes with us as we evolve and grow in awareness. We begin to tame the lion, remembering that we are spiritual beings moving through life, learning to grow in love, kindness, and compassion. We also begin to move away from lion-like anger, pride, and judgment. Simply *wanting* growth, awareness, and a simpler life is a huge step away from the growling, teeth-bearing lion and toward the sweet, soft, loving, lamb.

The beautiful thing is that we can choose. We can realize our joy doesn't come from circumstances, it comes from our state of mind, from the way we see things. We can be joyful during storms or in the sunshine. We are human, imperfect in many ways, but our true nature is not that of the grumpy, defensive lion. We may sometimes fall into old ways of thinking and act lion-like, especially when we're tired, hungry, or feeling bitter or negative, but we can take a deep breath, and decide to be the lamb, to be love and to have compassion even toward our imperfect self.

Sometimes it's hard to choose the way of the lamb, but we can train ourselves to find ways to get out of any bad mood we find ourselves in. Yoga works for me. Quieting my mind and moving my body, relaxing into the postures of yoga, lifts my spirits. And it helps release blocked energy and gets me back into the flow of positive energy. Taking a walk or a jog helps some, as does simply stopping to take a few deep breaths. Also, being around and supported by like-minded people can bring us back from the dark side.

When your positive energy is depleting, everyone around you is affected, so when those lion moments come, don't let them last long. The softness of the lamb already exists in you, it's just that sometimes you have to peel back the layers of lion to find it. To make life simpler, find what works for you to keep the lion at bay and stay connected to the lamb nature that is alive within you.

GAIN WITHOUT PAIN

At the gym, we've been told to work harder, do more reps, go faster, that if we aren't feeling pain, we're not making any gain. This never made sense to me. Who wants to inflict pain on themselves?

In life, most people struggle more than they really need to and they cause themselves unnecessary pain. We try to find answers to puzzling situations when there really are no answers. There are some things we aren't meant to understand. We don't need to endure the pain of trying to make sense of these things. We don't need to struggle. What we need to know will be shown to us, sometimes in mysterious ways, sometimes clearly. It's like light and dark. When we're in the dark and a light is turned on, the darkness goes away. We didn't have to struggle for this to happen. When we open our minds to a world without pain, dark turns to light, the struggle ceases, and we gain peace.

Sometimes pain works in our favor. If we touch something hot and feel pain, we immediately let go so we won't get burned. When we're buying a new pair of shoes and the ones we like hurt our feet, we don't buy them to avoid enduring the pain of ill-fitting shoes

When we feel the contrast of how bad it feels to hurt, against how good it feels not to hurt, we are motivated to make choices that take away the pain and open to making decisions that we gain from. Peace of mind is a game-changer. When making critical choices, if we take action from a place of composure rather than distress, of reason rather than reaction, our life is simpler, more peaceful, more relaxed, and we can enjoy this journey a lot more.

I recall the story of the frog who, when dropped into a pan of boiling water, jumped right out and ran away. Another frog was put into a pan of cool water which was gradually heated to boiling. This frog stayed put and was cooked. Like the second frog, we've learned to blur or deny some signals of pain. When we're in distressing emotional or physical situations where pain builds gradually over time, we kind of stop noticing the pain, and learn to endure it. But we don't deserve that kind of pain. We don't really deserve any kind of pain. Deep in our consciousness we know what hurts and what doesn't, and we can learn to take steps to avoid what hurts.

Gentle lessons are learned easily and there is no need to learn though pain. Gain without any pain will make your life simpler and more rewarding.

RULES FOR LIVING

Miriam Keare was a civic leader and a strong environmentalist. She died in 2000 at age 91 and left behind her now famous "Golden Rules for Living." They are twelve rules that, if followed, would simplify life for everyone.

1. If you open it, close it.
2. If your turn it on, turn it off.
3. If you unlock it, lock it up.
4. If you break it, admit it.
5. If you can't fix it, call in someone who can.
6. If you borrow it, return it.
7. If you value it, take care of it.
8. If you make a mess, clean it up.
9. If you move it, put it back.
10. If it belongs to someone else, get permission to use it.
11. If you don't know how to operate it, leave it alone.
12. If it's none of your business, don't ask questions.

This all sounds so simple, and each rule makes perfect sense. If we think about how much easier it would be to get around our home or workplace if these rules were followed, or how much time and energy we'd save by not having to look for things or clean up other people's messes, we might want to give these rules for living some consideration.

Maybe the rule we break the most is number 12. People tend to have an insatiable need to know *everything*. We want to know about other people's lives, and we want to know their secrets. Some people might just be nosy, but most of us simply want to be helpful. We don't have to know every little detail of the life of another, however, in order to be helpful. If someone you know seems unhappy, you can give them a pick-me-up just by being positive and maybe buying them a cup of coffee. If you can take their mind off their problem even for a short time, you have been helpful. That respite from the thoughts that are bringing them down can give them a chance to stop and take a look at what's wrong and perhaps come up with their own solution.

I have these Golden Rules for Living on my refrigerator, held there by a happy-face magnet, so I can see them every day as a reminder to keep life simple.

WHY DO I DO THIS?

We're all human, and every human has at least one innocent, sometimes silly, habitual obsession. I have a cousin who doesn't close drawers, cabinets, boxes, or anything with a lid. She's an otherwise intelligent, capable, fully-functioning individual, and she doesn't know why she does this. Maybe it's because she might need something else out of the drawer or cabinet and thinks it saves time to just leave them open. She just half-closes things like the lid on mayo or jelly jars and vitamin bottles, and the inner lining of the cereal box. This can become problematic when she pulls out the cereal and it dumps on the floor, or when she picks up the bottle of vitamins by the lid, the bottle drops, and the pills go rolling all over. She also leaves the drawers in her desk open. Is she airing out the pencils?

My own strange obsession is containers. I can't throw boxes or and jars away, and I love luggage. I have a drawer full of jelly jars with cute checkered tops that I've washed and removed labels from and stashed away for I don't know what. And my garage is full of cardboard boxes. I do find uses for some of them at times, and I can have my choice of sizes, but most of them just stay until I can't get to what I need on the shelves in the garage and have to purge boxes. And luggage—I would have to pack for a long sojourn to the North Pole to ever use all the suitcases I have in the attic.

Maybe my obsession for containers is my penchant for organization. I like to keep things neat, so I want to have containers to put things in. Or maybe I've felt like I've been contained throughout my life so I keep empty containers around to signify my breaking out of the box. My cousin sees her habit as a convenience, but maybe she comes from a family that was "cram and slam" and she's subconsciously rebelling.

Whatever your strange habitual obsession, as long as no one is hurt by it and it doesn't interfere with your everyday living, it's probably not worth worrying about. If you can laugh in the face of your obsession—like I laugh at my container overload—you'll be okay. If your obsession is truly a distraction in your life, however, or if it's dangerous, you can replace it with a new, better habit. Or you can change it any time you decide it's time to do so by thinking about it differently. Ask yourself, "Why am I doing this?" And if you don't have a good reason, you can stop . . . if you want to.

THE SUCCESS OF HAPPINESS

Which came first—the chicken or the egg? This is the age-old question that no one can answer. But here's another question to think about: Which came first—success or happiness? Are you happy because you're successful, or are you successful because you're happy?

USA Today did a survey of successful people, asking this very question, and found that twice as many respondents said that happiness led them to success as those who stated that success is what made them happy. In other words: Happy people are far more likely to become successful than successful people are to be happy.

Happiness is an inside job, it is a choice, it doesn't come from external conditions, it comes from intention. Conditions in our life go up and down. Relationships, jobs, cars, homes come and go, but our happiness needn't go with them because there are always new ones—better ones—waiting for us if our underlying intention is to find happiness . . . to *be* happy.

We all know chronically unhappy people. No matter how good their life appears to be, they can find something to complain about. These could be highly successful people, but their success hasn't really brought them happiness. They've chosen unhappiness. You may also know very happy people who are not necessarily successful. Success doesn't have to be financial, it could simply be finding success in a relationship, in raising a family, or in growing a beautiful garden. Success doesn't always bring happiness, but happiness more often brings success. The law of attraction plays into this. When we are happy, we are drawn to success because people—employers, customers, friends—are attracted to those who exude a certain joy.

Lighten your load! Choose happiness, and success will follow. If you're not happy, you may need to stop struggling to find success. Happiness attracts success. Sometimes success brings happiness, but you have to work harder for it.

It might sound too easy, but happiness simplifies our life. If whatever success we have is not making us happy we can change our outlook. We can choose happiness and allow more success to find us.

WHO ARE YOU?

Who do you think you are? Do you feel like you are under attack by the world you see? Do you think your hopes, wishes, dreams, and plans are at the mercy of a world you cannot control? Are you holding yourself back with self-defeating thoughts about yourself?

It's true that there are some things in life that we can't control, but we *can* control the way we look at these things, and how we respond. When we look beyond appearances and recognize the truth behind what we *think* we see, we will come to realize that what we believe about these appearances are images that we have created. By changing our mind about them, and more importantly, about ourselves, letting go of defeating, self-restricting thoughts, and allowing the truth of who we really are dawn upon us, our life will change and we will open up to opportunities we might never have thought possible.

When we can remember that we are children of God, and that perfect security and complete fulfillment are our birthright, we will see that it is our own thoughts that keep us from living to our full potential. When we forget this, the world we perceive can hold a fearful self-image in place, and keep us from seeing the truth of who we are.

God's will for us is perfect happiness, and God is patient. He will wait as long as it takes for us to change our mind. When we no longer wish to believe we are under attack, that the world is our enemy, keeping our hopes, dreams, and wishes unfulfilled, we can change our mind about how we see things—our perception of the world—and open up to the knowledge that who we are has been kept for us in the mind of God. We are one with the thought of God and we can look past appearances to see the truth beyond them. What we see—our vision of our self—is what we will be.

We see the world not as *it* is, but as *we* are. Changing our perception and seeing the world, people, things, situations, and circumstances differently, will change our outlook. That mind change is always available to us. We can take heed of the words of Wayne Dyer, "Change Your Thoughts and Change Your Life."

You'll be amazed at how people and situations change when you choose to look at them with a new perception, a new perspective, and see that when you change the way you look at things, things do change the way they look.

CRAZY HAPPY

I heard about a young man on a commuter train who was a bother to the other riders. He wouldn't stay in his seat. He ran through the car touching everything he could—seats, windows, bars, posters, and even some people. He squealed with excitement over each thing he touched. The other passengers were getting upset about this "crazy guy" and tried to force him to take a seat. The young man ignored them, pushing them away and continued moving around the train, touching and squealing. The offended passengers became very upset, almost to the point of violence. After a short time, another man joined the young fellow and seemed to enjoy what he saw him doing. This irritated the passengers even more. Now there were *two* crazies on the train! But their attitudes changed when they were told by the man that the younger man was his son, that he'd become blind as a small child, and that he'd just had a surgery which restored his vision. This was his first venture into a sighted world. He was so excited by what he could see that he wanted to touch everything around him. The passengers were shocked by this revelation. They cowed back to their seats, felt humbled and somewhat ashamed of the way they'd been treating this young man, realizing that their actions could easily have escalated and become dangerous.

We never know why people act the way they do. When someone is disruptive, it might be because they're experiencing a trauma, or a terrible loss or illness. They might be intoxicated. Or, they could be seeing the world for the very first time and loving what they see.

When we judge another's actions, we need to take a look at ourselves. What is it in us that makes us react? Why did all those passengers feel they had to interfere and try to make this young man settle down? This scenario could have triggered something in them that they didn't want to look at, so they blamed the "crazy-happy" boy for their discomfort when, if they'd known the truth, might have celebrated with him.

Our lives are so much simpler when we accept others just the way they are without trying to make them adjust to what we want them to be. If we can look at the world as millions of different personalities, each with their own reactions to life, giving them different reasons for doing what they do, we can become more accepting. We can live and let live, and the world can become a better, more peaceful place.

CONNECTION

There are people who are addicted to over scheduling and multitasking, who find it hard to focus on one task or one person at a time, giving neither their full attention. Darla, a good friend, was one of those people. She would plan a dinner or a casual outing and invite several people to participate. Although these affairs were fun, and it was nice to meet new people, there was never any substance to conversations or interactions because there was always something else calling for attention—a video, or a child dancing, or someone who dominated the conversation. I was always pleased to be invited to dinner at Darla's—she was a great cook—and looked forward to seeing her, but rarely got the chance to have meaningful conversation. There was always something else going on. Darla had a way of combining errands with a lot of stops when we got together alone. As a result, we rarely had a chance to talk, to really connect. We eventually drifted apart, I guess because I put more value on friendships with more meaning for me.

The funny thing is that recently, one of my yoga students was about to move to another state and I wanted to treat her to a lunch before she made her move. Strangely out of character for me, I invited two other class participants to go along. Was I somehow afraid we wouldn't have enough in common to keep a conversation going when it was just the two of us? Maybe so. As it turned out, she had to back out of the lunch and we rescheduled for a later date. When we did get together, we enjoyed a nice meal and stimulating conversation, just the two of us. We had a lovely time, never running out of subject matter. I got to know her on a deeper level and will miss her very much when she's gone.

What I've learned from all this is that our presence is the most valuable gift we can give to another. When we want to really get to know someone, we should try not to dilute our connection with outside influences. We want to be fully present for the person we're with, open our heart to them, learn about them, and let them get to know us on a deeper level as well. When we are open to giving *and* receiving, our heart will be filled, and our soul will sing with the reward of true friendships and relationships. In those one-on-one meetings, both lives are nourished.

IT'S ABOUT TIME

After facilitating the sale of the company I'd been managing for fourteen years and stepping into "retirement" I'd often wake in the morning not knowing what day it was. The daily routine I'd been living was gone, and I felt I was floating in a sea of, "What am I supposed to be doing today?" Thankfully, this feeling didn't last long. Because I am a "doer" by nature, I found ways to fill my time, to the point that I sometimes felt overwhelmed. Dreams and visions that had become latent while I was so busy taking care of business, came knocking at the door of my consciousness. I found myself prioritizing projects to get them all done. My days were so full that I often had to look at a calendar to see what day it was.

These days I still seem to be busy all the time. Only now, busy can mean teaching yoga, going to a movie, meditating, taking a walk, or pulling weeds. It can also mean reading, writing, spending time with family and friends, exercising, or watching my favorite television shows. The difference is, my time is my own. I created it and can use it as I wish.

When you feel pressured to get a project done by a specific time, do you become tense and fear you won't meet a deadline? When you were a youngster and were assigned a big project—be it building a volcano in fourth grade or writing a twelve-page essay in high school—did you get right on it, taking advantage of the time you had to do it well, or did you wait until just before the assignment was due and rush through it? Some people will say they work better under pressure, but tension and pressure actually offend the soul. We can use time wisely and constructively, or we can waste it. It is within our power to create our life on the values we choose, in the time we choose. If we stay awake to knowing what we want or need to do, relax, and take the time to do it well, our spirit will soar with the feeling of accomplishment.

In reality, there is no time; there is only *now*. When we can stay in the moment and let time work for us, our life becomes simpler. When we check in with our spirit and listen to guidance, we'll find there's time enough to do what needs to be done, and to do it well . . . whatever day it is on the calendar.

BOWL OF LIGHT

Modern day Shaman Hank Wesselman, in his book *Bowl of Light*, tells of an ancient Hawaiian tradition about how every child born into this world is like a "bowl of light," innocent, and imbued with a radiance of light. As the child grows, symbolic "rocks" are placed into their bowl and each rock begins to hide the child's original innocence. If there are many rocks placed in the bowl the child can become an angry, judgmental, negative, basically unhappy individual. But if few rocks are placed in the bowl, he will become happy, well-adjusted, loving, and joyful.

If there are many rocks in your bowl of light, they could have come from a number of sources. Your parents may have been strict and unbending, not allowing you the freedom to explore and learn, keeping you from experiencing new and exciting adventures, keeping you stuck by placing rocks in your bowl. Some of the teachers you've had along the way might have consistently pointed out your shortcomings. You might have been intimidated by certain friends, making you feel inferior. Relationship partners often add rocks. Bosses at your work might be contributors. Sometimes you put rocks into your own bowl by being defensive, self-denigrating, and argumentative.

The good news is that we don't have to accept all the rocks. We came into this world as perfection and pure innocence. Health and happiness are our birthright, and everything we need to live a full and successful life is within us. It is our "bowl of light."

We can remove the rocks from our bowl by recognizing our perfection and removing anything from our consciousness that inhibits the full expression of who and what we are. Negative beliefs and attitudes we've accepted from those who've given us rocks are not our truth. When we don't let our own light shine, when we doubt our own worth, our light is hidden by rocks.

In Sunday school, when you were a child, you probably sang, "This little light of mine, I'm gonna let it shine." If rocks have been placed in your bowl throughout your life, starting today, throw those rocks out and know that your light isn't *little*, it's the light of the world. See yourself in your "bowl of light" without the rocks, and let your radiant light shine.

WHO'S THE PHONY?

In a TV interview, a respected actor confessed to feeling like a phony. He said, "Sometimes I don't really know what I'm doing, and if people knew this about me, I might not be so highly-regarded." Maybe he is a phony, after all, what he does is *act*. But because he's committed to his trade, he does that very well.

When I was in high school, I was on the school newspaper staff. I interviewed teachers, honor students, and quarterbacks and wrote articles about them. I didn't really *know* anything about what they did, I just listened to what they told me and wrote it down, and I won awards. When I was accepted into the most highly regarded sorority on campus in college, I felt like a phony, thinking that if they really knew me, they wouldn't have invited me in. But I was in. I held offices and was a leader in many projects.

When I started my decorating business without much formal training, simply a knack for what looked good, I was successful and having more fun than anybody should ever be paid for. And when I began teaching yoga classes, again without formal training—only about 40 years' experience practicing yoga—I kind of felt like a phony. But as I watched my students become stronger, more flexible, and more balanced physically, mentally, and spiritually, I came to know that I am helping a lot of people, and that I'm in my right place. As I facilitate a *Course in Miracles* study group I've learned along with the rest of the people, and now, some 25 years later, I find that profound thoughts come out of my mouth, and I know they aren't really my thoughts—coming from a place of knowledge—but words that come from Spirit, through me. I might have felt like a phony when I started all these activities, but I was put in these places and circumstances to foster my own growth, and to help others in their growth.

Opportunities come into our lives, challenging us, balancing us spiritually, benefiting others, and changing our self-perception. The actor in the interview might have felt like a phony, but the messages that come through the characters he portrays get through to us. He's not a phony—and neither are you! If you feel led to be, or do, or join, or teach something, but don't feel *qualified*, go for it anyway. Learn as much as you can about the subject, and then learn so much more by doing. You will touch people in ways you may never know. Connecting with others and helping them is not being a phony.

HUMILITY

We've all known egomaniacal people. People who are so self-absorbed that they feel the need to find fault with others in order to make themselves look good. People who see the world and everyone in it as something to conquer. What these egotistical people may not know is that bragging about how wonderful they are actually makes them appear ignorant and alienates them from others. They think they're happy with themselves, and they think they are the winners in life, but there is usually a deep-seated insecurity that they don't know what to do with.

Judith Martin (Miss Manners) says, "It is far more impressive when others discover your good qualities without your help." We don't need to tell others how good, smart, and talented we are, we just need to be ourselves, to be authentic, and others will figure it out for themselves.

We have everything we need within us, we just have to put the gift of our talents and uniqueness into action. We don't need to brag in order to make others think highly of us. When we use our God-given gifts to bring happiness to others or to make a difference in the world, our reward is the feeling of achievement within our own heart and soul. We don't do the good things we do for others and for the world, for accolades, awards, or even a pat on the back, and there's never a good reason for causing someone else to feel less-than just to boost our own ego.

A big part of a beautiful person is that they always see the beauty in others. If we want to get ahead in life or simply live a happy, peaceful, productive life, we will put the needs and the feelings of others before our own. When we act at the expense of others, everyone looses. When we are humble, honest, helpful, and living authentically and in integrity, it shows. We don't have to point it out to people. We don't have to brag about how smart, capable, or strong we are. We simply need to live, and let others watch. Others will recognize our goodness and will admire us for it. When we remain humble, and open our hearts and minds to see the beauty in others, they will see the beauty in us.

HABITS

When one person's alarm clock rings, he turns it off, bounds out of bed, dons his exercise clothes, and sets off for his morning jog. Another person hits the snooze button and goes back to sleep. What these two have in common is a powerful force that keeps them doing what they've become accustomed to doing: The force of habit. You may have habits that you'd like to change, habits that are unhealthy or self-defeating, and you might find it hard to stop the habitual behavior. But you can do it!

If you are the snooze button person and would like to become the jogger, you need to lay out your exercise clothes before you go to bed, then get up and get out when the alarm goes off to break the habit of staying in bed until there's no time left for exercise. There may be others habits you'd like to change as well. You might have the *will* to change and tell yourself, "This week I'm going to start exercising, stop smoking, stop swearing, stop biting my nails, stop wasting time, stop eating junk food." But tying to stop all these habits at once is a sure way to stop none of them. It's best to focus on one bad habit at a time, make the change gradually, and reward yourself with a *way-to-go* when you've overcome it. Then start on the next bad habit.

We can speed up the process of changing habits by replacing a bad habit with a good one we can build on. For instance, if our habit is watching too much television, and we'd like to form the habit of connecting with family and friends, instead of turning on the television, we can pick up the phone and call someone we care about. If our habit is snacking on unhealthy foods, we can buy healthy snacks instead. If we don't keep the bad stuff in the house, we won't eat it.

The popular notion is that it takes 21 days to develop a new habit, but research has shown that to go from starting a new behavior to doing it automatically takes, on average, two months, or 66 days. This research also found that messing up every now and then has no measurable impact on long-term habits, and that a relapse isn't a permanent failure. But how long it takes to break a bad habit and cement a new one isn't the issue. It could take 50 days or 500 days for an old mental image to dissolve and a new one to jell, so we need to focus on the *goal*, not the *time*. If we become a little discouraged, we can remind ourselves that we have to *put in the work* to change an unwanted behavior or habit. When we do that, and we're successful, we'll find our life smooths out and we are happier, more relaxed, and life is simpler. And we might like ourselves a little better.

JUNK PILE

Thomas Edison said, "To invent, you need a good imagination and a pile of junk." When I lived on a farm in Canada, everyone had a pile of junk on their land. A good pile of the best junk was a mark of success. All this junk was somehow useful. When something needed fixing, you went to your junk pile and usually found just the part or piece you needed to fix whatever was broken. Things were built out of those junk piles. I saw animal pens, sawmill platforms, even porches that were built using collected junk. I didn't dare throw anything away. It all went to the junk pile. The mindset of the farmers was that everything has value.

Phil Glashoff is a renowned artist who has a ranch near where I now live. He creates magnificent sculptures from every conceivable kind of metal—from sheets of steel to bike chains and screws. His art is whimsical, fascinatingly beautiful, and is highly sought after. Every year he has an art show at his ranch and admission to this show is an old piece of metal. As the weekend progresses, the pile of metal grows exponentially. I have been a fan of Phil's art for years, but the prices were out of my league. Last year, though, I succumbed to the desire to have one of his sculptures. I bought an adorable girl with a jump rope. She's about seven feet tall, including the jump rope over her head. Her body is an oxygen tank, her skirt a wok, her head a large steel ball, her hair a bike chain, her eyes ball bearings, her eyelashes wire, her legs and arms pipe, and the base she's standing on is a heavy wheel. She's got fingers and toes, and a metal flower in her hair. She's painted purple, pink, and silver. My daughter named her Elizabeth. She's on my patio and I love seeing her every day. Her pieces might have been junk at one time, but she's a work of art now.

The dictionary describes junk as items that are useless or of little value. But seeing what Phil and the farmers in Canada do with junk is a reminder that nothing is ever simply junk. I've heard people say, "My life is junk." But no one's life is junk! Every life has value and purpose. When life isn't going well, we may feel useless, but the best way to come out of this junk funk is to reach out to help others. When we're at our most unhappy, if we can imagine a way to make someone else's life happier, to ease another's pain or lighten their load, we will recognize the value of our life. When we see the joy we can bring into the life of another, the joy in our own life expands, and we recognize that we are not even close to being junk. We are all valuable, important, works of art!

HOPSCOTCH

A *Blondie* cartoon by Dean Young and John Marshall, shows the mailman coming upon a hopscotch game drawn on the sidewalk. He hops through the game and says, with a big smile, "It's the little things that make my day."

This brought back a memory for me. I was asked to lead a workshop at a retreat I often attend. The timing of this particular workshop happened to fall right after the lunch break, and I found that a number of the participants weren't showing much interest. One man actually fell asleep and another was grouchy because he'd been dragged there by his wife and wasn't happy about it. I was doing my best to make the workshop interesting, trying to encourage everyone to participate, but soon discovered that it wasn't going to work. An idea dawned on me! I asked everyone to stand up and follow me outside. I divided the group into smaller groups, gave each group some sidewalk chalk, and asked them to draw a hopscotch. They were somewhat surprised, but gladly obliged. It turned out to be a fun activity with everyone hopping and jumping and laughing while playing this child's game. Everybody woke up from their after-lunch lethargy, and when we'd finished our games, we returned to the classroom and had a great workshop with full participation. (Even the grouchy guy was happy and took part in discussions.)

Sometimes when we're feeling tired or disinterested in what we're doing, it helps to lay the work aside for a while and just play. We can do something physical: Take a walk. Play with the dog. Put on some music and dance. Anything to take our mind off the task at hand. We'll be refreshed and find it easier to return to our project with a clear mind and enough energy to complete it.

It is said that all work and no play makes Jack a dull boy. And it's true. Play is important in our life, and practically anything can become playful if we set our mind to it. It's all in the way we approach things. If we think of a task or a job as drudgery, and we're doing it just to get it done, it becomes a chore that is hard to enjoy. But if we can look at it as fun, the drudgery becomes pleasure. When we have an opportunity to make a game of something, let's do it. We'll get the greatest pleasure out of the hardest jobs if we can see some fun in them. And when we come upon a hopscotch a child has left behind on a sidewalk, let's jump it. Like the mailman in the cartoon, it *is* the little things that make our day.

MINDFULNESS

Mindfulness is described as being connected to the present moment. It's different from meditation in that it can be practiced by anyone, anytime, anywhere. We normally think of meditation as sitting with legs crossed, back straight and unsupported, eyes closed, with concentration on the breath. This works for millions of people, and has for centuries, but for some, meditation is difficult.

Thoughts come into the mind of the mediator and they don't know what to do with them. In my yoga classes, during the final supine meditation, I tell students that if thoughts intrude, to simply be aware of them, then gently let them go. This sounds easy enough, but it doesn't always work. The thoughts are still there. They come and go and can cause a restlessness that negates the benefits of a deep relaxation meditation. If you are someone for whom meditation is difficult, consider mindfulness, clearing from your mind everything beyond what you are doing at any given moment.

Mindfulness can be practiced while washing dishes, giving complete attention to each plate, bowl, glass, spoon, or fork. When eating, mindfulness lets us enjoy every bite without rushing through the meal. We can also remain mindful while brushing our teeth or walking the dog. Mindfulness offers a rest for the brain. It increases productivity and the ability to turn off the unfulfilling autopilot of the daily grind, allowing us to live in the present moment.

Whatever we're doing, we can do it fully, letting it be the only thing we're thinking about. We're doing it in the present moment, and that moment is the only place that we can be. We can start by letting our body relax and our mind remain clear. Mindfulness is mental strength-training, training the mind to accept and enjoy this moment . . . every moment. The point is to prevent our mind from wandering and to give full attention to what's at hand.

Experts contend that mindfulness is the antidote to the fast-paced tech world we're living in. There's a slow backlash against this distracted, multitasking lifestyle beginning to give way to one that's a more self-aware, live-in-the-moment mindset.

Mindfulness, staying focused on what's before us at every present moment—be it a task or another person—will allow us to accomplish more without stress and bring us a peace we might not have thought possible in this hectic world. It's certainly worth a try.

WEARIN' O' THE GREEN

There are several images associated with St. Patrick's Day: The Leprechaun, the color green, the shamrock, and the driving out of snakes.

St. Patrick was not actually Irish, but his name has become an integral part of Irish heritage. As a young man, he felt a call to go to Ireland, where he inspired the masses with his preaching and the miracles he performed. The country had been overrun with snakes, and with spiritual guidance, Patrick drove the snakes into the sea where they all drowned, thus freeing the country of this scourge. He soon became known as the Patron Saint of Ireland.

Leprechauns are believed to be small, illusive sprites wearing large hats and buckled shoes, who relish in mischief and who war against the folly of greed—of trying to get too much too fast.

Shamrocks were sacred to the Druids of Ireland because their leaves formed a triad, and three is a mystical number in the Celtic religion. The green of the shamrock became symbolic for other reasons as time went on. In the 19th century it was a symbol of rebellion against being converted to Christianity. It was a period that spawned the phrase "The Wearin' O' The Green" and anyone brave enough to wear green during that time risked cruel punishment. The country has overcome the negative association with green, however, and now you might get pinched if you *don't* wear green on St. Patrick's Day.

What are your snakes? What habits, sense of lack, limits, oppression, or small thinking could you drive out of your life and into the proverbial sea to drown and be gone forever? St. Patrick listened to spiritual direction to eliminate the snakes, and so can we, if our mind is open to guidance and we have the willingness to follow it.

Do you have a Leprechaun to warn you about going too fast? It might be wise to slow down and make ourselves aware of benefits and possible pitfalls to life decisions before advancing headlong into actions that could backfire.

What is your symbolic green? What is as important to you as the Druids beliefs were to them. What are you willing to stand up for, to wear green for, risking banishment or ridicule? We must be strong in our beliefs, our morality, our self-confidence and self-respect. It's not necessary or responsible to engage in activities that affront our soul. We honor ourselves by living our truth.

If we drive out the snakes, listen to the Leprechaun, and take risks for good, our lives will be better and simpler for it.

AGREE TO DISAGREE

I'm always open to inspiration from life experiences or from things I read, and sometimes the best inspiration comes from the comics. I saw a little two-frame comic that made me think about friendships. It had a title of "How to be a Friend." The first frame showed two guys sitting together and was labeled WRONG. The first guy said, "I'm hurt, mad, and scared." The second guy said, "Let me tell you how you're wrong." The second frame was the same two guys, with the first saying, "I'm hurt, mad, and scared." The second one said, "I'm listening," and this one was labeled RIGHT.

One of the best things about having a friend, or being a friend, is having someone to listen to us and hear what we say and feel without needing to fix things or giving opinions. We all need to vent once in a while, just to get frustrations and anger out of our system, and this venting doesn't have to call for a response of any kind. A simple *I'm listening* or *I hear you* is enough.

I was recently uncomfortable about an action of someone close to me and was experiencing feelings of resentment. Because of the discomfort I felt, I spoke to this person in a gentle, loving way, explaining my feelings. It was, from my standpoint, a clear-the-air moment. It was met, however, with strong denial of the action, excuses, and clear defensiveness. I responded that there was no need for any excuse or explanation, that I wasn't accusing or complaining. I simply wanted to have my feelings acknowledged.

Although it was not my intent, apparently this person felt attacked by my comments, and the denial and defense were returned attack. The action wasn't an issue worth arguing over, and an argument was averted, but it was a learning opportunity for us both. For me, it was *know your audience*. Know who you can trust to hear your feelings and simply listen. For this other person, the lesson *could have been* to stay open to the feelings of another. Knowing this person well, and understanding the motivation for the action, I could see the defensiveness not as an attack on me, but as personal frustration.

There are two sides to every interaction, and when we are able to recognize our part in any kind of disagreement—or even a simple conversation—both sides can be clearly heard and understood. This doesn't mean one side has to give in to the other, but if clarity can be uncovered, even agreeing to disagree can have a peaceful outcome.

QUALITY OR QUANTITY

I'm not someone who should be giving dieting advice. I'm skinny and always have been. I was uncomfortable with my skinny body through my teenage years and into young adulthood. But, just as fashions change through the years, so do ideas of physical beauty. There was a time when roundness and curves were the standard of beauty for women. More recently, willowy figures are the hallmark of allure—at least in the fashion industry. I grew up in the wrong time. If I was a teen-ager today, I might not have had that self-defeating perception of my body.

When we come right down to it, though, it really doesn't matter if we're slim or plump, and nobody should be judged by their body type. Staying healthy in both body and mind is what's important. How we think about our body, though, can have a huge effect on our mind because we are what we *believe* we are.

There are those who live to eat, and those who eat to live. I fall into the second category. All-you-can-eat restaurants are a waste of money for me because all I can eat is not much. But some people tend to overindulge and would like to shed a few pounds. If you are one of those people remember this: It's not *what* you eat, or even how *much* you eat—its *why* you eat.

Eating is emotional. With some people, it's the only thing they feel they have control over in their life. I know people who follow strict dietary regimens, even weighing their food, but this concept is more concerned with *quantity* than with *quality*.

When we can love our self fully, just as God created us, recognize the *quality* person that we are, and know that *we* are in control of both how we think and how we eat, we might change our thinking, and those extra few pounds might begin to melt away.

It's not what we look like on the outside, it's how we feel on the inside that determines our self-worth and happiness. Confidence comes in all sizes. We can tell the image in the mirror that we are a beautiful child of God, loved unconditionally just the way we are, and then let that love shine through to everyone and everything. The *quantity* of our love, for our self and for others, can enhance the *quality* of our life, whatever our body type. And, with quality of life, life is simpler.

EVEN STEVEN

I do a favor for you—you owe me. You do a favor for me—I owe you. Isn't that sometimes the way we think? I helped you pack boxes when you moved, now you owe me something. NO! I helped you because I saw a need and was there, by your side, to help get the job done. We help others, not for accolades, returned favors, or rewards, but for the joy it gives us to be helpful.

Giving and receiving doesn't have to be evenly balanced, in fact, I believe that giving *is* receiving. When we give from our heart, we receive the warm feeling of knowing that we've made something easier for a friend, or maybe for someone we don't even know. That's why we have charities. When we take the clothes we no longer wear to the thrift store, we are helping not only the person who gets those clothes, but also the charity that the store is benefiting. What do we get in return? We get a comfortable feeling of pleasure, knowing we've been helpful. And . . . we get more room in our closet.

I remember a time, long ago, I contracted the flu. I was so sick I couldn't even lift my head, let alone get out of bed. My dear friend Dorothy came over, and out of the blue, started cleaning my house. She cleaned top to bottom until the house shined and smelled wonderful. Then she checked up on me every day until I was strong again. Although this happened decades ago, I still remember it because it meant so much to me. She acted strictly from her heart, expecting nothing in return, and she probably doesn't even remember doing it. When we give love just because we feel love, not expecting anything in return, life becomes a mutually beneficial give and take.

In truth, we are all one, what we give to another we give to ourselves, and the opposite is also true, what we give to ourselves, we also give to others. Love is about give and take, and we are all giving and taking all the time . . . but it doesn't have to be Even-Steven.

If we feel we are giving more than we're getting, we can feel grateful because we are able to help another. If we feel we are getting more than we're giving, we also feel grateful because someone cares enough to help us when we have a need. If we want to extend a favor, we can do it just for the good feeling it gives us, not because we want something in return. We don't keep score, because love doesn't have a score card.

IS IT LUCK?

I recently heard a story of a man who was travelling and came upon a religious shrine. There were many people gathered around the shrine, throwing money at it. The traveler asked why they were doing this and was told that the more money they threw at the shrine, and the harder they threw it, the more good luck they would have.

But life doesn't depend on luck. Even though you've heard people's experiences about being lucky in love, winning at gaming tables, or a multitude of seeming strokes of luck, it's not luck. It's guidance, it's timing, talent, knowledge, skill, hard work, and sometimes it's chance. It's believing in your own good. It's being aware of opportunities and acting on them.

Back in the 1970s, I heard of a prime piece of property that was to be sold at auction. It was a closed-bid auction, so I wrote a bid, sealed it up, and took it to the courthouse on the day bids were to be opened. My bid was accepted and I bought the property. The next day, about a dozen people came to the courthouse with their bids. I was one of only two people who showed up on the correct day. People told me I was really lucky. But was it just luck? I think not. I'd studied the offering, checked out the property, and knew when to submit my bid. Was it divine guidance? Maybe. Was it the result of my own investigation? That helped. And it was timing. It was an action that was ripe, my instincts were right, and it worked to my benefit.

Sometimes when things come out the way we want them to, we might say it was just luck, not fully believing in our own skills and knowledge. Attributing good outcomes to luck is a deception. The universe responds to what we think and feel. If we want good outcomes, we need to think positively, aspire intensely, and feel enthusiastically about what we want or need. Everything depends on us, what we think and feel inside. There are no coincidences, there is synchronism and design. When good things come to us it's because we've attracted them on a cellular level. We've *believed* we deserve our good.

Maybe the people at the shrine do believe luck will come to them, but it won't be because they're throwing money, it will be because they've opened themselves up to good outcomes. The only lucky ones at the shrine are the ones who gather up the money that's been thrown, but even that is planning.

EMBARRASSMENT

In a *Pickles* carton by Brian Crane, little Nelson and Grandpa are sitting on the porch. Grandpa says, "Oh, shoot! I've got a mustard stain on my shirt." Nelson offers, "I've got a Hello Kitty sticker that my teacher gave me. You could cover up the stain with it." Grandpa asks, "Don't you want to keep the sticker?" and Nelson says, "Nah!" and puts the sticker on Grandpa's shirt, saying, "That's what I like about you, Grandpa, nothing embarrasses you."

As we age, we do let go of petty embarrassments. So what if someone thinks it's silly to have a Hello Kitty sticker on our shirt; it's our shirt and it's our sticker. It has nothing to do with anybody else or what they think. If we're okay with it, that's all that matters.

It seems like we spend our lives worrying about what other people think of us. Some of the happiest, most out-going, well-adjusted people I know sometimes do things that someone else might be too embarrassed to do. They're not embarrassed because they accept themselves just as they are. They are comfortable in their own skin and are not bothered by little things. Like Eleanor Roosevelt said, "You wouldn't worry so much about what others think of you if you realized how seldom they do."

When we are embarrassed about something, we are probably the only one noticing it. Yes, there are people who feel the need to judge others and decide how they should look and act, but most people are more accepting than we realize. They're so consumed with trying to avoid their own embarrassment, they don't even think about ours. As we mature, we get past embarrassment. We know that judgment is more about the other person than it is about us.

Go ahead, wear that Hello Kitty sticker on your shirt if you want to. And don't worry about what others think of you. It's how you think of yourself that matters. If you are relaxed and happy, others will be relaxed and happy with you. If there are people who judge, they are likely to be embarrassed about something in themselves, and that's why they find things wrong with other people. Be accepting of those who judge, but stay true to your authentic self. Your kindness, your confidence, and your love will shine through. Perhaps those others will see past what embarrasses them and become happier and more peaceful as well.

FLOWERS & DIAMONDS

You've heard it said: "Bloom where you're planted." Too many people find this hard to do and can't get past the thought of *if only*. If only I was better looking, if only I was richer, if only, if only. Well guess what, your life is just the way you make it. You are responsible for what you see, and on some level, you ask for what you receive

We've seen plants in a garden blooming beautifully with one plant set apart from the others, also blooming. That plant didn't fail to bloom because it didn't have the benefit of attention that the others had. It bloomed where it was planted because it was created to bloom. We are all created to bloom, and the only thing stopping us is our own self-defeating beliefs about ourselves.

There is a true story of a farmer in South Africa who heard tales of other farmers who made millions by discovering diamond mines. These tales so excited this farmer that he sold his farm and set out to go prospecting for diamonds, but was never successful. Meanwhile, the man who bought the farm happened to be crossing a creek on the property one day when he noticed a bright flash of blue light from the creek bottom. He bent down and picked up a stone. It was a beautiful, large, crystal-like stone, and when he showed it to a visitor, he was amazed to learn that he'd found one of the largest diamonds ever discovered. There were many more stones like this one sprinkled throughout the creek bottom, and the property the farmer had sold turned out to be one of the most productive diamond mines in all of Africa. The farmer had owned acres of diamonds but had sold them for practically nothing in order to search elsewhere.

We are all standing in the middle of our acre of diamonds. When we recognize what we have before charging off to look for something better in other places, we'll find we are already abundant in health, happiness, peace, love, and unlimited possibilities. These are our God-given rights.

Abundance isn't something we acquire, it's something we tune into. If we can't see it, it's simply because we're not looking in the right place. The flower is within us, and when we stay open to this, we *will* bloom where we're planted. We will find we are standing in a diamond field. We have what we need, and the only things holding us back are our own self-doubts. We can *expect* every need to be met. We can *expect* the answer to every problem. And we can *expect* abundance on every level, because worry and self-doubt always block our good.

APPLICATION

"Spirituality" is defined as a broad concept with room for many perspectives. In general, it includes a sense of connection to something bigger than ourselves, and it typically involves a search for meaning in life. As such, it is a universal human experience, something that touches us all. Those who speak of spirituality outside of religion generally believe in the existence of different spiritual paths.

Although many people find spirituality through a connection with their religious affiliation, there are certain differences. Religion usually asks the question: What practices, rites, or rules should I follow? Whereas, Spirit asks: Where do I *personally* find connection and value? Both belief systems engender comfort, reflection, ethics, and emotional well-being. Where these questions overlap is in the individual *experience*—the deeply personal aspect—which affects the way we think, feel, and behave. Those who are deeply entrenched in a given religion are inclined to want to bring others around to their way of believing, while those who are more spiritual find it's a deeply personal journey, important to their own growth and development

Many students of spirituality spend a lot of time and effort in gathering information. They feel that the more information they can put in their heads, the more enlightened they'll become. There's nothing wrong with learning in order to give us a background, but it doesn't really lead anywhere. What matters, in terms of finding our spiritual comfort zone, is *application*, which leads to *experience*.

We can read dozens of books on spiritual subjects or philosophical speculation, and we can jump from one aspect to another, but what's important—the only way we'll really find our spiritual center—is when we find a path and *apply* its teachings, which leads to an *experience* of comfort and well-being.

If we search for only this and do not let theology delay us, a kind, understanding, empathetic person who glows with true, unconditional love for all beings, who is able to forgive all perceived wrongs, and who sees others as himself, has found a genuine spiritual path and can cease to search. When we find that deep spirituality within ourselves, there's no need to *tell* anyone about it. The way we apply it, and experience it, lights up our life and shines out to others. When we're living our spiritual truth, it shows.

LEARNING

We are in this world to learn. We learn from our parents. We learn in school. We learn at our jobs. We learn from each other. We learn by observation and by practice. Everyone and everything is constantly teaching us something, and from all this we learn what we want in life. One of the best ways of learning, though, is learning what *not* to do, how *not* to behave, how *not* to think. Almost as valuable as knowing what we want, is knowing what we *don't* want—then we can eliminate those things from our life.

I'm grateful to a woman with whom I spent a good amount of time several years ago. I'll call her Jane. Without knowing it, Jane taught me a lot about what I did *not* want. She was overly suspicious and had neurotic tendencies. And when I saw how these thoughts affected her, I decided I did not want to go down that path. Paranoia is described as intense anxious or fearful feelings and an irrational and obsessive distrust of others, thinking they're out to get you. Jane didn't trust people, she felt threatened by almost everyone and everything, and was constantly on guard—sure signs of paranoia.

When I was spending time with Jane, I began to see her mistrust and her belief that people were out to get her, and I saw her defensive measures—ways of getting them before they got her. Because I wasn't completely self-assured at the time, I found I was beginning to take on those signs of insecurity. But, because Jane was there, demonstrating her paranoia, and I didn't like what I saw, I learned that wasn't the way I wanted to live, and I changed my thoughts. I learned that I am what I am, and that what other people think about me is none of my business. I became more open and accepting, less fearful, and friendlier, knowing everyone didn't have to like me, but cherishing those who did.

I'm eternally grateful to Jane for the lessons I learned by spending time with her and observing her actions. For obvious reasons, though, I could never express that gratitude to her. I learned what I didn't want, I learned the way I didn't want to live, and with that recognition, was able to eliminate that kind of thinking and to recognize the signs of paranoia if they ever crept into my consciousness again, and to change my mind.

TIME FOR LOAFING

In a *Pickles* cartoon by Brian Crane, Grandpa says, "I broke down and bought myself a new pair of shoes today. I figure this pair will probably be the last pair of shoes I'll ever have to buy." Then Grandma asks, "What kind of shoes are they?" Grandpa answers, "They're loafers." To which Grandma responds, "Ah! How appropriate."

There comes a time in life when loafing actually *is* appropriate. We live our whole life—going to school to learn what we need to know to make our way in this world, then spend many years working to earn a living, raising a family, volunteering in our community, and generally keeping busy—filling every minute doing what needs to be done. Then comes a time when we're older, and kind of tired. We've instilled good values in our children, and they're out on their own. We may have travelled and seen the world—or at least the part of the world we wanted to see—and we've slowed down. It's time to loaf, and to wear loafers.

We don't stop living, we just live a little more slowly. Thoughts of getting ahead are behind us, and we can reflect on the things we did well and stop worrying about how we might have done some things better.

We can now be the voice of wisdom and experience for our children and grandchildren. We still eat well and get the exercise we need to stay healthy. We read, watch TV, do puzzles to keep our mind alert, but we are entitled to simply do nothing if we so choose. We can loaf, so loafer shoes *are* appropriate.

If you're still in the busy part of your life, take some time to appreciate your elders—the loafers. Listen to them, learn from them, and help them understand how their computers and cell phones work. If you don't have parents or grandparents who are living, you can visit your local senior center and find someone with white hair wearing loafers, and get to know them. My bet is they have stories that will curl your hair, that will make you think, and probably come to better appreciate your own life.

There are so many things about my parents that I never took the time to learn, and that's one of my greatest regrets. When I ever get around to writing my memoir, it will begin with these words from an African Proverb: "When an old person dies, it's like a library burning down."

THE FIVE W'S

The lead paragraph in any news story contains five W's: Who, What, When, Where, and Why. This gives the reader all the pertinent information in a nutshell so he can maneuver through the rest of the article which will contain more specific details, giving insight into what that news story is revealing.

The interesting thing is that without even realizing it, we all live our lives with those five W's. If we've figured out *who* we want to be with or share with, we can live with that decision and eliminate from our lives those that don't work for or with us. When we know *what* we want, we can work toward getting what it is we're striving for. If we can set a time for *when* we want to accomplish something, we can work within that time-frame. When we know *where* we want to end up, we can set a goal and work toward that goal. And if we understand *why* something is important to us, we can work to make it happen. When our Who, What, When, Where, and Why come together, our lives become more fulfilling, more peaceful, and simpler.

Many of us just plod our way through life, not really knowing where we're going, or why, when, or with whom we want to go. But often the best things in life come seemingly out of the blue with no planning or preparation. What we don't realize is that somewhere, deep within, we're working with that five W agenda. A certain person can show up in our life and become the *Who* that fills all the criteria we've unconsciously asked for. Many *Whats* come along and we grasp on to the ones that feel right and ignore the ones that don't. That's our choice to make.

Much of the time we can't figure out the *Why* of things, but in the long run, we don't really have to know why, we just need to be accepting of what comes to us, enjoy the good, and try to make the best of the not-so-good. *Where* and *When* can be carefully planned, or they can be totally spontaneous. Spirit has a way of guiding and leading us when we're open to that guidance.

Try keeping the five W's in mind as you navigate your way through your days and you'll begin to recognize them as they come along. They will give you a basic road map onto which you can add more specific details and gain insight that will lead you to fulfillment and happiness.

PACKING

When travelling, there are two schools of thought: 1) Take everything you might conceivably need while you are away from home, and 2) Travel light, taking only what you know you'll need, and nothing more, figuring if you've forgotten something, you can buy it when you get there.

I once traveled with a woman who took great pride in the fact that she managed to pack everything she needed for a 14-day trip to Europe in a back-pack. This wasn't a camping or trekking trip. We stayed in four-star hotels, had comfortable coaches to travel from place to place, and our luggage was attended to by the tour company. Her pack was not your ordinary backpack. It started at her neck, ended at her hips, and protruded at least two feet behind her. If she didn't give herself plenty of room to turn around, she knocked other people down with what looked similar to a tortoise shell on her back. And she took up two seats on the busses, one for her and one for her pack. But she, by gosh, had everything she needed with her at all times. She was one proud traveler—with a very achy back.

Another woman on that same trip had four suitcases to make sure she had a different outfit for every day. She also had contingency outfits, just-in-case. She had shoes that went better with contingency outfit number one than with main outfit number two. For that, she had another pair. She had *choices* . . . lots and lots of choices.

To make travel easier, we can take blouses, shirts, or sweaters that can go with each of the skirts or pants we've packed. We still have choices, but it takes fewer items to create different outfits. And, if we roll our clothes we can get more into our suitcase

The way a person packs for a trip, either a long journey or just a weekend away, says a lot about that person. Psychologists would say that over-packers have a fear of doing without. They don't want to take up mental space by worrying about changing weather conditions or whether they might spill something on their last clean shirt. They are ready for anything and everything. Packing light gives the illusion that we're freeing ourselves from being overburdened (even though we might end up washing our underwear in our hotel rooms).

There's probably not a *right* way to pack for travel, but if we do whatever makes us comfortable, we will enjoy the trip more and relieve the chaos of *do I have enough or not enough* in our minds.

WELCOME TO WAL-MART

You know how when you go to a new church, there are greeters at the door to meet you and make you feel welcome? Well, think about Wal-Mart; they, too, have greeters. It seems Wal-Mart has learned something from the church.

In the busy life people lead, it's a nice break to be welcomed where you go. How many times have you gone into a retail store to shop and felt completely ignored? Then you enter another store where, no matter how busy the sales people are, they acknowledge your presence. Which of these stores are you most likely to go back to the next time you go shopping? Nobody wants to be hounded by salespeople, of course, but when someone actually lets you know they know you are there, it feels easier to ask for help if you need it.

At times I've gone into a small store that is not necessarily filled with customers, where two or three salespeople are idly standing around in conversation with one another without even noticing that a customer has come in, and I've left that store. I feel like if I'm going to spend my money someplace, it would be nice to feel that those who are there to help at least know I'm there.

I was shopping at one of the big-name home improvement stores one day, looking for a specific item. I came upon a man wearing a store vest who was sitting on a stool. I stopped and asked where I might find the item. He simply pointed and said, "Try aisle 14." It took a certain amount of searching, but I did find the item, and when I walked past this man again, still on the stool, he asked, "Did you find it?" I guess that was his idea of customer service.

I don't go to these big stores much because there is a small privately-owned hardware store near where I live that I much prefer. The people there are welcoming and helpful. The person whose helping me stays with me until we're both sure we've found exactly what I need. I really enjoy shopping at this store, and even know many of the employees by name because I feel comfortable and cared for there.

If you are someone who meets the public—and most of us are, in some way—become a "Wal-Mart Greeter" and let people know that they, and their needs, are important to you. A friendly hello and a smile can go a long way to making someone's day a little better. And being friendly and helpful will make your day happier as well.

FEEL THE FEAR

John Wayne was a brave man, who said, "Courage is being scared to death and saddling up anyway."

Fear is not a comfortable feeling and is often hard to get past. There are lots of things that induce fear, like getting back on the horse after you've been thrown. Really bad weather conditions or thoughts of unrest in the world can bring about fear. This kind of fear, in itself, can be exhausting, but if we remember there is a greater good looking out for us, and we take necessary precautions, this kind of fear can be overcome, or at least lessened by looking at it with a new perspective and a positive mindset.

Public speaking is a fear for many people because of their self-consciousness. They think they're being judged, and they don't want to look foolish. But this fear is easily overcome with practice. When we have to speak in front of a crowd, we can write down what we want to say and follow our notes. And because it's easier to talk to one person than to many, we can find a single person in the audience to speak to. When we can imagine it's just our self and this person, our words will come easily.

Some people have a fear of heights, or of closed-in places, or of flying. To get past these fears we can, with the help of someone close to us whom we trust, experience what we fear. We can feel the fear and do it anyway. This can be hard, but if getting past the fear is important enough, it can work.

People fear what they can't control. A study at Chapman University in Orange, California identified major "domains" of fear, finding that *Crime, Economics, Environmental conditions, Governmental corruption, Man-Made Disasters,* and *Natural Disasters* topped the list of fears for the majority of people. There are real things in each of these categories that could conceivably happen, but worrying about them can hold us back from enjoying our good

When we live in constant fear, we're missing out on life's blessings. *A Course in Miracles* tells us there are only two emotions: Love and Fear. When we feel fearful, we can adjust our thinking back to what we love. We can let go of irrational fear of what *might* happen. Even if the thing we fear should come about, our fear doesn't have to control us. When we can take the necessary action to fix things and to take care of ourselves, we'll find the fear will dissipate, and life will be simpler.

ENTHUSIASM

When you have decisions to make, products to purchase, or vacations to plan, do you rely on what other people advise you to do? What tradition says will work? What you have historically done? What is cheapest? Or do you decide based on feelings of joy? Noted poet Ivern Ball said, "Knowledge is power, but enthusiasm pulls the switch." We can listen and learn all we want from the ideas and experiences of others or from study, but we ultimately make better decisions if we let our own enthusiasm guide us.

I had a little shop, for a while, where I sold plants and baskets. I called it *Wicker and Weeds*. When purchasing merchandise for the shop, I bought items based not on what I thought would sell, but on how much I liked them. I had interesting plants that weren't sold at local nurseries, and baskets that could be used, not just to hold potted plants, but as wall art, serving pieces, or simply grouped together to make an interesting statement in a room. A few of my customers were not impressed, but most were excited to get something out of the ordinary. My enthusiasm for what I was selling trickled down to those who wanted something different. We had a lot of fun figuring out how to best use these unusual baskets and plants.

When I worked in the custom decorating department of a large department store, my car's trunk was full of fabrics with many patterns, colors, and textures. Before bringing any fabrics into a customer's home, I discussed elements of style and preferences with them. I then brought in only fabrics that were suited to their taste. And they were never disappointed. Some decorators in the department felt they had to take everything into the customer's home, right off the bat, to provide lots of choices. But I learned to gauge what the customer was enthusiastic about and I was enthusiastic about their choices. Enthusiasm in one of us triggered enthusiasm in the other.

We make dozens of choices every day, and we are free to make them based on joy and intuition rather than history or standard procedure. When we let our enthusiasm guide us, our own joy will tell us we've made the right decision.

APRIL FOOLS' DAY

April Fools' Day, sometimes called All Fools' Day, is one of the most light-hearted days of the year. Although its origin is uncertain, some speculate that it dates back to 1582 France, when the switch was made from the Julian calendar with the New Year beginning on April first, to the Gregorian calendar which switched the start of the year to January first. Because circulation of news was very slow at that time, many people failed to hear of the change and continued to celebrate the new year on the first of April. In so doing, they became the butt of jokes and hoaxes for being unaware of the change. The jokes included having paper fish put onto their backsides by their trickster friends. These paper fish were called "poisson d'avril", or April fish, and became a symbol of an easily caught fish, or a gullible person.

In ancient Rome it was thought that Mother Nature fooled people with unpredictable weather on April first. The day was sometimes seen as a celebration related to the changing of the seasons. The drab days of winter were left behind, the days were sunnier and warmer, and because hearts were happy, people began to play tricks one another for light-hearted fun.

April Fools' Day spread throughout Britain and Scotland in the 18th century and the tradition of "hunting the Gowk" was introduced. Gowk was a word for the cuckoo bird, or fool, and people were sent on phony errands by their friends for a laugh.

In modern times people have gone to great lengths to create elaborate April Fools' Day tricks. In 1985 *Sports Illustrated* tricked many readers by running a made-up article about a rookie pitcher named Sidd Finch who could throw a fast ball over 168 mph. In 1996 Taco Bell duped the public by announcing it had agreed to purchase the Liberty Bell in Philadelphia and would rename it the Taco Liberty Bell. In 1998, Burger King advertised a "Left-handed Burger" on April first and scores of customers asked for this fake burger.

All this craziness was intended to be great fun, and even those who were fooled could laugh when they realized they'd been duped. You can have a little fun this April Fools' Day. Play an innocent trick on someone, as long as no one is hurt. And if you turn out to be the butt of someone else's prank, laugh a little, or laugh a lot. Life is more fun when you can find simple humor in simple things. There's a little fool in all of us. Celebrate that fool today!

BE GENTLE

There's a Karen Drucker song that says, "I will be gentle with myself. / I will love myself like a new-born baby child." We are all born anew every day, and if we treat ourselves gently, life is simpler.

When a baby is born, he has no doubts and no fears. All he knows is the love from which he came, and he fully trusts himself and those around him. As the baby grows, learns to crawl, to walk, and to ride a bike, he knows he can do these things because they come completely naturally to him. It's not a struggle. If he falls, he gets right back up and tries again. That is until someone tells him he can't. That's when self-doubt begins to creep in.

If you're reading this, you're certainly older than this baby child, and you've had your share of being told you can't. Your inner critic has taken up residence in your mind. But if you're gentle with yourself, you can overcome any self-doubt. When you make a choice to do something, try it on for size, and if it feels right, go for it. Kick out that inner critic and listen to the inner voice that's telling you that you *can*. Life is about ease. Relax, let it let go of struggle and stay with the easy flow of life.

When attempting something new—whether it's a physical feat, learning a new language, or playing the piano—if you're gentle, you won't simply say *I'll try*, you'll take the necessary steps to *do*. In life there is no *try,* there is only *do* or *don't do*.

I had a co-worker who, when he saw me obsessing over a decision or trying too hard to solve a problem, told me to stop "efforting." If a choice doesn't come naturally, or something just isn't working for us, no amount of effort will make it right. We might have to shift gears, make a different choice, or try a different way of looking at the problem. Doing it gently will make it a lot easier, and the right answers will come.

We can be gentle with ourselves. We can give ourselves permission not to be perfect. We can tackle the seemingly overwhelming projects in little bite-size chunks. When we think of that new-born baby child, we will be as kind and gentle with ourselves as we would be with him. We can love ourselves as if we were that innocent, trusting, fearless little person.

SHARING

Seventeenth century English author John Donne wrote, "No man is an island. No one is self-sufficient; everyone relies on others." No one can make it through this life alone; people need people. And to maintain a semblance of sanity, people need to share.

We all know at least one person who is so self-absorbed they don't consider anyone else's thoughts or feelings. Or we might know someone who is so timid they are afraid to speak up or to share. But wherever you are in life, don't ever be afraid to share because in honest, open sharing, you learn about yourself.

This journey through life is one of exploration and self-discovery, and the only possible outcome is to truly know ourselves. As we share our thoughts, feelings, adventures, even sadness and fears with another, we continue to know ourselves on a deeper level. Because we are mirrors to each other, each person we talk with reflects a part of us that we are ready to see. Often, we hold a distorted image of ourselves, and when we share, our minds are opened to our own truth.

I might have regrets for having done something I wish I hadn't done, or wishing I had done some things that I didn't do. But as I converse with others, sharing stories of times that were good, exciting, educational, and fulfilling, those distorted images of regret fall away. The self-discovery of sharing can sometimes be frightening, but if we walk through that fear, we will meet our self on the other side and discover our Divinity.

Namasté is an ancient Sanskrit greeting still in everyday use in India. Roughly translated it means, "The Divine in me bows to the Divine in you." The Divine in all of us is simply our light, love, truth, beauty, and peace. When we share these aspects of our self, we become aware that this is who we truly are. My yoga classes end each session with *Namasté* because we've just shared an hour and a half together deepening the connection of our bodies, minds, and spirits.

The Simon and Garfunkel song says, "I am a rock / I am an island / A rock feels no pain / And an island never cries." It's a good song, but the message is a little sad. We can make the most of this life! We don't have to settle for being a rock or an island! It's a whole lot healthier—both physically and emotionally—to feel some pain, and to cry some, and to share these feelings. When we discover ourselves by sharing, we are also helping others to discover themselves.

WHAT'S GOING ON?

A *Garfield* cartoon by Jim Davis shows Garfield thinking, "Whoa! Do you ever feel like you don't know what's going on? Then, smiling, he adds, "Isn't it Great?"

In our society, everyone seems to think they need to know everything, and they cause themselves stress by trying to anticipate the future or figure out why things in the past happened the way they did, and they miss the pleasures of the moment. Drawing from Eastern philosophy, Allen W. Watts, in his book *The Wisdom of Uncertainty* states, "It is only by acknowledging what we do not and cannot know that we can find something truly worth knowing."

Think of *Alice in Wonderland*. Who could have been more unknowing and confused than Alice as she experiences a topsy-turvy world where the normal order of things is completely reversed, and common sense turned upside down? She finds, in the end, though, that it wasn't important that she know the why of her experiences as she finds herself awake beside her sister, drinking tea. It was all a dream. In reality, our life is a dream . . . we make it up as we go along.

When we struggle to try to know the ins and outs of too much, we fill our minds with things over which we have no control. We think knowledge resulting from logic, reason, and intelligence offers us a form of security, but even in the best of times, security is never more than temporary. We can only determine what we need to know by seeing the world through an open mind, just as we can only see the sky through a clear window.

Children are probably the happiest group of people we'll ever know. They play, they laugh, and they offer unconditional trust and love. They do *wonder*, though. Talk with any two or three-year-old and you'll hear *"why"* so many times you'll want to scream. When my sons were little, they watched their grandpa tinker in the garage fixing things and asked him *why* so much he began showing them what he was doing. Today, they can both figure out how to fix almost anything that's broken. This is know-how, something worth knowing, and it serves them well. But it doesn't mean they have to understand rocket science, and they're okay with that.

It's said that knowledge is power, but as long as we know what's truly worth knowing for us, there's a comfort in the knowledge that we don't have to know everything. Like Garfield, we can relax and be grateful that we don't always have to know what's going on.

DRAMA

Everyone faces difficult situations in their life, and some people are over-the-top dramatic about their perceived problems. The rest of us don't have to buy into their drama, though, we can maintain our peace. A *problem* is something unwelcome that is asking to be dealt with and overcome. And most problems can be solved simply and effectively by calmly taking necessary steps toward resolution.

I once worked with a couple as they were planning their wedding and reception. The mother of the bride was a heavy drinker and the couple feared she would get out of hand and cause a disturbance like she'd done at a previous family gathering. I suggested they either not serve alcohol at the event, or appoint a trusted friend or family member to whisk the mother away if her actions became disruptive, and to inform her of that possibility. As it turned out, the occasion went off without a hitch, the mother was on her best behavior, and the couple has wonderful memories of their special day . . . without drama.

One of the adages I live by is, "It only matters if it matters." Drama is a choice. We can choose to have dramatic angst about our life situations, or we can find solutions which bring good—or at least fairly good—outcomes. If we make something matter to us and give it enough importance or power, it can become overly dramatic and cause unnecessary stress. But if we don't let it matter to the extent that it affects our life adversely, we can solve any problem with a clear mind.

I'm not suggesting that we become like ostriches, burying our heads in the sand. Problems aren't solved by denying their existence. Life still happens. But we can find peace anywhere, anytime, and bring that peace with us into chaotic situations as we work toward solutions. It takes focus and willingness. We can do it, and we can do it without drama.

If you are someone who really enjoys drama, indecision, and stress, you might thrive on this negative energy, but remember, your drama, indecision, and stress affect everyone around you, and you might, someday, be the one whisked away from an event.

To overcome drama, try taking things as they come. Face situations and find solutions while staying calm. You'll find life is much simpler without the drama.

SELF-RESPECT

A Course in Miracles states, *Trials are but lessons you failed to learn presented once again.*

I've always thought of myself as a fairly good judge of character. I felt like I could distinguish between people who were a good addition to my life, and those who were not. But as I look back, I can see that I was wrong as much as I was right. I seemed to allow relationship partners to take advantage of me, and when things went south, I tended to analyze their behavior to figure out why they were acting the way they were instead of telling them to knock it off or kicking them to the curb.

I'm a consummate people-pleaser but have learned that we teach people how to treat us. If, in all these years, through all these relationships, I had taken a good look at how I was allowing myself to be mistreated or taken advantage of instead of trying to figure out what someone else was thinking, I might have learned this lesson sooner without having to endure trial after trial. I can see now that it was not me being helpful, kind, and understanding, it was me being weak, and allowing my peace to be disturbed.

Not every relationship or friendship can turn out to be ideal, but they are all opportunities for learning. When we consider our own needs as well as the needs of others, a mutual respect can be achieved. And if it turns out that it's not a good fit, there can be a mutual agreement to part. Denial of our own discomfort does not serve us well, but honesty does. Authentic communication is the first step to mutually beneficial relationships, along with being aware of our own feelings and attitudes.

If we don't respect and take care of our self, who will? Knowing that we teach people how to treat us by our acceptance of the behavior of another, we can also know that bad behavior doesn't have to be tolerated. We can't dictate the choices of others, but we do have control over our own choices. We can't really love and respect another if we don't first love and respect our self. We must take care to nurture our most important relationship, the one with our self, then we can expect and accept respect and love from others.

Don't fail to learn this. By developing a healthily self-respect, we save ourselves from anguish and stress by not having to keep having more and more trials, and life is simpler.

NATURAL PROGRESSION

There's a story told of a man who came upon a cocoon which was shaking and quivering and beginning to crack open. The butterfly inside was trying to get out. As the man observed this cocoon activity, he took out his pocket knife and slit open the cocoon, thinking he would help the butterfly find its freedom. The butterfly came out of the cocoon, fell to the ground, flapped its wings a couple of times, then died. The man's good intentions stopped the natural progression of the butterfly's metamorphosis, releasing it before it was ready to live as a fully formed butterfly.

We all go through a kind of metamorphosis throughout our lives. We have noticeable changes in character, appearance, function, and condition. We transform, and whatever we leave behind is replaced by something more valuable. We go through pressure, hard work, and struggle that enables us to develop our internal fortitude, to keep pushing forward to succeed in life. We have ups and downs and eventually develop the muscle and spirit to walk on our own and to soar like a butterfly. It's the natural progression of our life.

Even crops in the field have a natural progression. Seeds are planted and fertilized by the earth. They sprout and grow, and eventually bear fruit which feeds humans and animals.

There is also a natural progression of spiritual growth. We came onto this earth to learn the lessons that are ours alone to learn. Some religions stifle this natural growth with harsh dogma, too many rules, and fear of punishment. When we are allowed to keep our minds and hearts open, there is a natural progression to a life filled with peace, love, and joy. We can't rush this natural progression any more than the man cutting open the cocoon could speed up the butterfly's maturation. Werner Erhart wisely said, "It's easier to ride the horse in the direction in which it's going."

Our passage through time and space is not random. We cannot *not* be in the right place at the right time. We will make mistakes, but even mistakes can be used for our benefit. We might not agree with everything we see in the world, but when we remember that God is in charge, and if we're patient with the natural progression of things, we'll save ourselves worry, pain, and struggle. So, get on the horse, ride it in the direction it's going, stay in the flow, relax, and enjoy the ride. You'll find your life will be simpler.

ENERGY SPEAKS

What kind of energy to you emit to people you pass on the street? If you are stressed, in a rush, or irritated, people you come in contact with will pick up on that energy. And if you're happy and peaceful, don't be surprised if people you don't even know smile at you. Your own energy passes to everyone around you, and inner peace passes to others when you accept it for yourself. We cannot have thoughts that do not affect others; thoughts are energy. We don't pass on this energy on purpose or consciously, it just happens. This is because we are all joined. Even dogs know this. Have you ever been feeling sad or sick or just not your best and found your dog nuzzling up to console you?

You may think whatever you're thinking is just in your own mind, that they're *your* thoughts, you're keeping them to yourself, and nobody else knows them. *But there are no private thoughts.* Everything someone thinks affects someone else in some way. Evidence of this is when we are thinking about someone, and out of the blue, they call us or we run into them at the market or the hardware store. Thoughts are like magnets, they attract to us the people, attitudes, and sometimes even actions we think about. If we remain upbeat and thinking happy thoughts, good is attracted to us. But if we're thinking negatively, things just don't seem to work out in the way we'd like

When we are at peace and accept inner peace for our self, that peace is sent to all others to some degree. At some time, we've probably encountered someone who is totally at peace with themselves and we suddenly feel peaceful in their presence. When we send peace and love, someone, somewhere is affected because thoughts are things, and things have effect.

The next time you find yourself thinking negatively notice how it affects others. They might begin to tell you how bad their life is, or they might gripe about this or that. Or, they might simply walk away because your negative thoughts have interfered with the peace they want.

The energy of positive thoughts—keeping our minds open to the good around us—changes our thinking to see only the good, and life becomes simpler, happier, and more peaceful. We can all live with a bit of Pollyanna. When we think happy thoughts, happiness will come to us.

PLAY

In a recent *Baby Blues* cartoon by Kirkman & Scott, the father is on the floor in Flat Plank position (a yoga pose where your weight is on your toes and your forearms and your entire body is lifted off the floor with a straight line from shoulders to heels). In the cartoon, Mom comes in and asks, "Doing yoga planks?" Dad responds, "Yeah. Working (grunt) on the abs." Then along comes mischievous little Hammie. He takes one look at Dad, then runs to find his sister Zoe and says, "Quick, get your bike! Dad is making us a ramp."

Kids see the world in a different way than those of us who are older, have lived through more, and pretty much do things for a reason or because it's expected of us. Dad's reason for doing yoga was to keep is body in shape, but the little boy saw it as an opportunity for play. What some of us don't remember, is that life *can* be play. On this journey we call life, we are beset with situations that worry us and problems that we need to find solutions for. We have to keep plugging along, working to make ends meet, and we ultimately forget how to play.

Play is defined as engaging in an activity for enjoyment and recreation rather than a serious or practical purpose. Because children don't have the weight of the world on their shoulders, they don't need a reason to do things. They see the fun in situations, and they go for it.

Freedom to quit an activity is another essential aspect of play. Children have short attention spans and can see the fun in the moment, then effortlessly move on to the next playful moment. But children do learn from play. They develop physical, intellectual, and social capacities, and play is a means of creating and maintaining friendships. In the adult world, we have jobs, but work doesn't have to be the opposite of play. If we make up our minds to enjoy what we're doing to the fullest, work can become almost like play. You've heard it said that if you earn a living doing something you love to do, you'll never work another day in your life. I've had jobs in my life at which I got so much enjoyment, learning new things and performing at my highest level, that it felt like an activity done strictly for enjoyment rather than something I *had* to do because someone was paying me to do it.

We can lighten up. We don't have to take life too seriously. We can make our work fun. We can remember to laugh and to play. (But don't ride your bike on your dad's back when he's in Flat Plank.)

THE ANSWER

Love is the answer to every problem that will confront us today, tomorrow, and all the days of our life. We keep trying to find answers to life's upsets with pills, money, fancy cars, and being around the "right" people in order to feel good and to be happy. But all these things are replacements for true love. When you face difficulties, pause a little, adjust your thinking, and see how you could perceive these set-backs from a place of love. Your life will change if you can approach hard times from the love that is alive within you. Wayne Dyer wrote, "When you change the way you look at things, things change the way they look." And love can be that change.

We are created in God's image, and God is Love, therefore *we* are Love. *A Course in Miracles* says that *ideas leave not their source.* God is our source. We are a part of God and therefore cannot be separated from Him/Her. God's Love lives within us all the time.

It seems a little strange and over-the-top to suggest we look at people we don't like with love, or do things we don't enjoy doing with love. But if we want our life to be simple, and we want to maintain peace of mind, love really is the answer.

You already know you feel better and are happier when you are with someone you love or doing something you love to do. So why not carry that inner happiness over to include everyone and everything? And don't forget yourself. Remember to love yourself! Talk to yourself in the mirror, telling yourself what a beautiful person you are, how talented, smart, capable, and loving you are. Put little sticky notes on your bathroom mirror reminding yourself first thing every morning to live from love. Love and happiness are your birthright. You deserve to love and to be loved. And the love that comes from you expands, trickles into the hearts of others, and touches everyone and everything you come in contact with. Animals can be the best examples of unconditional love. When they show their love for you, it's hard not to love them back.

Love is the answer, no matter the question. Let's stop trying to get past life's upsets with money, possessions, the right people, or whatever magic we think we need to bring stability, serenity of consciousness, and a calm demeanor into our life. The Beatles got it right: *Love is all you need.* Love will make you happy. Love is the answer!

YES OR NO

Relationships can become very complicated when we aren't open to what the other person is thinking or feeling, and when their perception of a situation is different from our own. If someone disagrees with us, the typical reaction is to feel attacked and to deny the accusation by attacking back. Just as it takes two to tango, it also takes two to start a fight, and fighting is *never* the way to solve a problem.

One way to avoid a fight is to give in and say, "Yes, you're right." But that would be to deny our own true feelings if we really mean "I see it differently, let's discuss this." Too much denial of feelings can cause a build-up of resentment which can lead to a really big blow-up later on.

Don't say *yes* unless you really mean it. When we are addicted to being *right,* we'll be caught up in wanting others to admit their own responsibility for an uncomfortable situation. But if we stop to explore how our own actions and responses might be affecting the situation, we will find that we might carry part of the responsibility for the unrest. If we want to say *yes* to peace and comfort in a relationship, we first have to honestly consider whether we've been saying *no* by our actions of self-righteousness. When we can say, "I didn't understand how my actions were making you feel," we've opened the door to communication, compromise, and understanding.

When we become aware of what others are thinking and feeling during any difference of opinion, we can communicate our own thoughts and feelings which will allow everyone involved the opportunity to say *yes* to the peace that comes with shared responsibility. But we have to understand that when we are saying *no* just to make ourselves right, we won't find that peace.

When dealing with something we simply can't say *yes* to, we need to emphatically say *no*. When we mean *no*, we need to say so. We need to get off the fence. But if we're in agreement, we need be able to say *yes* without holding any bit of *no* in our mind. To be honest with ourselves, *yes* has to mean *yes*, and *no* has to mean *no*. To truly say *yes*, we must say *no* to any contradiction that remains to keep us from peace and comfort. When we can do this, we will enjoy a simpler life.

I AM

How often do you have limited thoughts about yourself? I AM not talented enough, I AM not smart enough, I AM too weak, I AM too fat, I AM too tall, I AM not happy. You fill in the blanks. But if you take a good look at the words I AM, and think about the words that follow them, you will begin to see how you might be holding yourself back from being the best you can be, and you can begin to release any negative thoughts you're holding about yourself.

Anything we say after the words I AM is what we invite into our lives. When we say "I AM not good at this," or "I AM not worthy of that," we're planting seeds in our minds that make us believe that is the truth of us. If we say we're not good at something, it's a sure bet we won't be able to do it. And if we tell ourselves we're not worthy of our good, we stand in our own way, not allowing our good to come to us. When we replace negative I AMs about ourselves with positive I AMs, our whole thinking will change. Our lives will change.

When we change our mindset, and put positive statements after the words I AM, we will be able to rattle off a whole litany of positive things about ourselves. If we can say I AM happy, I AM peaceful, I AM loving and kind, I AM strong, I AM capable, I AM focused and unshakable, I AM calm, quiet, assured, and confident, I AM radiant, clear-minded, centered, and serene, I AM smart and I AM healthy, that is what we will be. When we catch ourselves saying I AM, we need to think about how we might be describing ourselves. Is it a put-down and a limitation, or it is an encouragement to boost to our confidence? Following I AM with a negative description is a habit we can change. It takes some discipline, it takes remembering, but we can do it!

What I AMs can you let go of and what I AMs can you add? Even saying I AM sorry, has a negative connotation. It might be better to say I regret, or I apologize, because *you are not sorry*; you're not a sorry sort of person, you're not in a pitiful condition. Even saying "I AM tired" plants the seeds of fatigue, and your productivity slows down. So, don't limit yourself with negative I AMs. Remember who you are, remember your good, and remind yourself of this as you learn to use words that follow I AM to build your self-image.

WHY NOT NOW?

We all seem to put things off until a "more convenient" time, or until a certain event occurs in our lives, or until we have someone to help us or to join us in what we want to do. Living like this can lead to frustration, to undone tasks, and to missed opportunities. It can even lead to depression over the chaos in our home, in our workplace, and in our life.

Every time I open a drawer, closet, or cupboard, I think I really should clean this out or get it organized. Then I close the drawer, closet, or cupboard and forget about it until the next time I open it and the same thought comes up again. If something needs to be cleaned out or organized, what better time to do it than *right now* . . . while it's right in front of us? If our child is hungry, we certainly take time to feed him. If our dog needs to go outside, we let her out, so why do we put off things that might keep us from living a more peaceful, stress-free life? There really is no good answer.

This procrastination doesn't just apply to tasks that need doing, it can also apply to embarking on a program to get physically fit, to beginning to eat a healthier diet, to taking a class we've been thinking about, or even to maintaining a more positive and grateful outlook on life. Sometimes we miss out on activities we would enjoy, passing them up because we don't have someone to enjoy them with us. There really is nothing wrong with going to a movie, a cultural event, or even a vacation trip alone. Granted, activities are more enjoyable when shared, but if we go alone, we can talk about the experience afterword, sharing it with friends and family, and relive the whole event.

I've had many opportunities to set goals or intentions, and I can do that easily, but I *miss* many opportunities to fulfill those goals and intentions because I tell myself it's just not the right time. What am I waiting for!?

If we've been putting things off, or if we *know* we want to accomplish a certain thing, we can ask ourselves, *Why Not Now?* Why not clean out the garage *now?* Why not go visit our parents *now?* Why not commit to a healthier lifestyle *now?* Why not clean out those drawers, closets and cupboards *now?* If we make *Why Not Now* our daily mantra—and follow through—we'll find that things are getting done and that we're feeling better about ourselves. We'll find that we are more relaxed and are enjoying this life that we've been given a little more.

ENLIGHTENMENT

This world seems to be a place of haphazard results, with each of us getting exactly what we are asking for at any given moment. We think we want freedom from illness, unhappiness, and from frustrating situations, but we sometimes appear to be stuck. If we truly want freedom, however, we can find it. And if we're not ready to reach for it, to fight for it, we will remain bound.

There is a story I like about a young man who longed to become enlightened. This young man came to a guru and asked him what he would need to do to become enlightened. The master took the student to a lake, pushed his head under water and held it there for a long time. When the young man became desperate for air, he fought his way to the surface and shouted, "Are you trying to kill me?" The guru calmly replied, "When you want enlightenment as much as you wanted air, you will find it."

Sometimes we want a change in our life, but we don't want it as badly as the young man wanted air. When we can find some benefit in not making the change, we stop trying. If we are stuck in any situation that is less than fulfilling, we can ask ourselves if we are receiving any perceived benefits from staying where we are. Maybe we're feeling sick. While no one would reasonably choose illness, the subconscious perceives many hidden benefits from it. It gets us out of work, we get sympathy, we don't have to face the issues in our life that trouble us, we may be receiving some kind of monetary reward for our disability, and on and on. While no one would consciously admit to choosing illness, on some level we do.

Many people complain about their dysfunctional relationships, yet staying in them often seems to outweigh the benefits of leaving. One thing is for sure, though, the moment leaving becomes more attractive than staying, it will no longer be an option. We are always free to choose, and we are always choosing.

When we have a burning desire for peace and simplicity in our life, longing to see all people and all situations from a place of peace and love, and we want it as badly as the young man wanted air, that will become *all* we want, and that is *all* we will settle for.

TAX DAY

Today is the day for filing our income tax returns. Nobody is excited about paying taxes, just as nobody really likes to pay utility bills, but these are facts of life. If we stop thinking of these payments as obligations, and instead see them as blessings, our life will become simpler.

Instead of grousing about how much everything costs, we can feel gratitude for the ease of flipping a switch to light a room, or turning on the heat or air for comfort, as we pay utility bills. We can be grateful for indoor plumbing, green lawns, and the plants in our garden as we pay the water bill. We can give thanks for the convenience of our telephone, internet, and television as we pay those bills. Looking at paying bills in a positive frame of mind and feeling grateful for the conveniences we enjoy changes our outlook on life, and writing those checks or logging on to make payments becomes an honor.

If you have income taxes to pay today, you might want to add a blessing to the subject line on the check you write. The overworked, overtired IRS agent who processes that check will feel and appreciate the love in that blessing, and it just might change his day for the better. He might be kinder and more friendly to his fellow employees, with love and kindness flowing through the office like a cool stream. Can you imagine a room full of IRS agents happy, peaceful, and loving what they do because of that one blessing? It could happen.

When we consider that the taxes we pay help to keep our roads in good repair, our public schools running smoothly, and our cities safer with up-to-date equipment for police and fire departments, we might feel better about paying taxes. And knowing that these taxes keep our country safer with support for our armed forces, and keep our government and cities viable, we recognize the need for taxation. We are governed by a democratic system, and I can't think of a better way to run a country. We can be grateful, every day, as we go about our business, we can feel safe and secure and able to express our opinions openly because of the freedoms we enjoy.

To have the safety and freedom of living in a well-run country with well-run systems of providing services to us and our homes, there *is* a price to pay. But if we take a look at the way some other, less civilized, countries exist, we will be happy to pay for conveniences and even to pay taxes, and to be grateful for that privilege.

MEDITATION

We all have problems in our life—at least things that we *perceive* as problems. But problems aren't really problems unless we make them so. What is seen as a problem for one person might be simply something to be solved then moved on from for another. When you think about a problem and look at it differently, you may no longer see it as insurmountable. Changing your view of life can have an immediate effect on your well-being.

Meditation helps get past problems. Getting still and quieting our mind, asking for guidance to see our problems differently, and being willing to change our perception, is like washing dishes. If there are food particles stuck on dishes or pans, soaking them in water helps to loosen and soften these particles. After soaking for a time, the stuck stuff washes off easily and floats away. Meditation helps the "stuck stuff" in our minds float away.

When we have a problem in our life that seems so big, so overwhelming that we feel we can't get past it, we can try meditating. Becoming still, clearing our mind, asking for and being open to guidance will help us to see the problem in another way. It can change our perception of the problem. We might say, "I sense a problem, I don't like the way I'm feeling, and I'm willing to see it differently." Then in our quiet mind we can feel the weight being lifted. Meditation can help us to see things differently and more clearly.

Meditation is an approach to training the mind, similar to the way exercise is a way to train the body. Seasoned meditators can sit for hours with clear minds, but this is extremely hard for beginners. A good way to start is to sit quietly and focus on your breath, noticing each inhalation and exhalation as you relax. Following your breath as you repeat a single word or mantra, listening to a repetitive gong, focusing your attention on a chosen object like a candle flame, or counting beads on a mala are ways that can help you relax and stop the thoughts that try to invade your mind. If you find your mind wandering as you meditate, simply notice the thoughts, without judgment, then gently let them go. As you begin to meditate, even if relaxation is not the goal, it is often the result. The main goal of meditation is not to achieve benefits, it is simply to be present.

What soaking does for the dishes, meditation will do for our mind. It will soften the troubling thoughts, and we will begin to view problems differently.

SUCCESS OR FAILURE

You are as God created you, not what you've made of yourself. You may be a success in the business world or you may excel at a given sport. You did this through hard work and dedication, and you may feel like you've made yourself into something pretty special. But the truth is, you were created to be successful, to excel, and you're simply living the life you were created for. On the other hand, you may be struggling, always feeling like you can't catch a break and nothing is going right, and you may think of yourself as a failure. If so, you've forgotten what you came here to do. What you're calling failure may have come about through your own thinking and attitude. But whatever the outward picture of your life, the fact is that you are a creation of the Divine, and nothing in your life—good or bad, success or failure—changes that, and to think you can change what God created, either elevating or corrupting yourself, is the height of arrogance. You were created for good, and that will never change.

We were all created wholly loving and wholly lovable, and we are still that, no matter what we think, what we believe, or what we have done. We were given a mind with which to think, and how we think about something—anything—is what it will be for us. If our mind tells us we can be successful, and we believe those thoughts, we will, with commitment and perseverance, become successful. But if the mind gives us limiting thoughts and we believe them, then life might not work out as well as we'd like it to.

When I started my first business venture, I truly believed I would succeed, and I brushed away any limiting thoughts. And because I believed I could make it, and because I knew I was created by a Master who wanted only the best for me, my business was very successful. And I was grateful. There have been other things in my life, though, that didn't work out as well. I was limited by self-deception, thinking I couldn't do it so I held back and chose not to keep trying.

We were created with unlimited knowledge and abilities, but we were also created with the power of choice. God created us for good, but somewhere along the way, *we* make the choice for success or failure. The good thing is, it's not too late. If we've made bad choices, we can make new ones. God will offer His strength to every little effort we make. We honor our Creator by being the best we can be.

TOOLS AND TELEVISIONS

Our minds were "manufactured" as a tool for the function of peace, love, forgiveness, and joy. Sometimes, however, we use our minds for unintended functions. We think this works for us, and sometimes it does . . . for a while, but we forget that using a tool for an unintended function can sometimes deem that tool unusable. Then it has to be repaired, returning it back to its intended use.

Consider the screwdriver. Its only function is to screw and unscrew screws. People, however, sometimes get very creative. Give a person a screwdriver, and he may use the handle as a hammer (which could break the handle), the shaft as a pry bar (which could bend the shaft), or the blade as a knife (which could chip the blade). All these are uses the manufacturer never intended. And, like misusing tools, we sometimes misuse our minds

Now, picture your mind as a television set. We all know when our TVs are working well, they have a clear picture, the colors are true, and the reception is good. We know that something is wrong when the picture has lines or waves, there is static, and we can't see images clearly. Just like the TV, our minds were designed to receive messages accurately, but sometimes our reception is poor and the pictures on our screen (our mind) are distorted so we cease to see our brothers and sisters and the world through the eyes of love. Other times the choice of channels can be the problem. We could tune into a soap opera and mistake the drama for reality and become upset over something that is not really happening.

But there's good news! Our minds are still under warranty. The manufacturer, God, has sent his repairman, the Holy Spirit, to help us. All it takes is *willingness* on our part. If we desire see the world through the eyes of love, all we have to do is ask. Guidance is always there for us—although God will never force us. We *choose* willingness, or we don't. How we see the world around us depends on how we choose to use the tool of our mind. We can use our minds as a tool for peace; we can correct our reception (our perception).

We were given the tools for a better life. We are unbroken and undistorted, and peace, love, forgiveness, and joy are our natural state of mind. So, if you don't like what you see, just remember your function, and use the tool of your mind to see things clearly, without distortion, and your life will become much simpler.

AMEN

We normally think of the word "Amen" as the ending of a prayer and that is, indeed, its general use. The word is derived from the Hebrew and means "certainty" "truth" and "verily" and can be expressed in endless ways, from a soft whisper to a joyous shout. Saying Amen is virtually saying, "This is the Truth." or "This is a certainty." In the Bible, Jesus often says, "Verily, verily I say unto you," which means what he's about to say is the absolute truth, without question. If someone says something that we totally agree with and believe to be true, we might say "Amen" or "Amen to that" indicating our agreement with the truth of what they've said. In a church service, congregants might shout "Amen!" after certain comments by a speaker, indicating their agreement.

Agreeing with the truth, or at least someone's version of the truth, is well and good, but when praying, we must be careful how we use Amen. Whatever we apply our Amen to, we declare to be a fixed and final truth, and that declaration can assume mastery over our life. If we pray in a beseeching manner, asking for something we feel we are lacking and end with Amen, we have affirmed the truth of that lack. If we pray, "O God, I am sick and troubled, help me. Amen," we are saying Amen to something we don't want. We are applying truth to the words *I am sick, I am troubled*. We are saying to sickness and trouble, "This is the truth of me. I believe it. I accept it." But if we pray saying, "This sickness or this trouble is not what I want. I'm willing to let it go. Help me to see it differently. Amen," then we've applied truth to a positive affirmation.

We must be thoughtful about what we're saying Amen to. We can reject the negative, limited, and weak thoughts we express about ourselves, and affirm the positive and constructive. We need to do more than speak words of Truth; we must accept the reality they affirm. We can declare a Truth such as; *I am strong, whole, and healthy*, then follow it with Amen. We must be careful to say Amen, literally and figuratively, only to those things that are good and true, only to those things that we want to see manifest in our life.

You are, and I am, healthy, wealthy, and wise. AMEN.

BECOMING AND BEING

Some people are ruled by their intellect, their ideas of what they can become if they work hard enough. Others are led by their hearts, their presence and their understanding. Our minds can sometimes be limited to thoughts, our mental understanding of something or someone. But there is no limit to a true heart connection. An intellectual connection is more about *Becoming,* while a heart connection is about *Being.* If a person is constantly working at *Becoming,* they find it difficult to simply *Be.* People focused on their intellect often seem to live on the surface and find it difficult to really get deeply into their heart. Others may be so sensitive, so focused on feelings, that they aren't open to developing their intellect. But by combining the intellect and heart, we can be fully open and present. We can learn, we can grow, and we can feel.

It's hard to *Be* when we are focused on *Becoming. Being* is something that can never be attained as long as we cling to the thought of attaining wholeness and completeness, not knowing that we already have it. Knowing something with our intellect isn't really Truth unless we can *feel* it in our heart. Focused on our intellect, we are always *Becoming,* always striving for more. In our heart, we know the truth of who we really are and we are *Being.*

Too often we are obsessed with becoming richer, more attractive, more popular, smarter, more successful, or whatever the intellect thinks it wants but doesn't have. But in a state of *Being,* centered in the heart, these things are no longer just concepts, they become what we are. We already have all we need. We simply have to recognize this and have the willingness and the fortitude to discover that it is within us now—that it is our *Being.*

Until we can connect thinking and feeling, we will continue *Becoming* with little hope of ever *Being.* In truth, *Being* is what we already are. It doesn't wax and wane with the changes and challenges of life. *Being* is like a clear mirror that reflects things perfectly, exactly as they are. With sincerity and commitment, the effort of *Becoming* can gradually transform into one unbroken state of *Being.* It's no longer a conscious effort, it's a simple resting in our self. We find our self walking on a needless path—a path that leads to where we've always been—and the struggle of *Becoming* becomes the peace of *Being.*

CHANGE

John Henry Newman, a 19th century Catholic Cardinal and Theologian, said, "To live is to change, and to be perfect is to change often."

Our lives are constantly changing. We're born, we become children, we develop into adolescence then adulthood, and we grow old. And through this lifetime we learn, and we certainly change. Some changes are easy, some are not, but it's not really the changes that form who we are, but how we respond to these changes. If we can take life as it comes and not fall apart over something we perceive as *bad*, but simply make the changes needed to get past it or make it better, we've learned how to do life. We can't change the world, but we can change our mind about the world. How we think about things is how things will be for us.

Growth and change are the only evidence of life. If a person is hesitant to step out to make a change, if he always waits to do something until he knows he can do it so well that no one could ever find fault, he would end up doing nothing.

Michael Phelps didn't come into this life knowing how to swim, but he managed to win 23 Olympic medals throughout his career. His life has been constant change, years of practice, learning new techniques and mastering them. He has learned by ever-changing trial and error.

If you're stuck in a rut, try making a change in your life. And, above all, change your mind. Staying open to positive changes can make you a new person. If you're shy, try being a little more bold. If you're judgmental, switch to love. Becoming aware of the goodness in others will increase your love for yourself.

We can give new activities a try. We don't have to be good at something to start doing it. Ability and talent come with time, with practice, with a goal in mind, and with change. According to Newman, we're not living if we're not changing. Many people are resistant to change because it's a little frightening, but most people get tired of the same-o, same-o and keep changing to keep growing, to keep living life to the fullest.

Don't be afraid of change. Again, it's not the change itself that should concern you, but the way you look at it. If it's a positive change, celebrate it. If the change you try doesn't work, try again, or try something else. To be the person you want to be, make changes, and make them often.

LOVE OR HATE

We all know that when we look good, we feel good. We've got a new outfit, our hair is perfectly coiffed, we feel a certain confidence, and we're ready to take on the world. But it's not the clothes or the hairdo that's making us happy, it's the way they make us *feel*. And looking good for ourselves is enough, we don't need confirmation from the outside world.

The strange thing is, though, that you *do* get confirmation when you feel good about yourself. People see the confidence in you, they see your strength and they gravitate to you. It's *you* that attracts them, not your hair or your clothes.

There may be someone who, because of their own insecurity, will judge us, find fault with us, and try to put a dent in our armor, but if we respond with love, they become the ones who are disarmed.

There are people who live to be unhappy, and they want everyone around them to join them in that unhappiness. But if we remember who we are as perfect, innocent, beautiful children of God, loved unconditionally just the way we are, we won't fall prey to these people even when we're not wearing stylish duds or when we're having a bad hair day.

No one can take our inherent goodness from us . . . unless we allow it. I recently witnessed two women in a dispute. One had fire in her eyes and was spewing all kinds of negative accusations while the other remained calm and responded with "I love you."

Life is a series of choices. We can choose to be disrespectful, hateful, and negative, or we can choose love. Just as we feel good about ourselves when we look our best, we still feel that goodness even in the face of adversity by maintaining a peaceful demeanor and answering hate with love.

If you truly love yourself, and trust in your goodness, you can turn a negative situation into a positive one, because a positive attitude will dispel a negative one every time.

HEAVEN AND HELL

Those who identify with a religion find a comfort there. They are taught what to believe, and that by living an honest and dutiful life they will gain favor in an afterlife. They also tend to believe that others who live a sinful life will suffer in the end. In my own belief system, there are no differing afterlives. I believe we make our own Heaven and hell right here, right now. The teachings of ancient Jewish mysticism and of Hindus and Buddhists is that Heaven is feeling a closeness to God, and hell is a distance from God.

When we're judging another, seeing him as separate from ourselves, or when we're angry, depressed, or feel discomfort, we lose the peace that is our birthright. That is our temporary hell. On the other hand, when we see others with acceptance and love, we've found our Heaven. We go back and forth from Heaven to hell throughout our lives—in some cases, throughout our day. We create our own Heaven and hell in our minds, through our thoughts. When we're feeling hellish we can come back to a heavenly feeling simply by changing our thoughts.

We were created in the image of God; not a physical image, but as perfect innocence, at one with God and with everyone else. When we're feeling a oneness with the perfection and innocence with which we were created, we are in Heaven. When we let our thoughts slip away from this creation, we slide into a self-made hell.

A good example of this back and forth phenomenon would be in relationships. When we fall in love, we're on cloud 9, somewhere above where our critical minds take us. There are songs written about this feeling, for example, "Heaven, I'm in Heaven / And my heart beats so that I can hardly speak / I seem to find the happiness I seek / When we're out together dancing cheek to cheek." Then if things sour, or there is trouble in that same relationship, we feel down, sad, and alone. There are songs about that feeling as well. In fact, there would be no country western music without heartbreak.

The thing to remember here, is that because we make our own Heaven and hell. We can choose which we want to feel. Happiness is a choice. Sunsets are heavenly, storms can be hell, and when we can remember the sunsets during the storms, we can stay in our self-made Heaven at any time and any place.

CHOCOLATE

My friend Katie once sent me a card that said, "Money can't buy happiness, but it *can* buy chocolate, and that's kind of the same thing."

Chocolate is a magic food, it's tasty and it's actually good for you. Dark chocolate, in particular, contains antioxidants, many vitamins, calcium, and magnesium. It can help lower blood pressure and cholesterol. It can boost energy and brain power. It's rich in fiber so it promotes weight loss. It's an immune booster so helps to decrease anxiety and depression. How many prescription drugs do people take to do these same things? And chocolate goes down a whole lot easier than a pill.

Chocolate is a vegetable. It's derived from cocoa beans and beans are, as we know, a vegetable. Most chocolate contains sugar, and sugar is derived either from cane or beets. Both are plants which puts them in the vegetable category. So how can chocolate *not* be a vegetable? Chocolate candy bars also contain milk, which is a dairy product. So, there's another of the food groups. Chocolate covered raisins, cherries, blueberries, and strawberries all count as fruit, and fruit is good for us, and most people can eat all the fruit they want

Chocolate is a traditional expression of love. Who doesn't appreciate a box of chocolates for a special occasion, and what kid doesn't love a chocolate bunny at Easter? My sister loved chocolate so much that whenever she was asked what she wanted for a gift, she always asked for a box of See's candy. She was known for her love of chocolate and, as a tribute, her daughter passed out boxes of See's at her funeral. Her friends and family honored her, and we all remembered her fondly as we enjoyed the chocolate.

Life can be unpredictable. Every day brings something new. Forest Gump said it well, "Life is like a box of chocolates; you never know what you're going to get." We may not be able to buy happiness with money, but we can buy chocolate, and chocolate equals happiness.

I'm going to step away from the computer now and go eat some chocolate. Will you join me?

LET IT GO

Unpleasant circumstances that occurred in the past remain in our subconsciousness and those memories sometimes pop up to cause us stress. Too many of these stressful memory moments can cause us to lose the peace and joy that are our birthright. We may become someone who is ruled by anger, judgment, or unrest, which can result in a negative frame of mind. And that is something no one really wants if he's being honest with himself.

The good news is, our past can't haunt us if we can let it go. There is a story I like about two monks who are walking along a stream when they come upon a woman who wants to get to the other side of the stream but is afraid to go into the water. Seeing her need, the first monk puts down his pack, picks up the woman, carefully carries her across the stream, then comes back to continue his journey with his fellow monk. Long after they've gone past the place where they'd encountered the woman, the second monk says to the first, "How could you have done what you did with that woman? You know that in our order we are forbidden from touching a woman." The first monk calmly replies, "I put that woman down miles back. Why are *you* still carrying her?" Because the second monk was so appalled by the first monk's actions, he continued to carry the thought of it with him, allowing it to cause him unrest.

Even when we've done something we are forbidden to do and no one was hurt in the doing, we can let it go. We can stop letting its memory affect our thinking, therefore affecting our life. This doesn't mean we can break laws or cause harm and just forget about it as long as we're not caught. Laws are in place for a reason and breaking them has consequences. But, if like the first monk, our actions didn't cause hurt or harm, or in this case, actually helped, it's just a moment in life that happened, and the memory of it can be released.

Lewis Carroll, when relating a terrible event in his story *Through the Looking Glass* wrote, "The horror of that moment," the King went on, "I shall never, never forget." "You will, though," the Queen replied, "If you don't make a memorandum of it."

Holding on to thoughts about things that are behind us can keep us from going forward in life. Living in the moment of what's happening right now will keep us present and allow us to move forward without guilt or regret. This will help to keep life simple.

IMAGINE

We've heard it said, "Act As If" and "Believing is Seeing" along with other positive mind-set quotes. These sayings might sound cliché, but if we believe them, and live by them, we will begin to *imagine* what we want so clearly that we can actually feel it happening before it happens. It's about envisioning an outcome, feeling it, describing it, and doing whatever it takes to make it real in our lives.

In a recent *Rose is Rose* cartoon by Pat Brady, little Mimi is wearing a tutu and dancing, with her shadow on the wall beside her. The caption in the first frame says, "Learn the basics . . ." In the next frame, Mimi is jumping, and her shadow is in a perfect Grand Jeté. That caption reads, ". . . and leap beyond your potential." We, too, can leap beyond our potential. It's only the limitations in our own minds that hold us back.

Birds were meant to fly, it's their nature. If a bird chooses to walk around and remain grounded, he doesn't stop being a bird, but his experience of life is limited. If we have a dream of being all we can be, but we choose to live in ways that limit our full potential, our experience of life is as limited as the bird that chooses not to fly. It's our nature to be the best at whatever we want to do or to be.

"Right Place, Right Time" is another saying we've heard, and that's not just chance or luck. If we recognize opportunities, stay open to them, and trust enough that we are prepared for what they offer, we can fly. Oprah Winfrey says, "Luck is where opportunity and preparation meet." A lot of what we see as luck is really a result of hard work. When we have a vision of seeing ourselves doing the thing that takes us to our full potential, there will be set-backs. The baby bird doesn't just fall out of the nest and fly away, there's some pain to the learning-to-fly process, some trial and error, but his vision is to fly. He keeps flapping his wings until he manages to get himself off the ground. The pain pushes him until the vision pulls him.

You can leap, you can fly. Mimi's vision was a perfect Grand Jeté. Your vision probably isn't a ballet pose done perfectly, but you can reach whatever your Grand Jeté is. Imagine your success, learn everything you can about what it is you want, feel it, describe it, believe it, and you can do it. When you believe something hard enough, the sky's the limit, and you *can* reach your full potential.

WILLINGNESS

How much of the time do you have a task to do, really want to do it, and really want it done, but are somehow unwilling to exert the effort to get to it? After a long, wet winter, the spring is breathtakingly beautiful. Grasses, trees, and bushes are a vibrant green, and flowers are dazzling with abundant bloom. It's a glorious sight! But along with the greenery and flowers, weeds are having a heyday. Realizing that weeds are simply plants in the wrong places, I fully understand their prolific growth, but for me, they are completely out of place in the garden in my back yard. These weeds need to be pulled. And the grass that has invaded the decomposed granite walkways to the point that it's hard to tell where the lawn leaves off and the walkways begin, needs to be sprayed with weed killer. For weeks now, I've been telling myself to get out there and dig out the weeds and spray the misplaced grass, but something is holding me back. That something is clearly unwillingness. I've chosen, so far, not to act and have laid a justifiable veneer over this unwillingness to make it okay.

Whatever it is that we want done but find our self unwilling to do can keep growing until it becomes an almost insurmountable task. We conceal our unwillingness behind a cloak of situations we think we can't control. We feel doing the task interferes with other goals that we hold more dear and more important. But the fact remains that those tasks are still calling us.

My friend Shirlee has a bookkeeping and tax business. She does very well preparing returns during the tax season, but only has enough bookkeeping clients to barely keep her going the rest of the year. She talks about reaching out to small businesses to grow that aspect of her business, but so far hasn't gone beyond talk. Maybe it's a lack of confidence, maybe it's not knowing where to start, but at the bottom of it all is unwillingness. She doesn't have the *will* to do what it takes to advance and is limiting herself, not allowing her business to grow to its full potential, to what she really wants it to be.

It just takes a little willingness to reach our goals. We have to be willing to stop thinking of excuses and take action. If I get out and pull weeds and spray, my yard will be even more beautiful, and if the Shirlee's of the world take action, success will be more than just talk. When we say a task is impossible, what we really mean is that it is inconvenient. Nothing is impossible, we just have to have the willingness to make it happen.

SEVEN UP

We would all rather feel good, to feel UP, than feel bad, to feel DOWN, wouldn't we? But it's sometimes hard to stay up all the time. Things happen that bring us down, and it takes work to stay positive.

Here are seven Ups that can help keep spirits high and keep us from going into that dark mood. Every day:

Wake Up. Decide to have a good day. Whatever we make up our mind to do, let's make it happen. Every day is a new opportunity to wake up and to and give thanks for the blessings in our life.

Dress Up. This doesn't mean we need to don our best clothes. The best way to dress up is to put on a smile. A smile is an inexpensive way to make us look good no matter what we're wearing. A smile brightens our day and the day of those around us.

Shut Up. We have two ears and one mouth, so we must be meant to listen twice as much as we talk. Nothing is more endearing to another than really listening to what they have to say. Sometimes we're so busy deciding what we're going to say next, that we forget to listen. If we can open our ears and close our mouths, we'll get to know each other more deeply.

Stand Up. Sometimes we become complacent about what's going on around us, and we need to stand up for what we believe in. And we need to stand up for ourselves. We all have a voice. If we stand up for ourselves, not allowing others to mistreat or take advantage of us, life becomes richer and happier. Remember, when you don't stand for something, you'll fall for anything.

Look Up. We have become a society that feels we no longer need devotion to a higher power. We need to take time to pray, to remember positive principles for life, and to live them. We can't do this life all alone, we need the safety of knowing we are taken care of.

Reach Up. Don't settle for a mediocre life. Let's never stop trying to better ourselves. We know our potential, and we know we can reach it if we never stop believing in it.

Lift Up. Sometimes in the craziness of today's world and the busyness of society, we forget to stop and talk to God (or whatever we call our Higher Power). Some think they only need to reach out when they are in a crisis, but if we can make our life a prayer, if we can lift up thanks for our good, grateful that we are here in this world to live these Seven Ups, our life will be more fulfilling and simpler.

TEACHING MOMENTS

When the student is ready the teacher will come. This is something I've come to learn when I've tried to force things in my life. If I can let go, and be open to learning, a teaching moment will inevitably turn up. Actually, every moment of life is a teaching moment. Even mistakes are teachers, we learn what works and what doesn't by paying attention to our mistakes.

When we're young, we find teachers at home, at school, or at church, and we take what we learn with us through the rest of our lives. As we grow, we learn that staying open to activities around us, listening to the experiences of others, being aware of what's happening in the world, and staying open and available to one another, bring teaching moments.

We are all students and teachers on this journey through life. Sometimes the lessons come easy and sometimes they're hard. The person in our life who upsets us the most and is the hardest to get along with is most likely to be our best teacher. We are mirrors to one another, and when we see a trait in someone else that bothers us, it's a sure bet we have some part of that trait in ourselves. Knowing this, and finding others expressing negative traits, lets us see what we might look like to others when we express those negative traits. We can let that awareness teach us to remain positive.

We've heard said, "Show up, pay attention, and don't be attached to the outcome." When we try hard to force a specific outcome and it just doesn't work out, we become stressed and frustrated. But if we set a goal, take the necessary action to attain that goal in a relaxed, open-minded manner, and trust that a teaching moment will come, we're more likely to be successful.

We need to stay open to the teachers in our life. These teachers don't have to be people. They could be something we read, see on TV or the internet, or simply a thought conveyed by an unknown source. If we are someone who is set in our ways, feeling our way is the *right* way and are closed off to other ideas, we need to broaden our awareness. Inspiration and opportunities for learning are all around us and are ready to be our teachers when we are ready to be an available student.

PERSONAL TRUTH

We all have a personal truth; what we believe about ourselves. If our personal truth is damaged by being told that we're not good enough—or if we're telling ourselves this—we have to decide if we're going to live with that damaged personal truth, or if we're going to repair it and move on. If we have a damaged personal truth, we generate the results we think we deserve. If we feel like a second-class citizen, we will generate second-class results. And we don't have to do that!

The choice is ours. We can shake off any negativity, emotional baggage, and mixed messages that others have put on us or that we have put on ourselves. We don't react to what happens in our life, we react to what we *say to ourselves* about what happens. If we *choose* to reject these mixed messages, we *can* reject them. If we decide to be someone who becomes a leader instead of a follower, we can do that. If we decide to choose joy instead of pain, strength instead of weakness, we can do that. If we decide to be a victor instead of a victim, we can do that. We can live our positive personal truth.

That's the beauty of this life; *we* are the decision-maker; *we* make the rules. Though it's inevitable that there will be times of turmoil, of stress and confusion, and there will be situations that we can't change, but what we *can* change is our perception of these situations, and how we choose to respond to them. Our personal truth is that we are beautiful, perfect children of God. We must not forget this personal truth. We must not allow ourselves to get sidelined when things aren't going the way we like.

Remember, too, that all things work together for good. This is no more clearly demonstrated than the experience of a young man who is close to me. He was convicted of a non-violent, victimless crime and sentenced to prison. Instead of moping around, thinking *poor me*, he enrolled in classes provided by a local community college and earned two AA degrees during his three years of incarceration. And he found work immediately following his release in a field he'd studied. Although he could have wasted his time there, he knew he was better than his circumstances. He never forgot his personal truth, and he's a successful business and family man today.

Kick any negative thinking out of your mind and out of your life! Forget the word *can't*. Tell yourself you *can,* and you *will*. It's not as hard as it may sound if you don't lose sight of who you are, and what you are. Remember your real personal truth . . . and live it.

MAY DAY

When I think of May Day, I think of flowers and sunshine and happiness. I think of my grandmother who was born on May first, and I think of the fun we had when I was a child, laying flowers on the doorsteps of our neighbors.

But that's not how this day was first thought of. The origins of May Day go back to the 1880s which was a turbulent and pivotal time in United States labor history. On May 1, 1886, more than 300,000 workers in 13,000 businesses across the country walked off their jobs, advocating for better workplace conditions and for 8-hour work days. There were scenes of violence as workers began picketing. When police showed up to disperse the picketing crowds, rocks thrown at police were answered with gunfire. People were shot so we could have 8-hour workdays. Homes were burned so we could have Saturday as part of the weekend. People fought and sacrificed for the rights and dignities we enjoy today.

It's hard for me to associate the upheaval of the worker's May Day with the May Days of my childhood. My grandmother, my sister, and our many cousins, recognized this day as a beautiful way of celebrating spring—a time of renewal, and rebirth. We danced around a maypole, weaving brightly colored ribbons around the pole by ducking in front of and behind each other until the ribbons formed a beautiful woven design on the pole. And the gathering of flowers from grandma's garden as gifts for friends and neighbors was a high point.

May Day was always a celebration of my grandmother, and I remember her fondly on this day. I also remember her crocheting. A recent *Pickles* comic strip by Brian Crane reminded me of this. The strip shows Grandma crocheting, and little Nelson asking, "What are you making, grandma?" Grandma says, "Doilies. I'm making doilies. They're so frilly and pretty. Don't you just love doilies, Nelson?" To which Nelson replies, "I think you have to be an old person to like doilies." My grandmother was an old person, and she liked doilies. She crocheted tablecloths, scarfs and hats, and even bedspreads (one of which won a blue ribbon at the Los Angeles County Fair). And she crocheted doilies. She loved crocheting doilies. I still have some of them and like to use them under vases of flowers to celebrate spring on May Day, or on any day of the year.

FAMILY

In families, fathers who take an active role in the care and interests of their children are praised as being "involved fathers". But their wives or partners who do as much or more with and for their children are never referred to, let alone praised, as being "involved mothers." Mother involvement is a given, it's expected, but dads who are equally engaged are seen as going above and beyond. Why is this, I wonder. It takes two to make a baby, so why shouldn't it take two to raise and nurture that baby throughout its life.

My own father was not very involved in my upbringing. He was a hard-working man and a good provider, but I guess he thought dealing the children just wasn't part of the job of being a parent. Consequently, I never had the nurturing of a man that is so important to a girl growing into adolescence and young womanhood. As a result, I didn't learn how to relate to men, and have been in and out of relationships all my life.

I don't blame my father for how my life turned out, but I do wonder if I had been able to talk with my dad about boys and relationships, getting advice and direction, I would have made better choices. I have a good life. I'm content and fiercely independent. I've learned to take care of myself. Maybe that's the take-away from an uninvolved father.

If you are a new mother, ask dad to change some diapers and to feed the baby, or hold and rock her. If you are a new father, get involved. Children are priceless blessings. Toddlers need a father to teach them what's right and to avoid dangers. Teenagers need an involved father to mete out consequences of bad or dangerous behavior. Boys need a man to show them what manhood looks like, and girls need a father to guide them and to be a soft place to fall when things don't go well.

It warms my heart to see how involved my sons and grandsons are in their children's lives. There's a beautiful bond between father and child. The children are happy and well-adjusted as a result. For children to get the benefit of fathering even when there isn't a bio dad in the picture, an uncle, grandfather, or a good friend can be a stand-in father figure.

Life is simpler when we've had guidance and nurturing throughout our life. And as a parent, we can give our children the gift of a better life by being involved, physically, emotionally, and spiritually. That's what families are all about.

GETTING OLDER

In a recent *Pickles* comic strip by Brian Crane, Grandpa and little Nelson are having a conversation. Grandpa says, "Do you ever stop to think that old people weren't always old? I wasn't always old. I used to be young like you are now, and some day you will become an old man like me." to which Nelson innocently replies, "Cool. Maybe we can share clothes then."

When we're children, that's all we can see. We are around grown-ups all the time but we don't think about them growing older. Our lives, as children, are lived in the moment, without thought of change. Just as Nelson believed he'd someday be someone who could share clothes with his grandpa, children don't give thought to themselves or to those in their lives growing older. Old people, to children, will always be old people and children will always be children.

I have two sons, one three years older than the other. When the older one was able to do things that the younger one couldn't do, the little one would watch longingly and say, "When I'm a Mike, I will be able to do that." In his innocent mind, he didn't realize he would one day be as old as his brother was. He somehow thought he'd *become* that older boy.

The Bible tells us to become as little children. Little children perceive life differently. They have an innocence that allows them to see things with an uncluttered perception. They see things exactly as they are. If we can be as little children and see only loving thoughts as our reality, we will laugh at our fears and replace them with peace.

As I grow older, I'm seeing what's right in front of me. I'm not making up scenarios for what's coming. I'm living and loving every moment. I'm also sharing clothes with my twelve-year-old granddaughter. I gave her a pair of Mickey Mouse pajamas I'd purchased, that were neither appropriate, nor fit me. Maybe not inappropriate—is anybody ever too old for Mickey Mouse? But they were, in fact, too small for me.

Let's all hope that as we keep getting older, we also keep getting wiser. A wise grown-up can help a child become a well-adjusted adult. There is something to be said for the wisdom of the aged. In aging, we develop a deeper understanding of life. When we're able to let go of perceived problems and false self-images and rekindle the innocent mind-set of a child, we can live life in the moment and life does become simpler.

YOUR BEST MOMENT

What was the best moment of your life? Was it when you first fell in love? Was it when your child was born? Was it the day you got your dream job? If you asked a group of 100 people to tell you about their best moment, you'd get 100 different answers. Some might say their best moment hasn't come yet, and that they're sure it will come very soon. But if these people continue waiting for their best moment, it may never arrive.

In truth, the best moment of everyone's life is *this* moment, the one we are having right now, because this moment is the only true reality. We can enjoy memories of past moments and hold them dear, and we can hope for good moments in the future, but this moment is truly all there is.

No matter what's going on in your life right now, you can transform this moment into your most wonderful moment by not running to the future, not obsessing about the past, and, instead, looking at each moment in a different and more positive light. Even if you don't feel like this is your best moment, you can take heart in knowing that this moment will pass. In fact, it passed while you were reading this.

In every moment that we can open our eyes and enjoy the sunshine, the beautiful sky, the adorable children and wonderful people around us, that will be our best moment. Staying open and aware in this moment, breathing in and out consciously, we will feel calm, fresh, solid, clear, free, and we will welcome the present moment as the best moment of our life.

Breathe in the moment, enjoy it fully, and let all worries go. Your life is in good hands. God will see you through any bad moments and will celebrate all the good ones. With a clear mind and a positive outlook, this moment—and all moments—will be the best moment of your life, and life will be simple.

LET THEM KNOW

How often do you think about contacting someone, but just don't seem to get around to it? And how good do you feel when a friend or family member contacts you out of the blue just to touch base? Somehow, in this fast-paced society we live in, letting others know how much we care about them takes a back seat to whatever it is that we think is more important.

When my sister died very suddenly, I was in shock, and I felt such regret that I hadn't called her every time I'd thought of doing so, just to catch up. I miss her immensely. I miss being able to talk with her. I miss seeing her. I don't know if she even knew just how important she was to me.

My parents lived with me and I cared for them for the last four years of their lives. The blessing in their prolonged decline was that it gave us a chance to say and hear everything that needed to be said. They knew how much they meant to me, and I knew how much I was loved and appreciated. I miss them terribly, but have no regrets. They were both 91 when they passed—my father first, then 14 months later, my mother—and they lived good, happy lives.

So many people now days feel like they're staying in touch with friends and family through Facebook, texts, e-mails, Instagram, or tweets, but these are quick little contacts, not deep, meaningful connections. Seeing a picture of a lunch plate at a nice restaurant in a text doesn't really make me feel closer to the sender. What I'd really like is to be with them at that restaurant, sharing time and talk. I'd like to share thoughts that aren't out there in cyberspace for the world to see. I'd like to share on a more intimate level, face-to-face, to let them know that they mean more to me than a minute or two at the computer or cell phone.

We all have people in our lives who mean a lot to us and to whom we mean a lot. Social media is an easy way to stay in touch, but there is nothing better than a personal connection to let these people know how we feel. Let's remember not to let *stuff* get in the way of connecting to the people we care about. Today, tomorrow, every day, we can let someone know how much we care, and maybe someone will do that for us. We can give love the final say—before it's too late.

CONFIDENCE

When we look at all the people we know, we see some who don't seem to be quite sure how to interact with others, who appear shy. We also see those who are angry and combative. And there are those who laugh at inappropriate times. The shy ones kind of hide away. The combative ones try to make themselves right even when they know they're not. And the ones who laugh inappropriately are covering their feelings with humor. All these behaviors stem from insecurity and a lack of self-confidence.

I have to admit I've gone through phases in my life in which each of these behaviors have felt like they worked for me, especially laughing to cover insecurity. But through years of mental, spiritual, and physical maturing, I've gained a confidence that feels a lot better than any cover-ups.

When we're feeling a lack of confidence, we can make changes that will make life simpler. We can think about the people we are most comfortable with—the people who know us best—and take a good look at how we act around them. This will help us begin to see our real selves. We will become comfortable in our own skin and won't be so concerned about the impression we're making. Confidence is not caring so much about what other people think or say about us, confidence is doing what makes us comfortable. We can channel what it is that we love about ourselves, and we can *own* that. We can live to our own rules with confidence, not having to cover our feelings.

Confident people have an aura about them that, by example, encourages others to feel more comfortable and confident. Confident people don't have to hide, they can be who they are, expressing their own thoughts and ideas. Confident people don't have to be combative because they don't feel like someone else is running the show. Confident people are happier and laugh because they're happy, not because they're covering discomfort. Confident people can say *no* if they want to so they aren't led into things they would rather not do. *You* are a confident person. Even if you don't feel it all the time, it's there within you.

Without cover-ups, take a good look at yourself, find your confidence, live with that confidence, and life *will* become simpler.

L. F. C.

Life doesn't have to be as complicated as many people make it. A simple life boils down to three things that we all have a capacity for: Love, Forgiveness, and Choice.

With *Love* in your heart, you can look beyond the horror of some of the things you see on the news to the demonstrations of love that follow tragedies, and you'll see another world. For every person who causes pain, there are millions who are feeling love for, and are ready to help, those who are hurt. Fred Rogers, "Mr. Rogers" of TV fame, said, "When I was a boy and I would see scary things in the news, my mother would say to me, 'Look for the helpers. You will always find people who are helpers.'" You would be hard-pressed to find anyone more loving and helpful than Mr. Rogers in his Neighborhood.

Fear and hate are cancers on our world. Love and helpfulness will drive out those cancers. Whatever we encounter that upsets us, if we look at the love in those who turn up to help, pretty soon we'll see everything from a place of love in our own hearts.

Forgiveness helps us find the love. Forgiveness is a deep relief to those who offer it. We might think that there are acts that are simply unforgiveable, but if we can hold forgiveness in our hearts, we will realize that it is not so much the person who acted, but the action itself that seems unforgiveable. Forgiveness isn't something we do for another person, forgiveness is a gift we give to ourselves. When we hold on to thoughts of wrong doing or of being victimized, we are condemning ourselves to discomfort. We lay chains of imprisonment on ourselves when we lay them on anyone else. Forgiveness doesn't make right what is clearly wrong, it simply frees us from the prison we keep ourselves in by allowing it to consume us. Forgiveness breaks chains, slays dragons, and lets us move forward to live a simpler, more peaceful life,

Life is about *Choices*. Even when we've made bad choices in the past, we are free to make new choices now. We can choose love and we can choose forgiveness, and no matter what happens, we can always choose again.

Life is simpler when we choose love over hate, peace over conflict, and forgiveness over a self-imposed prison. It's our choices that determine our happiness. Let's let Love, Forgiveness, and Choice direct our lives so we can live peacefully, happily, and simply.

ATTACK / DEFENSE

When you feel attacked by someone who makes an unkind remark, do you feel you must defend it as untrue? When someone who has a point of view about something that differs from your own, do you feel the need to defend your beliefs? It's a natural tendency to answer attack with defense, but defense is really returned attack. It's a vicious cycle. There are no winners, only losers. And what we lose is our peace of mind.

Have you ever had an argument in which the other person throws up his hands and says, "Okay, you're right. I'm done" and felt like a winner? Probably not. The accepted belief is that to win, someone else has to lose. Agreeing to disagree is sometimes the best action. When no one loses, everyone wins.

What we feel as attack usually isn't, it's just someone's idea or thought. It's their version of something and it doesn't warrant defense, even if we think differently. There really is no right or wrong, no good or bad, there is only what *is*. What *is* requires neither attack nor defense, it simply *is what it is*.

You may be thinking, "What if I'm attacked physically, shouldn't I defend myself?" Yes, of course you should, that's why self-defense classes are offered. The kind of attack and defense we're talking about here is in the mind. Something in your mind attacks something in mine, and my mind wants to attack back. It's minds that need to be changed to stop the attack/defense cycle. Minds that are closed and warring are not going to change unless we consciously change them.

Debates are good, discussions are better, and a meeting of minds is best. Nothing outside our own mind can attack us or make us happy or unhappy. Our peace and happiness is strictly a decision we make in our mind. We cannot find happiness in attack and defense. We think attack comes from somewhere outside ourselves, not realizing it stems from our own thoughts of unworthiness. If we think we are worthy of attack, we will see attack. If we have a healthy sense of self-worth and feel confident in who and what we are, attack will roll off our back like water off a duck, and we won't feel the need to defend ourselves, to return attack with further attack.

Let's hope all people of the world, or at least the ones in our own life, can work to break the attack/defense cycle and begin to live a simpler, more peaceful, and happier life.

ART

Art comes in many forms. It could be a painting, a song, a play, a novel, a building, or a simple piece of pottery. And, we *look* at art in many different ways. When we are familiar with the artist, we can see it as a reflection of that person, which can color our thinking about the piece. We can also see it as a reflection of the times in which the piece was created. If we look at art with a technical mind, thinking about how the artist accomplished it—Johann Sebastian Bach's use of mathematical patterns and forms to create music, and William Shakespeare's use of iambic pentameter to write plays—we see the artistic matter in a completely different way.

When I look at a piece of art, I tend to *feel* it. Does it stir me in some way? Does it speak to my life? What is my response to the subject matter, the colors, and the composition? I have several great paintings in my home. None by famous artists, but all with some meaning for me. I never get tired of seeing them because of the emotion they generate. I have pieces of sculpture that are my own creations. When I look at them, I can still feel the clay on my hands and between my fingers and it gives me great pleasure. I also have some paintings I've done that are in the back of a closet. One, in particular, is of a barn which I did in a class with constant input from an instructor who was a stickler for precise, life-like detail. By the time I'd finished that piece, the only emotion I felt was frustration. Most art that appeals to me is free and has movement, and the picky little detail of that barn made me crazy, so I don't even want to look at it.

The purpose of good art isn't to create history, to honor the artist, or to be an ode to language. The goal is to stir the spirit, to touch the heart, to evoke emotion, to make us think, and most of the time, to make us feel good.

We could say our life is a work of art. It contains many details, it brings about changing emotions, it's sometimes beautiful and well composed, and at other times fragmented and chaotic. But in our life, *we* are the artist, the composer, the sculptor, and we have the ability to choose, not necessarily what happens in the composition of our life, but how we respond to it. We are all magnificent works of art. When we cherish every aspect of our life, we will touch the lives of others with its beauty and we will evoke emotions that will be remembered and appreciated by everyone we come in contact with.

RISK AND REWARD

When I hear of famous people changing professions, I wonder why. I see dancers who explore careers as actors, and actors who leave film and move on to Broadway, and I wonder why these people leave lucrative careers to venture into untested waters. Then when I look at my own life, I begin to understand why. It's a "been there, done that" kind of thing. When the thrill is gone and the emotional reward has dwindled, we feel led in a new direction, to do something that will challenge our talents and abilities.

My life has taken many new directions. My parents lived through the depression. They moved from place to place to find the next job. They had rice with tomatoes for dinner and rice pudding for dessert and called it a great meal. Not wanting their children to feel that kind of insecurity, they made sure we had consistency in our lives. I lived in the same house all my growing-up years, and thought that was all there was. I married young, started having babies, and thought *that* was all there was. But when my marriage went south, and a second one lasted only six years, I started to wake up. I began to recognize there was more to this world than the boxes I'd been living in. I went through what some might judge to be an irresponsible time. I changed jobs and moved often and I left relationships when they got uncomfortable. All this made me appear to be unsettled, but for me, it worked. I was living with enthusiasm and my spirit was free. I retained the good values which had been instilled in me by my parents and didn't do anything stupid, but I enjoyed life to the fullest. I travelled the world, met interesting people in interesting places, and I learned a lot. I took classes, gained new skills, and my psyche was fed by associating with people who challenged me intellectually. I made investments that my father would have been appalled by, and made them work for me. To this day, I still live in the moment. I'm spontaneous, and if something comes along that I want to explore, I'm drawn to it.

I'm not advocating throwing all caution to the wind, I'm only suggesting stepping out of our comfort zone a little. Taking a leap of faith and trying something new and different. My parents meant well by wanting security for their daughters, but for me, security lies in adventure. So, I say to you: Reach out! Take a risk! Without some risk in life, there can be no genuine reward.

TAKE A NAP

In a *Blondie* cartoon by Dean Young, Alexander, the son, tells Dagwood of a brain study saying, "Ha! This study says your brain can actually get full!" Dagwood then asks, "Full? How?" Alexander reads from the study: "Over-stimulation! Napping actually prunes the unneeded brain files, like weeds in a garden!" Dagwood brightens and says, "I knew it!" The last frame shows Dagwood lying on the sofa as Blondie approaches saying, "Honey, I've got a job for you." To which Dagwood replies, "Sorry, sweetheart, my brain is full." Dagwood, being an avid napper, gets out of doing the chores Blondie has lined up for him, using this brain study to justify his napping.

The truth is, Dagwood is right. Taking time out from work to nap, or just stopping and thinking of something more pleasant than work for a little while, does increase productivity. When we become fatigued, our thinking and reasoning powers slow down, and we aren't as sharp as we are when we're rested and refreshed.

A nap needn't be hours long, and we don't even need to lay down for a quick nap. My own best naps are when my head just falls forward when I'm watching television or reading and I sleep for five or ten minutes. This kind of "napette" refreshes me and allows my brain to recharge and begin to hum again.

The time for a good long, lying down nap is when we don't feel well. The more rest we can get when we're sick or run-down, the faster we'll get well and feel better. And if we can take breaks from our work when we *are* well and healthy, the less likely we are to get run-down and become sick.

So, don't feel guilty if you feel you need a nap, feel empowered! Just knowing we can revive and renew our productive energy by taking a little nap can make life simpler.

WANT VS NEED

My friend Barb had a long-time tradition with her grandchildren. Every year on each child's birthday, she took that child out to lunch and shopping. She allowed them to pick out two gifts, one to be something they *need*, the other, something they *want*. The needs were often new underwear or socks, a backpack or something else they needed for school. The wants were toys, games, a special article of clothing, or a big old hot fudge sundae. This ritual taught the children the important difference between want and need. There may be things children want but don't necessarily need, and other things they need but aren't what they'd choose as a gift. Barb's ritual worked for everyone.

This is actually a good lesson for all of us. Barb's grandchildren are adults now, with their own families, and they've learned the value of distinguishing want from need so they're less likely to buy things on impulse.

There are a lot of things we'd like to have, but to get them, and pay for them, we have to stop and give thought to what we might overlook. There might be a needed item that we would have to do without if our money was spent on more frivolous things, just to fulfill an urge for instant gratification.

We wouldn't go without making our mortgage payment to have a mani/pedi and a massage on a whim, for example, and we wouldn't go without groceries for our family in order to go to a fancy expensive restaurant for a one-time decadent meal. We have to set priorities, there's a balance between want and need, and unless we have unlimited funds, we often have to make a choice.

I've taught my own grandchildren this valuable lesson and often see them with their palms up, raising one hand then the other, weighing the options of want or need—I *want* a new pair of jeans, but my kids *need* school clothes.

This doesn't mean we can never treat ourselves to something special, but we have to understand that wants and needs are not always the same . . . but sometimes they are. When we take the time to think clearly and consider priorities, often times the happy outcome is that a want is also a need, and this is where a balanced, happy, simple life happens.

FEAR

A Course in Miracles teaches that there are only two emotions: Love and Fear, and that anything not loving is based in fear. Once, in my *Course* group, we made a list of different emotions: anger, sadness, envy, anxiety, doubt, mistrust, worry—and the list goes on. When we took a good look at the emotions on the list, it was easy to see how each one was based in fear. Fear engenders loneliness, frustration, stress, and guilt. Jealousy is a fear of insecurity. Even anger is mostly a fear of being wrong. All these emotions are needless. When we stay in a place of love, there is no room for fear.

Love is the only reality, and if we're feeling fear, no matter how it manifests, we have invited it into our minds and into our lives. We have accepted it as real. The good news is that if we choose to look at our fears and see them differently, not identifying with them, we can overcome these fears. When we act out of fear, we are in its grip and the fear runs us. But when we can look on fear dispassionately and respond to it with mercy, we can heal instead of going into panic. It's the difference between saying, "I am afraid" and saying "I am having fearful thoughts." Thoughts of fear don't define us, we are simply the thinker of the thoughts.

This changed, or altered, vision of fear does not necessarily affect us alone, it affects everyone. When we see ourselves differently, without fear, we will see others differently as well.

When thoughts of fear enter our mind, we can recognize them as a stranger, and uninvited interloper, and know they don't belong there. We don't need to accept fear. But we don't need to fight against it either. Some wise person once said, "What you resist, persists." We can simply see our own thoughts of fear with compassion and understanding, recognizing them as a mistake then dismiss them. We can also see others in the same light. When we observe others caught in fear, we can see them with forgiveness, kindness, and mercy rather than with judgment.

Fear can be equated with a storm at sea. We can accept it as something we cannot beat, or we can find a way to work around it. Chuck Chamberlain, in his famous book *A New Pair of Glasses* wrote, "It is the set of the sail that determines where the ship goes, and not the gale." The wind can't take the ship off-course when the sail is set against it. It's not what we look at that matters, it's what we see. When we see fear as unreal, our life will become simpler. Without fear in our hearts, there's a whole lot more room for love.

CLEAR OUT

When I moved into a place with a very large closet, I moved all my clothes over instead of going through them and getting rid of what I don't wear. Now, because there's room for everything, I've lost the urge to clear out. But I was just inspired by an article I read. The tip was: On a date that you'll be sure to remember, like your birthday, turn all of the hangers in your closet backwards, with the hook opening facing outward, toward you. Then, during the year, after wearing something, hang it up with the hanger hook facing the back of your closet. On that same date the next year, take a good look at what's still hanging backwards and consider giving it away. Notice I said *consider*, there are seasonal clothes that are only worn in extreme temperatures or on special occasions.

I had a friend in elementary school whose mother didn't want to do unnecessary laundry, so when Dottie changed after school, she hung her clothes inside-out. This way she knew she'd worn them before and they were to be put in the laundry after the second wearing. Some people date their clothes and hold on to them for only a limited time. Others have a certain place they put clothes they wear a lot, and the pieces that never make to that place get discarded.

There was a time that, whenever I bought a new item of clothing, I'd make myself get rid of another, and reuse the hanger. This worked for a while, but since I tend to keep items of clothing way too long, I sometimes surprise myself by coming across something I haven't worn in literally years, and it's like getting a new sweater or shirt or jacket. So, I just keep buying more hangers.

I try to go through my pantry periodically and toss out-of-date items and half-empty jars and packages of stuff that I don't know how long they've been there. This works with cosmetics and lotions in the bathroom, too. If we haven't used a certain face-wash, or hair spray, or moisturizer because at some point we've found something else that we like better, why keep the old stuff around?

Clearing out can be empowering. When we're done, we're left with only things we really need or use, and the old stuff isn't there to confuse us anymore. We would all be more comfortable and peaceful if we would simplify our lives by clearing out our closets, cabinets, drawers, refrigerators, freezers, garages, and any place we *put* things. I'll try it if you will.

TRUST

I've always felt that a person who trusts others is also trustworthy. I therefore hesitate to trust someone who doesn't trust others. Trust is the essential ingredient in a relationship. Some people have been so hurt or taken advantage of through their lives that they find it hard to trust anybody. But trust can be built, and there is a process.

To learn to trust, you first go through a period of *undoing*, of changing external circumstances, removing yourself from the person or situation that has been proven untrustworthy and caused you pain.

Then you do some *sorting out*. Decide whether trust is helpful or harmful. If you perceive value in a situation, you trust it can be good for you. But if you feel strong resistance, question that trust.

You then enter into a time of *relinquishment*, giving up what doesn't feel right. You may think you're letting go of something desirable, but if trust is not *fully* warranted, it's not there at all.

Then *settle down*. Take time to really consider what is worthy of your trust and what is not, what has value to you and what does not.

This leads to a time of *unsettling*, questioning if you've put your trust in the right persons or situations. Lay aside all judgment and see only what serves you in every circumstance. See the valuable and the valueless, and you will see what deserves your trust and what does not. Somewhere inside, you know the truth. You have an inner guidance . . . trust that guidance.

At the end of all this comes a feeling of *achievement*. When you've learned to trust only what is worthy of your trust, you can rest assured that your trust will not be misplaced and that your thinking can be counted on in any emergency, as well as in peaceful times.

Only trusting can afford honesty, not only about what a person does or says at any given time, or what a situation looks like or feels like in the moment, it's about consistency. If that person or circumstance *seems* to be something we can trust, take a look at history. If we've been deceived before, we're likely to be deceived again. We need to be cautious and trust our own instincts When we trust only what has been proven to have value, it's hard to go wrong.

People who find it hard to trust live a tortured life. Life is indeed simpler when peaceful trust is a part of it.

SUBTRACT YOUR BLESSINGS

People often tell us to count our blessings when we're feeling down. That's good advice, because reminding ourselves of our good helps us get through the tough times. But, consider this: Instead of counting your blessings, subtract them. Think of your life without the good things, without your loved ones, your good job, your pets, all the things you love and enjoy and that make you happy. Now, imagine what your life would be like without these people and things.

It's easy to count our blessings, but if these blessings were taken away, subtracted from our life, it would make us feel worse than the blessings make us feel good.

Sometimes we take the good in our lives for granted, we believe it will always be there for us, that we'll always have those blessings. But to really appreciate the good, there's a new-found appreciation when we can imagine life without it. This exercise isn't meant to be a downer, it's simply a reminder not to become complacent, not to forget the people and things that make us happy and are blessings in our life, and to enjoy them to the fullest.

When the owner of the airport I managed, and had complete control of for fourteen years, decided to sell, I was given the task of finding a buyer. I did that, and negotiated a very good transaction. The owner walked away with a lot of money, I was out of a job, and my hefty income stopped. I could no longer afford to do the travelling I'd been doing. I had to very carefully watch my spending. I no longer had contact with the employees and tenants I'd come to know well. My whole life changed. I'd been living a blessing. It was hard, energy-taxing work, but I loved it. I had never given a moment's thought through those years to what my life would be like without it. I didn't count my blessings, I took them for granted and didn't fully appreciate what I had. Then my blessings were subtracted.

I still have many blessings in my life—my family, a beautiful home, good friends, and opportunities for adventure and fun—but I no longer take them for granted. I'm deeply grateful for every day of my life because, through the airport experience, I've learned what it is to have the blessings in my life subtracted. I now take comfort, however, in knowing that sometimes when the blessings are subtracted, new blessings can multiply.

CRUCIFIXION & REDEMPTION

Crucifixion and Redemption are something we do to ourselves. As we go through life, we may encounter episodes of being attacked or abused. I'm not talking about physical attack where our bodies are hurt by the actions of another, but a subtler, verbal or neutral attack. Bullying falls into this category. But what the bully doesn't know is that by debasing another, he is also debasing himself. When we ignore the bully, not allowing the attack to hurt us, he is neutralized and the attack usually stops.

When we know our own worth and are confident with who and what we are we cannot be attacked, because we know that whatever feelings of attack we think we're getting from others is really something we're doing to ourselves. It's our own crucifixion. It's *believing* the attackers words and actions that brings the hurt. If we don't let ourselves believe them, knowing they're not true, we can maintain our peace. This is our redemption.

Attack and abuse are motivated by fear, and if we accept another's fearful thoughts, letting them affect us negatively, we have allowed them to take away our peace and freedom. But if we recognize these actions by another as their own fear, insecurity, and lack of self-worth, we will be unfazed by them. The way we interpret things others do to us is a reflection of how we feel about ourselves. People who find fault with others unconsciously see those same faults in themselves. When we are attacked or abused, verbally or emotionally, it's not about us, it's about the attacker or abuser, and we have the power to rise above the actions and remember that we cannot be hurt unless we allow it.

I learned this lesson the hard way, the way most hard lessons are learned. In my first marriage I was both verbally and emotionally abused. I allowed myself to be crucified by someone who had so little self-confidence it made him feel better about himself to make me feel worse about myself. I was so naïve, vulnerable, and inexperienced that I gradually crumbled into a tiny shell of myself. I had been in the top percentile in school and was a natural leader in many pursuits, and it wasn't until after my divorce and I was forced into the work world that the strong, intelligent, capable, woman I had been emerged again. I had been crucified and was redeemed when I woke up to who I really am and learned that his actions only indicated how little he honored, or even knew about, himself. Through my crucifixion and redemption experience, I learned that life could be simpler.

PHOTO ALBUMS

I love to look at photo albums, turning those big pages and reliving memories and good times. The younger generations today don't fully appreciate photo albums. They have all their pictures on their computers, tablets, or cell phones, and can access them anytime and anywhere. This is a good thing—can't knock technology—even *I* enjoy passing a phone around so everybody can take turns seeing the pictures. But with a photo album, people can talk about different aspects of the pictures. My grandkids, from the oldest to the youngest, love to sit on the sofa with me looking at photo albums and seeing what the family they know looked like ten or twenty years ago, or seeing themselves as babies and through their growing-up years.

In a recent *Garfield* cartoon by Jim Davis, Garfield the cat has a big book open in front of him and is approached by a mouse who asks, "What are you looking at, Cat?" Garfield responds, "A photo album." The mouse says, "A photo album? What's that?" to which Garfield replies, "It's where we old folks used to post our selfies." The mouse, still looking stumped says, "Ah . . ."

Selfies are the photo albums of today. Because it's so easy to do, people take pictures of themselves with friends, at interesting, and sometimes uninteresting, places, and even with meals on a plate, and they send those pictures to everyone they know.

We don't have to cart around a clumsy camera any more, and we don't have to take rolls of film to the drug store to be developed. Pictures are now instant gratification, and if you don't like the first one, you can take another. It's easy, even for me, and I'm one of the old folks Garfield referred to. Even being an oldie, I still swipe pictures from my phone and send them to Costco to be printed so I can add the prints to my photo albums. I look at my photo albums often and enjoy going back in time to bring back memories.

Photo albums might seem passé to you younger people, but you "old folks" reading this, know what I mean. Say cheese!

LEAD ME

Do you ever feel subtly, subconsciously, led to do something that feels a little alien to you, not knowing where the thought is coming from? Sometimes you might be driving on a familiar road and something is telling you to alter your route to avoid a certain area, then you find out later that there'd been an accident on your regular route, or the street was closed for repairs. The big question is, do you follow that nudging, or do you put it out of your mind and go merrily along your way until you come upon a danger or delay that you could have avoided if you'd followed that subtle lead?

Very often I feel led to do something—to alter my route, to call a certain person, to invite someone over, to attend an event I don't feel like attending— and I've learned to follow those leads, those inklings. I don't always know the why behind what I'm being led to do, but it usually turns out to be a positive action.

When my niece was in her 30s, she felt a strong urge to have a mammogram. Doctors told her she was too young and, even though she had no symptoms, she felt strongly led to have the test. She had to fight for it, but the mammogram was finally performed, and a very aggressive cancer was discovered. She went on to have a double mastectomy and is living healthily now, more than 25 years later.

Cynthia was invited by friend to go to a dance. She had no interest in going, but she felt a distinct urge to go. She fought that strong urging, finding all kinds of excuses, but the feeling was so strong that she finally gave in and went to the dance. While there, she met a handsome, friendly, respectful, kind, young man and—fast-forward—they've just celebrated 33 years of marriage. That nice young man was my oldest son.

When we feel led, we can fight the feeling if we want to, but following those unconscious leads is often a short-cut to peace. The process goes like this: We feel led. We fight the feeling. We eventually give in and act on the lead. We feel relief. Wouldn't it be easier to simply follow what you're feeling led to do and get to relief sooner, eliminating all the resistance in between?

When you feel led by some unknown or even unfamiliar feeling, nudging you in a different direction, act on it . . . it's the universe working for your safety, health, and happiness.

GOOD FOR YOU

When you see someone you feel is better off than you, who has a bigger house, a newer car, a better job, who appears to win at everything he does, do you feel happy for that person or is there a little bit of envy? Or when you excel, when you feel better off than others around you, is there a pride that makes you feel superior?

According to most faith traditions, we are all equal, we are one in the eyes of God. Even the Constitution of our country tells us that all men (and women) are created equal. But sometimes we don't feel so equal. When our life isn't going along smoothly, when we can't seem to catch a break, when we feel left behind while watching others excel, we find it hard to fight feelings of being less-than.

These feelings come from a mindset based on comparisons. Rather than being proud of, and happy for, our fellow man, we tend to compare his accomplishments to our own, and one of us comes up lacking. The antidote to this kind of comparison is gratitude. We can be grateful for our own good and also for the good of others.

Watching sporting events, we often see the losing team congratulating the winners, and the winners praising the ones who didn't win for a game well-played. When we compare ourselves with others, we split them off from the unity we share as beings in this world. But when we lay comparisons aside, hatred, envy, and disappointments are forgotten and we feel gratitude for what we have, and for what others have as well.

When we see someone excel, we can be there with a resounding, honest, "Good for you!" We can be grateful for their success. And when we have a win, we can be equally grateful for our own triumph, with no feelings of *better than*. There are really no winners and losers because when one person is diminished, we are all diminished. We can be grateful for who we are and for what we have, and be equally grateful for the good in the lives of others. If we would all choose togetherness over competitiveness, letting love be our driving force instead of competition, all our lives would be simpler.

Although some competition can be fun—a friendly pick-up game of basketball or playing Scrabble or Monopoly—but it doesn't really determine who is best. The best person is not the one who wins the game, it's the one who is grateful for the opportunity to play the game. Whether you win or lose, Good for you!

THEN – NOW – WHEN

To live simply, we must let go of the past, not worry about the future, and stay in the present. We've heard this said in many ways, but it really is that simple. Maybe not easy, but simple.

There are things in everyone's past that they'd rather not think about, but because they *are* in the past, the only way they can affect us *now* is by thinking about them in the present.

The same thing can be said of the future. We have no way of knowing what will happen in the future. We only have a mental imaging of what the future *might* hold. Thinking too much about what has not yet happened can have an effect on our life in the present. Only by mentally letting go of the past and the future can we be free from their apparent effects, and be fully open to accept what is ours *now*.

When we find something in our present life somewhat threatening, it likely has come about from our perception of some past event. The only thing we really know is what we've already seen and experienced. If we aren't seeing or experiencing those things in the present, we can let them go and live our best life now, not giving thought to how they will affect us going forward into the future.

We may have had bad relationships in the past which have made us leery of any new relationship. We may have made some bad decisions that we regret. But if we look at these life experiences as learning tools, if we recognize the lessons we've learned from them, we can avoid similar experiences in the future.

The past is behind us, but what we've learned from it can help us in the now. The future lays before us and we have the power to let it be better than our past. On the other hand, if our past was filled with only good, we can feel that good in the present and carry it with us into the future. It's all up to us. It's the way we perceive things in our own mind that makes them real for us.

Your past was *then*; learn from it, cherish it, or let it go, it's your choice. Your present is *now*; make the most of it for current happiness and peace. Your future is *when*; it's yours to create. Life is a series of present moments laid before you that you can make the best of. Whatever happens will be a result of your present thinking, and keeping your thoughts positive can make life simpler.

PEACE, BE STILL

At Unity Village in Lee's Summit, MO, there is a tiny chapel. It has heavy drapes on all the walls making it virtually sound-proof. It also has a stained-glass window inscribed with the works, "Peace, Be Still." So many prayers have been offered up in that little chapel that the peace of God is palpable. It can be felt physically in the body. It's probably the most holy place I have ever encountered. After spending even a short amount of time in this chapel, you can't help but feel peaceful and safe.

The aim in life for all of us is to truly feel that inner peace, to feel safe as we go through each day, doing what's ours to do. That peace is our reality. It is the truth of us.

When we watch the news on television or read the newspaper, it's easy to see that not everyone has a deep peace in their heart. There is a storm in the mind of so many, causing them to forget that their inherent reality is peace. I feel appallingly sad for these troubled souls who live in a completely different world, apart from their reality.

Everyone in this world, sees what they want to see. Alan Watson, long-time student and teacher of *A Course in Miracles*, explained it well in his writings. He pointed out that there is a "blind spot" in our eyes. It's a place on the retina where the optic nerve attaches to it that does not pick up the light shining through the lens. Our minds fill in this blind spot with what *ought* to be there. None of us really *sees* this blind spot at the side of our vision, but it's there, and the mind simply makes up what it thinks it should be seeing. Our mind then sends out its information gatherers to find what they think they seek. If the mind tells them to find guilt, they find it. If it tells them to find evidence of attack, they attack in return. The mind sees what it *wants* to see and makes it real to the seeker.

If we allow our mind's blind spot to see peace, our mind will fill it with peace. If the mind tells us to seek for love, we will see love in all things, and in each other. When we live in a peaceful place in our mind, we bring peace to others. We become, as St. Francis prayed, an instrument of peace.

If you don't feel peace within yourself today, reach out to help someone who needs the comfort of inner peace. In doing this, you will recognize it in yourself. And when you feel yourself losing your peace, become still and pray, "Peace, Be Still." Your blind spot will be filled with love, and your life will be simpler.

DANGER

There seems to be danger all around us. Our water is unsafe. Smoking can kill us, even being around smokers can be deadly. Preservatives and coloring in the foods we eat can cause illness. Too much time at the computer or watching television can ruin our eyesight. Unaware drivers on the freeway are a danger. Feeding the critters at the zoo can be risky. Even using our land-line phone during a thunderstorm can cause electrocution. Danger! Danger!

It's a dangerous world we live in, and constant thought about the dangers can be debilitating. But the good news is: We don't have to be in continual worry. We don't want to purposely put ourselves in dangerous situations, but we don't have to live in non-stop fear either.

If you can live your life in perpetual peace without worrying about what could go wrong, life *can* be simple. I'm not suggesting you be a Pollyanna, thinking nothing bad can ever happen. There are events that sometimes do go wrong, and we need to be aware of things to look out for and to avoid. But don't be so fearful that when something goes wrong you shrug and say, "I knew it! I knew this would happen if I let my guard down."

It's the way we look at danger that makes the difference. If we keep our cool when faced with the prospect of danger, we can take the necessary steps to remove ourselves from that danger or to neutralize the situation. Even if we do get hurt, or sick, or so afraid that we wet our britches in the face of peril, we can rest assured we'll be okay. There is always help available, and just knowing this can relieve the tension in our shoulders, the knot in our stomach, and the rapid beating of our heart.

I knew of a woman who, when shopping at the mall, noticed a man who appeared to be following her from store to store. When it came time to leave the mall, she turned to this stranger and asked if he would walk her to her car because it was dark and she was afraid to go out there alone. The man obliged. When they got to her car she got in, locked the door, and drove away, leaving the man looking dumbfounded. This scenario could have had a very different outcome, but the woman remained calm and neutralized the situation by acting in complete opposite of how she would have if she had shown fear.

Don't court danger, but don't let it disable you either. Just as mommy and daddy told you that you'd be okay when you were afraid or had a bad dream, you can tell yourself that today. You *will* be okay, whatever the outcome.

MAKE A LIST

It's a rule at my house that if you use, eat, or drink the last of something, put it on the list. There is an on-going grocery list on the counter in my kitchen, and if everyone follows this rule it makes grocery shopping much easier and things don't get forgotten.

This is only one of my lists. I am a consummate list-maker. When I run errands, I make a list with the destinations in the logical order of their location so I can easily go from one to another without back-tracking. And I make a sub-list for what I need at each of these places. I cross the destinations off as I leave them. I also list jobs I have to do around the house, and I cross them off when they're done. If, through the day, I add a destination or a household chore that isn't on the original list, I write it on the list just so I can cross it off. *I love crossing things off lists.* Sometimes when I go to the market and only need four or five items I won't make an actual list but will think of first letter of the items I need and make a word out of those letters. For example; if I need bread, eggs, grapes, apples, and detergent, it becomes BEGAD. If I keep saying the made-up word as I'm shopping, I don't forget anything.

I also put sticky notes everywhere. Even some of the pages in this book are a compilation of sticky notes on my desk. I get so busy sometimes that things slip my mind and I end up thinking about them at the end of the day when it's too late to take care of them, so I need lists and notes as reminders throughout the day to keep me on track.

Psychologists would say list-and-sticky-note people are either absent-minded or very organized. Maybe I'm a little bit of both. Lists give me structure, a plan I can stick to, and they are confirmation of what I've achieved. After I've completed everything on my list and crossed them off, I can simply erase them from my memory and my brain will be ready for new thoughts, new plans, new lists.

Making lists can actually make your life simpler. Thinking about tasks you haven't yet done can be distracting, and just making a plan to get them done can free you from anxiety. And you get a feeling of accomplishment when they get crossed off the list. Making lists certainly works for me. Once I write something down, I can free my mind to think of other things, knowing I can come back to the list whenever I need a reminder.

STICKS AND STONES

Every little kid has chanted, "Stick and stones can break my bones, but words will never hurt me." And they're right. But self-condemnation *can* hurt us. Not our body, of course, but our mind, and when our mind is hurt, our body reacts.

Whether we realize it or not, we do a lot of self-condemning. We criticize ourselves when we have a bad hair day, or when we don't do well on an exam, when that new recipe doesn't turn out right, our golf game is off, or for a multitude of reasons. Sometimes we try to make ourselves feel better by vilifying others, condemning or judging them, and blaming them for our own shortcomings. We see this kind of disparaging as attack on another, but it is really an attack on ourselves. When we attempt to hurt others with our thoughts and our words, we are actually hurting ourselves. *A Course in Miracles* says, *The spears of attack you hurl out at the world all come back to stab yourself.*

Self-condemnation comes from inside and is projected as outward-directed criticism. Anger, mistrust, prejudice, hatred, resentment, dislike, or even discomfort with another are really symptoms of self-condemnation and mistrust of ourselves. But because we have the power to change our mind about how we see and feel about ourselves and others, we can cease to condemn ourselves for our perceived shortcomings and begin to see our own glory, our own perfection. We can also see past our judgment of others and see their glory and their perfection.

It's true, stick and stones can sometimes hurt physically, but the only thing that can really hurt us is our own condemnation, and we can let that go. When we feel a rush of judgment within our mind, whether directed at ourselves or at another, we can bring our case to the court of our higher mind, open our heart, and feel dismissal of the case against us.

Using sticks and stones to act out negative feelings is using your body as an expression of conflict. And conflict won't really solve anything for you or for anybody else. So, let life be simple, dodge the sticks and stones and let the words roll off your back. When others try to hurt you, they are only hurting themselves, and when they see that neither sticks and stones, nor words have any effect, they might learn to be kind and loving as well.

AN OFFERING

When I was in the Fiji Islands staying in a hotel room that opened out to a vast white-sand beach, I attended a church service where a great deal of fresh fruit was placed on an altar as an offering to the gods. After the service was over, a group of tiny monkeys came in from outside and carried away the fruit. I was surprised by this, but was informed that the gods to which the offering was made chose to give the fruit to the monkeys. That opened my eyes to the true meaning of an offering. Who was I to say who got to eat that fruit? It was offered to the gods to do with whatever they wished.

When we give an offering of any kind, be it fruit, love, something of monetary value, or even advice, we've *given* it—it's not ours to say what the recipient does with it. If we try to control the destiny of a gift, then it's not a gift at all, it's some kind of bargain.

Honest communication is also an offering. When you are truthful with someone, you release any expectation of what they do with that truth. They may thank you, ignore you, argue with you, or they may not respond at all. But you can be comfortable in knowing you've communicated honestly. You've done your part and the recipient is free to do his.

I once gave copies of a couple of my favorite books—books that contained insights that changed my life—to a friend who was floundering spiritually and emotionally in a sea of *who am I, what am I here for, where am I going?* I believed if she read these books her thinking might be changed, as mine was, and her life could become simpler. After a time, I asked her if she'd read the books, and she said she had not, that she'd given them to her daughter. Much later, I learned her daughter *did* read the books and shared with her mother what she'd learned. In future conversations with my friend, she began to relay to me some of the insights she'd gained as though the ideas would be new to me. The message I'd wanted to give to her got to her, but not from me, and that was okay, it was the giving that was important, not who got credit for the outcome. Her life did turn around, just as mine had, and she became happier and more fulfilled.

When you give an offering or a gift, let go of it, and don't be attached to any outcomes. If we mean it for good, good will come of it in one way or another. Giving warms the heart and feeds the soul, so if you want the gods to have the fruit, offer it to them, and if they want the monkeys to eat it, be happy for the monkeys.

WILL FOR PEACE

When you're in a compromising situation, or have a difficult decision to make, you might pray "Thy will is my will." I know I do, and when I let go and let God, I can allow myself to relax, knowing the outcome will be what is meant to be. Much of life is far beyond our own control, and what we think is our will can often be nebulous, cloudy, or vague. We all have wishes and dreams, but it's *will* that's the driving force that pushes us.

We might be seeking or hoping for wealth, fame, or some form of worldly security. We might be hoping for romance, or a great adventure, or simply a quiet family life. We *think* these are the things we're longing for, but these are wishes and dreams. Outcomes are what we believe these things offer us. If our will for something is strong enough, and our actions effective enough, we often do realize those wishes and dreams.

The real will that we all share, is for inner peace. These other wishes, dreams, and goals may be part of the path to our real will, but true will is for a sense of completion, a sense of worth, a feeling of belonging, of feeling valuable. It's something inside of us, not something we gain from the world. Only when we remember the truth of ourselves, only when we remember our connection to Love itself, will we find what we're seeking.

When you wish for something, be it a tangible item or an experience or adventure, stop and ask yourself, is this desire going to give me an inner peace? It may give you a sense of pleasure for a time, but it won't last forever, and it won't give you a deep, lasting peace. The only everlasting peace comes from a will for Love with a capital L. And that capital Love is God's will for you. You'll have lots of small loves in your life, as you should, but abiding Love and Peace are your birthright and shine above all else.

We can have all the adventures we can, all the fun we can fit into our life. We can have wealth, fame, security, romance, or a quiet life. Wherever we find the happiness that makes life feel worthwhile remember, God's will for us is peace. Our *real* will is for the love and peace that comes from within. This will for deep peace allows us to face the trying times with composure. A mental calmness and evenness of temper is our true will and is the only thing that will bring us simple, lasting, calming, peace. It's the peace we've been seeking and that has always been in us. If we will for peace long enough, and strong enough, it will come to us. It will make everything in our life seem simple.

MULTITASKING

Are you a multitasker? Doing one thing with one hand and something else with the other? Starting a task then allowing another to take part of your attention? Study while watching television? Text while driving? If your answer is yes to any of these actions, think of the words of Dr. Phil, "How's that workin' for you?"

In our busy do-as-much-as-we-can society, many of us think we can concentrate on more than one thing at a time. We can, to some extent, but when we do, our thoughts are divided and nothing has our full attention. As a result, nothing gets done in the best way.

Too often we see people so busy they just brush off their children when they come to mom or dad with a question, thinking they are the ones in charge and the children can wait. What message does this give the children? They might throw tantrums, not because they are bad children, but because they can't get the attention they crave. Or they go off on a wrong path with someone who does pay attention but who doesn't have their best interest at heart.

I marvel at my oldest granddaughter who is raising seven children, four that she bore and three more who came with their father when they married (one just a nine-month-old baby). If you visited her home you would find laundry stacked up, toys strewn about, and the noise level sometimes a bit high, but the kids are clean, happy, well-behaved, and well-adjusted. And, they are *heard*. There are so many tasks to be done that they sometimes overlap, but she can step away when the needs of her children take precedence. Her children are her main focus and they do their part. She involves them in tasks and chores, and has taught them to be helpful and to work together.

It was Maya Angelou who first said, "I'm doing *one* thing now, and I'm doing it well." That's a good thought to hold. When we focus on one thing at a time, we are more likely to do it well. Maya's words have become my mantra because I know this to be true. I actually get more done in less time, achieve better results, and am able to accomplish more when I'm not jumping from one thing to another.

When we have a lot to do, we can focus on the first thing first, get it done well, then go on to the next thing, and do it well. We'll have less frustration, be less stressed, and life will be simpler.

INSIGHT

I have a lovely little book that I like to pick up and read when I need insight into what I see, feel, or think. That book is called *Your True Home,* and contains everyday wisdom of the Buddhist master, Thich Nhat Hanh. The book was compiled and edited by Melvin McLeod, and he wrote, "Insight is a mysterious, almost miraculous experience. A flash of insight can come upon us in a moment, without warning, like the opening in a cloudy day that suddenly illuminates the landscape below. We see simply and clearly what had before been hidden in the shadows of concepts and confusion. . . A phrase, a single word, a blow, or a shout can be enough to wake us up."

True insight is the ability to see and understand why we think and act the way we do. It's the ability to see without distortion. Insight is not complex, nor does it require a lot of words. It is not merely wise ideas or statements of principle to cheer us up or inspire us. True insight can be transformative and instructional. It goes deep below the surface level of intellect, to the heart.

Insight is often confused with inspiration, but we can be inspired by something without having real insight into it. We might say that inspiration is a thinking process, and insight is a feeling.

True insight is a deep and accurate intuitive understanding of something. To gain deep meaning of the nature of reality, an awakened wisdom that we can feel in our body, is insight. The word itself says it. We intuitively see *inside* the external, the visual, and the obvious. Insight is knowledge. It is seeing the motivational forces behind what the eyes see. It is a deep, and sometimes sudden, understanding of a complicated problem, situation, or concept.

Sometimes we can read something that suddenly makes a concept we've been struggling with make sense. When I read Eric Butterworth's *Discover the Power Within You,* I was new to the Unity Church and learning about how we are all one with each other and with God. Butterworth gave the example of God as the ocean, and each one of us a bit of water in the ocean. Each of us is responsible for the whole ocean because each one of us *is* the whole. We can't be separated from the whole ocean (God) or from any part of it (all of us). This was a light-bulb moment for me and I suddenly understood oneness.

Insights can come in a single moment from a single thought, and if we stay open to it. Insight can make our lives richer.

FREEDOM

We hear songs about freedom: "Freedom is just another word for nothing left to lose," "Born free, free as the wind blows. . . free to follow your heart." When we hear these songs, we think, "Yes, that's what I want! I want to feel freedom!" In our everyday life, we're not being held hostage against our will, but do we really feel free? Are we free to follow our heart? Is our mind free of thoughts and attitudes that keep us from being free?

The word *free* in *freedom* comes from the German *frei,* which means "to love." The word *friend* has the same origin, so we can think of freedom as having the choice to love or befriend anyone we wish. Freedom is defined as the power to act, speak, or think without external restraints, hindrances, or limits. Freedom is not granted or withheld by anything external, but only by our own thoughts. Freedom is a choice. When we can remove the blocks we've erected in our mind that keep us from feeling free, keeping us from the love that *we are*, we will find freedom. When we feel free to give, we will receive. When we feel free to love others, that love will come back. When we freely help others to heal, we will be healed.

When we feel trapped by circumstances, we aren't free. When we're feeling judged, we don't feel free. When we are judging or comparing people or situations, we are not free. When we're feeling sad, hurt, angry, or any other uncomfortable emotion, we are not free. Freedom is a state of not being imprisoned or enslaved, and if we're not feeling freedom, it's only our own thoughts that are keeping us imprisoned or enslaved.

Freedom *is* just another word for nothing left to lose. I have a friend who was a prison guard for a number of years. He relates stories of inmates who, after a time of incarceration, actually felt more freedom than they did before they were locked up. In their life outside, they were constantly striving to prove themselves. When they began to see they were only hurting themselves with these thoughts and actions, rather than feeling they had *lost* by going to prison, they realized they had nothing *left* to lose, so they could stop fighting. They relaxed, and they felt freedom.

When you know who you are, you are free to be *what* you are, and what you are is love, and living with a heart filled with love is freedom.

TIMING

Do you ever have days where nothing seems to come together? The people you need to talk to are not available. The check you've been waiting for isn't in the mail, again. The item you ordered is on back-order. You finally throw up your hands and declare, "I give up, I'm going to a movie!"

All this delay is a hint from the universe. Things don't always happen when and how we want them to. Joseph Marie de Maistre, an 18th century French philosopher said, "To know how to wait is the great secret to success." It's all in the timing. Sometimes the timing just isn't right when we attempt to do something, but when we wait a bit, periods of nothing coming together are followed by periods of everything coming together. People return calls. The check comes in the mail. The item your ordered gets delivered . . . all in the same day.

The level at which human force operates is small and impotent when compared to the mighty strength of spirit to manifest your good without struggle. This is why it's useless to try to force the universe to do anything. If we give up fighting to make things happen and open up to the vibrational harmony of what we want, and are energetically unified with our vision, the universe will lay it at our feet.

Everything has right timing. If we pick a fruit from a tree before it is ripe, it's hard and tasteless, but if we leave it on the tree too long before picking, it's squishy and not fit to eat. True artists and geniuses are sensitive to right timing. They refuse to rush into something they're not ready to do. And when spirit moves them, telling them the time is right, they refuse to wait.

If someone is pressuring us to take on a project before we're ready, or to sign a contract we're not sure about, we must find the confidence to speak our truth. When the time is right, we will know it! On the other hand, we don't want to let an action that is ripe wait past its fertile moment. Our internal guidance will alert us to right timing. When we feel moved by spirit, the time is right.

Stay open to guidance, strike while the iron is hot, but don't try to force it. Let the iron lay when it is cool.

DON'T STRUGGLE

When I was recently asked to participate in a project that didn't feel comfortable to me, I declined, saying, "This feels like a struggle to me, and my life is about simplicity, so, thanks for asking, but no."

There is something inside each of us that tells us that we are bigger than what is sometimes asked or expected of us. If we can believe in ourselves enough that we can refuse to participate in anything that feels like a struggle, and relax into what we are doing because we love to do it, we can let our life be simple. Even when we are required to do something about which we feel a sense of strain or struggle, we can ask ourselves, "How could I be seeing this task differently, and be willing to let it be simple?"

English author, Stuart Wilde said, "Life was never meant to be a struggle." That's a powerful statement. But some would question, "If we don't struggle to get where we want to be, how will we ever get there?" Living life simply doesn't mean lounging on the sofa watching television, expecting someone else to do everything for us. Letting life be simple means honoring our aliveness, acting from the place within us where life is meaningful, and letting go of the idea that we are required to participate in any activity that feels like drudgery or struggle. Granted, there are things in life that we have to do in order to keep the balls in the air, but when we can act from joy and enthusiasm rather than perceived obligation, we will have more energy, creativity, and vibrant health than if we struggle through everyday tasks. Struggle is a choice. Ease is more rewarding.

Keeping life simple will allow us to have infinitely more power to choose, and will serve others in the process. We will feel a deep and abiding peace, allowing our light to shine into the world.

Life does entail a certain amount of necessary actions, but struggling to get them done makes everything harder. Release yourself from the thought of struggle. Rest into simplicity. Enjoy everything you do. Flow with the events of life. All pain is born of resistance. Pain comes about when we fight against what's happening, and peace comes from accepting what is.

Think about what you're resisting, what you're struggling with, and choose to do those things with ease and relax into them. Then consider the peace you'll find by simply allowing life to be simple, and stop the struggle.

QUIET AND CONFIDENT

When I visited Salisbury Cathedral in England, a banner on the wall beside the entry caught my attention and has never left my mind. It read, "In Quietness and In Confidence Lies My Strength."

Some may think that strength comes from having ample energy and stamina to overcome difficulties and not surrendering to defeat. But the strength this quote spoke to was inner strength. Inner strength is the opposite of aggression. People act aggressively out of defense. When we feel we are not strong enough to resolve a situation, we might resort to aggression or even violence. Aggression is actually a means of covering weakness. Inner strength is staying in peace, not allowing outer circumstances to fluster us and maintaining an undisturbed tranquility.

We can lift weights, jog, cycle, or participate a number of activities to build muscle and strength in our body. Inner strength can be a little harder. It takes a while, because our eyes see and our ears hear the unrest that constantly surrounds us, and it's hard not to let that turbulence disturb our peace.

The way *to* peace is a way *of* peace. We need not be upset because we can't be perfectly peaceful all at once. Peace is a process. It's a muscle we build. To lose what peace we have because we're not *perfectly* at peace is not productive. We can actually maintain peace by *being* at peace. It's the same as building mental strength which takes study, concentration, and a goodly amount of time. Building the strength of inner peace also takes study, concentration, and time. We can instruct our mind that peace is our goal. When disturbances arise, we can dismiss them by quieting our mind. When we have the confidence to do this, our inner peace becomes strengthened. It takes mental vigilance to get to the point where we no longer allow disturbances to disturb us. We can calmly and quietly shut down distraction and do it without anxiety. There is no stressed-out way to the strength of inner peace.

Quieting our mind takes practice, yet with confidence in our ability, our self-assurance, and belief in our potential success, the strength of inner peace can be ours. When we find ourself feeling out-of-sorts, or worried, disappointed, frustrated, or angry, we can *stop*, calm our mind, be quiet and confident, and we will find our strength.

WORDS

I am a lover of words but am glad that English is my first language because with all the synonyms, antonyms, and homonyms, learning English is difficult for those who speak another tongue. Whoops, there's a homonym: Tongue (a spoken language) and tongue (the flappy thing in our mouth).

Homonyms are words that sound the same and are spelled the same (like tongue) but have different meanings. A pitcher is the guy who throws the ball to the batter OR a vessel to pour from. Chair is someone who leads a meeting OR something to sit on. Lie is either an untruth OR a prone position. And, there are different kinds of homonyms:

Homophones are words that sound the same but have different spellings and different meanings, like: to (a preposition), too (also), and two (a number). And: there (a place), their (belonging to them) and they're (a conjunction of they are). Plus, buy (to purchase) and by (near to). And, pear (a fruit), pare (to peel), and pair (two things that go together). Others are ant and aunt, eight and ate, cord and chord, peace and piece, led and lead. The list goes on.

Homographs are words that are spelled the same but have different meanings and are pronounced differently: Minute (a short time) OR minute (very small), tear (crying) OR tear (rip), bass (a fish) OR bass (a low voice), entrance (the way in) OR entrance (to delight), evening (smoothing out) OR evening (after sundown).

The fun comes in using these homonyms in sentences: Looking out over the horizon with *rapt* attention, I could *see* the *sea*. *Wrapped* up in my emotions, I was thrilled with the *scene* I had *seen*. I took a *walk* along a *walk* and stepped into a *hole* that was about a *foot* deep and covered my *whole foot*.

I could get carried away with silly sentences as examples of these forms of language, but suffice to say, they can be quite confusing. I am a fan (admirer) of words but need to fan (implement for moving air) away the urge to go on. It is true, however, that the more we know about words and how to use them, the better we can express ourselves, and the more simple, easy, and uncomplicated (all synonyms) our life becomes.

HAPPINESS

We seem to live our lives trying to find someone or something to make us happy, but as hard as we look for happiness outside ourselves, we will never find it, because happiness isn't *out there*. Happiness is an inside job.

Don't let this discourage you, it's actually *good* news because knowing this, you no longer have to depend on someone or something outside yourself to play its proper role, to do what you want, to meet your needs, or to do anything. You can let go of relying on someone else to make you happy. You can let everyone else off the hook.

Imagine the freedom we'd feel if we could tell the world, "You are no longer in charge of my happiness, and I no longer hold you responsible for any unhappiness in me. I now know that my being happy is my job, not yours."

We might be thinking about someone or something that we feel is making us happy right now. But we'd be wrong. It's not actually that someone or something that is *making* us happy, it's how we *feel* inside ourselves that is bringing that happy sensation. Also, when we're unhappy, it's never anything outside that's the problem. Unhappiness also comes from within.

A Course in Miracles tells us that *projection makes perception*. Whatever we're seeing outside ourself (perception) that is causing us grief is only the projection of self-condemnation inside. We *project* what we *think* we see. If we see ourself as unhappy or undeserving, we will find it hard to project the happiness that is within us. If we can change our perception and see ourself as worthy of all the good we deserve, we will feel happiness whether or not that someone or something we've been relying on to make us happy is present in our life.

So free your lover or your friends or your dog from the responsibility of making you happy by finding that happiness inside yourself. The goal of a simplified life is to be happy, period. Not happy because of . . ..

NOT OUR BODY

Our body is the vehicle that moves us around and with which we communicate. We relate to our body—we feed it, wash it, clothe it, and rest it. We also use our body as a barrier to guard our mind, keeping us separate from other bodies. We see our body as *what* we are, but our body is not *who* we are. We are not our body. We are who the mind inside our body has chosen for us.

If I'm not a body, you might ask, then what is this image I see in the mirror? I see a face, hair, arms, legs, hands, and feet. And when I look at other bodies, I see male and female, tall and short, fat and thin. All these bodies look different. Seeing bodies as different, however, doesn't make each one *who* that person is.

When we look past these apparent differences, we see the sameness in all of us. It's the mind, the consciousness, the awareness of love that makes us *who* we are. Our minds are joined with all other minds, and with the One Mind of our Maker.

Seeing differences in bodies breeds judgment. When we see a body that looks different from ours, we tend to judge it. If we choose not to let our sight— what our eyes see—stop at the differences and go beyond them to the oneness of all people, connected at a soul level, we will see others through the eyes of love, not just as a body in competition with our own.

If we didn't have such a strong attachment to our body, if we realized that what we *truly are* transcends the body and dwarfs its significance, we would know that the body serves the mind. If we change our minds about what we think the body is for, our body will begin to serve a new purpose. Bodies can be used to express unity with other bodies. We touch, we embrace, we help each other, and we teach through our actions. That is the true purpose of the body.

We know people whose bodies are broken or twisted, yet we see a certain happiness in them. These people have learned that there is more to them than their bodies. They have learned to see past their limitations to the love and gratitude that is in their hearts, and to express and extend that love.

No matter the form or look of our body, it's not that *visible* part that determines *who* we are. It's the *invisible* part that is felt by one mind to another through love and caring that makes us *who* we are. When we remember this, life becomes simpler.

BE HERE NOW

My parents lived through the depression years, often not knowing where the next meal was coming from. My father's stepfather lost everything: his farm, his investments in the stock market, and his income. Seeing this, my dad developed a strong lack mentality. He didn't trust banks, he didn't spend freely—only enough for absolute necessities—and he squirrelled away as much as he could to be protected from future bad times. He looked at life from memories of a bleak past and visions of a possibly bleak future. He missed out on much present happiness and fulfillment due to this belief in lack. My father wasn't looking at what was *here*. Neither past nor future is *here*. The present is all that is *here*. We need to do our best not to waste it.

How nice it would be if all we saw, and concentrated on, was present happiness! What if we had corrective lenses that allowed us to see the world differently? Lenses to see only the truth of today. Lenses to dissolve any pain of the past and any fear of the future. Lenses to witness love, joy, and peace, looking within for happiness. Lenses that allowed us to stop looking at what *isn't* here. The past isn't here. The future isn't here. Only today is here. We are already happy because we were created to be happy. Nothing in the present can change that as long as we don't approach it from a sense of past pain and future fear.

People keep *approaching* the future, wondering or fearing what will come if they were to let down their guard and relax. We can't *approach* the future, though, because very quickly, the future becomes the present. We're already there. The best way to approach the future is to make it the way we want it to be by making the changes we want to see *now*, this very minute, because what we do *now* will carry over into the future.

We can control our mind; therefore, we can control our future. Pain from the past and fear of the future are thoughts in our mind. So is our present happiness. There is little effort in life if we see it through the lens of happiness and peace. This doesn't mean pretending the tribulation and unrest in the world isn't happening, it just means not buying into the turmoil.

Do what you can to make your present peaceful and happy. Leave the past behind, let the future be what it will be, and let life be simple today.

GOLDEN RULE

I ran across a cartoon recently, showing a man standing next to a large trash can wadding up some paper and throwing it on the ground. A girl who was close by asked why he didn't put the paper in the trash can. He responded with, "I didn't think anyone was watching." Do we do the right thing only when someone else is looking, or do we do the right thing because it's the right thing to do?

We all know, and hopefully try to live by, the Golden Rule . . . *Do unto others as you would have them do unto you.* I've rewritten that rule. My edited Golden Rule is, *Do unto others as you would have others do unto others.* Wouldn't it be nice if everyone treated everyone else the way they'd like to see everyone treat everyone else? Then it wouldn't be only you treating everyone else well, it would be everyone treating everyone well.

Whatever we do in life somehow affects somebody or something else. It all boils down to respect. Respect means not being impolite with someone because we're having a bad day. It means not judging someone who looks or thinks different than us. It means not gossiping or spreading lies. It also means not leaving a mess for someone else to clean up. To have a well-functioning society, being kind, polite, and thoughtful needs to be non-negotiable.

When we are polite and kind, there is a trickle-down effect. The same goes for when we are rude or unkind. When we exhibit anger or selfish behavior, a negative charge is emitted into the atmosphere and gradually spreads, affecting the thoughts and emotions of others in its wake. Consider the science of the Butterfly Effect. The flapping of butterfly wings in New Mexico has been attributed to causing a hurricane in China. It took a long time, but the scientific connection is real.

Actions and emotions are contagious. If we are in business and treat employees and customers well, likely outcomes are increased productivity and customer satisfaction. Integrity and honesty are also contagious. As you go through your day, watch to see how what you do and say affects others. Notice the way others relate to you in return. Life is indeed simpler when we are honest and stay in integrity with strong moral principles. We must remember to treat people with the respect we'd like to see people treat other people.

THANK YOURSELF

A good friend Toni, was lamenting recently, about how much she's accomplished in her life and how she'd like to be noticed for that. Not that she wanted fame and fortune, she simply wanted recognition for raising a child alone, for having a career in which she gave her best, and for being able to take care of and support herself. She'd like to be recognized for her ability to learn, and to grow into the kind, loving, capable woman she is today. She is proud of herself, and rightly so, but she sometimes feels she'd like to have someone else be proud of her as well.

As I was thinking about Toni's discomfort, I thought of a lesson in *A Course in Miracles* that says, *It can be but my own gratitude I earn.* Yes, Toni has done well and is someone who is looked upon by society as successful and happy, but she might not be recognizing that she has earned that, and she has earned gratitude for that. There is a part of her that is continually moving and motivating her in the direction of inner peace and acceptance of her greater self. When she becomes aware of being both the giver and receiver of love and gratitude, a whole new appreciation will open up.

A wise person once said, "Life if God's gift to us. What we do with that life is our gift to God." Toni is using her gift from God very well. Her successful life is her gift to God. And God is grateful. And she is grateful. Our own truth lives untarnished in our own mind. It is this truth we discover through every thought that nudges us in the right direction as a gift to ourselves, from ourselves, and we can be grateful for that. We can all, along with Toni, be grateful to ourselves and recognize that we are deserving of our own gratitude. That's all we actually need and want.

I can fully understand Toni's desire for kudos, I feel like that myself at times When we can learn to be completely grateful to ourselves for what we have learned and achieved, we can feel a sense of accomplishment. We were all given certain skills and abilities. It's how we use those skills and abilities that make our lives successful. God has been with us all along the journey, but we have made life what it is and has been through our own efforts. We can take comfort in recognizing and accepting our own good, knowing that other people recognize it too, even when they don't say so.

PROMISES

This is the traditional month of marriage—the June Bride and everything that goes with that. At every wedding ceremony we hear the bride and groom promising to love and honor each other through all sorts of situations, good and bad. We can also look at friendships the same way we look at a marriage. Even though we don't go through a ceremony to make promises to our friends, we still maintain a good friendship through good times and bad. Maybe not for as long as we both shall live, but for as long as we are connected. A true friendship is a relationship that can survive the test of time and remain unconditional.

Friendship is a combination of affection, loyalty, love, respect, and trust. There is emotional safety in a true friendship. It means not having to weigh our thoughts or to measure our words. True friendship goes beyond simply sharing time, it is a long-lasting bond.

We often refer to people we spend time with as friends, and many people talk about their many friends. We might have certain friends who like to fish, so we go fishing with those friends. Others who like to bowl, we go bowling with. Those who love the 49ers, we watch football with. Situational friends come and go, but most of us have just one or two true friends throughout our lives who are by our side through difficult life changes, and through our happiest times. One or two people who know us inside and out and stand by us no matter what. It's been said that the person who finds a true friend has found a priceless treasure.

Friendship is a two-way street. To have a friend, we must be a friend. Friendship is a mutually beneficial relationship between people who click psychologically and emotionally. James Taylor said it in his song *You've Got a Friend,* "When you're down and troubled and you need a helping hand . . . Just call out my name . . . I'll come running . . ."

What a treasure to have the kind of friendship where we know there is someone we can call on at any time and they'll be there for us, and we'll be there for them. The fortunate ones find this in their marriage as well, but even the happiest married couple also needs good friends to turn to in times of need and to enjoy good times with. With people needing people, may we all find the kind of friendship that enfolds us in safety, trust, love, and peace. True friendships make life simpler.

ANGER

Anger is a wasted emotion, it causes loss of perspective and judgment, and it doesn't solve anything. Anger creates bad feelings, it can ruin relationships, and it eats away at our heart. Some think of anger as a tool for getting what they want. Weighed against its perceived usefulness, however, anger is impractical and unhealthy. No amount of anger will cause others to change, but it can reduce us to a state of stress that is harmful to every cell in our body.

Anger isn't just getting mad, it can run the gamut from petty resentment to aggression. It can escalate to violence, crime, and even war. Anger is dangerous. It can get us into situations where we might get injured, or worse. When anger meets anger, there's no telling what can happen.

Our anger is all about *us*. We can't always blame someone else or other outside influences for our anger. Anger can be channeled, but we can't deal with it until we take a good look inside ourselves to find our trigger points. If we keep looking for endless people and reasons to blame for our anger, or keep spotting something or someone that enrages us, we are giving *power* to anger. Anger is always personal, and only when we sincerely seek to end our cycle of anger will we see how entangled it is with our whole personality, our daily actions, beliefs, and worldview, and come to see the image of ourselves that we present to the world.

Mark Twain said, "Anger is an acid that can do more harm to the vessel in which it is stored than to anything onto which it is poured." When we realize that anger is our own doing, that it's an unconscious choice, we can choose against it. By collecting our thoughts, stating our concerns clearly and directly in a non-confrontational way, without saying things we might regret, we'll find people respond to us in the same calm manner. Life becomes simpler when disagreements can be settled without outbursts of anger.

When you feel angry, take a time-out, maybe take a walk. In discussions that might lead to anger, stick with "I" statements rather than hurling criticisms, and above all, don't hold grudges. To get past anger, choose not to give it power, and your life will be more peaceful and much simpler.

MIND-CHANGE

As I write these pages, I start with an idea or an inspiration. When thoughts come to me, I write them down. Sometimes other thoughts come to mind, and I work them into the message. Pretty soon I'm not even sure what I'm writing about. In a way, I'm writing for myself, and my hope is, if I can inspire myself, I can also inspire others. Just as a teacher teaches what he needs to learn, I write what I need to hear. My goal is that you, the reader, find what you need also.

There is a lot in these pages about mind-change and perception. The way we perceive things is the way they will be for us. If there are things in our life that keep us feeling uncomfortable, victimized, helpless, or even angry, we can change our perception. We can change the way we look at, feel about, and respond to these things.

It sounds simple, I know, and it actually is, but we have to take responsibility to do it. We must take back our power and live our best life instead of allowing our life *be lived* by outside forces. In the past, my own limited vision had kept me imprisoned until I chose to look at things in a different way. I came to understanding that I can, by changing my mind, turn thoughts of pain, unworthiness, or fear into thoughts of peace, love, joy, and confidence.

Different people have different means of changing their way of thinking. Therapy works for some. It takes a drastic experience for others. But what works for me, and has worked for a long time, is taking my troubles to the Holy Spirit. I might say something like, "Holy Spirit, I am distressed about this, help me see it differently." Then the mind-change comes. I can look deep into a problem and recognize that it's how I'm *thinking* about the problem that is causing me distress. When I say *you can choose* how to think and how to feel, I believe it. It has been demonstrated to me countless times. It can also work for you.

We don't have to be religious to ask for guidance, we simply have to be open to listen, and be willing to enact change in our thinking. To let life be simple, we simply need to look at things differently. We can change our mind about how we see distressing or uncomfortable situations. Then we can bask in the feeling of peace that comes with our renewed frame of mind.

LITTLE FREE LIBRARY

There is a little wooden box, with a door and a roof, perched atop a post in front of a small church that I pass by on my morning walks. One day, being curious, I opened the door of this box expecting to find information about the church inside, but instead, found books. All kinds of books. There was also a sign inside the door that read, "Take a book or leave one." I did select a book one morning, and after reading it, returned the book to the box along with a couple of others that I'd already read. What a nice thing for this little church to do, I thought. Then in the newspaper more than a year later, there was a feature article about "Little Free Libraries."

The concept started with a man in Wisconsin who built a wooden model of a one-room schoolhouse as a tribute to his mother who was a teacher, and who had instilled a love of reading in him. He filled the little schoolhouse with books and placed it on a post in front of his house. He found that books were being taken, and more books given back. The positive reaction generated by this house of books prompted him to build several more and give them to his friends, so they could set up their own little library.

From this humble beginning, a non-profit organization, naming itself *Little Free Library* was launched in 2009, promoting the idea of these little lending libraries. The idea took off, and currently there are 60,000 Little Free Libraries in 60-plus countries. Five or six of them, it turns out, are in my own home town in front of churches, businesses, and private homes. They can also be found in coffee shops and public spaces.

Books are portals to adventure, knowledge, entertainment, and many kinds of learning. Having them tucked into little wooden boxes where people pass frequently making them easily accessible, is a remarkable idea. Local libraries wholeheartedly support the Little Free Library concept, believing that reading opens minds and expands people's worlds. Librarians feel that anything that puts books into the hands of people is to be applauded.

On your journey, keep your eyes open for these little Little Free Libraries, and when you find one, stop and borrow a book. The book you choose might enrich your life. Learning never stops, and what better way to find a source of learning than a little box of books in your own neighborhood.

GREEN-EYED MONSTER

In my yoga classes, at times someone will say they are envious of the way someone else can perform a posture. I tell them that just as everybody is unique, every *body* moves in its own way, to never compare themselves to another, and certainly not to feel jealous. Yoga is not a competition. Each person does the postures in the way that works for *their* body.

Jealousy or envy denotes a belief in lack or limitation and has power over us only if we believe we are less than the person we are envious of. The truth is that there is no lack. There is enough of everything for everyone. Because someone else can do, or have, something we cannot do, or do not have, does not mean it cannot be there for us if we set the positive thinking part of our mind to doing or getting what we desire. We can actually let that person we feel envious of be a motivator. We can see the good of another as our own good. Someone else receiving their good does not diminish our own good, it actually adds to it.

Thinking we lack some thing, or some ability, will keep us limited. But if we let our envy motivate us, telling ourselves, "If that person can do something that well, or have something that good, so can I." No one can rob another of their good.

Being jealous of another's good is a disguised attack on ourselves. When we are confident of our own worth, and accept ourselves with love, any jealousy or envy we feel will turn into acceptance, or even admiration, of another. We can respect another's ability and be happy for their good fortune. The emotion we feel when we experience envy can encourage us. It can attune us to the perception of doing or having our heart's desire. This perception is the first step in manifesting what we want. The way we see things in this world—through the eyes of envy or the eyes of confidence—is what we will see for ourselves. There is no lack or limitation! We are as capable as we make up our mind to be.

Never sell yourself short by feeling jealous or envious of another. Instead of counting someone else's blessings, count your own. You are the perfect *you* and no one can take that from you.

FATHER'S DAY

This is the month we recognize and celebrate fathers. The tradition of honoring fathers began in the Middle Ages in Catholic Europe, but was not brought to America until the 20th century. It was meant to complement Mother's Day by celebrating fatherhood, honoring male parenting and the influence of fathers in society. It's now celebrated by families all over the country.

Several presidents attempted to designate a holiday to celebrate fathers, but none were successful until Lyndon B. Johnson who, in 1966, issued a proclamation designating the third Sunday in June as Father's Day. It wasn't signed into law, however, until 1972, when it became a national holiday. I don't know why or how it took so long for the governing bodies to make honoring fathers official. Surely all those law-makers had fathers who were an important part of their lives.

In typical families, fathers are kind of "directors," while mothers are "nurturers." Some fathers help children simply by spending time with them and being a positive role model. A father's emotional support, and everyday assistance in monitoring behavior and providing clear boundaries, makes for positive social skills, fewer conduct problems, greater academic success, and higher self-esteem for their children. In today's world, there are many families where the father is absent, and mothers pick up the slack. I raised my children as a single mother and proudly enjoy Father's Day cards from my daughter and two sons.

All fathers might not be perfect examples of good fathering. Some might have unachievable expectations for their children or be unsupportive. Some might be neglectful or uninvolved. And some might even be abusive. Even if you don't have a good relationship with your biological father, on Father's Day you can honor someone who has been like a father to you—an uncle, a grandfather, a family friend, or even your mother. Love, nurture, support, understanding, and time spent together is a priceless blessing for all, no matter where it comes from.

Celebrate Fatherhood, cherish your father or your father figure, and let him know how much you care, not just on Father's Day, but *every* day.

TRUTH IS TRUE

Here's something to think about: Truth is true, whether we believe it or not. We often deceive ourselves by making real what we *want* to be real. As a result, we live in a world of illusion, thinking the illusion to be true. But illusions are not true. Only truth is true.

There are some truths that are somewhat difficult to believe. One of these might be that to give and to receive are one in truth. We think that when we give something away, we don't have it anymore. This may be true on the physical level when what we're giving is a tangible item, but truth goes deeper than that. When we give an item to someone else, there is some love that goes with it, and the more love we give away, the more love comes back to us. When we offer quietness, gentleness, and peace of mind to another, those same feelings are felt in our own heart. We receive as we give.

Another truth is: We can change our life by simply changing our mind. Even in the hardest of times, in sickness, sadness, or loss of any kind, we have a choice of how it will affect us. We can sink into despair, or we can adjust our thinking. We can recognize these feelings as part of life, and know that we have the power and fortitude to overcome. We all go through ups and downs and some tough times, but when we look at situations with a positive mindset, we can see there's some good in every situation. We can decide to focus on that good and see the truth in it by finding ourselves happier and feeling better.

One more truth: Pain is a wrong perspective. Pain is deception, joy is truth. The world may seem to cause us pain, but in truth, the world is causeless. The world we see does nothing. It has no effect at all. It merely represents our thoughts, and it changes entirely as we elect to change our thinking.

You were created perfect and radiant in holy joy, unchanged, unchanging, and unchangeable, forever and forever. This is your truth! So, approach life without defense, laying down all thoughts of danger and fear to the truth of you, and when you do, your world will be filled with gratitude, forgiveness, love, peace, and joy. When you accept truth as true, letting go of belief in the illusions you are making up with wrong-thinking, your life will be simpler.

THE REAL WORLD

Words, or names for things, are merely symbols of symbols. The word *tree*, for example, is not actually a tree, it only stands for the object we see, and call a tree. It's the symbol, the name, for the symbol. Similarly, we see a bright light in the sky and call it the sun. But the word *sun* isn't the actual sun, it's the symbol we use for naming the bright light. We give names to things, but the names, the symbols, are not the real things.

We may think the world we're seeing is the real world, but it's not. It's a world we have made up and called our world. We create our own world with our thoughts, beliefs, and actions. The world we think we see is nothing but a symbol of our thoughts of fear, or thoughts of love. The world, itself, is not the reality of anything. It merely stands as a symbol for something that exists in our mind. *A Course in Miracles* calls this *an outside picture of an inside condition*. Whatever we think, see, and feel internally is what we will think, see, feel, and express externally.

The Real World is the world we seek. It is the symbol for a world of peace, love, and joy. It is the antithesis of unhappy thoughts. The Real World is a world viewed through quiet eyes and a peaceful mind. The Real World is a world of forgiveness, kindness, and gratitude, with thoughts of guilt, fear, anger, and danger left behind. The world we seek, then, is not a changed world, but a changed perception of the world. When we listen to fear, we see things that justify that fear. When we listen to love and forgiveness, we see things that justify love and forgiveness. The mind *inside* determines what we see *outside*, and we can *choose* what we want to see. We can change the symbols.

The Real World is a symbol telling us that we are no longer dreaming. We have glimpses of that symbol when we see nothing to condemn, telling us there is a higher order of reality. When we perceive safety, peace, and joy telling us that only love is real, and fear does not exist, then we are seeing the Real World.

We are now in the process of letting perceptions be corrected, which is what forgiveness does. As we do this, we will see the Real World more clearly and more frequently, until it's all we see. The symbol for the Real World will become our reality and life will be simpler.

LIMITLESS

There was a time in my life that I feared happiness because I couldn't let myself believe it could last. As a result, I sabotaged my goodness, and what do you know, the happiness *didn't* last.

I remember a movie from a long time ago in which the main character is on the run when he comes upon a woman in a small town who befriends him, cares for him, and offers him unconditional love. But the man is so afraid of love that he continually fights the feeling. I don't remember the name of the movie, but the emotions I felt watching it made a lasting impression. It hit close to home. I kept hoping the man would relax and let love have him. But he never did.

This character was limited by his fears, by what his life had been before, and I found I was similarly limited in my own life. Since that time, I've learned to take life as it comes, enjoy the good times, and stop sabotaging my goodness by believing in limits.

In truth, we are limitless. There are no limitations on any of our attributes, whether strength, happiness, peace, joy, or whatever. Can you imagine limitless strength? Limitless peace? Limitless joy? It's hard to conceive of what limitless happiness would feel like. Happiness without limits! Wow! I do know what love without limits feels like. It's what I feel for my children, grandchildren, and great grandchildren. It's what I know God feels for me. But joy without limits? I've known a great deal of joy in my life. There have been many times when I've been so joyful it was hard to contain, but that joy has been fleeting.

We might put mental limits on our peace and happiness. When things get too good, something in our mind tells us to "Watch out, this can't last forever." We also feel there's a limit to our strength. Certainly, physical strength is limited by many factors, but inner strength—resilience, the ability to handle difficult situations or cope with stressful circumstances—has been instilled in us by God, and it is limitless. Each of us can be a limitless force for good in this world if we transcend our *belief* in limitation. The power of love is limitless because there is nothing *real* to oppose it. Love is the *only* reality, it has no opposite.

When we're feeling limited by circumstances, we can open our minds to the limitless power of love, and know that everything we need has been given us. When we can let go of limiting thoughts, our life will be so much simpler.

TWO LANDS

There are two make-believe lands in the story of our life: The Land of Plenty and The Land of Not Enough. We were born into the Land of Plenty, but somewhere along the way we slipped into the Land of Not Enough. The good news is, we can climb out of Not Enough back into Plenty, because these opposing lands live in our mind.

The Land of Plenty is a wonderful, thriving place—it's the truth of us. In this Land, we know what love and fulfillment are. We know we are whole and perfect just as we are, no matter what we look like or what we do. There is nothing missing in us, we have all that we need. The answers to life's questions are here in this Land, and we have nothing to prove because we are enough. We don't need to earn love, because we *are* love. Oh, to live in this Land of Plenty all the time!

There is the other land: The Land of Not Enough. When we stop believing in ourselves, when we forget where we came from and begin doubting our own worth, we slip into the Land of Not Enough. While in this land, we feel we have to prove ourselves worthy. We see lack—lack of time, lack of money, lack of love—and we feel fear. We don't feel loved, and we don't even feel lovable. When we're in this Land, it can feel quite real but, luckily, it's not. It's our mind telling us that we're not enough. It's an illusion born from the stories we tell ourselves or hear from others, and choose to believe.

Because we create our own reality with our thoughts, we can move out of the Land of Not Enough back into the Land of Plenty. We are called to be the best we can be. We can create our perfect reality. We can be who we truly are, and our heartfelt dreams can be realized. When our minds are right, when we believe in ourselves and our potential, we can play, soar, and demonstrate all of the inspiring possibilities that are bubbling up inside us waiting to be expressed in the Land of Plenty.

When you feel yourself being pulled down into the Land of Not Enough, remember who you are. Change your thinking. Let go of any doubts. Soar back into the Land of Plenty, and be the best that you can be, knowing you are worthy of all the good that comes to you. Happy Landing!

LOOK FOR THE GOOD

It's easy to find circumstances in the world to despair about, to be critical of, or angry about. But to make the world a better place and to live more simply, doesn't it feel better to focus on our potential, to motivate rather than denigrate? People who are cynical, finding fault or blaming others for their discomfort, find it hard to look for the good in anything. They often mistake optimism for naiveté, and positivity for simplistic thinking. In the long run, don't optimism and positivity trump cynicism? Doesn't a smile feel better than a frown?

A while back, the church in which I was active had a "Look for the Good" campaign. They had buttons made to wear as a constant reminder to look for the good in all things. Wearing these big round buttons also conveyed that message to the people we came in contact with wherever we went. Looking for the good doesn't negate the fact that bad things do actually happen, but when we maintain a positive attitude, we find there is some kernel of good in every situation. When we keep our focus on the good parts, the bad parts take a back seat. They don't necessarily stop, but their power over our life diminishes. A positive outlook is a conscious choice . . . and *we* are the chooser. We choose what to hold in our mind. Our thoughts determine how we see, and feel about, the world.

We are currently in a rather tenuous place in our country with talks of war, of tax increases, of people losing health care, of escalating prices of fuel, food, and other necessities of life. There isn't much we can do about it except to voice our concerns, and hope our squeaky little voices are heard. If we don't allow ourselves to despair about all this, and can keep in mind that no matter how bad things look, we can let hope be our guide. We can look for the good, and what we look for, we find.

Every bad thing in our life, and even in the world, is usually followed by something good. New technologies are discovered and developed following breakdowns of communication. New regulations and laws are put into place when older regulations and laws have failed. Storms of winter are always followed by flowers of spring. We can't conceal evidence that bad things happen, but we can't be afraid to keep looking for the good. Let the cynics be critical and unhappy if they choose, but we don't have to go down that road. We can choose to look for—and find—the good!

PLAN AND RELEASE

The day I got married, I made a pair of capris to take on my honeymoon. When I tell people this, their reaction is usually something like, "How could you have been calm enough to sew on your wedding day?" I was calm and collected because I already had all the plans for the wedding and reception in place and I felt good about them, so I could allow myself to relax. And, for me, at that time, sewing was relaxing. A whole lot better, anyway, than worrying if everything would work out exactly the way I'd planned.

When we plan an event, carefully tending to every detail, we can let the event run without worry, knowing we've done all we can do, and that we can't control how other people will respond. If we're a candidate for office and have run a good campaign, we can relax on Election Day because, by then, it's out of our hands. Being tense and frantically watching progression of the voting on television isn't going to change the outcome. What's going to happen is what's going to happen. The only person we have real control over is our self, so why torture ourselves with worry!

It's the same with raising children. We can instill good values in our children and hope and pray they remember them as they embark upon independence. I know of a woman who raised her much younger brother after the death of their parents. Her brother was blind, so her job was particularly challenging and she felt overly protective of him. After they were adults and making their own way in the world, he called one day to tell her he had become engaged to a woman he'd met just three weeks earlier, who was also blind. The woman was shocked, and instantly felt that underlying need to protect. She questioned the rapid progression of the young man's love affair, and his response was, "Don't worry, Sis, even the blind can experience love at first sight." She had done everything she could for her brother and now it was time to release him and allow him to live his life in the way that was right for him.

Plan and Release is a wise way to live this life. We can plan and act responsibly, but then we have to leave space for outcomes, to allow the universe to manage the details. Life is much simpler when we can plan and release. Fretting and worrying will never make anything better, it only increases our stress level. When we know we've done our job, and done it well, then we can let go and let God take over.

NOT ME

As we go through each day, we encounter other people. These people might look different than us, or speak a different language, or act in ways that we do not. We think of these people as *somebody else*, not *me*. We see ourselves separate from these other individuals. What we're *not* seeing is that we are all creations of God, that we are all connected. We are all one, and we cannot be separated.

Think of a hologram. When an image is captured on a holographic plate, light shined on the plate produces a three-dimensional image. If the image is of a dog, for example, it will be a life-like picture of a dog and can be made to look different by moving the picture, allowing light to shine on it from different angles. Now, consider breaking that holographic plate into four fragments. We might think we'd see four *pieces* of the dog. But it's not as we imagine. Instead, we would see four smaller images of the same dog. We'd see that the whole dog is in every part, in every fragment.

This is what God's creation is like. There are many fragments of the Whole, and creation is reflected in every tiny part. All of creation is in you, and in me. The *wholly whole* is God's will complete in every part, fragment, or aspect of the Whole, and every part, fragment, or aspect *is* the Whole.

We think of, and see, people as separate individuals, but in truth, each one of us is an aspect, or a part of the Whole Sonship, yet we are, at the same time, each one of us, the Whole. Even the seal of our great country affirms this: *E Pluribus Unum*: Out of all, One.

Somewhere along the way, we have over-identified with our *part-ness,* our fragmented self, and have lost touch with our oneness. We tend to think of ourselves as our own individuality and consider our individual self as "me." What *A Course in Miracles* calls the holy relationship—oneness with another, a shared self—is designed to break down our sense of part-ness and isolation, and to strengthen our identification with the Whole. All thoughts are shared. What I think affects you, and what you think affects me. What I give to you is given to myself. When I forgive you, I am released. This breakdown of part-ness gives way to the realization of Wholeness. It begins to be generalized and transferred to all aspects, parts, and fragments of creation . . . all the people we have been thinking of, all this time, as "not me."

SERENITY, COURAGE, WISDOM

A man I know, who is well into the second half of his life, has decided he wants to run a marathon and then hike the Appalachian Trail, and has embarked on a grueling training program to reach these goals. His wife thinks his too-rigid training must be depriving his brain of much-needed oxygen and questions the wisdom of his quest. She reminded him of the words of the Serenity Prayer: *God grant me the* Serenity *to accept the things I cannot change, the* Courage *to change the things I can, and the* Wisdom *to know the difference.*

This man can't change his age, of course, but he can change his physical ability and stamina with a lot of hard work. He has the courage he needs and is determined and willing to do the work required to get his body in shape for his desired feats. His wife, however, thinks he needs to work on the wisdom part. She feels he's determined to change only what he wants to change, not giving thought to what he really cannot change. She says that, even though he has kept his body in good shape and is vigilant about his health, given his age, she isn't sure he knows the difference between what a young, athletic man can do, and what *he* can do. He feels very courageous—maybe even a little foolhardy—when it comes to things he wants to change but perhaps falls short of knowing the difference between acceptance of what is, and unrealistic goals.

As for now, he is still training, determined to get his body and his mind to a place where he can accept the serenity of the changes he is making. He's certainly built up the courage to make those changes. Maybe soon his wisdom will demonstrate for him the difference between going forward and hanging back.

I say, more power to him! If he doesn't complete one, or either, of his two goals, at least he'll know he did his best. He will be in better shape physically, and will feel the serenity of acceptance, the courage of change, and the wisdom of knowing the difference.

SIGN HERE

When you sign your name to a document, do you do it out of fear or out of generosity? We sign some documents to protect ourselves, and others to procure some needed things to keep us safe and comfortable. Signed documents can prove ownership, if proof becomes necessary, or to underscore terms of agreement that might be disputed at some later time. There's a certain amount of fear connected with these documents, fear that someone might try to cheat us or hurt us in some way. When we sign them, we are actually giving someone permission to hurt us. If we default on a mortgage agreement, for example, we've given the bank permission to take our house if we don't keep the payments current. If we fail to make payments on a car loan, we can expect a visit from the repo man in the middle of the night.

No one wants to live in fear, so there's another way to look at the documents we sign. Signing them is a promise that we'll live up to certain stipulations. It's a sign of our integrity and honesty. It's an agreement to agree.

Much of what we put our signature to is done in generosity. I recently had a Living Trust drawn up. I signed documents after document until my pen ran out of ink, but I did it happily because I know the fruits of my life-long labor will benefit my children after I'm gone. I don't plan on going any time soon, but I'm comfortable knowing my assets will help to make someone else's life easier.

I also sign lease agreements with tenants that are fair and have protections for both of us. And when I pay utility bills, I sign the checks with gratitude for the services provided.

I first began signing my name when I was in junior high, only it wasn't my own name I was practicing, it was my first name and the last name of my puppy-love boyfriend. Silly, I know, but I'm willing to bet that every woman reading this will identify.

Your signature is your bond. If you're asked to put your signature on something you don't feel good about, don't sign it! And whatever you do sign, do it with confidence and do it with generosity. Not with fear.

GUILT

The dictionary defines guilt as: The fact of having committed a breach of conduct or violating law and involving a penalty. But guilt has another meaning having to do with consciousness. *A Course in Miracles* defines guilt *as a judgment on yourself, a belief in your own unworthiness.* When we see ourselves as not worthy of love and respect, we imagine we've done something wrong or displeasing, and we feel guilty.

When people become belligerent or commit crimes, it's often to show how strong and in charge they are, but they are actually covering the insecurities they feel about themselves. Whatever we see and act out in the world is a judgment on ourselves.

The guilt of feeling unworthy can take many forms. I know people who, when they feel they don't add-up, get angry, mean, or defensive, and are not pleasant to be around, which only exacerbates their feelings of unworthiness or guilt. Guilt can cause not only our own life, but the lives of others, to go off-track.

In this age of broken families, a single mother might raise her children out of the guilt of not having a father in the home. She could be too lenient, thus failing to teach them to make wise decisions and to develop self-confidence. Or she might allow the children to disrespect her, thus learning it's okay to be disrespectful. Even with two parents in the home, their jobs might be more important to them than interacting with the children, which can result in giving the children too much. They give out of guilt and let *things* replace attention. These children grow up believing the world owes them something, and they don't develop the drive to work for what they want and need.

No relationship—parent/child, husband/wife, friend/friend—can survive where one party feels the guilt of unworthiness because guilt, in this sense, is used to avoid the reality of a situation. The penalty for judging ourselves unworthy is keeping ourselves imprisoned. Our reality is love, and it's hard to see that reality through the lens of guilt. If we are truly honest with ourselves, and remember who we are, we can overcome feelings of unworthiness by maintaining healthy boundaries, thus risking someone else being upset. We teach people how to treat us. If we allow disrespect, not standing up for ourselves, the disrespect will continue. But if, when feelings of unworthiness creep in, we can dash them away with confidence in ourselves, we will find that life will be simpler.

JUDGEMENT DAY

In days past, the sidewalk preacher on his soapbox warned, "Judgement Day is near! Prepare to meet your Maker." It was a message of fear declaring, "Watch out! Soon you will be standing before the judgement of your God, and if you aren't ready, you'll be damned for eternity!"

But fear is not the way into eternal Heaven, love is. Fearing God's judgement is fearing the very thing we want, because God's judgement does not damn, it redeems. God's loving judgement is complete release from suffering and a return to peace, security, happiness, and union with our own true identity. God's creation consists of pure joy, pure love, pure peace, pure safety. God waits for us, not to punish, but to enfold us forever into his everlasting arms. God is Love. And, in the end, Love is all there is.

You might know people who have had near-death experiences, who have actually died long enough to see the other side, then come back into this life. These people all report the experience as beautiful, and some are a little reluctant to come back. They've seen paradise, and they've found it is not a place of judgement of the wrongs they've committed, but a peaceful, loving, forgiving, wholly accepting place. Those preachers on their soapboxes were wrong. There is nothing to fear on Judgement Day.

When we pray to whatever deity we hold sacred, we often call it Father. We don't, or didn't, all have the perfect earthly father, but if we can call upon the *image* of the perfect father, he would be very much like our Heavenly Father, who is near, available, and accessible. Our Heavenly Father is a source of safety and protection, providing for all our needs, and making sure we're not lacking anything we require. God's desire for us is happiness. Just as does our earthly father, our Heavenly Father regards us as part of himself, a continuation of his line, of his very identity. He gives us all of his love and passes to us all that he has.

We don't need to fear Judgement Day or the Wrath of God. God has given us a promissory note to be redeemed at the end of this journey. A promise assuring us that we will end up in His loving embrace forever. We are there now, and always have been, that's why the end is secure, and we need not fear it.

AIMLESSNESS

Why do we do what we do? Are we so oblivious that we do certain things because they're expected of us, or do we do them because they make us feel good? When we can stop trying to please all the people all the time and do things to please ourselves, our life can become much simpler.

When we can walk, simply for the sake of walking, not because we have to get somewhere, walking becomes a kind of meditation. When we can sit, simply for the sake of sitting, this can be a mind-adjusting time. When we do any activity simply for the sake that activity, and not for some perceived urgent reason, that activity can become aimless.

We need to aim for aimlessness, doing things without a particular goal in mind. When we do that, we heal ourselves, and by healing ourselves, we help to heal the world. Aimlessness allows us to know how to enjoy and to live deeply in a very simple way. In aimlessness, we don't want to waste our time anymore, and we can begin to cherish the time we are given.

When we are faced with a long line at the coffee shop waiting for our morning boost, we can practice mindful breathing, focusing on enjoying our relaxed state of mind and the presence of the people around us. The line isn't going to move any faster if we get fidgety and allow ourselves become upset. When we relax and not let our immediate aim, our intended mission, lead us into a lack of patience and become stressful . . . that is aimlessness.

The first time I went to England, I planned nothing further than my plane ticket. I had no agenda, I learned things when I got there and let the trip simply evolve. It was one of the most enjoyable trips I've ever taken . . . that's aimlessness.

On the highway, we often encounter slow-moving traffic and other delays. If we can accept the situation as it is, knowing that we'll eventually get where we're going, even if we don't honk at other drivers and weave from one lane to another . . . that's aimlessness.

Keep paying attention to what's going on, but consider staying aimless. Being aimless and undirected allows you to enjoy and appreciate every moment, to meet and greet your unknown fate, and to let life evolve. Do what you have to do but be aimless when you can. It will simplify your life.

WHAT'S IN A NAME?

What's in a name? Shakespeare's Juliet said, "A rose by any other name would smell as sweet." She argued that it does not matter that Romeo was from her family's rival house of Montague. Juliet compares Romeo to a rose, saying that if he were not named Montague, she would still love him and would be able to marry him. It was his name that forbade their union.

And think about Hatfield and McCoy. Descendants of these two families have been feuding since the Civil War; a feud that began over ownership of a hog and led to killings and house-burnings. The two families have now reconciled and their feuds are memorialized in Kentucky with annual reunions involving competitions like races and a tug-of-war. If you are named Hatfield or McCoy, though, you are still assumed to be at odds with the other.

Children use unkind names to antagonize or to hurt other children. We all learned to say, "Stick and stones can break my bones, but names can never hurt me." We said this to deflect the hurt done to us, but it didn't always work. Name-calling *can* hurt, just as sweet names can instill a warm feeling.

Every name has a meaning. There are books written about the meanings of names—which makes me wonder if people live up to the meanings they've heard, or if those meanings are really accurate. My name, Judith or Judy, means "Woman of Judea" or "She will be praised." I have never been anywhere near Judea, but am I praised? Maybe, by some who know me well and love me, but I'm not making any headlines. Just for fun, look up the meaning of your own name and see if you live up to it.

We use names to classify things. It's not only people that are named. Businesses and products are named to denote their activity or their use. Movies and plays are named to give an idea of their context. Even storms have names. Babies learn the names of things as they begin to talk. And another person's name us usually the first thing we learn about them. Their name becomes a part of who they are, and when we hear their name again, it brings up an image.

Names differentiate things from one another. Just think how confused we'd all be if nothing was named. You can name what you want to accomplish, and how you want your life to be. When you believe in what you've named, that is what life will become for you. What's in your name? You are. And that name is goodness, light, and love.

TRUE OR FALSE

A great statement of truth is, "What is false is false, and what is true never changes." The truth of ourselves as children of God has not changed, nor will it ever change. Any beliefs and opinions we've come up with to dispel this truth, and to convince ourselves otherwise, are false. The problem is that we don't always believe it.

Our problems can be summed up by becoming aware that, so much of the time, we have taught ourselves to believe what is false is true, and what is true is false. What is true is that spirit, holiness, innocence, love, and eternal life are real. What is false is sin, guilt, suffering, sickness, and death. As we go through these life experiences, what we believe to be real *becomes* real to us because we've made them real with our thoughts.

When we change our perception of the world, when we learn to look at it with open minds and open hearts, we will begin to understand that we haven't always been seeing things rightly. The learning process we appear to be going through is teaching only one lesson: What we thought was real—our own sin or sin in another, attack, and separation—are shown to be false, and the love we were too closed off to see, is real. With this shift in perception, where we thought we saw sin, we now see innocence. Where we thought we saw attack, we now see a call for love.

Think about what it would be like to have a situation which now seems to justify anger turned into something that justifies love. With the shift to seeing what is false is false and what is true is true, all we will see is love, because love is the only unchanging reality. What is true is that love is always justified.

This learning process can begin by simply looking at situations from a different angle, a different point of view. Closed minds can't see past the falsities they've made real, and they aren't open to entertaining other ideas. Go outside and look at something—a tree, or maybe your house—then move a little in one direction or another and look at the same thing from a different angle. It looks different, doesn't it?

Life is illusion, it's impressions. What we see is what we *want* to see, and we believe what we've *imagined* to be true, even if it can be proven false. Without illusions or impressions, what we see clearly is truth. Seeing things as they are—beyond what our eyes see to what our heart feels—is seeing truth. When we've learned to keep our mind and heart open to love, we will have learned the difference between true and false, and life will be simpler and more peaceful.

IT WOULD BE NICE

Are you a goal-setter? Do you have your life all figured out, knowing what you want and when? I'm not. I'm kind of a *winger*. I tend to go where the winds of life take me. Some adamant goal-setters might see me as wishy-washy, not knowing what I want or how to get there, but there really isn't a right or wrong way to live, there are simply different ways of approaching life.

When I was working in real estate, some opportunities came along that I jumped on with no eye to the future. An agent came into the office one day and asked if anyone had a client who'd like to buy a little house in a certain very good neighborhood and assume the loan. Without even seeing the house, I immediately wrote an offer to purchase the house myself. My offer was accepted and I'd bought my first rental property. Another time, a friend told me of a multiple-unit property that was to be sold at auction. I submitted my bid, which was accepted, and purchased the property at a great price. My income property inventory was growing. My goal had never been to become a real estate mogul, but simply by chance—right place, right time—it started happening. And rents from these properties is what supports me now. I had no conscious goal in mind, but it worked out well.

It seems when I set specific goals with specific time frames, I hit walls and have to alter my plans. Goals are kind of like prayer. We often set our mind on something and ask for it in prayer. Many people pray fervently for specific outcomes and are disappointed when the prayer is not answered in the way they desire. When there is something I pray for, rather than being specific, I say, "It would be nice if the right outcome would be revealed to me." This kind of prayer leaves my mind open to accept whatever comes along. Sometimes it's what I desire, sometimes it's something else—often something better. Whatever the outcome, it's okay. We pray, "Not my will, but thy will, be done," because God's will for all of us is perfect happiness.

It would be nice if everyone could reach every goal they set and have exactly what they want, or think they want, in life, but that's not always the case. I'm not suggesting you throw caution to the wind or abandon goals you've set. If you continue with what you've worked hard for, still keeping your mind open to new opportunities, sometimes what comes along can be a pleasant surprise. Remain flexible, see the good in what does come to you, and life will be simpler.

PROTECTION

No one wants to be wrong, so we come up with all kinds of defense mechanisms to protect ourselves from appearing wrong. It's not really ourselves we're protecting—we are whole and perfect just as we were created—it's our egos that we feel need protection. Defenses are what we use to protect our egos from the outside world.

Denial is one means of defense. We lie, or we hide. Some dissociate by dulling their minds with alcohol or drugs so they don't have to admit, or even look at, the truth. Denial is the primary defense we used as children. When we got into trouble, with wide-eyed innocence, we would say, "It wasn't me."

Projection is an obvious form of defense. We find someone or something to project blame on. "Billy broke the cookie jar." or "The dog ate my homework." Projecting blame lets us feel we are more pure and maybe even more important than those we point to. How many times have you said, "It's not my fault" or "It's not me who's being unreasonable, it's you!"

Anger is another means of defense, as is *Attack*. Most anger is actually inwardly directed, unconsciously, of course, and because we don't want to see ourselves as wrong, we direct that anger outward to somebody else to alleviate our own insecurities. When we can get angry at someone and attack them for being wrong, we think it makes us appear right. Through anger, we are refusing to acknowledge our own responsibility. We, in essence, are saying, "The problem is not me, it's you, and that makes me angry and gives me the right to attack you."

We can ask ourselves if we'd rather be right or happy. I, for one, choose happy. When I'm wrong, I admit I'm wrong, and if any damage has been done by my actions or my words, I take responsibility to correct that damage, whether it's damage to some object or to someone's feelings. And, if I've been wronged, I find forgiveness—perhaps not for the wrong, but for the wrong-doer.

When you feel yourself going into protection mode, remember Shakespeare's Hamlet saying, "Nothing is good or bad but thinking makes it so." You don't need protection, you need wisdom; wisdom to know that the ego isn't real anyway, so you don't have to protect it. Denial and projection sidestep truth. Anger is never justified. Attack can't occur without judgment, and judgment is thought. You can think yourself happy, without needing defenses.

HAPPILY EVER AFTER

The June weddings and graduations are behind us now, and couples and graduates have begun their journey to the rest of their lives. But what makes "Happily Ever After?" How can all of us, not just newlyweds and graduates, learn to relate to one another? How can we learn to let life be simple? Here are a few tips that can help bring happiness:

1. Never miss a chance to make a good memory. Enjoy every moment. Some things may not seem important now, but one day they might become cherished memories.
2. Don't harbor secrets. Be open and honest. Don't be afraid to let others see the real you.
3. Talk to others about important things, not just about yourself. Ask questions, pay close attention to what is said and what is not said. When you stay interested, it makes you more interesting.
4. Laugh a lot. When you can even laugh at yourself, laughing becomes easy.
5. Don't criticize. Never expect perfection from others or from yourself.
6. When you're wrong, apologize. Always being right can be a lonely place.
7. When you're right, shut up! Someone else might be looking for an argument, but you don't have to defend or prove yourself. Peace feels better than conflict.
8. Whenever you feel dislike for another, remember that people need love the most when they are the most unlovable, so treat everyone with love.
9. Be patient. Not everyone is on the same time frame as you, or does things exactly as you do, so don't expect everyone to keep up with you or to be like you.
10. Be content with what you have materially and honest with where you are emotionally. Remember, we're all still growing.

If we can recognize that everyone is on their own personal journey and that we will probably not click perfectly with anyone in every way, it is possible to get along with almost everyone. With these tips in mind, our life can be simpler, more peaceful, and happier in the long run—in the happily ever after.

GIVING AND RECEIVING

Giving and receiving are the same. We may think that by giving something away, we no longer have it. This may be true when we give away an item we no longer have need of, or when we give a gift. But in giving, we are not only blessing the receiver, we are being blessed ourselves with the good feeling we gain by knowing we have helped someone or cheered them up.

While cleaning up a rental house, getting it ready to re-rent following a tenant who had left it in a sad state, there was a lot of work that I couldn't physically do myself, so had planned to hire it done. Then my son and his wife showed up, and without my asking—even without my knowledge—began the hard work of repairs and cleaning. There aren't words that come close to the gratitude I felt for their unbidden assistance. When I offered my thanks, they said they were grateful for the opportunity to help, saying it was the least they could do for all I'd done for them through their lives. What a beautiful picture of giving and receiving. It is a true win-win.

When my parents moved from their longtime home to live with me, my mother's only living relative—a cousin—sent her a sizable check to help with expenses. I saw this as a loving gesture that gave the cousin great pleasure, but my mother saw it as charity and sent the check back, saying they didn't need charity. I was appalled, and told her I felt it would be a deep disappointment to her cousin. Since my mother had spent her life giving to and helping others without any thought of getting anything in return, she felt uncomfortable with her cousin's gift. She hadn't experienced the concept of giving and receiving as being the same. She saw the gesture only as receiving rather than as the loving gift her cousin meant it. If she had understood that giving and receiving are the same, she would have been grateful just knowing the pleasure it gave her cousin to be able to give that gift.

We need to keep in mind that whatever we give, we receive in abundance. When we give in love, love comes back to us. When we give things away, new things come into our life. When we give help, someone shows up to help us. We don't give to receive. The reward for giving comes without effort or expectation. Giving and receiving is a very simple concept. If everyone understood this, and lived with this knowledge, the world would be a simpler place.

EGO

What is Ego? The dictionary defines ego as: A person's sense of self-esteem or self-importance. If you say someone has a "big ego" you are saying he's full of himself.

A certain amount of ego is good, it keeps us on our toes, striving to do our best. But the result of too much ego can be that the better we do, the more we elevate ourselves in our own mind, thinking we're somehow superior. If we find ourselves in a feisty discussion and we just can't back down until we have won the argument, that's our ego talking. When we constantly compare ourselves to people who we feel are not as good as us, that's our ego at work. When we blame others when things don't' go our way, again, that's our ego talking.

Egoic people may think their pride makes them happy, but criticizing others or always having to win keeps them in constant competition, and this is not a happy way to live. The interesting thing is that the bigger the ego, down deep, the more insecure these people are. They have to keep puffing themselves up, clawing their way through life, trying to prove their worth.

Egotists are often hard to be in company with. They need to surround themselves with others who will play into their egos, and those others often get lost in this battle. I know this to be true because, for six years, I was married to one of the biggest egos I know, and it wore me out.

Being a student of *A Course in Miracles*, I see ego in an entirely different way. The *Course* defines ego as idolatry: *Seeing the body as a separated self, an idol to be worshipped, set apart from all other bodies.* The ego of the *Course* is precisely what we are NOT. It's an imagined self, separate and independent from the will of God. The ego is not real, it's illusory. It sees the strengths of innocence, gentleness, and love as weak, and attack is seen as strong.

We often have the choice of listening to the voice of the illusory ego on our left shoulder, or the voice for God on our right. To listen to the voice for God instead of the ego means letting go entirely of the distorted concept that we are something apart from God, and affirming the truth of our identity with everything. Rather than expressing ego thoughts, we can expel them, and when we understand this, life will become simpler.

AMERICA THE BEAUTIFUL

O beautiful for spacious skies, / For amber waves of grain,
For purple mountain majesties / Above the fruited plain!
America! America! / God shed His grace on thee,
And crown thy good with Brotherhood
From sea to shining sea!

When I hear these words, a mental picture is conjured up for me. It's a picture of the brotherhood of man, hands joined, reaching across this great nation, loving and respecting everyone regardless of creed, color, sexual orientation, ethnicity, or any other perceived differences. A brotherhood celebrating its unity and honoring its diversity.

On this day, America's birthday, let's figuratively—or even literally—take the hands of our brothers and sisters of this land, sing this song, really feel the words in the depth of our hearts, and give thanks for all that America is for us.

We may be thinking that everything isn't always rosy. It's true that we don't all have a perfect life. We may have a physical limitation. We may not have the kind of job we would like. We may not have the money to buy what we desire, or the talent to do some of the things we would like to do. But in this great country, our highest good is available to us. If we set our mind to it, and do what it takes to make it so, there are no limits to our good despite any of these constraints.

We need only watch the news on television to see how fortunate we are to be living in America—the land of the free and the home of the brave— this land of opportunity where anybody can be who and what they want to be with hard work and dedication, and a belief in self and country. We are not persecuted as so many across this globe are, and the vast majority of us have homes, food on our table, and the love of our family. Today, let's celebrate America, our home sweet home, and feel gratitude for the good we have.

A CAT'S LIFE

As I write this, my beautiful little black cat is sitting on my lap. This is a more-than-average independent cat. She insists on just the right kind of food. She wants to come in when she's out, and she wants to go out when she's in. Whatever she does has to be *her* idea, so when she sits on my lap, it's a relatively rare occurrence. It happens mostly when I'm reading or writing. She positions herself between my book or writing pad, and my eyes. To keep her happy, I adjust the position of my book or pad to suit her comfort. Is she spoiled? Yeah, I think so. But isn't that why we have pets, so we can spoil them? They can also spoil us with unconditional love, asking nothing more than a warm place to sleep, good food, and a soft lap when it suits them.

Cat's lives seem to have few complications. Instinct rather than anxiety governs their actions. Happiness, for them, consists of enjoying life in the immediate present, not in the assurance of future of joys. Despite their acute sense of hearing and smell, cats have a somewhat insensitive brain. It's more specialized than ours, which makes them a creature of habit, unable to reason and make abstractions. They have limited powers of memory and prediction.

There is no question that the very sensitive human brain adds immeasurably to the richness of our life, allowing us to experience intense pleasure. But it also makes us vulnerable to intense pain. Life is a contradiction, because consciousness must involve both pleasure and pain. To strive for pleasure to the exclusion of pain is, in effect, to strive for loss of consciousness. This begs the question of whether life has gone too far in this direction, and might it not be better to turn the course of evolution backwards—to the relative peace of the cat.

For the cat to be happy, it's enough that this moment be enjoyable. Man is much more concerned with having enjoyable memories and expectations in order to put up with a possibly miserable present.

For us to be happy and to live simply, we can take a page from the "book of the cat" and stay in the moment. We can enjoy memories of past good, and stop worrying about the future. For now, find a warm place to curl up, and feel the peace and comfort of your cat. Purrrr.

DON'T CHANGE

If we ask almost anybody to tell us the three best things about themselves, it might take a while for an answer, with some hemming and hawing and stammering. But if we ask them to tell us the three worst things about themselves, we'll usually get a quick answer.

Why is it that we so easily see what's wrong with us, but find it hard to list our own best qualities? I'm not talking about physical attributes or abilities, I'm talking about our inner beauty, how we see ourselves relating to others. Are we kind, understanding, patient, loving, caring? Does our inner light touch those we come in contact with? Do we love and accept who we are? Can we list these things when asked about our best qualities?

People who find it hard to relate to others usually feel an inadequacy or a need to change something about themselves to be accepted. But we don't need to change so people will like us. We don't need to meet someone else's standards.

There may be something about ourselves that we feel we'd like to change. If we're impatient, quick to judge or to anger, for instance, these are things we can change by looking at situations differently. How we feel about ourselves determines how we appear to others. If we are true to ourselves, the right people will be attracted to us. These will be people who motivate us, encourage us, inspire us, enhance us, and with whom we feel comfortable. But if we have people in our lives who do none of the above, and who want us to change to be what they want us to be, we can let those people go. Abe Lincoln said, "It is difficult to make a man miserable when he feels worthy of himself." It matters less what others think of us than what we think of ourselves. If we feel worthy, it's easy to list our best attributes and to release thoughts of needing to change to appeal to someone else.

As we let go of the qualities we don't like about ourselves and focus on the ones we do like, we can think how we would answer if asked to list the three best and worst things about ourselves. If we can easily list the good things, but have some difficulty listing the worst, we have come to know ourselves well, and to feel worthy. When we have the right people in our lives and someone asks us to name three things we like about ourselves, we can list those people and the attributes they admire in us. Life is simpler when we recognize our good qualities, and when we can love and take pride in who we are.

BE AN UP-LIFTER

How often do you encounter really happy people? And how often do you find people who don't appear to be happy and who resent the happy ones? And the bigger question: Which one are you?

Happiness is a choice. Some people actually choose misery and think that's happiness. They feel limited in their ability to be happy. They feel locked into unhappiness and believe they don't have the power to change. We might know people like this. Sometimes it's hard to be around these people, which leaves them alone, thus contributing to their unhappiness. Sometimes these people are very close to us. They might be a good friend, a family member, or someone we work with, someone we don't want to lose connection with or simply can't avoid. But we don't have to join them in their unhappiness. Instead, we can be up-lifters. We can see them as calling for love, and we can love them. We can express our own happiness and perhaps they will see us as an example, follow our lead, and become happier as a result.

Unhappy people are not doomed to unhappiness, they have the ability to change. If they can recognize that happy people are demonstrating a possibility for them and realize that they can use that as inspiration to become happier . . . change can happen.

Unhappy people may believe that misery loves company and might try to bring us down to their level of misery. But misery has enough company. What we need in this world is happy people who can be up-lifters for the unhappy ones.

If we're not happy, it might be because we have given power to what makes us unhappy. We might have made a substitute for happiness, a substitute for God's will for us, and we don't believe we have the internal fortitude to change. But, if we're unhappy, it's what we've chosen. *A Course in Miracles* tells us *We are responsible for what we see; that we choose the feelings we experience; that everything that seems to happen to us, we ask for, and receive as we have asked.*

It's true that circumstances in our life might not always go smoothly, but we can choose how we respond to these circumstances. We can sink into despair, and think the world is out to get us, or we can rise above the experience and carry on. This doesn't mean we won't mourn losses. Happy people also have losses, and somehow their underlying happiness isn't affected. Happiness is a choice, and so is unhappiness. We can be a downer, or we can be an up-lifter. Which will we choose?

WELL-WATERED

I have a very large yard. There is a lot of grass, making it park-like. There are also big trees and lots of flowers. My yard is my sanctuary. I love watching the birds flit around and the squirrels scamper up and down the trees. But I had one big frustration . . . the sprinkler system in the lawn. There were areas that weren't getting watered and the grass was suffering. I kept adjusting sprinkler heads in an effort to balance them out so all the grass got ample water, and no matter what I did, there were still places that weren't getting the life-giving moisture. When I got tired of having to water these areas by hand, I called the landscaper who installed the system. He insisted it was right, that the sprinklers watered head-to-head, but when he came out to take a look, he found there were indeed places that weren't getting water. He added sprinklers, moved others, and now my lawn is well-watered.

This, I think, could be a metaphor for life. When every aspect of our life is watered—or tended to—we become well-rounded, and parts of us don't suffer. But when our watering pattern doesn't go "head-to-head," when parts of our life get a lot of attention and others not enough, our whole system feels off, and certain aspects of our life tend to wither.

Some people are so obsessed with their own thoughts that they pay little attention to what's going on around them. They miss out on a lot and find it hard to carry on a conversation about things that interest others and could be of interest to them. Others can't seem to focus, spreading themselves thin by jumping from one preoccupation to another, diverting their attention in so many different directions that they, like my sprinkler system, skip over places that need attention. Still others are so consumed with their work that they don't allow time for fun and relaxation and miss the beauty that is evident everywhere. Quoting Leo Tolstoy: "In the name of God, stop a moment, close your work, and look around you."

Just as I had to get my sprinklers adjusted, leaving no dry spots, you can adjust every aspect of your life to connect with all the others. Simply fine-tune your sprinklers, modify your life, not allowing any area to get left out to wither and die. When all aspects of your life are watered evenly your life becomes full, balanced, simple, and none of the beauty is lost.

WHO DO YOU BLAME?

When we feel victimized, or experience pain in our life, we think it's got to be someone else's fault. The truth is that how we feel about whatever befalls us doesn't come from outside, it comes from inside our own mind.

A Course in Miracles says, *It's your thoughts alone that cause you pain. Nothing external to your mind can hurt or injure you in any way.* Accepting this is foundational to release from suffering. As long as we think there's an outside cause for our pain, we will not look within for the thoughts that are really at the root of the problem. If nothing outside us is causing our pain, then we must be doing it to ourselves. There's no one else to blame.

That's actually the *good* news. If nothing outside us is causing our pain and we're doing it to ourselves, we can, therefore, stop doing it! Since our thoughts are *our* thoughts, we can change them. Even the unconscious ones. We can be liberated and released from our self-imposed prison simply by changing our mind, by thinking differently.

We think we can solve our problems with more money, with drugs and medicine, or by surrounding ourselves with people we think give us what we think we lack. But since these are external solutions, they will all fail, because the real problem is in our own thoughts.

Think about this: What does it cost us to hold a grievance? What does it cost us to insist on being right in an argument? What does it cost us to constantly see ourselves as victims? What it costs us is loss of peace of mind. What it costs us is living a life of fear. What it costs us is investing in the world's reality by denying our own. And all these costs give us nothing in return. We pay an immense price in suffering in order to hold on to our treasured ego.

When we have learned that our own power of decision determines all outcomes in our life, either by chance or by conscious choice, our life will be simpler. We can stop trying to figure out why we're feeling like the world is stacked against us, and we can stop placing blame on other people or circumstances when things don't go our way. How we see the world is not always the way the world really is, it's simply the way we *think* about how we see the world.

You control your life and your happiness by controlling your mind. When you find you're blaming some outside influence for your pain or discomfort, take a good look at how you're thinking. No situation is inherently good or bad, it's how you think about it that makes it what it is to you.

A SEAT IN THE FRONT

Do you sometimes feel like a misfit? Like the world is a tuxedo and you are a pair of brown shoes? Like you are marching to a different drummer? I think we all feel like that at times, and although it may be a bit uncomfortable, it's actually a good thing. We all present differently, we exude different energies, we have different personalities, different wants and needs, and one of our major life-lessons is to find and to claim our right place in this life. We might feel embarrassed or uncomfortable about being different, but in truth, we are living exactly the life we came here to live. We simply have to recognize it.

During my long life I've finally learned that I don't have to *fit in*. I've found it serves me well to do my own thing, to be my own self without reservation, and to play my own game instead of someone else's.

When we think we have to be like everyone else, to think like others think or to believe what others believe without question, we lose ourselves, and the *who* that we are disappears. We actually become less interesting, and not much fun to be with. When I discovered that I could let appearances go, stop trying to please everyone, and stop doing what others told me was *right*, I became a happier, more peaceful, even more interesting person.

I once had a tee-shirt with the word ME emblazoned on the front in large letters. I worked in advertising sales at the time, and wore a badge bearing the name of the company. A restaurant where I often had lunch had seating in the front, and more in a back room. One day the hostess led me to a seat in the back and I asked if I could be seated in the front. She noticed my badge and asked me what I was advertising. I bravely pointed out the letters on my shirt, and said, "I'm advertising ME, that's why I want to sit out front."

When I learned to express myself without apology or compromise, my confidence level increased. Just because some things might be right for others, they don't have to be right for me. I am an individual; the world has a place for me. *You* are an individual, and the world has a place for you. When you discover where and how you fit into the jigsaw puzzle of life, when you seek out people who match you at your core and let them be who they are, you will be free to be who you are, and life will be simpler.

WHAT DO YOU SEE?

A lot goes on in our minds that we are not even consciously aware of. Some of it is positive thinking, some of it is not, and some of it is scientific.

It's a fact that, when we look at something, the image projected by the lens of our eyes onto the retina is actually upside-down. Our mind literally turns the upside-down image right-side-up. In scientific experiments, people were given glasses to wear that inverted images so that they were right-side-up on the retina, but their minds saw them upside-down. Their minds were so accustomed flipping the image, they flipped it even when it was right. After a few days, however, still wearing the glasses, the minds of these subjects adjusted and they again saw images right-side-up. After the glasses were taken from them, these people, with their bare eyes, saw images as upside-down. The mind has the power to literally change how we see things, physically.

No matter what we see with our eyes, the mind has the power to see it differently. Often, what we see as false, our minds have learned to interpret as true. We often see bad as good, ego as strength, love as weakness. This is why it's so important that we keep a close watch on our minds, and rather than being taken in by the distorted images, we stay on the high-road of what we know to be true and real.

Love is real. Hate is a distorted belief. Forgiveness is real. Punishing ourselves or others by holding grudges or thoughts of revenge, is distorted thinking. Self-respect and self-confidence are real. Judging and finding fault is a distortion.

When we see an upside-down world, full of hate, dishonesty, murder and egos, we can pull out those glasses that invert what we see, and discover love, honesty, compassion, and humility. All the good is out there, and more importantly, it's in us. We see the world not as *it* is, but as *we* are. If our mind is capable of seeing upside-down images as right-side-up, surely it has the ability to turn any negative impressions into positive ones.

Let's look at the world as we would like to see it, and find it changing before our eyes. By changing our own vision, and living our own truth, others will recognize our good and just might turn their own upside-down perception into a right-side-up one. Mahatma Gandhi wisely said, "You must be the change you want to see in the world." Simply by changing your mind, you *can* change the world.

OBSESSION

It's easy to become obsessed with something we enjoy doing, but we can't let our obsessions take over our lives. One obsession that affects families today is video games. These games are fun, and they do help develop hand-eye coordination and quick thinking, but for some—especially teen-agers whose brains are not yet fully developed—they can become a problem.

I recently talked with a woman whose thirteen-year-old son was so obsessed with video games that he would get up in the night to play, because he knew his parents wouldn't let him play as much as he wanted to during the day. This woman tried hiding the controllers to curtail her son's habit but, like a kid looking for Christmas presents, he found them. This boy lost interest in everything in life except his video games.

My granddaughter, who has two teen-agers, has discovered solutions. When she asked her son for help with a chore, without looking up from the game he was playing on the computer, he said he would help her, but made no move to accommodate. When it became apparent that he wasn't going to leave his game, she turned the electricity off and the game went dark. This got his attention, and he did what he was asked to do, then went back to his game. On another occasion, her daughter was concentrating on a game on her phone. When asked for help, she said, "Okay," but continued playing. A little while later she asked her mother what it was she had asked her to do, and was told to figure it out. The girl then switched the laundry, emptied the dishwasher, and cleaned the kitchen. She wasn't listening when her mother told her what she needed, so she covered all the bases. She found what needed doing, and she did it.

Psychologists who study obsessive behaviors, tell us obsession with video games can be overcome, either with outside help, or by the greater-than-we-believe power of our own mind. They tell us time spend video gaming can be replaced with constructive activities that stimulate the brain in a more positive way. These activities could be exercising, reading, learning to play an instrument, being out in nature, writing, or getting involved in activities that help others.

Life is simpler when we use our intelligence to choose how to spend the time we've been given in a productive way, but it takes desire, diligence, and patience.

There is really no good reason for playing video games excessively, although they *can* be fun in moderation. "All things in moderation," is a good guideline for keeping life simple.

GOSSIP

Eleanor Roosevelt said, "Great minds discuss ideas; average minds discuss events; small minds discuss people."

With the advent of social media, there is so much damage done when people discuss other people on line. Cyber-bullying has become an epidemic. Sadly, we hear about young people who are in such pain over the lies that are broadcast about them that they choose to end their own lives. This is not only sad, it's an unfortunate reflection on our society.

When I started working as an interior decorator at a major department store, there were three other decorators working in the studio. Two of these women asked me to go to lunch with them one day, and at lunch, began to *warn* me about the third woman. They told me she was sneaky and would take my clients. They told me not to trust her. They had all sorts of reasons for me not to like her. I listened politely, then told them that I'd like to take the time to get to know this woman and to make up my own mind about her. It turned out that I didn't find her to be all the negative things I'd been told. The truth was, she was very good at her job, made lots of sales, and had repeat customers. The other two didn't like her because they were jealous of her success. She and I became good friends. We alternated being top-sellers in the department each month, and when a new decorator was hired later on, I wouldn't be surprised if the first two women took her to lunch to warn her about me.

Eleanor Roosevelt was a wise woman, and her statement should be a page on the blueprint of our lives. We all have great, God-given minds. We can learn and get inspiration from the ideas of others, and hearing about events others have had in their lives helps us get to know them on a deeper level. There are so many interesting, positive topics to discuss, there's no need to revert to gossip. Let's keep life simple by refraining from idle talk or rumor. Gossip is for small minds, it's mean, it causes pain, and possibly even worse.

My mother was also a wise woman, and still today, I can hear her saying, "If you can't say something nice, don't say anything at all."

DO NOTHING

We have put so much faith in our body as our source of strength, that we look to our body for comfort, protection, or enjoyment. But our real strength lies not in our body, but in our mind.

The body is always remembering or anticipating, but never experiencing *now*. Only its past and future make it real. Time controls our body. If we could forget that we have a body, if only for an instant, we would discover a mind at peace. When we can detach from our body, knowing that our body is not *who* we are, we can recognize that it's our mind that controls us, not our body, and that trying to find happiness or fulfilment through our body is futile.

Many people find detachment from the body through long periods of deep contemplation or meditation. Although these methods are ultimately successful, they are tedious and time consuming, and they are looking to a *future* moment for release from a *present* state of discomfort. To find peace and the simplicity of life, what we really need to do is *nothing*.

Unhappiness is not a condition of lack, it's a condition of denial. We actually negate happiness by trying to do something with our body to find solutions, when the solution is to *stop doing something*. We can put an end to the bodily activity that is obscuring our happiness. When we let our body relax and our mind shine though, we find the clouds clear away and we see the brightness that is always there.

We have taught ourselves that we are a constant mental activity that manifests in our body, and that if we let that go, there will be nothing left. In truth, all we need to do is to *stop doing*. What we are, without any bodily activity at all, is enough to support perfect, constant happiness. We don't *make* ourselves happy, we simply stop finding things that eclipse our happiness.

Give your body a break. Don't make it fight your battles. When we can allow our mind to find solutions, we come to realize that doing nothing with our body is, much of the time, the answer. Our body doesn't need to get involved. If we can make the choice to look at things from a peaceful place, we'll see that, to find peace, our *body* need do nothing.

WHO WILL YOU FEED?

A man shopping in a pet store, looking at tiny sharks, asked the salesman how big a shark would grow. The salesman told him, "It depends on the size of your aquarium. If he's kept in a small bowl, he'll stay small, but if he's put into the ocean, he will grow big enough to eat you."

Sharks, like goldfish, will grow proportionate to the size of their environment, as will our thoughts and aspirations. Whatever space and food we provide for our positive thoughts and our will to succeed, will determine our success and the shape of our life. This is the power of potential. We are free to make anything we want out of our lives—we have the raw material to do so—but we must feed the potential we choose for ourselves.

There's an old Cherokee teaching about feeding choices. A young boy came to his wise old grandfather saying there was a terrible fight going on inside him. The fight was between two wolves. One wolf is good, peaceful, loving, and kind, and the other one is evil, angry, and arrogant. He asked his grandfather which of these wolves would win the fight, and the wise old man simply replied, "The one you feed."

When we have choices to make in life, we can look at the outcome each choice would bring and we have the option of feeding either one. Our life will be simpler if we make choices using wisdom and strength, feeding and nourishing the good, the positive, the more peaceful, and the true.

The ancient Roman poet Virgil, who represents reason and wisdom, said, "They can do all things because they think they can." Henry Ford said, "Think you can or think you can't, you'll be right either way." Thinking is feeding. Whatever thought system we feed will be the way we will look at life and will determine our frame of mind.

If we feed our positive can-do attitude and don't impose limits, we will grow in proportion to the life we allow for ourselves. But, if we retreat into a small world in our mind, we will stay small and will not live up to our full potential.

Who will you feed? Do you stay small and unfulfilled, or do you expand and live a full, rewarding, richer life? The choice is yours.

FINDING YOUR SELF

I often refer to *A Course in Miracles* in these pages. Even though I try to stay away from specific faith traditions, since my primary spiritual path is the *Course,* I find it hard not to talk about its tenets and its principles. We are on a journey to find our Self—the self with a capital S—and in the teachings of the *Course,* we find it through Salvation and Atonement.

Salvation is the undoing of the separation from God through a shift in perception. It's being saved from our belief in mistakes as sin. It's also releasing the belief in our unworthiness which we see as guilt. It's the belief that forgiveness brings about the corrected perception, which is the miracle the *Course* speaks of.

Atonement is the Holy Spirit's plan of correction to undo the false self we made as a substitute for the Self which God created, and that we call ego. Atonement heals the belief in separation, and will be completed when every separated Son has fulfilled his part in the Atonement by total forgiveness. It's the principle that the separation from God never occurred.

Throughout our life, we seek for the comfort of salvation. We think we have to go through a special ritual for salvation to occur but, in fact, all we need to do is *change our mind.* The means of getting to salvation is not *out there,* it's within each of us, therefore there's no need to *seek* because we already *are* what we are seeking. The only reason for a continued search is when we have *forgotten* who we are.

The search for salvation is guaranteed to be successful because we are seeking only for our Self, our true identity as a Son of God, and where can our Self be but within us? *We are the way and the means to salvation.* And when we can accept the Atonement (Oneness) for ourselves, knowing we are sinless, and that forgiveness will release us from the shackles of the ego, our seeking can stop.

Try saying to yourself, *I am the good the world is searching for.* Just try it, and see how it feels. Notice what it is that you've been believing about yourself that keeps you from truly believing these words as you say them. Feel yourself as an integral part of the Whole, letting go of the belief that you are separated from your spiritual brother. When you can accept your part in the salvation of the world, the healing of all minds, and believe that with Atonement, everyone will awaken to love, you can rest easy. You'll know you are here to be truly helpful, not just to make a name for yourself or to achieve temporal things that you think of as goals. You are here to find forgiveness in your heart for yourself and for others. You are here to help, to heal, to bless, and to save the world.

ALL BY MYSELF

We spend a lot of time with other people. We live with them, we work with them, we socialize with them, and we connect with them almost everywhere we go. But how much time do we really spend alone—all by our self?

I know women who are actually afraid of being alone, and feel they need someone else around to ensure their safety. And I know men who *can't stand* being alone, and feel they need someone to take care of them. I know others, both men and women, who need someone to guide them through life, or to keep them from slipping into a lonely depression. Personally, I enjoy time alone.

Not long after I married my second husband and moved to a new area, he went on a weekend hunting trip with his new buddies. The wife of one of the men called to see if I wanted to get together while the fellows were gone. I gave it some thought, then declined. I'd been alone for four years between marriages, was kind of missing the solitude, and was actually looking forward to the weekend all by myself.

A recent study about being alone has shown that more people enjoy aloneness than I would have guessed. When participants were asked if they identify as an introvert or an extrovert, 42% said they are primarily introverted, compared to just 10% who identified as extroverts. The other 48% claimed to have qualities of both. When asked if they enjoyed being alone, a whopping 95% said yes, and 90% said they had no fear of being alone. The study showed, however, that only 32% of responders enjoyed eating alone. There's something about the connection of dining with others that makes us feel good.

Being alone allows us to do things that we might not do with company. Things like meditating, reading, journaling, napping, watching what we want to on television, and not having to do things on someone else's timeline. And when we're alone, it's okay if we hang out in sweats or sloppy clothes, or even in our underwear.

I've always said when I'm alone, I'm in good company. Once in a while, though, as I'm enjoying my aloneness, the thought of people needing people comes to mind, and I wonder why I feel so content when I'm all by myself. Maybe it's because I'm enough. Each of us can be happy alone because each of us is enough. Although it's great to spend time and do things with others, there's nothing wrong with spending time all by yourself. It can, in fact, be very comforting.

PREORDINATION

Some believe that our lives are preordained, that no matter how we fight it, our lives will evolve in a preplanned manner. Some religions actually teach this preordination and ask believers to embrace it, wait for it, and live by it. But, so much goes on in this crazy world that it's hard to tell when we're doing what we were preordained to do, or if we're making it up as we go along.

Personally, I don't believe in strict preordination. I do believe, however, that we each have a particular role to play, a role that brings help and comfort to others. It's our job to discover that role and to live it, and we do have spiritual guidance along the way.

The message of love, forgiveness, and healing can be shared in many ways. For some, it manifests large and grand in the public eye, but for most of us, it comes in smaller ways. It could be simply raising our children from a perspective of love, goodness, kindness, and sharing. Or it might be tending bar and listening to patrons with a quiet understanding and forgiveness. Or it could be healing just one specific relationship. Whatever our particular function is, it will be some form of healing, some aspect of alleviating feelings of unworthiness in another, or in ourselves, some way of bringing grace into the world. Healing hearts and minds is our function here. As we fulfill that function, we find our own peace and happiness.

I also believe that we don't have to go out *looking* for our function. The answers to our questions are inside us. We just have to be open and willing to listen to guidance and accept our role when it is presented to us. And we will know! When we see even one person's perspective change, or one person's life turn around as a result of our own love, forgiveness, and grace, we will know we're doing what we're here to do.

Even a smile to someone on the street, someone we don't even know personally but see as our spiritual brother or sister, can change their day, and maybe even their life. When we're living our function of love and healing, we leave people in our wake without even knowing it. We're not in it for kudos or thanks, we're in it to do our part to heal the world.

When we remember that we *are* love, there's no way that we can *not* demonstrate love. We are preordained to love. And love heals!

ATTA-BOY

People who live alone, as I do, are forced to be their own cheerleader. When we do a job we're proud of, it's hard to reach around to pat ourselves on the back, but sometimes we really need an Atta-Boy.

Since summer is here and the rains have subsided, it's time to get out into the yard and do a lot of cleaning up. Yesterday, as I was weeding, I discovered a dozen or more of the tallest, strongest, meanest-looking dandelion plants I'd ever seen. They were like dandelion *trees*. Some were as tall as I am and growing up into a flowering vine along the back fence. I spent a long time digging them up. The root-balls were six to eight inches in diameter. When I was about half-way through this chore, my daughter-in-law stopped by. I took her out to see what I was doing so she could be impressed. I know we're not supposed to ask for praise, but I really needed someone to see those huge plants I was dealing with, and to tell me I was doing a great job. Someone to give me an Atta-Boy.

It gives me great pleasure to see the results when I've done a hard job, and I sometimes reward myself with popcorn, and a movie on television. Other times I just move on to the next job that needs to be done.

My life is full, and I like it that way. I like spending time with family, friends, and people with interests similar to mine. I like sharing things in my life, and I like hearing what others are up to. And, I like giving Atta-Boys as much as I like getting them. As Maya Angelou said, "I try to be a rainbow in someone's cloud."

We all need to know when we're doing a good job, and that what we are doing is appreciated. It's also okay to appreciate ourselves, to praise ourselves for a job well-done.

People will come and go in your life, but the person in the mirror will be there forever. Be good to yourself. Be your own cheerleader. Be proud of your accomplishments. When you do this, you will be pleasing the most important person in your life—yourself. Now, give yourself an Atta-Boy!

THINK FIRST

It's a well-known fact that people think faster than they can speak. This is because the neurons in the brain fire faster than it takes the muscle contractions of the tongue to work, therefore, the physical mechanisms of speech are slower than the electronic mechanisms of thought.

Even though we know this fact, we all-to-often let our tongue start flapping before we've listened to what our brain is telling us what to say or not to say. We blurt out things that we haven't given enough thought to, and end up having to say, "I didn't mean to say that, I wasn't thinking." And that isn't good enough. When something is said, it can't be un-said.

It's best not to say things too quickly, before engaging our brain. Before we say anything, we need to ask ourselves, "Is it true? Is it kind? Is it necessary?" and speak only if the answer to these questions is *yes,* and speak sincerely. The habit of speaking kindly and giving appreciation and praise will train our thinking to find the good around us.

Speaking before thinking can get us into trouble. Relationships can suffer, or end, if we say unkind things before thinking them through. Careers can be stalled at a level below our talents if we speak in the heat of the moment, without taking time think about the message we want to convey. Speaking before thinking can, indeed, alter our future.

Our words are a way of underlining our thoughts and reinforcing them. If we take a moment to think about what we want to say and consider the right words to use—what they will mean to the person we're speaking to and how they will make them feel—we will be less likely to offend or anger that person. We also have to think about what the words we speak say about *us* as a person, or about the good things we may be neglecting to focus on.

Remember that we are responsible for what comes out of our mouth. It's up to us to control our tongue. We need to let the muscles in our mouth rest while the muscles in our brain re-align the thoughts we want to convey as we speak. There's a saying, "The tongue is a good servant, but a terrible master." Let's allow thinking to be our master so that what we say will serve us well.

FREE WILL

We seem to feel we know what's best for ourselves. We think being happy and at peace comes from something we're doing or something we have, but true peace—the peace that passes all understanding—comes from God. On some level, we know this to be true. Even with this knowledge, we still get caught up in thinking we need some tangible thing to make us happy, when what we really want is ease, peace, and comfort. Tangible items might make us feel good, but it's the *feeling* we really want, not the *thing*. And God knows this.

Our life is a gift from God, but we've also been given free will, and what our free will tells us we want can sometimes get us off track. When we want something specific, we ask God for it in prayer. Then we dictate the form in which it must show up for us. We know that God's will for us is perfect happiness, but too often *we* decide the form that happiness must take, then tell God that's what we want. We try to fulfill our own will rather than being open to God's will.

The sometimes-frustrating truth is that when we think we know what we want—our own will—we don't really know what's best for us. Our free will gets in the way of God's will. Since we've been given our own free will, God will not force His will on us. God is patient. He will wait until we're ready to become quiet and listen to His voice. He knows what we want and what we need, and wisdom on our part, is listening to His ever-available guidance.

I remember a time, when I was a little girl, I asked my father for a jawbreaker. He offered me a yellow one, but I wanted the red one. He told me the red ones were hot, and that I wouldn't like it, but I was bratishly adamant, and he acquiesced and gave me the red one. It was hot! It burned my little child's mouth and tongue! and I spit it out. This was a lesson in father knows best. Just as my father knew what was best for me, our Heavenly Father knows what's best for us.

The answer we want from any prayer, whether we're actually praying or simply wishing, is peace, despite what we may think to the contrary. When we can let go of our insistence that answered prayer must come in a certain form, we will find that, in its own way, in its own time, peace comes to us in a form we could never have anticipated had we stuck with our own free will. God's will for all of us is perfect happiness. Let's put our own will aside, and listen for the will of God. Praying, and listening for guidance, makes our life simpler.

EEK! A MOUSE!

When I was a newlywed, at the ripe old age of 19, my new husband and I rented one half of a duplex. The owner lived in the other unit. My husband got up for work much earlier than I had to, and I drove him to work so that I could have the car. We had a cat named Kitty (short for Kathryn). One morning, after taking my husband to work, I let the cat in and went back to bed. When I got up a little later, the cat was in the hallway between the two bedrooms. She had a mouse. Kitty looked proud, the mouse looked a bit stunned, and I was totally creeped out. I mustered my courage and managed to coax the cat, with the mouse, into the bedroom at the other end of the hall and closed the door. But I had underestimated the mouse, who managed to get out under the closed door. Now the mouse was loose in the hallway between me and the cat. I was afraid to step over the mouse to get to the door to open it, and the mouse was sitting in the hall wiggling his nose at me. I was panicked. I had to do something, so I got a shoe box out of the closet, plopped it over the mouse, and stacked four of my husband's size 13 shoes on top of the shoebox. Then I went next door and, almost in tears, told the owner about the mouse. He came over, and when he saw the shoes on top of the shoebox he laughed hysterically, saying, "Did you really think that little mouse could have gotten out from under that box?" He rescued me, took the mouse away, and I let the cat out of the bedroom. I was saved from that creature, but I felt uncomfortable all day.

I can laugh at this episode now, but I wonder why I feared that little rodent so much. It was, I've realized, because my perception was skewed, making my fear automatic. The mouse in the house was outside my normal experience, and I had allowed it to take away my peace, as well as my reasoning skills. That mouse had no power over me, but in the moment, I felt fear. The poor little guy was probably as afraid of me as I was of him, and even though the fear was real, the danger was minimal.

When we perceive something as dangerous, our fear goes into overdrive. But when we stop and take stock of a situation, there is always a way to work things out without losing our peace. We invent the world we see, and we give things whatever meaning we make up with our thoughts. When we can challenge our thoughts, and see things and situations differently, we can maintain peace, and life is much simpler.

SOAR

Kahlil Gibran, poet, philosopher, and author or the immortal *The Prophet*, observed, "God has created your spirits with wings to fly in the spacious firmament of Love and Freedom. How pitiful to lop off your wings with your own hands and suffer your spirit to crawl like vermin upon the earth." How very true! I don't think many of us actually crawl like vermin, but we do lop off our own wings when we forget that we have been created by God to be the best we can be—with wings to fly in Love and Freedom.

When we are self-denigrating, listing only our faults and shortcomings, not believing our self to be the perfect, innocent being that God created, we are lopping off our own wings. When we have a need to prove ourselves, we sometimes see only lack. We think about what we can't do. We feel like time is not on our side. We are fearful of life itself. It's hard to feel love or even to feel lovable at these times, and we question our own worthiness. If we stay in this space, with our wings lopped off, we will always feel that we are not enough, no matter what we accomplish, how much we give, or how hard we work. To get out of this self-defeating space, we can change our outlook. We can see the beautiful, whole, complete, and perfect child of God that we are. We can see—and know—that we *are* enough.

When we remember who we really are, that we are called to fly on wings of love and freedom, to be eternal creators with infinite potential, we don't have to justify our place on this planet. We simply have to know that we are enough, that we are perfect, and that we are love. Knowing this, we don't *have* to create, we *get* to create. We can play in the sandbox of life, making castles and rivers and anything else we can dream up.

We are the creators of a world of love and peace and freedom. A world where what we *believe* we are is what we *will be*. The truth of us is that we are not lacking. We are amazing. Where we give love, we will receive love. Where we want to see perfection, we will find it.

We get to be here in this world to play, to soar, and to express all the inspiring possibilities we have inside us, just waiting to find expression through us. So, fly! Express yourself proudly, never question your own worth, and soar in the spacious firmament of Love and Freedom.

YOUR KINGDOM

Many of us don't think of ourselves as a King or a Queen, but we all have a kingdom to rule. That kingdom is our own mind. We, alone, are the ruler of what we see in our lives—not always *what* happens, but what we *see* happening—our perception.

You may feel like there are all kinds of external forces imposing themselves on you, but the truth is that it is just your own mind playing games with you, making life difficult with bad decisions, wrong choices, hasty judgements, and negative reactions. The good news is, there is hope. You can turn things around. Your mind is your kingdom, and you are the King or Queen of your mind. You rule it; nobody and nothing else does.

At times it doesn't feel like we are the ruler but instead, that our kingdom rules us. We think our mind is telling us what to do and what to think. We think about our problems and let our mind run wild instead of ruling it. We forget that our mind is our kingdom and we are its ruler. When we let our mind magnify our problems, our kingdom gets out of control.

Problems are only problems if we allow it. We make up the problem, we project an image of the problem onto our mind and then we blame the *image* for being the problem. In other words, we're reversing cause and effect. We are the cause and we made the effect, but we think the effect is the cause. It's not the problem that's the actual problem; it's whatever meaning the mind puts on the problem, thus making the *meaning* the cause and the *problem* the effect.

The mind is a tool, given us to serve. The mind does nothing except what we ask it to. The problem is that we sometimes stop watching what we've asked the mind to do. When we ask for pain, we're given pain. When we've asked for lack, we've been given lack. We get what we ask for, even when we aren't consciously aware that we're asking for it. When we see wild insanity in the world and in our lives, the result is *that's* the world we see and the word we live in, the world our minds have created. We're doing this to ourselves because we're not controlling our kingdom.

As ruler of our kingdom—our mind—we create our responses and our reactions. There may be things that happen in our life that we really don't have control over, but it's how our mind responds to these things that make our life what it is. We are the ruler of our kingdom, and if we can remain calm, seeing things for what they are, and maintain control of our kingdom, our life will be simpler.

WHOLESOME JOY

Being joyful isn't just about being upbeat all the time. It's a trait we develop that helps us recognize moments of happiness and fully welcome the good in life. Happiness reminds us that even when things aren't going well, those times will pass, and we will find our joy again.

The happiness that joy brings creates resilience, it keeps us from getting stuck in a negative state of mind. There's joy in staying open to sweet moments in our life—big and small—and to really taking them in and acknowledging them. Joy is all around us. A friendly exchange with another can bring joy. The warmth of the summer sun can make us feel joyful. Skyping with our bi-coastal family members can bring joyful, happy moments.

Happiness can be learned. It's a kind of mind-training, and when our mind is trained on happiness, we will discover joy in so many ways . . . ways we've never dreamed of. We often think of happiness as a side-effect of some outside stimulus, but *wholesome joy* comes from within. We have a natural, deep reserve of joy that is readily available to us at any time, and that reserve never runs dry.

Happiness is contagious. Just try to stay in a bad mood when everyone around you is finding joy and expressing happiness. Joy isn't something you can keep to yourself. It radiates, shining like a beam of light. It expresses in generosity. It has a domino effect. The more joy we generate, the better we feel, and the easier it becomes to be generous with others. In addition, our acts of generosity might very well inspire someone else to act kindly toward another, further spreading the joy.

We can spread joy by smiling at a stranger, by showing appreciation to a friend, or by telling a loved one how much we care. Making others happy adds to our own happiness quotient. Wholesome joy, arising from things like sharing and giving, is as good for our well-being as wholesome food is for our body.

Just as we are careful to consume wholesome food that feeds our body, we can feel and express wholesome joy that feeds our heart. Practicing wholesome joy makes life simpler.

JUST STOP IT!

I was watching some old television one day, and *The Bob Newhart Show* came on. In this show, Bob Newhart, a very funny man with a dry sense of humor and a straight face, played the part of a psychiatrist. In one episode, a woman came into his office for counseling. Dr. Newhart told her his fee was five dollars, to be paid in advance. She questioned this fee and the need for advance payment, and was told, "I charge one dollar a minute, and this will only take five minutes. Payment in advance saves time when the consultation is over." The woman agreed to the stipulations and Bob asked, "How can I help you?" She said, "I'm afraid of being buried in a box." and he said, "Well, Stop That!" The woman said, "You mean I should just stop thinking about that?" to which he firmly replied, "Yes. Just Stop It!" The woman kind of shook her head and said that she had yet another problem. Bob asked what that was, and she said she lets people take advantage of her, and he said, "Well, Stop It!" Her five minutes were up, and she had the answers she needed.

Problems aren't always corrected as quickly as they were in this little encounter, but the principle is the same. It really is that simple. When we finally realize that we have a choice, that it is our own decision whether to allow our problems to rule our life, or simply stop obsessing about them, we will no longer be plagued by indecision and we won't need a psychiatrist to tell us to Stop It!

Thoughts are judgments. Whatever we encounter, our thoughts put some sort of judgment on the situation. We judge ourselves: Does this outfit look okay on me? Am I having a good hair day? And we judge other people: Am I condemning someone for what I see as wrong? Am I defensive when my opinion differs from someone else's? So much of what we judge is actually inconsequential and meaningless. When we can see things simply the way they are, instead of putting our own meaning or judgment on them, watching our thoughts for condemnation or criticism, we can retrain our minds to think twice (or more than twice) about what we see before judging it. If we can see how we are forming judgments about pretty much everything, we can learn to stop doing it.

Begin to look at the world without adding anything to it. Just see it as it is, and let it be what it is. Watch your mind; see how you judge what you see. With an open mind, you'll see what you're doing, and if you find yourself judging, you can tell yourself to Just Stop It!

THE SCIENCE OF ARGUING

When we are at peace, and our life is simple, we don't think much about arguing. But there are times when we feel like we have to stand up for what we think, and we tend to argue to make ourselves right. This *fighting* leaves us stressed and uncomfortable, even when we win. Honestly, there are really no winners in an angry confrontation. Even when our opponent comes around to our point of view, we still have a discomfort that takes a while to dissipate.

There is a scientific component to an argument. Elements in our brain control our reaction to perceived attack and create feelings of defensiveness. Epinephrine, also called adrenaline, is a neurotransmitter of energy hormones that bring on a surge of energy causing us to talk louder and to interrupt when we argue. We can actually become addicted to the rush of battle.

The stress hormone cortisol is also released when we feel attacked, fearful, or misunderstood, causing our hearts to beat faster, to experience shortness of breath, and to feel physically uncomfortable. When we win an argument, feel-good chemicals like dopamine are released in the brain, making us feel dominant and invincible. But this invincibility is a false feeling of being too powerful to be defeated or overcome. Nobody wins *all* the time.

There is another chemical that is activated by *positive* human interactions; that chemical is oxytocin. Oxytocin opens up the prefrontal cortex, sometimes called our *executive brain*, which increases our ability to trust our beliefs and to open ourselves up to sharing rather than arguing. When we share feelings calmly, our ideas can be heard and considered as we listen to and consider the feelings and ideas of another.

I recall a time when one of my grandsons asked me to hear differing ideas he and his wife had about a child-rearing issue. I was struck by how politely they disagreed. No anger, no name-calling, just discussion. I gave the input they asked for, they both gave it consideration, and the disagreement was ultimately resolved without anger or upset.

We don't need to get swept up into a battle-mentality when we have a disagreement. When we resist the tendency to fly off the handle, we can stop a moment to clear our mind, allowing oxytocin to do its work, and we will be able to approach any disagreement calmly, maintain our peace, and come to a compromise that we can all live with. Doing this will keep life simpler.

KIND AND GOOD

A Course in Miracles asks us to *look on everyone as our brother, and to perceive all acts as kind and good.* To see everyone as our brother, is to see them as equal, without judgment.

Even as we see homeless people in our towns, or people who may not have the niceties of life that we do, or people who have riches that afford them much more than we have, they are still our brothers. What has been given to them by God is the same as we have been given. Within each of us, we are equal. It's what we do with our lives that can make us appear to be unequal. We must remember this when we are tempted to judge others as better or worse than ourselves and know that all people are equal in God's eyes and that they need love and caring the same as we do.

To see all things with kindness is to realize that even what appears to be an attack does not make the attacker unkind. It is fear that drives the apparent attack, and behind that fear is a kind and gentle heart. There could be many factors contributing to the fear that compels attack. It could stem from an abusive or loveless childhood, or an undiagnosed mental illness, or even drugs. But deep within the attacker is a heart imbued with the love of God. People who appear to be different are, in reality, more similar than different.

We can all acknowledge that we've made mistakes in our lives and that we have, at times, acted unlovingly, yet we know that underneath the mask of anger and selfishness, our hearts are kind. We don't want to hurt ourselves, or anyone else, but we sometimes feel driven to it by circumstances, and we feel it's the only way we can survive. The *Course* asks, *Do you not think the world needs peace as much as you do?* To receive peace, we must first give peace.

When you feel driven to judgment, remember that beneath an exterior that may appear otherwise, at their core, everyone is kind and good . . . including you.

BALANCE

In a *Baldo* cartoon by Cantŭ & Castellanos, little Gracie says to her friend, "Nora, good friendships have a natural balance!" The next cell shows Gracie and Nora on opposite ends of a teeter-totter, balanced, with the board straight across, and Nora says, "Then our friendship is perfect." To which Gracie responds, "I'd say so!"

Balance is an important aspect in life, not only in friendships with mutual respect and affection between people, but for every facet of life. We must maintain the right balance of activity and rest, of security and freedom, of earning and spending, and of work and play. When our life is out of balance, we feel unsteady, fatigued, and our brain feels foggy

We all know people who never seem to stop activity. They find it hard to simply do nothing for any length of time. I can relate to this. When I find myself with nothing to do, I pull out a crossword puzzle.

Feeling safe is important to us, especially in our homes, so we install alarm systems, and sometimes we become paranoid about what could happen if we let our guard down. But excessive need for security can keep us from being free to enjoy life. We need to let our hair down, and sometimes even take a little risk. We can be both secure and free by remaining alert and making wise decisions.

When earning and spending get out of balance, and we don't manage our finances well, we've got trouble; we become overdrawn at the bank or our credit card balance gets dangerously high. Learning to budget can be a huge step toward maintaining financial balance.

A balance between work and play is also critical. We've all heard the old adage, "All work and no play makes Jack a dull boy." There's truth in this. Even if we enjoy our work so much it feels like fun, we need to leave it behind sometimes and play a little. Play ball with your kids, hike in the hills, join a club, find activities that give you joy, and have something to think about besides work. My grandson, Jason, works hard at a grueling and potentially dangerous job, but when he's off work, he plays with his *toys*. He rides his quad or his motorcycle through the hills, gets muddy and wet, and thoroughly enjoys himself. Still a bit dangerous, but so much fun!

If the board on your teeter-totter of life stays balanced, you'll find that a balanced life is a simpler life, and a simpler life is a happier life.

FAITH

In Hebrews, the Bible defines Faith as the assurance of things hoped for, the conviction of things not seen. The Dictionary defines Faith as a belief that does not rest on logical proof or material evidence. *A Course in Miracles* implies that the mind can be made ready to conceive of what it cannot see and does not understand. Simply put, Faith is trusting in something that we cannot explicitly prove.

When we hear the word *faith*, most of us give it a religious connotation. But throughout our life we exhibit faith every minute of every day. When we step into the shower in the morning, we have faith that the water will be warm and that we won't slip and fall. When we get in our cars to drive to work, we have faith that we will get there safely. We go into jobs, marriages, and having children with no absolute proof that things will work out well; we're living with faith. If we didn't have faith, if we had to have solid proof that nothing could go wrong, we would be frozen in fear, and we would never be able to experience much of the good in our life.

Sadly, many people don't have the kind of faith in *themselves* that allows them to have what they want in life. They are not ready to *see* what they don't *understand*. They seem to need some sort of proof before they can act. If these people will only learn to believe in their own good, in their own abilities, in their God-given right to be successful and happy, they could keep their minds open and step out in faith.

Our minds *choose* what they want to see. Therefore, we must change our minds before we can see the evidence of our own good. We make choices on faith every day. We often desire something that we cannot yet see or understand, but in order to see, we must *want* to see. Faith follows desire, and that is the kind of faith we need.

Faith is a choice, a decision we make. Only by going forward, without solid proof or evidence, can we allow our good to manifest. With faith in ourselves, in each other, and in the goodness in the world around us, life becomes much simpler.

PERSPECTIVE

Perspective is defined as a particular attitude toward something—a point of view, a way of seeing events. Letting life be simple is a perspective. Serious illnesses and accidents can be debilitating, and maintaining a positive perspective can become a challenge. But no matter what limitations befall us, it's our perspective that determines how these seemingly negative things affect our life.

About fifteen years ago I began to lose feeling in my feet. Doctors could find no reason for this and simply said, "Don't go barefoot." Easy fix? Not so much. A well-respected neurologist finally did nerve channel excitability testing on me and determined that the nerves in my spine are deteriorating, causing the nerves in my feet to be affected, and there is nothing that can be done to fix it. That wasn't good news, but because it is what it is, I have learned to live with it. It does limit my life some; I find it difficult, and even dangerous, to walk in places where the ground is unpredictably uneven, or in the dark. But I've adapted and am grateful that I can walk at all. My perspective is positive.

An uncle of mine had this same affliction, and he opted to just go to bed and stay there. His perspective was that if he couldn't do everything he wanted to do, he didn't want to do anything. He ate in bed, he read in bed, and he watched TV in bed, all despite urging by doctors, family, and friends to get up and keep moving. He ultimately contracted pneumonia because of his inactivity, and he died in bed.

A happier story is that of Victoria Arlen, who, at age eleven, was diagnosed with two rare neurological diseases that caused sensory deficiencies in her extremities. She had to learn to walk again, and with determination, she became a Paralympian swimmer and, still unable to feel her legs and feet, competed on *Dancing with the Stars*. She simply refused to allow not being able to feel her legs and feet to stop her. She sees her life from a can-do perspective.

I found what I think is the perfect description of perspective: 1) Something happens. 2) It means nothing. 3) We make up a story about what it means. 4) The story we made up creates our reality, it creates our world, it creates our belief in what's possible and what's not possible.

Our perspective, our point of view, determines how our lives will be. It's the old glass half-full or half-empty concept. If we can look at life from a positive perspective, life does become simpler.

SQUARE CORNERS

When you walk through your house, or your office, or any other building, you'll notice that almost all the corners are squared off. This is, after all, the most efficient and cost-effective way to construct an edifice. But the next time you walk through your yard or a park or a grove of trees or on a beach, take note of the angles you see and you'll find that, unlike the buildings you go in and out of every day, there are no right angles in nature; there are no square corners.

Small rocks on a beach are always rounded, and larger rocks in a riverbed are similarly rounded because they have been formed by water rolling over and around them. You may think that trees are at right angles to the ground, but no tree grows precisely straight up. If you look closely, you'll see that every tree rises from the ground at a gradual angle.

Nature is gentle, it isn't precise. Nature is easy, it isn't complicated. That's God's way. And that's God's way for us as well. We may be living our life at right angles, feeling that there is a certain way things need to be done and, by golly, we're going to do them that way. But if we can take a page from nature, relax, be gentle with ourselves, and *let* things happen naturally instead of always trying to *make* things happen, our life can become simpler.

As an experiment, take a walk in nature, even if it's just a short stroll down the street you live on, and notice trees, bushes, flowers, rocks, even puddles. See how free-flowing they are, and notice how their freedom makes you feel. Then go back into the square-cornered building you came out of and see if you still feel that same freedom. This is why interior designers use soft furnishings, pillows, mirrors, plants, and paintings with images that give the impression of motion; they are creating the ease of nature in a squared-off space.

If you want to simplify your life, look no further than the natural beauty that surrounds you. When you stay open to this beauty, you will find the same beauty inside yourself. Your body and your mind were created to move, to be aware, and to be as graceful as nature. If you feel you are limited, stuck in a square box, break free, celebrate yourself and the beauty that you are, and let your life be as simple as nature.

HUMAN CONNECTION

When I had some work done at one of my properties, the tradesman wanted his payment in cash rather than a check. I didn't just happen to have the amount of his invoice in my back pocket, so I asked him to go to the bank with me so I could withdraw the cash from my account. He suggested we go to the ATM, but I said I'd prefer to go inside and deal with a live person. In any transaction, whether a bank or any other business, I almost always choose to have a human connection rather than using a machine.

In this world of machines and time-saving devices, we are gradually losing out on our human connection. Connecting with each other personally is a spiritual experience, and anything we can do to personalize our life will offer us rich rewards. When we rely totally on computers, ATMs, automatic payments, and such, we miss out on the opportunity to interact with another person; to feed their soul as well as our own. Every contact with another is a blessing . . . even if it takes a little longer.

Like most people today, I do a lot of texting, but they are short, mostly informational texts. When I have a lot to say, or just want to really connect with someone, I will make a phone call. My soul is fed by this human connection. Even when I have the choice to go online for certain information or to wait on hold on the phone for a few minutes, I'll choose to wait, in order to talk to a real person.

Unlike most people today, I still pay my bills by writing and mailing personal checks, and I sometimes write a little blessing like "Make it a great day" or "Smile" or "Relax" on the subject line. I know the envelope I send will be opened by a person, and that person might be having a bad day and my little positive thought might cheer them up. We never know how our connection with another will affect their life, but it's worth a try to possibly brighten someone's day.

Every day, every minute, offers a choice. The next time you have the choice of a machine or a human, choose the human. It will enrich your life, and possibly theirs as well.

UNCLE JOHN

When my uncle John was a very young man, he read Napoleon Hill's book *Think and Grow Rich,* in which Hill writes about using vibration and energy to create success and prosperity. John was so impressed by Hill's prescription for life that he followed his advice and started a business when he was in his early twenties. This was at the beginning of WWII, and John had been working at an aircraft factory on the production line. There was a little L-shaped piece of scrap that went into a trash bin on this line. Remembering Hill's words, John felt a vibration in these scrap pieces, saw a use for them, gathered them up at the end of his shift every day (with permission), and began building venetian blinds for small travel trailers using this scrap piece at the top of the blind to open and close the slats. But he didn't stop there. In just a few years John began building prototypes of travel trailers in his mother's garage and, soon after, his full-fledged recreational vehicle manufacturing company was born. This company was Fleetwood Enterprises and quickly became the biggest manufacturer of its kind in the nation. John never stopped developing bigger and better products.

John put Napoleon Hill's vibration and energy to work in his consciousness and became hugely successful and very wealthy. But my uncle is not alone in this. Everything we experience in life is based on vibrational frequency; better known as our thoughts. Unseen mental dynamics have resulted in the technology we all take for granted today. Our thoughts generate the frequency that creates success in our life. Unfortunately, these frequencies can also create failure. If we set our *tuner* to our desired frequency, our thoughts will draw to us the outcome we give energy to: a life of success and prosperity, or one of failure and frustration.

Be aware of your thoughts, the energy you hold in consciousness. There is an invisible force behind our every thought, and we can use that force for our own good, and for the good of others. When our energy is expended to serve others, or to create something that makes the life of others more comfortable and enjoyable, then we can be living in the positive vibration that allows us to think and grow rich—monetarily rich or simply rich in the knowledge that we've made a positive contribution to the world.

YOUR WORST ENEMY

There are certain names attributed to certain people: Your Honor for judges, Your Holiness for revered spiritual leaders, Your Majesty for royalty. But are these people really more honorable, holy, or majestic than you? I think not. I don't mean to disparage those in high places, but you, too, are in a high place in the eyes of God. The trouble is, you may not feel that way about yourself.

We are often our own worst enemy. We tell ourselves we aren't good enough, smart enough, talented enough, or attractive enough. We may have been disrespected as a child or by someone in our life and this may have left us feeling unloved, unlovable, and powerless. We may have turned to actions that are unbecoming or even damaging as a result. But socially unacceptable acts are often no more than awkward attempts to get attention, to feel the love and power that is our birthright.

What's happened in our past is gone. It has brought us to where we are today, and we have gained important lessons. But an imperfect past needn't define us in the here and now. Honor, holiness, and majesty are not attributes given to just a few; they are given equally to everybody. When we think of judges, spiritual leaders, or royalty by their honorifics, we can think of ourselves in the same way. We can honor ourself, respect our own majesty, and recognize the perfection of our spiritual self, to become our own most ardent admirer.

Respect is something we learn, and wherever we are in consciousness, it's not too late to learn to respect ourselves, to hold ourselves to the high standards of people in high places, to love ourselves, to know that we *are* good enough, smart enough, talented enough, and attractive enough. When we believe this about ourself it shines through us and others see us in this way. They may not address us with the honorifics they give judges, but they will respect and admire us, and we will feel like royalty.

We can get out of our own way. We can stop being our own worst enemy and become our best ally. We can be brave enough to step out and believe in our power and our majesty and let others see that beautiful part of us, our attributes of greatness. We were created for this greatness. If we can find it in ourselves, we will see it in others. If we see good, honor, holiness, or majesty in others, we *know* that same good is in us because *there is no private good*. Good for one is good for all.

WHAT IS BEAUTY?

Society tells us that the definition of beauty is perfectly styled hair, big eyes, long lashes, full lips, and perfect facial features. The beauty industry makes billions by telling us that we need to buy more products to obtain that illusive beauty. They sell us straighteners to tame our curly hair, and curling irons to curl our straight hair. They want to make our lips fuller, our lashes longer and darker, and our hair thicker. Women—and also men—spend thousands of dollars to look different from the way God created them and usually have jars and bottles of beauty aids under their bathroom sinks, which they've often abandoned because they didn't produce the desired effect. The real question is, do we buy into the beauty industry because we think we're not attractive enough the way we are naturally, or are we trying to look beautiful for someone else? Think about the people you've been attracted to in your life. What was it that drew you to them? It was likely something far deeper than any surface beauty.

Real beauty is authenticity. Real beauty comes from the heart. I've had many big holiday parties through the years, bringing together people from all facets of my life, and it has warmed my heart to watch them interact. One year, my friend Leo was there. Leo is bald, and wore a T-shirt emblazoned with the words, "Bald is Beautiful." Another friend, Troll, who was undergoing chemo and had lost all his hair, was also there. I noticed the two men talking together, and the next thing I knew, Leo had taken off his T-shirt and given it to Troll. *That* is beauty. That is love, kindness, caring, and generosity, which are the most beautiful attributes I can think of.

Authentic beauty doesn't come out of a bottle or a jar. Authentic beauty comes from within. It matters little what we look like on the outside; if we extend love to others, become aware of their needs and take action to help them, or simply compliment them, brightening their day, we are certainly beautiful in their eyes.

I'm not knocking getting dolled up for special occasions, or even just because we like the way we look with makeup and styled hair. But if we believe how we look, how we think the world judges us, is who we are, we need to think again. When we free ourselves of expectations of society and feel confident in who and what we are, we can become our authentic self. There is nothing more valuable that we can offer the world. Live, love, laugh, and be happy! True love is true beauty, and happiness is the best cosmetic for beauty.

THE BLAME GAME

We are the author and the main character in the drama of our life. If something in our story doesn't go the way we think it should, we tend to blame someone or something outside ourselves for the discomfort we feel. But the truth is, however we choose to feel is in the script we write. Outside people and circumstances are not always to blame for our predicament. Very often, we are. Although we don't ask for cancer, for a drunk driver to maim someone we love, or for any other tragedy, many challenging circumstances *are* of our own making.

It's easy to lay blame. People are defensive and don't want to be wrong, and when we can find something or someone to blame for problems in our life, we think we've taken the burden off ourselves, and we get to feel what we see as justified anger toward that person or thing. What we're really doing is trapping ourselves in a self-imposed prison, and it becomes hard to see out through the bars. When something goes wrong and we lay blame on something outside ourselves, we'll never find the solution to our problems. When we blame someone else, we're actually perpetuating the problem. More important than placing blame for how or why something goes wrong, is to consider how to make it better. We'll never discover how to do this if our focus remains on who or what made it happen. There's an old adage that says, "Holding onto anger is like drinking poison and expecting someone else to die."

Successful people don't make themselves right by making someone else wrong. When we take responsibility for our own thoughts, for the way we respond to conditions and other people, and seek solutions instead of laying blame, we will find we are happier, less stressed, and our life is simpler.

The only purpose for a problem is to motivate us to find or create a solution, to move us in a new direction. When something goes amiss, we need to take a look at our own thinking, our own reaction, and instead of trying to lay blame, go inside ourselves to find a way to fix it, or just to allow ourselves to accept it and feel better about it.

The upside of our life script is that we are the authors of the good in our lives, too. When all is going well, we can take comfort in knowing that we've created these experiences for ourselves. Are we going to lay blame on someone or something else for focusing our mind on positive outcomes? I think not. When things go right we have no one to "blame" but ourselves.

SING ALONG

Why is it that I can forget what happened yesterday, but can remember all the words to songs from the 50s and 60s? I have stations with the old songs on my car radio and love to sing along. I "Cry" with Johnny Ray, find my thrill on "Blueberry Hill" with Fats Domino, I "Walk the Line" with Johnny Cash, and I sing back-up doo-wop to the likes of Chuck Berry, Paul Anka, and the Platters. I find it hard to sit still when I hear "Stardust" or "In the Mood" by Tommy Dorsey and Glen Miller's "String of Pearls," the songs I learned to ballroom dance to. And, of course, the Beatles always make me smile with "Hey Jude." I remember these old favorites because they were popular during my younger years when life was simpler.

Younger readers might regard this as ancient history, but I'm sure you can come up with songs that bring back memories of emotionally charged times in your own life. What songs remind you of first dates, school dances, first loves, and even of breakups and heartaches? The music that is playing during emotionally-laden experiences becomes linked in our minds, and the pivotal memories come back when we hear those songs. In our teen-age years, when our minds are still developing, the music we hear gets wired into our brains in a way that the music we hear later on in life does not, and it offers us a benefit that other music can't. That benefit is nostalgia. Nostalgia is defined as a sentimental attachment to a time or place with personal associations. Remembering these past times—even the not-so-happy ones—boosts our sense that our life has meaning. Recalling memories of the good times in our past makes us more optimistic about the future.

You probably experience this nostalgia whenever you attend a wedding. I'd be willing to bet that at every wedding reception you've attended you've heard "Shout" and "YMCA." This is because DJs know these songs will have a positive effect, reminding us of happy times and prompting us to move onto the dance floor.

Let's keep singing along with the old songs, and with the new ones (if we can understand the words!). It will lift our spirits. Remembering the good-old times will allow the present time to become simpler.

DON'T FORGET TO LAUGH

Life seems to be cyclical. We go through stages of development on the way in, then again on the way out. My parents lived with me for the last years of their lives. (They both lived into their 92nd year, then passed away 14 months apart.) My dad was easy-going, and not much bothered him, but my mother became more and more demented as time went on. Caring for her was kind of like caring for a child, only backwards. The difference was that a child develops and learns along the way, but a very old person declines and forgets.

This experience could have been very frustrating, but I managed to keep my peace—and my sense of humor. I always told my parents that if you lose your sense of humor, you've lost everything. Even in her decline, I wasn't going to allow my mom to become morose and ill-tempered.

I ran across this humorous description of success in life. It puts the whole process into perspective . . . in a funny way:

At age 4 success is not piddling in your pants.
At age 12 success is having friends.
At age 17 success is having a driver's license.
At age 35 success is having money.
At age 50 success is having money.
At age 70 success is having a driver's license.
At age 75 success is having friends.
At age 80 success is not piddling in your pants.

People told me I was a saint for taking my parents in, but it was actually one of the major blessings of my life. It *was* hard, both physically and emotionally, but I felt honored to do it and grateful that I was strong enough to take on the task. I celebrate the opportunity.

Laughter helped me through those years, and I often recall some funny things my mom said or did that we all got a kick out of. She didn't always know who I was. Sometimes I was her mother, or her sister or my sister, but whoever she thought I was, that is who I'd be. I didn't try to explain because she was happy to relate to these people.

Aging can be hard, but it *is* inevitable, so we might as well enjoy it. Samuel Ulman said, "Years may wrinkle our skin, but to give up laughter wrinkles our soul."

IMPERMANENCE

In a *Garfield* comic strip by Jim Davis, Garfield is looking down at big puddle of water on the ground and asking the puddle, "How's the summer treating you . . . Mr. Snowman?" I chuckled, and was also reminded of one the basic characteristics of existence in the teachings of Buddhism—impermanence. Nothing lasts forever. People, conditions, even snowmen are inconstant and transitory. Garfield's snowman could have been a work of art in the cold of winter, but when the weather warmed, he melted into a puddle of water.

When I was much younger, I had a fear of change. When things were good, I thought this is it, this is perfect, this is comfortable, this is my life, and I lived wanting things to stay the same. But they never did. I often fought changes, doing my best to hold on to this good. What I didn't know then was that when we stay open to change, appreciating what we have and at the same time allowing the natural order of impermanence to enter, something better often comes along. At other times, challenges may come our way, and the good thing is, these challenges are also impermanent, and we learn from them. When we can stay in a place of peace in our mind, we can accept and appreciate the good times, and we can also accept and appreciate the not-so-good times.

A few years ago, a cancer grew in my breast. When the growth was discovered, I knew it was impermanent and that with proper medical care it could be treated, cut out, radiated, and be gone. When things aren't to our liking, instead of taking on a why-me attitude, we can simply take the steps and action necessary to deal with the situation. I don't mean to sound blasé about cancer. I was fortunate that the one in me was caught early and was treatable. It wasn't a permanent condition, I didn't *survive* it; it was simply something that passed through my life. It was impermanent, and it doesn't define who I am.

When we can stay open to change, keeping peace in our heart, we know that nothing is permanent, and we are able to celebrate the good in life and overcome the bad.

Life *is* simple, if we let it be. Let's remember to *let* it be because, like it or not, it's going to change. That change can keep us on the road to peace of mind, confidant in our good, and happy in our heart.

LIFE'S MESSENGERS

There are different kinds of messengers in our lives. The mailman brings messages of what we owe for power and water or the credit card company. Our telephones have the ability to record messages from people who call. Even our televisions bring us messages alerting us of weather and climate activities and of traffic delays. But the best messenger we have is our own body. Our body is the messenger that is with us all the time, the one that we can't turn off.

Unfortunately, this is a messenger we often ignore, even though the messages our bodies give are ones that most affect our well-being. When we're deep into a project and begin to feel tired, we tend to ignore the fatigue and tell ourselves we've got to get this done! But even when there's a deadline for completion, it's important to pay attention to the messages our body is giving. Each of us receives physical reminders that tell us when to slow down. It might be a headache, shoulder, hip, knee, neck, or back pain, or simply general fatigue. When we get these bodily messages, instead of taking a pill to dull the pain and soldiering on, we can learn to listen. What they're telling us is that our body is out of balance and it's time to reclaim our well-being.

We often fight to subdue the body's messages, or we don't even recognize them. Our body is, however, the best indicator of our needs. We don't want to shoot the messenger or push it aside and ignore it! When our body tells us to take it easy, we can listen to its message and take a break to regain our equilibrium. We don't have to stop what we're doing permanently. We simply need to take a little time to restore balance. We will accomplish much more when we are refreshed.

The Japanese have a word for working oneself to death (which occasionally happens in Japanese factories). That word is *karoshi*. When we say the word it kind of sounds like a sneeze, and even a sneeze can be a message from our body that we are over extending and it's time for a break. In this country, people in the workplace are not just encouraged, but required to take short breaks throughout the day—a break to relax, revitalize, and re-think so they can come back renewed.

At concerts and theater productions there are intermissions. At ball games there is the seventh inning stretch. Even in the yoga classes I teach we take short rests between sets of postures. When our body gives us the message to stop and take a break, we need to pay attention. Life can be simpler and more productive when we listen to our messenger and work and play in a more relaxed way.

CHANGE YOUR THINKING

We would all be happier and more comfortable if we knew life could be simple. What makes life simple is to look at it differently. Notice I said "simple," not "easy." Some things aren't really easy. We go through trials that don't feel at all easy, but if we can change the way we *think* about those trials, life *can* become simpler. There's a process to changing this thinking.

The first step is to give *lip-service* to your thinking. You have to *tell* yourself that you *know* the idea of the mind-change is true and that you'd like to believe it. Then believe it! For some people, journaling helps with this. Writing down your thoughts helps you see them clearly and helps you become more willing to change your thinking.

When you've developed a *willingness* to believe you can change your thoughts, step two in the process is to repeat the idea to yourself over and over and over. If you are angry, for example, you can say to yourself, "I am angry and I'm willing not to be. Let me think about this differently." If you say this *every* time you have even a tinge of anger, your thinking process will change. When you find yourself thinking negatively about something, or placing blame on someone else for your discomfort, simply stop and tell yourself to look at the situation in a different way. When you find situations problematic, causing you discomfort, remember that what is seen outside as hurt or frustration is first seen in your thoughts. This second step can take a while, and it isn't always easy, but it works!

Step three brings thought changes to *specific* experiences that validate the truth of what you've been repeating to yourself. If you've been feeling treated unfairly, or taken advantage of, you can get a handle on these problems by changing your mind, changing the way you're thinking about the problem. If the origin of the problem is in your thoughts, then the solution is also in your thoughts.

The fourth step is *experiential repetition.* The cause of problems, and therefore the solution to them, is entirely within our mind, and entirely in our control. If you find that the idea of the mind-change proves to be true in one situation, then you can apply it to another, and another, thus validating the idea of changing your thinking.

The final step is *acceptance* of this truth. What starts as a mental concept gets stronger with frequent repetition. As we begin to apply it in our experiences, it gradually encompasses more and more of our life. Knowing that we can change our life by changing our thoughts will make life simpler.

BAGGAGE

We all carry a certain amount of baggage, things we bring along with us from the past. Much of the time that baggage keeps us from living our best life in the present. When something triggers an uncomfortable feeling in us, often it's not caused by what's presently happening, but by a memory from the past. We might feel anger over some instance, then realize that anger represents how we were treated by our parents, a childhood bully, or other "shadow figure" from our past, and that there are unresolved feelings from these earlier events. But if we can realize that these events are not real in the present and have no hold over us now—unless we bring them with us—we can detach from them. We can leave our baggage behind.

I remember a time when I was entering into a new relationship. Because I'd been hurt or disappointed by previous relationships, I was leery of this new one. I had a hard time trusting my own feelings. Rather than letting my baggage hold me back, I shared my thoughts with this new friend, and he wisely said, "So do I have to pay the price of what others have done?" Bingo, he was right. I was holding back emotions that were still packed in my baggage. I relaxed and enjoyed my time with him

Any present distress, anger, or discomfort is not caused by the past, but by a *decision* to bring the pain of the past into the present. All that really exists is a thought in the mind, a memory, and that thought is imperfect, slanted to the perception of that memory. We simply remember what we saw, what we heard, what we felt, and our thoughts about it. These thoughts became baggage.

Present feelings are caused by viewing events through the filter of past thoughts. As we go through life, we keep collecting baggage, and letting go of baggage is a hard lesson for many. When we can detach from the pain of the past, we can lighten our load and recognize that our thoughts are all that are keeping us from letting life be simple. It's important to make changes in thinking *now*, this very minute. Whatever baggage we take with us on this journey will weigh down our future if we allow it. We can send our baggage to the lost luggage department and enjoy life more by living fully in the present.

A. I. R.

Life is an ongoing process of Action, Interaction, and Reaction. We take action, usually right action, but not always. We interact with one another, doing our best to make those interactions positive. We react to whatever comes our way, trying to keep our reactions loving and constructive, bearing in mind that the way we react says a lot about who we are as a person. If I were to list all the bad decisions and choices I've made throughout my life, it would certainly more than fill this page. But I've learned some simple guidelines that keep me positive.

- Speak your truth without judgment, blame, or shame.
- Respect the values and beliefs of others.
- Keep your thinking clear, and express it honestly.
- Take personal responsibility for your situation in life.
- Be open to results rather than attached to them.
- Use positive and negative experiences to heal and grow.
- Place greater value on learning from your own life experience than from the teachings of self-proclaimed "authorities."
- Recognize any prejudices you may have and replace them with love.
- Trust in your Higher Power, no matter what name you give it.
- Have compassion, warmth, and tolerance for those who have lost their way.
- Make the expression of love your primary goal every day.

When we make our own list and live by it, the world becomes a better place and life is simpler. As we travel this journey, keeping A.I.R. (action, interaction, reaction) in mind, we will remember that love is letting others be themselves just as we can be ourselves, and allowing our personal expressions to be in harmony.

A SIMPLER TIME

When you're bogged down with the responsibilities of life—working at a job or running a business, cooking, cleaning, paying bills, chauffeuring kids to music lessons or baseball practice, or just figuring out how to survive from day to day—do you ever feel like you'd like to tender your resignation as an adult and accept the life-style of a seven-year-old?

Not everyone had the benefit of an idyllic childhood, of course, but those who did can remember when you were seven and thought McDonald's was as good as any fancy restaurant. The biggest competition you felt was who could blow the biggest bubble. You got to drink Kool-Aid from a pitcher with a smile on it. You thought M&Ms were better than money because you could eat them.

Maybe you remember when all you had to deal with were spelling words, multiplication tables, and learning the words to TV theme songs. You weren't bothered about your limited knowledge because you didn't know what you didn't know and you didn't care.

Kids with happy childhoods believed that almost everyone was good and kind and honest, and that anything was possible. You got excited over a new Hot Wheels car or a cupcake with sprinkles. And one of the worst things that could happen was some mean kid at school saying you had cooties.

Good or bad, our childhood is behind us now. We've come a long way and we know so much more. We don't have to resign from adulthood! Even with computer crashes, depressing news, and heavy responsibilities, we can remain an adult and we can believe in the power of a smile, a hug, or a kind word. We can keep an open mind to truth, peace, justice, and the imagination of mankind. We don't have to relinquish our checkbook or our car keys or our cell phone. We can choose to love our life and to appreciate our strengths and our wisdom—the things that come with maturity.

When we dream the magical dreams of a child, we can make them a reality because, as an adult, we know what it takes to get that new Hot Wheels car, or even a real car, and we can have a cupcake with sprinkles any time we want.

Growing older is mandatory; growing up is optional. Whatever your life was like as a child, even if it wasn't great, you can be a great adult now. You can set a good example for the precious children of today.

COMPASSION

The etymology of the word "compassion" is Latin, meaning "co-suffering." Compassion involves *feeling for another* and is a precursor to empathy or *feeling as another*. Some might think that compassion and empathy are the same as sympathy, but there is a difference. When we feel compassion, we really want to alleviate another's suffering. Empathy is the ability to understand the feelings of another, feelings we may have felt ourself at some time. Sympathy, on the other hand, is *feeling with another*. It's a feeling of sorrow for someone else's misfortune.

We have to take care of ourselves on this journey through life, but we also need to have concern, or compassion, for others. Just as no one is dearer to *us* than ourselves, others are equally dear to *themselves*. If we care about ourselves, we won't harm others because we know how it would make them feel; we have compassion for them.

Matta, what Buddhist teaching calls loving-kindness, is often translated as concern for the welfare of all beings. When we see a person or an animal being hurt or mistreated and we rush to do what we can to help them, that's compassion. When we bear witness to another's pain, loss, or heartbreak, and come to them with help, that's compassion. Compassion is the antidote to cruelty.

Another form of compassion is *Mudida*, Buddhism's word for sympathetic joy, which is feeling pleasure in the happiness and good fortune of others. For many, this can be challenging. Out of envy or competitiveness, it's often easier to take comfort in someone else's misfortune than to delight in their success. In cultivating sympathetic joy, however, we overcome indifference and can be happy for another; we can be happily compassionate for them.

It's not hard to develop compassion. When we send loving-kindness to others, wishing them safety, health, happiness, and inner peace, we will become truly compassionate. We can start by sending thoughts of good-will to those close to us, then expanding those good-will thoughts to neutral persons, people we have no connection to and neither a positive nor negative feeling for. When this practice is well established, we can turn our attention to an enemy, and before long a sincere feeling of compassion is felt for everyone everywhere. Practicing compassion makes life simpler for everyone.

FINDING PEACE

There was a time a while back, when I'd get fed up with the trials of life and want to run away. I wanted peace. At these times, I would drive up through the hills that surround the town I live in, or drive to the beach and just sit in the sand. I did find the peace I was looking for, and I always felt better when I came back home. But it was not always convenient to run away from responsibilities of work, home, and children.

What I didn't know then, but have since learned, is that peace is within me. I don't have to go looking for it. *A Course in Miracles* tells us, *Peace is clearly an internal matter. It must begin with your own thoughts and then extend outward. It is from your peace of mind that a peaceful perception of the world arises.*

Imagine what it would feel like to have the kind of peace that would come with having no lingering regrets over the past, no fear of the future, and not a bit of a sense of failure. Most of us have a vague uneasiness haunting us. We keep looking over our shoulder and feeling a slight anxiety that something will go wrong. We build a defense mechanism that wants to put the blame for our uneasiness on someone else. We do this because we feel a sense that something is lacking in ourselves. All these fears contribute to our perception of the world. If we were truly at peace, if our minds were at peace, we would see the world differently. We would see the world without the filters that distort our vision.

Peace—true peace of mind—can be found and felt when we can walk through the day without a hidden agenda, without looking for outward things to give us purpose, and without any "secret mission." We find peace when we tell ourself, "I will be *love* in this situation, no matter how hard or frustrating. Nothing else matters because nothing else is real."

It's not what's going on around us that robs us of peace, it's the way we think about these things, the way we respond to situations. We make the *choice* for peace. Our life is about love and forgiveness, and that's *all* it's about. We are here in this life, on this planet, to be only what we are, and what we are is love. Peace of mind is the result of our *being* love.

We can go into the hills or to the beach just for fun if we want to, but we don't need to go there *looking* for peace, because we already have it. It's inside us. It's part of us. And we'll find it when we relax into this truth and find a mind at peace within itself.

PIZZA, BURRITO, OR TACO

In a *Frank and Ernest* cartoon by Bob Thaves, a slice of pizza, a burrito, and two drink cups are having a conversation in a cafeteria. One of the drinks says to the other, "I know everything about a piece of pizza the moment I meet him, but a burrito is mysterious, keeping much about himself hidden."

This gives us something to think about. Being too open could sometimes be a problem, yet a little mystery can keep life interesting. Do you want to be a pizza, or do you want to be a burrito?

I've known pizza people who broadcast everything about themselves at the first meeting, and it's exhausting. One such person was a woman who was dating a friend of mine. The first time we met, she told me her entire life story, in detail, in one fell-swoop. This was definitely way more information than I wanted to hear, or that I even cared about at that point. My friend remained my friend, but I found I'd rather see him apart from this woman.

On the other hand, we don't want to be a closed burrito, so buttoned-up and secretive that and no one can ever really get to know us, or for us get to know others. Conversation is difficult with burrito people.

For both pizza people and burrito people, it's important to practice being a good conversationalist. A one-sided conversation doesn't allow an opportunity for give and take. And having to pull information out of a person to get to know them is difficult and could sometimes be seen as rude. A good conversation is one that encourages a mutual respect—speaking *and* listening.

Pizza people are mostly friendly, candid, communicative, and pleasant to be around. In conversations, they share equally with others and are good listeners. Burrito people, who are more closed and reluctant to share, often hide their feelings and sometimes live a lonely life. But there might be a happy medium—we could be a Taco person, one who's layered, with some of the ingredients out in the open and others somewhat hidden.

The choice is ours: We can be a pizza—too much too soon with everything out in the open. We can be a burrito—hiding our true self and our innermost feelings. Or we can be a taco—disclosing what's on top right away, leaving what's underneath to be discovered later.

TWO WORLDS

I'm sure you've heard the quote, "I am the Master of my fate, the Captain of my soul." These are the final two lines of *Invictus,* a short Victorian poem by William Earnest Henley and is telling us that *we* are in charge of our own destiny. That anything happening in our life is orchestrated by *ourselves.* Wow! Most of us would rather place blame on something or someone outside ourselves when things go wrong. That's human nature. But this master and fate concept can be life-altering. We think outside events and influences control outcomes, but it's actually quite the opposite. *We* can control our destiny. *We* can go where we want in life. *We* can achieve what we want to achieve. There are no limits, unless we believe there are.

As human beings, our actions are constantly being influenced by two worlds, *The Outside World* (the news, books, opinions of others), and our *Inside World* (our mind, spirituality, and beliefs). This can make our life very confusing, and many of us just don't want to believe it. When things go awry, we don't want to accept responsibility, because we don't want to be at fault. The problem is that we lose control of our life and its outcomes when we let the Outside World dominate our Inside World. We want so badly to be accepted by society that we let ourselves be influenced by outside forces. Whether it's by skepticism, or just plain laziness, our fate becomes what others determine for us.

To make life simple and to gain control of our life, we can build ourselves from the inside, with our own thoughts and beliefs, and with total focus on those beliefs. When we take the necessary steps to succeed, what the Outside World tells us becomes secondary. We can take back our power. The way to do this, the way to become the master of our fate, is to change our philosophy about life.

That power is inside us, and has always been. We might not feel it all the time, but it's there. The way to put it to work is to acknowledge it, to believe it, and to act on it. We have to become the cause behind the results we get in the Outside World by listening to the dictate of our Inside World.

Decide what you want, write it down, read it often, and say it out loud to yourself every day. You can chart your own course. *You* are the master of your fate and the captain of your soul. Let yourself be great!

AFTER LIFE

I attended a memorial service, recently, for a very dear friend who I met in high school and remained best friends with all these years. It was a sad day. Being at Dorothy's service started me thinking about people's lives and the memories that live on when those lives are over.

When someone passes, an obituary is often printed in the newspaper. Obituaries paint vignettes about people's lives that, no matter how well we think we know them, reveal surprising details that we didn't know. New aspects are also revealed at memorial services and funerals. What we learn from these gatherings gives us a deeper understanding of the deceased, and we often wish we had the chance to talk to them about some detail that is new to us. Most obits cite information about what the person's profession or career was, but more likely what they reveal eclipses professional accomplishments and tells about activities like hobbies, sports, volunteer work, and other interests they had outside of their jobs.

Dorothy's life work was in horticulture, but what was revealed at her memorial was that she was an accomplished vocalist, which I knew because we'd spent many hours singing together in the past. What I didn't know was that she was also a talented artist. Our only contact, in later years, was by telephone, and the subject had never come up. I was impressed by the excellent paintings on display at her service. I, too, have done my share of painting, but I doubt Dorothy knew that about me, either.

Everybody has a story, and their story is always deeper and more interesting than what we see on the surface. Let's remember to really get to know the people we care about. Let's reach out, ask questions, learn about their life. That way we'll always have a more complete understanding of friends and family to remember, and to cherish, not only after they're gone, but while they're still with us.

ILLUSION

When you watch a movie, you might weep when a character you identify with suffers a loss or dies. You feel this emotion in your body even though, in reality, you know you're just watching a story. It's not real. Our life is like that movie. It's a story that we've created for ourselves with our thoughts and perceptions.

It all started in the Garden of Eden. Adam and Eve were happily living in paradise until that nasty serpent and tempted them to eat the fruit that God had distinctly told them not to eat. They were free to eat anything they wanted, but the fruit of that particular tree was off limits. Even though they knew better, they allowed the rascally serpent to convince them to eat the fruit. When they did, the knowledge of good and evil entered their minds. Up to that point, they had known only peace and love. With this new knowledge, they found they had to handle challenges. They had to make choices. Their perceptions changed, and they began to see things as good or bad, right or wrong, real or unreal. Fear began to taint paradise, and has corrupted our world ever since.

Throughout our lives we've come to believe in fear, have projected our illusions and made them real to us. We fear consequences, we fear death, loss, and sickness. We even fear wars and plagues. These things are all a part of life, but if we live in fear of them, we are giving reality to the illusion—whatever meaning we *choose* to give to a situation. When we can accept these things calmly and peacefully and do what we can to make ourselves feel better and be safe, not letting unhealthy emotions rule our thinking, life is simpler.

Nobody consciously wants to live in fear, but in some way, we do. Because we think we're a body, we guard that bodily image thinking our existence is defined by separation, that we are alone and have to protect ourselves. But this belief is not real, it's illusion, and nothing and no one can hold us to this world of illusion unless we give them the power to do so. Just as Adam and Eve chose to listen to the serpent, we can choose to change our thinking. We can give up illusions, stop making them real, and acknowledge that we are not alone, that we are all part of God and of each other.

Our only purpose in this world is to love and forgive. We can cease to fear what we perceive as bad or fearful. Life really is simple when we know that we, alone, have control over the way we see and respond to experiences. Our interpretation of things is what makes them real for us, not the illusion.

HOUR BY HOUR

A Course in Miracles teaches that our function in this world is forgiveness—not just forgiving someone who we feel has wronged us, but forgiveness of anything that brings us pain, distress, or anxiety. Forgiveness is the hidden lesson in every distressing event of our lives. Whenever we feel anger, injustice, or any other uncomfortable emotion, if we can remember to say, "I will forgive, and see this differently," we will find our life feels more untroubled and serene.

When we hold grievances and vow to never forgive some wrong, we are not only holding the person or circumstance that brought about our anger or distress in bondage, we are also holding ourself captive. Every time we feel a stab of anger, we are holding a knife to our own heart. That knife keeps us condemned and sentenced to a life of discomfort. When we can find forgiveness, however, we will also find freedom.

Forgiveness doesn't always happen instantly. It happens over time. As we forgive, we begin to see things differently. Our perception of everything changes. Remember, perception is whatever meaning our mind puts on something—a person, experience, or situation. These perceptions change as we remove stigmas from our minds and begin to see things more clearly, truly, and without energy-sapping negative emotions.

Peaceful freedom happens hour by hour. When we've allowed ourselves to feel upset, we can stop for a moment every hour to give thought to the happenings and emotions of the hour just past, and remind ourselves to live the next hour free of distress, anger, and pain. If we don't allow the shadow of a bad hour to darken the next hour, and the next, and the next, we will gradually find a peaceful freedom. When we remember to forgive hour by hour, distress disappears and we are freed from the prison we've placed ourselves in, now remaining unbound and in peace.

We've heard it said in many ways, that the past is gone, and we can't change it. The future is yet to come, and we can't know what it holds. All we have is the present moment. If we spend each hour holding in mind the peace that forgiveness brings, every present moment becomes happier, more fulfilling, and life becomes simpler.

THE COLOR OF EMOTION

Color adds interest to just about anything. Without color this world would lose its aliveness, its vitality. Colors can influence emotions. Colors can influence our mental or physical state. For example, warm colors like reds, oranges, and yellows can bring about a range of feelings from warmth, courage, confidence, and excitement to hostility, danger, and anger. Shades of blue, green, and purple—the cool colors—spark feelings of calmness, freshness, security, and healing, but they can also bring about sadness, moodiness, and insecurity.

Have you ever gone into a restaurant and felt just a little uncomfortable? Have you entered another and felt relaxed and calm? If so, there's a good chance the colors in those places played a part in your emotions. Colors can have a profound effect on our frame of mind . . . in any environment.

The colors we wear or paint the walls in our homes or bring out in furnishings and accessories say a lot about what kind of person we are and how we feel. Because colors are apt to trigger both positive and negative emotions, we work with the ones that make us feel good. Even black and white can be pleasing to wear or to decorate with. White is the color of purity, goodness, and innocence, but too much white can feel cold, pristine, and empty. Black, on the other hand, can be impressive and bring about a feeling of protection, formality, and drama, but also mystery and evil.

Colors influence perceptions that are not always obvious, like the taste of food. That's why some foods have added color so they seem to taste better. Even the color of medications can have the perceived effect of enhancing their effectiveness.

During the years I worked as an interior decorator, I had a lot of fun with colors. In model homes, I would make up stories about the people who would live in the homes, then pick colors that created excitement or calmness. It didn't really matter what style of furnishings I chose. I created environments with the color of emotion.

To keep life simple, it's important to be aware of what has an effect on our emotions. When we decorate our home, buy clothing, or buy a car, it's important to sit with the colors for a while to see how they make us feel. If there's a tinge of any discomforting emotion, we need to keep shopping until we find what makes us feel at ease. We spend a lot of time with the colors we choose, and life is simpler when we get it right.

SECOND CHANCES

I give thanks every day for the good in my life. Sometimes that good seems fleeting, but if I trust in guidance from Holy Spirit, I know I will be directed to another chance to feel that good again.

We all have second chances—or third, or fourth, or more—so if you've experienced a missed opportunity or a failed attempt to get what you want, don't lament and repeatedly wish, "If I only had another chance . . ."

With each new day, each new moment, God gives us another chance to further our career, to begin or renew a relationship, or to improve our health. Our only responsibility is to stay open to recognizing each opportunity as another chance, and then go for it!

We must not just sit back *waiting* for second chances. To obtain what we desire, we have to take action. We might have to take classes that qualify us for a new job or advancement in our present one. We might have to pick up the phone and contact someone about healing a relationship, or reach out to seek a new one. If we've allowed our health to decline, we can alter our eating habits or start a new exercise regimen. God not only gives us second chances, but also the wisdom and strength to be successful in them.

In years past I've written hundreds of news articles and ad copy. I have even tried my hand at writing fiction. I took classes and subscribed to an online course with an "expert" coach but felt so shot-down by this coach's snarky remarks and directions on how to change the story-line that I got frustrated and gave up. God had a better idea for me, a second chance. With guidance from Holy Spirit, here I am today, writing my second book geared toward helping and inspiring others for a better life rather than simply informing or entertaining them. This book is based on very real prompting and guidance from a Higher Power, and I'm trusting in my own God-given talent and wisdom to go forward with confidence.

Never give up on your dream. God is working with and for you, and there will always be second chances.

FRIENDS

Janie was my best friend in kindergarten through second grade. Janie's family owned the dairy farm where we bought our milk. It was raw milk, unpasteurized, unhomogenized, straight from the cow—and I'm still here and healthy. Go figure!

I spent a lot of time at Janie's playing in the hayloft. She came to my house, too, to play paper dolls and to play on the swing my dad built behind the garage. Janie and I were fast friends, and I cried when the dairy farm was sold and the family moved away.

Television ads tell us what children need when they start a new school year—new shoes, clothes, backpacks, binders, paper, pencils—but what they need most is friends. They need to know they have the ability to be a friend, and to offer friendship to someone else. The best way to make friends is to *be* one.

We may have moments of insecurity, afraid of how other people think of us. These insecurities can rob us of potential friendships. The truth is that we are everything we need to be. We don't have to be prettier, smarter, or more popular to make friends. We just need to be kind. When Janie left, I had to reach out to other children, to offer them friendship through kindness. Even the most self-conscious, insecure children—and adults—who find it hard to meet people, need friends. If we can offer our friendship, we can be a catalyst to change lives for the better.

Some say they don't need friends and squirrel themselves away, hiding from society to the point that others are not comfortable approaching them. Sadly, these people are overlooked and under noticed, so they never break out of their shell. Then there's the child—usually in their teens—who becomes so obnoxious that no one wants to be around them. This unacceptable behavior is often a result of not being fulfilled in their family situation or feeling insecure in some way. These people, and the majority of others we come across in our lives, are in search of friends. They need to know they will be accepted and loved, that they are loveable. My mother used to say that a person needs love the most when they are the most unlovable

Kindness is the answer. An offer of kindness is one of the greatest gifts we can give *and* receive. If we identify with the person who is hiding away, or with the obnoxious one, an offer of friendship is a precious gift we should graciously accept. We can never know what someone else is dealing with in their own life, so we need to be kind. It's that simple.

TREES

In a *Rose is Rose* comic strip by Pat Brady, Rose is often shown leaning on her "Let Things Be" tree when things aren't going well. She claims that leaning on that tree connects her to its power.

I actually have a "Let Things Be" tree, only I call it my "Huggy" tree, although I can't really hug it because it's too big to get my arms around. When I touch it, or even stand close to it, I can feel a healing, calming energy. A big tree with roots going deep into the ground, bringing up the earth's energy, can make us feel grounded, and stress and worry just kind of dissipate.

I attended an inter-active art class a while back in which the group was given large sheets of paper and instructed to sketch whatever we were led to draw. I drew a tree with a very big trunk, branches, leaves, and big roots beneath ground level. We were then instructed to stand up and dance, and the dance was to represent our drawing. Everyone started dancing around the room, but I couldn't move my feet. My arms and body were swaying gracefully, but my feet stayed right where they were. It was a strange feeling until I realized I'd drawn the roots of my tree so large and strong that my feet—my "roots"—had become connected to the floor and, in my dance, only my branches and leaves could move.

The idea of a "Let Things Be" tree isn't just something in a comic strip, it's real. There's a powerful energy field that emanates from trees—especially very large trees—and it really is a healing energy. That's why parks are peaceful places. It's not just for their beauty and their cooling shade. We need trees to keep us calm and grounded. A tree is one of God's wonders, and they *do* help to reduce stress. Joyce Kilmer knew this when he penned his famous poem, *Trees*.

> I think that I shall never see / A poem lovely as a tree.
> A tree whose hungry mouth is pressed / Against the earth's sweet flowing breast.
> A tree that looks at God all day / And lifts her leafy arms to pray.
> A tree that may in summer wear / A nest of robins in her hair.
> Upon whose bosom snow has lain, / Who intimately lives with rain.
> Poem are made by fools like me / But only God can make a tree.

The next time you're feeling sad or lonely, find a tree, lean on it, feel its power, take a deep breath, and let things be.

MINIMALIZE

Imagine moving from a 2000 square foot house with a double garage and a large yard into a 600 square foot apartment with no storage other than a bedroom closet and kitchen cabinets. Before that, imagine how much two people can accumulate in a house, garage, and yard. Now, imagine the tedious task of deciding what to take to the new place and how to part with what you can't take. My friends Carrie and Lance lived through that scenario. To make matters even more complicated, they moved to Hawaii and everything they held on to had to get there by boat.

Paring down possessions to the barest minimum can be difficult and stressful, but it can also alleviate the stress of having to take care of too much of stuff in your home. My friends first had to decide what had special meaning. For them, it was Carrie's art supplies. She is a talented artist. Lance is an accomplished musician, and his musical instruments had to be included. Through some heart-wrenching choices, Carrie and Lance managed to release emotional ties, let go of psychological baggage, and flew away to their island paradise with only what they chose to keep. As they were going through their possessions, they found that the reasons they were holding on to things were unimportant, so more items kept going into the donate pile.

Several years ago, I went overboard with Christmas decorations. I took everything off the mantle and the book shelves that flank the fireplace and replaced them with Santa figures, lights, and garland. It was beautiful for the holiday, but when I took it all down, I was struck by the beauty and simplicity of the open spaces, so I didn't fill them up again. I replaced only a few books and little things that had meaning for me. I felt, and still feel, comfortable with the clean, minimalist look.

There is a psychological basis to our materialistic culture, and there's often a new kind of happiness to having less. Fumio Sasaki discusses the benefit of minimalism in his book, *Goodbye, Things*. He points out that when we discard something, we gain more than we lose; we gain time, space, freedom, and energy.

To keep life simple, be brave and minimalize. You don't need clothes you haven't worn in years. You don't need old magazines. You don't need things that you might need "sometime." You don't need things you've kept just to impress others. Life does get simpler when we don't have *stuff* weighing us down. Get rid of it, and surprise yourself with the realization that you don't miss it at all.

MISTAKES

We're just human beings here, doing our thing. We get it right some of the time, and sometimes we make mistakes. But whether we're right or wrong, it isn't the end of the world.

Some organizations, employers, churches, even parents make a habit of punishing mistakes, meting out shame that makes us feel small or imperfect. In truth, mistakes are essential in the human experience. Mistakes are the key to learning. Our human vulnerability emerges when we make mistakes because if we weren't vulnerable we wouldn't have emotions, and without emotions, life would be static and boring.

We need random acts of failure to move forward in society and in the world. Even without genetic mistakes—mutations—the variability that life needs to continue into future generations would not happen.

Our natural reaction to having made a mistake is often to try to cover it with excuses or even blame someone else. When we have the confidence and self-assurance to own up to our mistakes, though, we are demonstrating strength. It takes a strong person to admit to being wrong or failing. Mistakes can inspire the healing emotion of forgiveness, both for someone else and for ourselves. As psychologist Kelly McGonigal points out, ". . . the process of failing—when you're willing to pay attention—is often what leads to the greatest successes."

Staying aware of mistakes can trigger a brain-shift—a mind change—that decreases our over-reaction to things not going as planned. We become more resilient when we are aware that life is not smooth sailing all the way.

Mistakes happen with ease. We don't have to *try* to mess things up. Messes await just around the corner, and if we remain resilient and accept mistakes as a temporary thing—something that can be corrected—and recognize when we've made a mistake, fess up to it, and do what we can to fix any damage the mistake has caused, life will become simpler.

Don't beat yourself up for making mistakes. Instead, learn from them, grow from them, and let the process of failing lead to your greatest successes.

WIN OR LOSE

Have you ever wanted something so big and so expensive that you dreamed of winning the lottery so you could afford this wonderful thing? I know I have, but then I remember that you have to buy a ticket in order to win a lottery, and since I don't buy lottery tickets, I can laugh at myself for my ridiculously foolish longings.

Of course, having a financial windfall sounds nice, but not all lottery or big-money winners suddenly have better lives and are happier. Many winners face huge emotional challenges. Suddenly they have "friends" they didn't know they had who pop up out of nowhere. Family feuds sometimes erupt and, if they have children, they might fear for their safety against potential kidnappers.

Some big winners don't know how to manage their new-found wealth and spend too much too fast. Within a few years, they find themselves right back at the financial level they were before winning the lottery. There are also winners whose lives go down a dangerous path. Some become alcoholics, and some even commit suicide. Because of the likelihood of these outcomes, some states provide support groups for lottery winners to help them maintain their mental health. Winning the lottery isn't always a dream come true—it can sometimes become a nightmare. You might win the lottery, but it may cause you to lose your mind.

Other winners, though, thoroughly enjoy their new-found prosperity. They spend—and save—wisely, their quality of life is greatly enhanced, and they are indeed happier. Much of their contentment is found by having the financial means to help others.

Studies have shown that big-money winners who were happy before winning are happier after winning, and those who were somewhat unhappy before winning are even less happy after winning. It isn't money and riches that make or break a person, it's how they respond to it. It's whether they make decisions from wisdom or from folly—because any prize not tempered by wisdom can become a booby prize.

Using wisdom when good comes to us can enhance our life, the lives of our loved ones, and others that we choose to help. When we moderate winning with wisdom—then we are a *real* winner.

GROWTH

A hundred years ago, our life would have been far different from what our life is today. We would have continued to live in the town where we grew up. We would have been married once—for life. We would have practiced one profession. We would have attended one church and would never have questioned the beliefs we were taught, and we would have taught those beliefs to our children. Those children would have followed this same pattern of life until, little by little, attitudes began to change, beliefs began to expand, life lessons began to come more quickly, people began to break the mold, and individualism became a way of life.

Rather than taking an entire lifetime to learn, lessons come to us every day. It might take multiple relationships or marriages for us to learn how to do it right. We might have several professions before we find what's the most satisfying. We may question the religious beliefs we've been brought up with and strike out to find a spiritual path that fits more closely with our thinking and speaks to our heart.

Changing thought processes, jobs, and relationships might make us appear to be unsteady but, in truth, every thought, job, or relationship offers us valuable insight and strength and can bring more depth to what follows. In today's world, we can become a "learner of life," gaining valuable wisdom and enjoying several successes.

I went through a long period of change when I was younger. Each relationship was a little shorter than the one before, and I changed jobs about every two to three years. This wasn't because I was unstable or incompetent. It was because I was learning. I was growing. I was finding myself. I was breaking out of the mindset that everything is forever. I was willing to grow through rapid changes and to be blessed by the lessons I was learning. I hold as gifts what I learned through all these changes. I value every experience, and I'm a better person for what I've been through.

Don't be afraid to make changes—a lot has transpired through the years—but make those changes with wisdom and thought, and do it for growth, reminding yourself you are living *today,* not a hundred years ago. It doesn't have to take a lifetime to learn a lesson, and every lesson is another rung on the ladder of your growth.

PEOPLE NEED PEOPLE

I still read the newspaper, and I'm pleased to read about people helping people, and the love they have for each other. There have been devastating fires in the northern California area where I live—not close to my home, but close enough to have friends who are personally affected. Some of them have lost their homes and have had to begin the long road to rebuilding their lives. There were entire neighborhoods reduced to ashy rubble, and stories emerged about how people whose homes were spared stepped up to help those who lost theirs, providing shelter, food, clothing, and lots of love. One man, whose home was still standing, remarked, "On one hand we want to celebrate, but on the other, our hearts are crushed for all the people who lost their homes."

A man who was a caregiver for an elderly woman who was unable to walk wrapped her in wet blankets and carried her to safety, escaping her burning house. Restaurants provided food for the more than 100,000 evacuees who could not return to their homes, or didn't have a home to return to. Some even opened their doors to provide free meals, one calling itself, The No Pay Café. People in the fire areas realized that the love in the air was even thicker than the smoke.

Historical landmarks were lost in the fires. One still standing was of the town's founder draped with signs thanking firefighters for risking their lives and for their valiant effort at fighting the fires. The statue was wearing a face mask, just like all the people, to ward off the smoke.

Barbara Streisand sings, "People who need people are the luckiest people in the world." We're all lucky because we all need people. We need each other. Even through news of political unrest, nuclear weapons, mass murders, and violence in our streets, we hear of people sheltering others from harm and helping them in times of need. This demonstration of love works to restore my faith in humanity.

Since what we are is love, it's heartening to see that outpouring of love displayed. If we can keep love alive in our own heart, we'll find it in others. When we can make life simpler for someone else, our own life is more rewarding.

FOLLOW YOUR FEET

The human body is an amazing piece of equipment. Our internal organs and our physical body usually work the way they were designed to. Even if some body part doesn't work the way it was intended, God gives us the strength to modify our movements and actions, allowing us to live a happy and productive life. We can walk, talk, eat, think, and make choices that affect our well-being. Our arms and hands do what our brain tells them to, and our legs and feet support the whole wonderful anatomy. Everything is in balance . . . except when we walk.

When we walk, our body is actually off-balance *half* of the time. With each step we take, one foot has to come down somewhere and the other foot has to come off the ground to follow it in order to carry us forward. This happens without any thinking on our part. We don't stop to ask ourselves how to take our next step, we simply put one foot down, balance our full weight on it, then pick up our other foot, swing it forward, put it down, and balance our full weight on that foot. We don't even think about being off-balance because it happens in a passing moment.

While walking, we mostly look ahead in the direction we're going without much thought about our feet. We do have to be careful to sense our footing, but our brain and our eyes are very good at rapid assessment of ground conditions and at giving direction to our torso, limbs, and feet so that each step is one of perfect balance in motion.

When we're on a hike there may be some tricky spots. While climbing over rocks or facing steep inclines, our mind makes split-second decisions about where to put each foot in a way that conforms to the terrain and of what's underfoot at the moment. Covering ground on foot always unfolds out of the uniqueness of the present moment, and our mind and our feet are in tune,

Our body works automatically without conscious thought. That's the beauty of its design. Walking is automatic. Our feet know what to do because they naturally obey instructions from the mind.

Follow your feet; they know where to go. Let them take you where spirit leads you, and be grateful that God designed your body to work in the perfect way it does.

THIS IS IT

A cartoon in the *New Yorker* shows two monks in robes and shaved heads sitting in lotus posture on pillows on the floor, meditating. One monk is old and the other, young. The younger one is looking at the old monk with a questioning "What's next" look, and the old monk quietly says, "Nothing happens next. This is it."

When we undertake any kind of exercise, ritual, or activity, we usually expect some outcome for our efforts. But meditation is not like that. Meditation is probably the only intentional, systematic activity that is not about trying to improve oneself in some way. It's not about advancing, because in meditation, you're already there. As the old monk said, "This is it."

In most forms of learning we see signs of progress which encourage us to keep going. But with meditation, when we let go of *wanting* something else to happen, we are taking a giant step toward being able to see what is here now, in this moment. In meditation practice, the best way to get somewhere is to let go of trying to get anywhere at all.

Meditation is more about *being* than *doing*. It allows us to let go of thoughts of the past or plans for the future and puts us right smack in the moment. People think they should have a certain result from meditation, such as experience of a higher state of awareness, a great epiphany, a special vision, or becoming free and enlightened. These are all valid reasons to meditate, but we are bound to be disappointed if we *expect* those things to happen. In fact, if we look for signs of progress and don't feel something, we might begin to wonder if we're doing it right. If our body is relaxed, our mind is still, and we're simply *being*, we *are* doing it right.

We meditate simply to meditate, not to see what happens next. Chinese Zen master Wu-Men Huikai said, "If your mind isn't clouded by unnecessary things, this is the best season of your life." Quieting our mind and emptying it of everything except the acceptance of the present moment brings a clear acknowledgement that *what is happening is what is happening*. What happens next is what we choose to do out of an understanding of this moment—a deep knowing of "Nothing happens next. This is it."

R & R & R

When we feel strongly about something, we tend to get emotional. We feel anger, pain, sadness, or some other negative emotion when things go wrong. We also feel happiness and joy around good experiences. Different people have different ways of dealing with emotions, but the three most common are to Repress, to Recycle, or to Release.

Repressing bad emotions isn't always healthy. Bottled-up feelings can actually cause us to become sick. When we press feelings down, out of our awareness, they aren't really gone. It's like trying to hold a beach ball under the water; it just keeps popping back up to the surface. Repressing emotions is temporary, at best.

Recycling is another somewhat unhealthy way to deal with negative emotions. It isn't a permanent solution, either. When we recycle a feeling, we play it over and over in our mind. We ruminate about it. We tell ourself a story about why we're feeling the way we're feeling, and we tell other people the story, thus keeping it in our consciousness. Some people have remained angry over a circumstance or situation for years because they keep recycling the anger. When we recycle a negative emotion, it has control over us, and we are never free.

Releasing emotions is probably the healthiest choice. If we can identify the emotion and think about the feelings associated with it, we can act out those feelings—either with body movements or sound—and most negative emotions will pass through our body within a few minutes. Then we can get on with our day. We can also release negative emotions by stopping when we find ourselves thinking about them and replacing them with positive thoughts.

When something goes wrong in our life, bringing up negative emotions, the choice is ours: Repress and feel uncomfortable or even sick; Recycle and hold on to your story, telling it over and over to anyone who will listen; or Release and feel the discomfort melt away.

We can make this choice with positive emotions as well. We can Repress them, not demonstrating our happiness. We can Recycle them, letting others know of our good fortune. Or we can Release them, expressing them in ways that make those around us feel happy.

Ridding ourselves of negativity and celebrating positivity makes life simpler.

SELF-TALK

We may think we're the master of our thoughts, but that's not always so. Some thoughts are conscious. They're the ones that keep us out of trouble and guide us through our days. The subconscious thoughts, the ones buried deep in our minds, circulate in a constant internal dialog, and that's something that we have little control over. And it's not always good. There is a physiological component to what we think. Our thinking affects us in ways we're not really aware of. We can tell ourselves that we are blessed, strong, wise, capable, and confident, but that subconscious internal dialog—that self-defeating self-talk—can convince us otherwise.

Because our conscious and subconscious thoughts differ, we sometimes have to *look* for the good in our life to find it. We have to bring our self-talk to a conscious level and keep it positive. We have to give ourselves permission to manifest our good. We have to *believe* in our good to convince ourselves that we *are* good. This may sound a little egotistical or narcissistic, but becoming our best self is what we are working toward.

When I was in fourth grade, there were try-outs for the school choir. I liked to sing, and I sang pretty well, so I wanted to audition. My subconscious thoughts—my self-talk—about not being good enough kept my confidence level low, so I asked a friend to go to the audition with me, thinking she would boost my confidence just by being there. She had no interest in joining the choir, but the director talked her into trying out. She made it into the choir. I did not. My self-talk and insecurity over-ran my belief in myself, and I didn't do my best.

Wayne Dyer said, "Self-worth comes from one thing—thinking that you are worthy." If you can let your subconscious negative internal dialog catch up to your conscious positive thinking, and turn self-talk into self-admiration, you will find that life will be simpler. The good you deserve will come to you, you will be happier, and life will be simpler.

(By the way, by junior high, I *was* in the choir, and I've been singing in choirs ever since!)

WHAT'S YOUR PROBLEM?

Do you have problems? Is it easy to find solutions to those problems? It might be easier than you think. The solution might simply be to look at the problem from a different perspective.

Problems come in many forms. One problem could be a difficulty calling for a solution. Another, could be a trouble or a worry. It might also be a complicated situation that you don't quite know how to handle. The origin of the word *problem* is from the Greek *proballein,* which means to throw forward. But throwing problems forward can easily create further problems. I remember the *I Love Lucy* episode with Lucy and Ethel working at the candy conveyor belt. When the candies began coming so fast that they couldn't keep up, they popped the candies into their mouths and stuffed them down their shirts so their failure to handle the problem wouldn't become evident. Obviously, this "solution" caused further problems.

Much of what we consider a problem is that we're seeing something in a situation that isn't really there. In order to solve a problem, we first have to become aware of what the problem is. When we can entertain some doubt about the reality of our *version* of the problem, we can begin to find a solution. If we're having a misunderstanding with another, we can take a look at our self and consider what part we are playing in what feels like a problem. As Dr. Phil says, "No matter how flat you make a pancake, it still has two sides." When we can look at a situation from a new perspective we can usually come to a reasonable resolution.

We're not defined by our problems, we're defined by how we respond to them. Most problems can be dealt with in a calm and civilized manner, taking any needed action to find a solution. If the problem is that we are unable to rectify the problem, we look for outside help. Therapists, clergy, and even wise friends can often help us gain a new understanding, allowing us to change the way we're seeing the problem. When the problem is resolved, we need to remind ourselves to accept the answer! We don't want to saddle ourselves with problems that no longer exist.

When plagued by situations or people that are problematic, a fresh look with new eyes can usually bring relief and ease our mind. A new perspective lets us see a problem in a different light and to change our mind about it. Sometimes, when the problem isn't really ours, but something that someone else is trying to pull us into, it's okay to simply say, "Not my problem."

HOW OLD ARE YOU?

I recently saw a YouTube video about a nonagenarian named Tao Porchon Lynch, a yoga instructor who was performing yoga postures far more difficult than I can now, have ever been, or will ever be able to do. These were postures that I've only seen in magazines performed by very young, seemingly double-jointed people. She started doing yoga in India at a very young age and is not letting her 90-plus years slow her down now,

In 1948, Tao Porchon came to the U.S. from India, where she'd been a model. Her modeling talent was discovered here, and she went on to become very successful. When she was 80 years old, she took up ballroom dancing and embarked on a second career. Through the years she has kept her mind balanced and spiritually centered and her lithe little body flexible and able to move easily. She believes this is what has kept her so spry in her advanced years. She claims, "Nothing is impossible because all you want and need is already within you." She cautioned us "Not to let anyone tell you that you can't, and not to procrastinate. If you want to accomplish something, don't wait until you think the time is right because tomorrow never comes. Today is the time to take action."

Colonel Sanders comes to mind as I ponder her advice. He was well into his 80s before his recipe for Kentucky Fried Chicken was introduced to the general public, and look at KFC today—it's a staple in American cuisine.

There is an insert in my local newspaper called *The Other Side of 50*. It contains stories about people who have started new ventures in their 50s, 60s, 70s, and beyond. Some of the ventures are businesses and some are hobbies—physically active hobbies like scuba diving, running marathons, or pole-vaulting, not stamp-collecting—and they've become successful. They are all happy and feel good about themselves. For them, age is just a number.

What these experiences have taught me is that we can do pretty much anything we set our minds to. The only thing holding us back is a belief in our own limitations. Age doesn't have to stop us; we are only as old as we think we are. Satchel Paige once asked, "How old would you be if you didn't know how old you are?" When asked her age, Tao Porchon declared that she is 96 going on 22. She believes that, and she lives her life acting on it. Don't hold back because you think you are too old. Go for it! Life isn't over until it is.

UNFORGIVENESS

We can't know what light is until we've seen the dark. We don't know what peace of mind is until we've known inner pain. We can't know what happiness is until we've experienced unhappiness. We can't know what real comfort is until we've known discomfort. We don't know what forgiveness is until we've known unforgiveness.

According to *A Course in Miracles*, forgiveness is the path to peace of mind. Sounds simple, right? But even the most peaceful and loving among us find ourselves in a state of judgment and unforgiveness at times.

My friend Julia once called her friend Bobbi to rant about a mutual friend who she felt had wronged her. Bobbi and Julia were both long-time students of the *Course*, and during Julia's rant, Bobbi kept her peace and held her tongue, letting Julia talk until she ran out of breath. Then Bobbi quietly said, "Are you ready to see this person from a place of love and to forgive him?" "No", shouted Julia. "Well," Bobbi replied, "when you are, you will feel much better." Then she hung up the phone. No more conversation was necessary, Bobbi had made her point.

Our perception of another is a choice we make, not a fact. By holding on to perceived wrongs in one another, we are keeping *ourselves* from feeling peace of mind. By continuing to judge this friend and refusing to forgive, Julia was choosing inner pain for herself. Had she been willing to see the situation differently, and to find forgiveness, she would not only be forgiving the friend, she would be forgiving herself, and she would indeed feel much better.

Sometimes we hear stories of ultimate forgiveness and wonder how they do it. One such story is of a woman whose son was killed in a senseless act by another teen-aged boy. The boy was convicted, served his sentence in juvenile detention and, when he was released, the woman took him into her life. She found him a job and a place to live—an apartment next to her own—and she helped guide him onto a positive track in life. The woman's forgiveness was so complete that she treated this boy just as she would have treated her own son if he were still alive.

Unforgiveness is a cancer that grows within us. Unforgiveness hurts us far more than anyone we are not willing to forgive. When we are ready to forgive, we are free, we are at peace, and we *do* feel much better.

THE END OF CONFLICT

We cannot live simply until our mistaken thoughts of conflict are corrected. Any conflict we perceive in a situation must be squarely faced and forgiven in order for our lives to be simple and free of stress.

Unresolved conflict doesn't just go away. When we keep our heads buried in the sand long enough, we suffocate. Although we know forgiveness frees us from the discomfort of conflict, we still manage to come up with defense tactics that we think will alleviate the problem. The problem in any conflict is our loss of peace.

We sidestep issues by going shopping, watching television, or staying busy with some evasive strategy that allows us to avoid facing the conflict in our minds. We might shelve the issue for later consideration, a later that never seems to come. We sometimes disguise the issue, blaming our upset on a bad mood, a bad day at work, a headache, or hormones. We might even cover our rage with a smile or with humor, choking down anger and pain.

We sometimes deny what is really conflict by giving it another name. We might call it "righteous indignation" or "standing up for what we believe," but if we are to resolve conflict, we cannot deceive ourselves. Rather than trying to cover up the feelings that conflict engenders, we need to recognize it as what it is. Once we get in touch with our feelings of conflict, we will understand that, in conflict, we see ourselves alone in the universe, clawing our way through life. We lose our peace. If we are not peaceful and joyful, there is a reason. We may be clinging to some mistaken thoughts that we are denying.

Whatever the conflict, we impart the reality it has for us, and we do so for some hidden, unconscious reason. We hide our fear of love through conflict. We disguise our true feelings through conflict. We punish ourselves through conflict. Only when we are willing to go through ruthless self-examination, taking total responsibility for our own thoughts, will the defenses to conflict be lifted.

Forgiveness for ourselves and for others is what transforms all conflict and all doubt. When we realize we've been acting in absurd ways to move past conflict, and that they don't work, we can decide that we will no longer accept the madness for ourselves. We can then find the end of conflict, and life will be simpler.

EMBRACE YOUR WORTH

Many of us, no matter how centered and spiritual we believe ourselves to be, still face the challenge of honoring ourselves by embracing our self-worth. For some, feelings of unworthiness are the result of wounds from childhood. For others, it may stem from perceived failures in relationships, in business, or even as a person. We keep trying to prove our worth, not only to others, but to ourselves. However, nothing can shift *for us* until there is a shift *within us*.

Trying to prove our worth often has exactly the opposite effect. Do you know someone who is outwardly egotistical, and continually boasts about how good he is? Do these traits make you see him as smarter, more capable, self-confident, or even happy? I don't think so. The best way to prove our worth is just to be who we are, and let others discover our goodness. You *are* smart, you *are* capable. You have self-confidence within you, and you deserve to be happy. When we can honor and embrace our own good, no one can take that away from us.

Abe Lincoln said, "It is difficult to make a man miserable while he feels worthy of himself." When we respect ourselves, and live with that respect, others gradually do the same. They not only interact with us differently, they begin to interact differently with themselves. They like themselves when they are around us because our self-confidence gives them confidence. It's a quiet transmission. Quietly confident people are honest, trustworthy, and can admit mistakes. These traits are evident to others, just as the egotistical, brash, boastful ones of the braggart are, but they are a lot more likeable.

You *are* good. You *are* enough. To engage the fundamental truths of self-esteem, simply affirm your value and your worth throughout every day. Release any thoughts that hold you back from loving your life fully and in joy, that keep you from loving yourself. Open up to being healed and renewed on a cellular level. Remember, no one can make you miserable while you feel worthy—not even yourself.

JUST DO IT!

When I was on the board of a non-profit organization there was a great deal of planning: one-year strategies, five-year goals, ten-year intentions. Surveys were taken, good ideas were presented, agreements were made, but not much materialized. The membership of the board changed during these planning phases and plans were slowed as we stopped to bring each new member up to speed. At one meeting, an outspoken woman plainly said, "Why all this planning. Why not do it?" She was expressing what I had been thinking and I silently cheered her remark. Because it's important that we choose our commitments carefully, I left that board when I realized it was not my work to do.

The Buddha said, "There are two errors that keep great projects from coming to life: Not finishing, and not starting."

Some people might put off starting a project because they feel conditions are not perfect. By simply starting a project, however, conditions often come together naturally to effectively make the project successful. Sometimes projects take on a life of their own and we do the work as it presents itself.

To get things done, we must *start*. If we wait until we're absolutely ready, with all the ducks in a row, some projects might never get off the ground. Even if we have to learn along the way, we can let things be simple, because complexity of a project doesn't always improve its quality. The ducks will line up for us as we progress.

Nike had it right when they said, "Just Do It!" If there's something we want to do, we just need to do it. Whether it's starting an exercise program or painting the living room, putting things off only adds to distraction, and distraction complicates life. We lose enthusiasm when we procrastinate. We all have the ability and the good sense to know that when something needs doing, life is simpler when we get it done.

Having strategies, goals, and intentions can give us a plan of action, but why wait? If you have a good idea, act on it. If you have a plan, work the plan. Patience is a virtue, but procrastination is a waste of time and money, and it keeps life from being simple.

RULE OF HEALTH

The *Regimen Santiatis Salerntanum*, also known as *The Salernitan Rule of Health* is a medieval didactic poem believed to have been written in the 12th or 13th century. It concerns domestic medical practices. By the 16th century, the work had come to be highly revered as a scholarly medical text. One of the teachings of the Regimen is that to be close to God we must "Use three physicians: First, Dr. Quiet. Next, Dr. Merryman and Dr. Dyet." And this is still good prescriptive advice today.

The quality of our life is in our own hands. No external force has power over how we feel or what we believe. The first prescription from Dr. Quiet is essential to our well-being. If we don't take some time to be quietly with ourselves, meditating, walking, or just being in a peaceful place, the outer world will take over our mind and keep us from hearing the voice of God. We will find it difficult to look within for the peace that is meant for us. God isn't out on a distant cloud somewhere. God is within our heart and, in being quiet, we will feel God's presence and we will feel peace.

Dr. Merryman sounds like a joyful soul. Joy and happiness are as vital to good health as air. Don't fall prey to images of God as a somber, mournful old man. God is the joyful presence that lives within us. When we go out and play, get silly, and cast our cares to the wind, we will feel the peace of God far more fully than we would in gravely somber moments. God can be playful, too, but doesn't play hide-and-seek. God is with us, in us, and all around us.

Dr. Dyet will teach us how to help our body function properly, stay healthy, and maintain a high level of efficiency. Eating fresh, whole, pure foods, free of artificial ingredients and preservatives, and avoiding sugar, fat, and processed foods will keep our body in harmony with nature. When we take time to eat slowly and to really be *with* our food, when we thank God for it, and when we digest it calmly, our body will reward us with robust health.

Health is our natural state. It is within our power to maintain good health. Any idea to the contrary is a limiting belief. When we take the advice of the three doctors and have quiet moments, playful fun, and eat the right foods meaningfully, we will be more peaceful, more fun, and healthier. And our life will be simpler.

DAY BY DAY

Sometimes life just doesn't feel simple and we feel like there's no way out of the doldrums we've fallen into. A lack of self-worth is swallowing us up. But, if we really want our life to turn around, we can do it. The main thing we have to do is change our outlook or shift our thinking. But it isn't magic and it doesn't just happen overnight. Major change has to be done on a day-to-day basis.

One way that's worked for me is to set *three goals* for every day. Each morning, I write down three things that I take note of and want to think about differently. They don't have to be complicated or difficult. They can be as simple as the act of getting out of bed, or eating well, performing an act of kindness, or finding something I see beauty in and enjoying the beauty. At the end of each day, I can reward myself for reaching my goals by crossing them off my list.

If we set three goals for every day, and accomplish them, at the end of the first month we will have met 90 goals, our outlook will have begun to change, and we will feel a shift in perception and priorities. We will have begun to find purpose and to see how much we are now *giving* to the world instead of *taking* from it. We're all part of the system of the world and we each play our own role. If we've become involved in high-risk behaviors like alcohol, drugs, or conflict, we can behave our way to success by being honest with ourselves about these risky behaviors. We can learn to value ourself as much as we would value a small child in our care, and to treat ourselves with as much love as we would give to that child.

We sometimes get lost in life and need a road-map to find our way. We have to be *ready* to change, however. Ready to *read* the map. Dr. Phil has what he calls The Four Stages of Readiness to Change: 1) When we're compelled by authority; we either change or go to jail. 2) To escape criticism; if others are constantly after us to change, we could make that change just to get them off our back. 3) When we become intellectually motivated; when we can stop thinking *I know what's best for me but I just don't want to do it.* 4) When we are mentally and emotionally ready; when we are desperate to escape the circumstance we've found ourselves in and can look in the mirror and say, *I will not accept this for myself one minute longer.*

Change *is* possible. When we're ready, and when we change the way we look at life, change *will* happen, and our life will become simpler . . . day-by-day.

SILENCE THE ECHO

We are free to give anything we hear others say about us whatever meaning we want to believe. A tone of voice, a facial expression, the set of a body, or the use of certain words can relay a meaning that is hurtful, unkind, or damaging, and it can hold only the power we choose to give it. If we lack even a little bit of self-worth and the words we hear and the meaning we give them have a negative connotation, we tend to internalize them. On some level we believe hurtful or unkind things others say about us.

In this age of social media, people can criticize, blame, or trash other people mercilessly with no consequence to themselves. But there *are* consequences. Too often, what is said is believed by the person who is being attacked, and there is emotional damage.

It is essential for us to remember that whatever a person says about us cannot change us in any way. The actual words have no power and no lasting effect—it's the *echo* that hurts us, the words we say to ourselves about ourselves.

We have all experienced someone saying hurtful, mean, and untruthful things about us, and because they're not true, we should simply ignore the statements. All too often, though, we echo them. The actual words of another can't really affect us because they are just words. The damage is done when we doubt ourselves and begin to echo the hurtful and untrue words to ourselves. If someone calls us stupid, for example, the word has taken up residency in our mind, and we may respond to ourselves about something we do later on as stupid. We remember the words, and we echo them.

We can squelch that echo by remembering that we are perfect and innocent children of God. No one and no thing has any power over us unless we allow it. When people disparage other people it's because they feel inadequate and say things about others to make themselves feel better. If what is said about us is untrue, we can simply dismiss it and not let the echo have a voice. If there's a kernel of truth to what's said and we hear an echo in our mind that makes us question ourselves, we can take a look at it and make a change if we need to.

Let's probe our past and find any lies we have echoed, then let them go, silencing the echo forever, and regain the self-confidence that is our birthright.

IMPORTANT OR URGENT

When you're watching a movie, do you ever think about how your attention is kept on a primary character or action and not on background people and movements? Probably not. This is because cinematographers have techniques for highlighting key characters and scenes. They can focus on one aspect of a shot and allow everything else to be out of focus or blurred.

Movies follow a carefully written script with total focus on what the director wants us to pay attention to. But our everyday lives are different. When we are peacefully working on a project or doing a chore, we sometimes lose focus when another voice or another movement grabs our attention, and if we're not careful, our project—along with our peace and joy—can be blurred into the background.

When we set our focus on goals that are important to us, all too often something else comes into focus to draw our attention away from those goals—something that seems urgent. Steven Covey, in his book *The 7 Habits of Highly Effective People*, writes about "the tyranny of the urgent." When something comes up that seems more urgent than what you're doing, you leave what's *important* and turn to what's *urgent*—the apparent emergency. Notice that I said, *apparent emergency.* Unless there's fire or blood, you can usually remain focused on the important task or activity at hand, see it through, then shift your focus to what seemed so urgent.

A Course in Miracles tells us *inner peace is the only goal that really matters.* If you have peace of mind—inner peace—you have all you need, and you can easily shift focus when the scene changes and still keep that peace.

To maintain your inner peace, instead of tearing yourself away from what you're doing that's important to you, think of one of Covey's 7 Habits, and "Do what's important, not what's urgent." Set priorities and stick with them. Stay focused on the main character or the main scene and allow your focus to shift to other actors and movements when they become important and the time is right.

When we can keep our interest centered on what we're doing and stay focused, we are happier, more peaceful, and life is simpler.

LIVE AND LEARN

Throughout our lives, we never stop learning, and we never stop teaching. Simply being with others is both a learning and a teaching experience. Because no two people's lives progress down identical paths, our experiences differ, and each has something unique to share with another.

Chinese philosopher Chao-Chou is quoted as saying, "If I meet a hundred-year-old man and I have something to teach him, I will teach; if I meet an eight-year-old boy and he has something to teach me, I will learn." We just keep teaching and learning!

I've learned the meaning of FWIW, AFAIK, LOL, ROTFL, BRT, OMW, and many more texting abbreviations to keep up with the younger generation. I also learn by taking time to talk with really old people about their lives, their adventures, successes, and even their failures.

These are some great lessons I've learned that might also be helpful to you. They apply to both young and old. STAY ACTIVE—We have to keep moving! When we stop moving we start to die. HAVE A PUPOSE—When we don't have a purpose, a way to advance ourselves, boredom sets in, and our brains begin to atrophy. LAUGH A LOT—*Laughter is the best medicine* isn't just an axiom, it's the truth. Laughing releases endorphins that help us to heal. VALUE FRIENDSHIPS—People do need people, and friends can be a valuable support system. BE GRATEFUL—As we get older we get past "want." Wanting things is the root of unhappiness. The more grateful we are for what we have, for what we've been, and for where we're going, the happier we'll feel. NEVER STOP LEARNING—There will always be something we don't know yet, and it's never too late to learn. LISTEN TO OTHERS—Listen without judging. Everybody's story is different, and a patient listener will appreciate another's stories and gain friends by doing so. STAY FOCUSED—Drawing our mind, awareness, and attention together brings us to a point of total concentration. If we know what we want we can get it by maintaining focus. PLAN AHEAD—We don't know what's in our future. Having a plan will allow our future to be more comfortable. And, above all, STAY TRUE TO YOURSELF—There are some things in life that we *don't* need to learn. When we know who we are and are true to our values, we won't let ourselves be led astray.

PARENT YOURSELF

When we were children, our parents were always there to nurture us, to teach us and to set us on a positive track for life. But now that we've grown into adulthood, there's no one who's around all the time to remind us to behave, so we have to be our own parent.

When a child gets tired and cranky and throws a tantrum, a parent will step in and say, *you need a nap*, and whisk them away to their bed. But, as adults, we can also become irritable and cranky when we are tired, hungry, fearful, overworked, or stressed, and we throw a kind of tantrum by lashing out at others. Our parents were patient with us, but others may not be, and our tantrum could build irritation in someone which could result in an ugly confrontation. Where is our parent to step in and remind us that we need to rest, rehabilitate, and change our attitude?

We need to learn to parent ourselves. We cannot be effective for ourselves, or for anyone else, unless we stop to charge our batteries when we get off-track. Our parents used to feed us physically, emotionally, and spiritually, and now we need to do that for ourselves.

Twelve-step recovery programs have an acronym that can be useful during challenging times: H.A.L.T. Stop and nourish yourself when you are Hungry, Angry, Lonely, or Tired. When our energy is depleted and we're running on empty, there is an internal sensor—an internal parent—that reminds us to stop and take stock of our feelings and emotions, and to re-group, even if it means we actually do need to take a nap.

When we stop—HALT—and take a good look at the course of events that led us to our tantrum, we can see things from a different perspective. We can discover how to respond more calmly and find a healthier way to solve any problem or misunderstanding.

If we can remember the nurturing our parents gave us and behave in the "polite" manner we were taught, and if we can love ourselves enough to take care of ourselves and to help others, life will be simpler.

FOUR SUBLIME ABODES

The "Four Sublime Abodes"—or the *brahma-viharas*—of Buddhism are: Loving Kindness, Compassion, Sympathetic Joy, and Equanimity. By his example, the Buddha showed that a mind imbued with good will, courtesy, and concern for others is a liberating force, and that caring counters anger, cruelty, self-seeking, and indifference. Sounds like a nice way to live!

The teachings of Buddhism are ancient but no less applicable in today's world. Seeking happiness by hurting others is the epitome of foolishness, which is why wars don't make sense. "Hatred never destroys hatred, only love does," is Buddhism's eternal law. When we understand the basic interconnectedness of all people, we learn that when we hurt another, we are also hurting ourselves. Knowing how hurt makes *us* feel, why would we ever want to hurt another?

Loving kindness is often translated as friendliness or good will, concern for the welfare of all beings. *Compassion* is empathy; bearing witness to another's pain is the antidote to cruelty. *Sympathetic Joy* is pleasure in the happiness and good fortune of another. *Equanimity* is the ability to stay balanced and neutral in the face of difficult people and situations. These ancient truths can be developed in each of us if we cultivate them, realize their truth, and learn to live by them.

Imagine a situation where you came across a stranger who suddenly became seriously ill or injured far from a hospital or assistance of any kind. You know he needs help, and you think *I'd better help him or he might succumb on the spot.* That's loving kindness and compassion. Now think about someone who is annoying to you—someone you don't like very much—in a situation where he calls to you for help. Is this person any less in need of assistance than the stranger? Just like the stranger, this annoying person also needs loving kindness and compassion, and you are in a position to give it to him. Imagine that annoying person's life having been turned around—he's found peace and happiness and is no longer annoying; now you can feel sympathetic joy for him, happiness in his happiness.

If we can learn to stay balanced and neutral—in equanimity—in all situations, toward all people, just imagine how happy and simple our lives would be.

ANSWER THE PHONE

One of my favorite comic strips is *Zits* by Jerry Scott and Jim Borgman. The antics of Jeremy, who is forever sixteen, remind me so much of my own sons at that age, aggravating his parents by doing things in his own—sometimes strange—ways.

In a recent strip, Jeremy's mom gives him a piece of mail and he asks, "What's this?" His mom says, "Grandma sent you a post card from Florida." "A what!?", Jeremy asks, and Mom explains, "It's a picture someone mails to tell you they were thinking of you—a week or so ago." Jeremy, looking at the picture says, "But she's not even in it." And mom explains, "Well, no, she didn't take the picture, she probably bought it at a drug store." Jeremy, looking puzzled, puts his hand to his forehead, looks at the card again and says, "Okay, start over from the beginning." And mom says, "It's like snapchat on a rotary phone."

Things have changed so much and so quickly through technology that a sixteen-year-old can't even fathom a mailed post card with a message that was written more than a week before, and the picture isn't even a selfie. His only exposure to written communication is texting, email, or some other social network like snapchat, Instagram, or twitter. And what the heck is a rotary phone?

Believe it or not, we didn't always carry tiny computers around in our pockets. We used paper maps to figure out how to get where we needed to go. We made flyers to tell people about up-coming events, and mailed invitations to parties. There was no such thing as Facebook or E-vites.

We looked things up in books instead of asking Siri or Google. When we had to write papers for school, we did research at the library, and we wrote the papers on a typewriter. For entertainment, we played records on a turntable, listened to the radio, or watched tiny TVs. We didn't have video games, we had board-games. We kept phone numbers in a book, and when we took pictures, we waited two or three days while they were being developed at the drug store.

Another comic strip made me smile a second time. In *Pickles*, by Brian Crane, the phone rings and Grandpa looks at the caller ID then clicks it off without answering. Little Nelson asks, "Who is it?" and Grandpa says, "Nobody I want to talk to. In the old days when the phone rang, you couldn't tell who was calling." And the boy asks, "Then how did you find out who was calling?" and Grandpa says, "You just answered the phone."

Perhaps not as expedient, but life *was* simpler in simpler times.

SILENCE

When I moved from bustling southern California to a small town in northern California, I was struck by the silence. I had not been aware of how continual the noise was in the big city until I didn't hear it anymore. At first, I missed noise and the fast-paced lifestyle, but I quickly learned to find a peace in silence that was refreshing. Silence can allow our mind to think deep thoughts because it doesn't have to compete with what's going on around us.

For many years, I attended a conference at Unity Village in Lee's Summit, MO, every summer. These were week-long assemblages, and one whole day and night was spent in silence. This was my favorite part of the conference (except for the talent show) because it gave me a rare opportunity for introspection. I noticed things that hadn't entered my consciousness before—birdsong and wind in the trees. I breathed deeply, relaxed, and in the silence, discovered that I really am in charge of my own mind. When there's no chatter around me, I can disengage with my thoughts, not condemning or approving them, simply noticing them and seeing them of no consequence. There is real mental peace in the silence.

Silence doesn't mean simply not talking, and it doesn't mean isolation. There were still a lot of people around me during these times of silence, and people acknowledged others with a nod or a smile, but we all remained silent. We walked in silence, we ate in silence, and we met as a group in silence. I'd find that I saw people differently in the silence. Without talk, I could see into their hearts, see the love there, and feel the love coming back.

Mental silence is an acquired habit. It takes practice, and learned well, the practice of silence can spill over into our whole life. Silence is something that could benefit everyone in every walk of life. If we could step back from negative thoughts for a moment of silence, and think before we act, a lot of unpleasantness could be avoided. In silence, we see things more clearly. When in the throes of a disturbing situation, taking a moment of silence in which to choose our response before we react can disarm an uncomfortable encounter.

Today, try silence. Set aside some time to practice silencing your mind, and just *being*, without letting thoughts or emotions drive you. Mental silence is good for us. Silence, cultivated mindfully, can allow life to become simple.

ARE YOU HAPPY?

Although people differ in the way they think, the way they act, and the way they live, all people want to be happy and to have the feeling of pleasure or contentment that being happy brings.

When we encounter someone who is judgmental or negative, who sees other people's needs as different from their own, we can still see them from a place of happiness within ourselves. Those negative ideas usually come from a place of fear, and their projection of their fears may be all they are seeing for themselves. But when we look at our interpretation of their actions, we will see that person's fear, which often manifests as attack, is really a call for love and is witness to the belief in love and happiness within their mind.

God's will for everyone is happiness, and when we can meet others with a face shining with joy, they will hear God calling to them in our happiness. Those we encounter want love, joy, and happiness, just as much as we do, and our happiness heals their sorrow, pain, and despair. God's plan is happiness for everyone and our job is essential to this plan. *A Course in Miracles* says, *Without your smile, the world cannot be saved . . . all laughter echoes yours.*

Happiness doesn't depend on anything outside our mind, or anyone else's mind. Getting upset with anything or anyone doesn't change anything, it simply causes unrest. Only happiness brings lasting change, and happiness is contagious. When we can stay in a happy place in our mind and heart, it will broadcast out to others, they will feel our joy, and they will catch it. The greatest gift we can give to those around us is our happiness. Our gift of joy increases as we give it to another.

In truth, everyone has the capacity to be happy; we simply have to claim it. Our job today, and every day, is to be happy. In order to be happy ourselves, we can simply seek and find the happy truth in everyone.

I LOVE YOU

My son called this morning, and simply said, "I Love You." Actually, this happens often, and it makes my day. On the road of life, there are ups and there are downs. Sometimes my son has downs and asks me for help. When I extend love in a way that helps him, he always shows appreciation, sometimes in big ways, sometimes in small ways, like calling to say, "I Love You."

When we're in a down time, maybe feeling depressed, lonely, or just unmotivated, we will pick ourselves up if we show love to somebody else. We cannot extend love and feel depressed at the same time any more than we can eat crackers and whistle at the same time. Whistling blows the cracker crumbs out just as love blows the depression away.

My life is full, and much of it involves helping others. There are times that I just don't feel like teaching my yoga classes or leading the *Course in Miracles* group, but because they are obligations, I do them anyway. When I get there and find the class or group members so focused and eager to participate, I am energized and feel one-hundred percent better. By the end of the sessions I am so inspired that I wonder why I didn't feel like going.

Although we all need some alone time, we can save that time for when we're feeling good about ourselves. When we feel sad, lonely or depressed, we'll feel better if we reach out to give love or to help somebody. Love is the best cure for depression and loneliness, and there are countless ways to extend love. We can read to children at the local library, visit someone who is not as healthy as we are, and maybe even take them a meal, or we can volunteer at the local animal shelter. Caring for our fellow man—or animal—is the best way I know to lift our own spirits and feed our soul.

Love is healing. People in rehabilitation centers are found to heal faster if they have a plant to care for. At one time I had no less than twenty plants in my living room alone. As I fed them, I found myself singing and dancing through the task. I felt love. I felt healthy. I felt needed.

There are really only two emotions, love and fear, and we can choose to live from either one. Love heals. When we give love, love comes back to us. Fear begets more fear and can leave us feeling isolated. If we want to make our self feel better, we can make someone else feel better. We can visit a friend, perform an act of kindness, or simply call someone to say, "I Love You."

DAYDREAMS

My 10-year-old great-granddaughter is a champion daydreamer. If I want to say something to her, I have to first get her attention, then make sure she's looking at me when I speak so she doesn't go back into the daydream state. This is not because she can't listen or learn. She's whip-smart, constantly surprising me with her knowledge and ability. She's simply a dreamer. I don't know what she's dreaming about—she might be devising a way to build a house on Mars or conjuring up a new video game. Her dreaming is a way of visioning. For every great thing that has ever been invented, there was a person who dreamed a dream, who had a vision.

Visioning is every bit as important as doing. Letting our mind play with possibilities will get better results than working on something for hours without a vision behind our work. Artists have a vision for their finished piece, writers have a vision for their stories, and entrepreneurs visualize their inventions. Visioning lets us explore realms we would not ever reach if we simply followed a rational thought process.

Children are often punished for daydreaming in school, but I think they should be encouraged, not punished. Maybe a period of time should be set aside every day just for daydreaming. Just think of what could come out of these young, imaginative, impressionable minds if given a chance to explore ideas. Maybe if kids were given a chance to surf on the sea of imagination instead of surfing the net, new and wonderful things might evolve.

There is value in daydreaming. For four years, I envisioned what my first book, *For the Love of Yoga,* would look like, how it would teach, and the value it would hold for those who read it and used it. I saw it finished, right down to the weight of the paper and the lay-flat binding, and I held on to that vision until it became exactly what I dreamed it would be. It was so good that it won first place in a book contest.

Trust your dreams and your visions enough to bring them to life, and allow the children in your life to daydream. Who knows what they will come up with. Steve Jobs, George Lucas, Jeff Bezos, Bill Gates, and Mark Zuckerberg were dreamers, and look at what their dreams—their visions—have done for them.

FORGIVENESS

Learning to forgive is probably the most important lesson you can ever learn, and sometimes it's the hardest. If you've been wronged or hurt by the actions of another, you have a right to be angry, but if you allow yourself to be consumed by that anger, feeling like the wrongful act is so heinous that letting go of the anger would be tantamount to accepting the act and making it okay, you are hurting nobody but yourself. You don't realize what damage you are doing to your own mind by holding on to grievances. However, through forgiveness it *is* possible to let go of grievances. It isn't really a matter of possible or impossible, it's a matter of choice. Forgiveness is a choice. Forgiveness means to *give up*. You *can give up* any grievance. The question is, do you want to? You won't be doing it for the sake of the wrongdoer, you'll be doing it for your own well-being, your own peace of mind.

Forgiveness is a gift we give to ourselves. Holding grievances can cause us to lose sight of our self and to become angry with the world, thus betraying our self as the Love we were created to be. Forgiveness can release us from something that can eat us alive, that can destroy our joy and our ability to love fully and openly.

The person you're forgiving doesn't even have to know of your choice to forgive. Much of the time, they not only don't know, but they also don't care. Somehow, energetically, they *will* know and are likely to feel peace surrounding them. I learned this lesson fully a few years back. I felt wronged by someone close to me and as the anger and hurt built up, I read the words; *Forgiveness is a gift you give yourself.* It was like a light had been turned on, and I forgave completely without saying a word to the wrongdoer. Sometime later, I ran into this person and told him of my forgiveness experience, and he said he knew exactly when it happened because a peace had come over him when he thought of me.

When we forgive someone, we release them from judgment, but unless they can speak the truth about what they've done, a relationship of trust is not always possible. Forgiveness doesn't mean that once we've forgiven we need to welcome the wrongdoer as a friend. Forgiveness doesn't mean we pretend what happened didn't happen. But forgiveness, forgiving ourselves for holding onto ill will toward someone who has wronged us, will release *us* from the pain, the sorrow, the anger, and allow us to open our mind and heart to love and peace. There's a simple magic in true forgiveness.

SELF-COMPASSION

If you are engaged in an endless round of self-criticism over some perceived failures, don't do that! Be nice to yourself! Stopping the criticizing and appreciating your gifts will not only make you happier and less stressed, it will also help you achieve your personal goals.

To ramp up yourself-compassion, try writing a letter to yourself about something you've been struggling with. Imagine you are an empathetic friend and think about what this friend would say to you about what you're going through. You can be empathetic with yourself, but it's somehow easier to imagine hearing it from someone else. When we try to make ourselves feel better, that ugly self-criticism wants to creep in.

You could also use a mirror. If you're going through a hard time, stand in front of a full-length mirror and talk to yourself as if talking to someone else. Tell the image in the mirror that he or she is competent, talented, loving, kind, or whatever comes to mind having to do with the particular circumstance that is making you question your worth.

You can flirt with yourself. When you catch your reflection in a store window, say, "Hey there, you're looking good today." and give yourself a smile. This might feel a little weird at first, but it helps to look at yourself without judgment or criticism. (I don't recommend saying these words out loud in public, though—that *would* be weird.)

Talking to your reflected image might sound a bit egotistical, but it works. When you can see yourself as others see you, in a more positive light, self-compassion increases and self-criticism loses its grip.

We all have hard times and disappointments in our lives, but they don't define who we are. They actually help us grow. They make us think. If our thinking is about how to get past those hard times and disappointments, we emerge stronger and more self-assured.

If you find yourself enmeshed in self-criticism, stop and take stock of your thinking. Write yourself a letter, tell yourself you are a wonderful human being with wonderful qualities, gifts and talents. Talk to yourself in a mirror and see the beauty that is you. Flirt with yourself. Build up your self-esteem.

We may think we need acceptance or approval from others outside ourselves, but the most important approval and acceptance comes from inside. Life is simpler when you can love yourself.

STOP THE ROAR

For the Love of the Game is a novel by Michael Shaara. The manuscript was found after his death, published posthumously in 1991, and later made into a movie starring Kevin Costner. In the story, Billy Chapel, a fictional character, was a major league pitcher who was aging out of the game and being forced to retire or be traded. He had also just lost the woman he loved and was feeling lower than he'd ever felt. Being somewhat distracted, Billy took to the mound for his final game, and into the last inning realized he was on his way to pitching a perfect game. The crowd was going wild, and the roar in the stadium was deafening. But Billy had found a way to shut out all this noise; he called it his *Disengage Mechanism*. With his mind, he was able to disengage with the din of the crowd and to concentrate on his pitching and nothing else. He ended up pitching that perfect game. At the end of the novel, and the movie, Billy retires from baseball, his loved one comes back to him, and the story has a dramatically happy ending.

There is a constant "roar" in all our lives. We have people after us to get a job done, we have appointments to keep, we have things to do and people to see. We go from one responsibility to the next and can get crushed by the stress of it all. I know this because I've lived it.

A few years ago, I found a small disengage mechanism that worked for me. It was a bracelet that had a tiny battery inside that could be set to vibrate at certain intervals. When I felt that pulsation on my wrist, it prompted me to stay in peace, or come back to peace if I'd gotten distracted. There was no sound to the bracelet's vibration, but I heard its message loud and clear. I wore that bracelet for a long time, and now I'm able to remind myself to stay in peace without it. When I start to feel overwhelmed, I think of the bracelet and its vibration, I take some deep breaths, and I come back to peace.

Billy Chapel was fictional, but disengage mechanisms are real, and there is one in you. You can learn to shut out the "roar" that distracts you. It could be repeating an affirmation of peace, a prayer for guidance, or even *knock it off!* When you can remind yourself to come back to peace and find clarity in the moment, you can rise above any outer challenges. You can step back from the chaos of the world and connect with the wisdom and peace that is within you. Your game can be perfect, and you can be dramatically happy.

W.H.E.N.

When will I find what I seek? When will I find contentment? When will I find the perfect job, house, car, or whatever it is I think I lack?

When we change our thinking, the word *when* takes on a whole new meaning. We can see how W.H.E.N. can stand for We Have Everything Now. Now! Already! Our goodness is right in front of us. We have everything we need. Our good is our birthright; it has been given us by Divine Power. We simply have to open up to it. When we feel lack, we can remind ourselves to take a look at the good in our life—*it is there*—and we can be grateful.

If you feel you're lacking something in your life right now, it's temporary because *lack is a state of mind*. The truth is, there is no scarcity anywhere within or around you. It is simply fear and small-thinking that are blocking the flow.

We may think the grass is greener on the other side of the fence, but if the other guy's pasture appears to be greener, it's not that he has a better pasture, it's just that it's getting better care. Negative thoughts, or thoughts of lack, can keep our own pasture from thriving.

You already have everything and already are everything. You are spiritually good in all forms: health, happiness, wealth, love, fulfillment, and unlimited possibilities. You have within you the power to satisfy all your needs and to make your dreams come true. True abundance doesn't just *come along*, it's there all the time. If you can't see it, it simply means you're not looking in the right place. Abundance isn't something you acquire, it's something you tune into. Abundance has many faces. It's not just monetary, it's peace, love, joy, and contentment, and it's family, friends, and happiness. Stop asking "When?" When is *now*, and when you can convince that stubborn mind of yours that there is nothing lacking in you, the whole world belongs to you.

"This may be so," you're thinking, "but there are still a lot of people who have more than I do." Someone else might have more possessions than we do, but no one—not any person—has any more capacity for love that we do. Love is what keeps our pasture green, love for others, and love for ourselves. WHEN is NOW. We Have Everything Now! When we give abundantly, we receive abundantly. When we remember this, life becomes simpler.

ANGELS

The dictionary defines *Angel* as a spirit that is believed to watch over and protect a person or place, or a helpful person. There are angels all around us. When we are at a breaking point and someone shows up to help, we consider that person an angel. When we have a close call in traffic and are saved, that's our guardian angel. We might even envision little fairy-like beings flying around us, keeping us safe. These are the angels I think of.

When I was six or seven years old and walking on the top cross bar of the fence in my back yard, I wasn't thinking of any danger. I was just having fun. But there was danger. This was a six-foot fence, so I was six feet above the ground, and a fall from six feet could do some harm to a little girl. As I was balancing, I saw little fairy-like beings flying around me. When I came down from the fence, the beings disappeared. These were, I believe, guardian angels. And they kept me safe.

Another angel I know of was the fiancé of my friend Patty. His name was Rick. On the way home from a trip with two friends there was a terrible car crash, and Rick was mortally wounded. When first-responders arrived at the crash site the car was engulfed in flames. The other two men were also injured but had been pulled from the wreckage before the fire started. They were alive. They told police that Rick was the one who pulled them free. Rick was pronounced dead at the scene. Rick, broken as he was, had been able to pull his friends free before he succumbed. Rick was a guardian angel to his friends.

As a 7.5 earthquake hit Indonesia, an air traffic controller was able to safely talk a plane on the runway into the air before the resulting tsunami occurred. More than 100 passengers on that plane were saved, but the controller lost his life. He was truly an angel.

In my mother's last weeks, she often reached up from her bed and remarked, "Did you see that? It was an angel." I believe it was. She was being watched over by a spiritual being getting ready to take her home.

Guardian angels are real. We can rest in the knowledge that we are being kept safe by something beyond ourselves. Even though we usually can't see the angels, we can trust they are there for us. Angels are everywhere; they are God's helpers. Just in knowing this, our life can become simpler.

IT ONLY TAKES A MOMENT

Got a moment? That's long enough to generate happiness, comfort, or any meaningful action any day of the week, any time of the day.

When things are going well for us, we can be oblivious to someone else's difficulty or discomfort, but when we know how bad our own difficulty and discomfort feels to us, we can understand how much it means to another to receive an offer of help from a friend. If we keep our hearts open to the needs of others, there are usually little things we can do to help. A simple note of support, a phone call, or a bouquet of flowers from our garden are small ways to let someone know they're in our thoughts, that we wish them well, or that we are grateful for their friendship. It only takes a moment.

When engaging in conversation, we can be a good listener. Instead of mentally planning our next statement, we can pause and check in with ourselves, examine our energy, take a breath, and really listen to what's being said. It only takes a moment.

The next time you're out walking the dog, taking your lunch break, or checking the mail, stop and listen. Allow the environment to come alive. Let the wind, city noises, birdsong, lawn mowers, children at play fill your attention, and for just a moment, be a spectator letting your ever-whirring mind take a break. It only takes a moment.

When someone—a waiter, a bank teller, a sales associate, or anyone who performs any kind of customer service—goes above and beyond to be helpful, kind, or super-efficient, let your gratitude be known. Thank them graciously, and also send a note to their manager or supervisor. This will not only communicate that the employee deserves credit, it also lets the business know what they're doing right. It only takes a moment.

If someone is kind enough to hold a door or an elevator for you, when the cashier rings up your purchase, or when the barista hands you your latte, lift your gaze and make friendly eye-contact. Offer a gentle smile that says, "Hey, hello there, fellow human being. I recognize your worth." Good vibes are shared, spirits are lifted, and it only takes a moment.

These moments are simple. Just small, effortless actions can help us wake up and plug in to the life that pulses around us, to notice what is important and give it some thought. It only takes a moment.

LAZY BRAIN

Are we becoming a society of smart phones and lazy brains? Storing memory in our brain requires considerable mental effort, but when we know where and how to find any piece of information on our little hand-held devices, taking very little effort to do so, we are less likely to remember that information and to be able to pull it from our memory when we need it later.

This is not a new phenomenon. It's happened before. Plato, for instance, whined about the spread of the written word, saying it would decimate people's ability to remember if they didn't have to hold every bit of information or knowledge in their brain. Writing, as it turned out, did not bring about a cognitive decline, but modern scientists are now finding more and more evidence that smart phones and internet use are, indeed, affecting cognitive function. When we know we can find the answer to pretty much any question with a touch on a screen, we don't need to commit it to memory.

Memory is essentially a long daisy-chain of neurons in our brain, and when we march down that chain we strengthen the synapses that connect one neuron to the next. This makes it easier to retrieve a memory and to recall it the next time we need it. But if we succumb to "just let me google that"—which has become ridiculously easy—that march down the chain of neurons doesn't happen, and the memory of the information doesn't last.

I almost hate to admit that I am one of those let-me-google-that people. And when I've made a note of something on the calendar—and set a reminder on my phone—for appointments, birthdays, and such, the information goes out of my brain. I no longer *have* to remember things, so I don't even try. It's there with a touch if I need it.

Unfortunately, when facts are no longer accessible to our conscious mind—only look-up-able—creativity suffers. New ideas stem from combinations of disparate, seemingly unrelated elements that are floating around in our brains, and the more elements, the more chance for a new idea or innovation.

To alleviate the risk of threatening the very foundation of creativity, set aside your smart phone for a while and work to store things in your brain by engaging in mentally stimulating activities like board games, puzzles, and reading. Participate in social situations to create more backup circuits so you can store more memory. Let your brain work to do its job and you will find life more interesting, and in the long run, simpler.

HAPPINESS IS A CHOICE

If we were asked to make a list of everything we think we *need* to make us happy, we might list things like a car, a computer, or a different house. We might think we need to be married, or divorced, or have a better job. But even if we had all the *things* on our list, none of them would make us truly happy. Happiness is a choice.

A couple of years ago I thought I needed a single-story house. I was tired of going up and down stairs, so I bought another house and moved truckloads of stuff into it, but I couldn't bring myself to actually move in and live there. I didn't feel at home in that house, so I moved the truckloads of stuff back to the house where I did feel comfortable. It wasn't a different house I needed, it was peace and comfort I was looking for. I had that in my old house, even with the stairs.

When we're feeling an emptiness inside, our mind translates that into a physical craving. We may think we're hungry and eat too much. We may think we're lonely and enter into meaningless relationships. We may drink too much, sleep too much, or watch television too much. We will try to fill the emptiness by doing something with our *body* to change how we feel. But that doesn't work. Peace doesn't come from our body, and we can never be at peace when our life is filled with cravings. What we really want is to be at peace within ourselves. We want to feel fulfilled, happy, and content. The good news is, these feelings are instantly available to us when we choose them. We don't find them through our body or anything else external. We find them in our mind and in our heart.

We really only require one thing on our *need* list, and what we need, we already have. All the things on our list having to do with our body are substitutes for the peace and happiness that is within us, and we find that peace and happiness by choosing it, by remembering that it is available to us all the time.

This isn't to say we shouldn't have things that bring us happiness, but the external *bodily* things don't last and don't become part of us. Life is much simpler when we can feel an inner peace that saves us from searching for something *better*. Sometimes when we get some of the things we think we *need*, we find that we don't really want them anyway—like my new house.

Don't stop growing and learning and developing a happy life, but let that happiness come from the inside, from a place of comfort, not from anything you *think* you need from the outside. Simplicity is more fulfilling than craving things that wither and die.

THE APPLE TREE

A sweet little book whose pages I read often and that I gain inspiration from is a compilation by Melvin McLeod of the wise words of Buddhist Monk and Zen Master, Tich Nhat Hanh. Just today I read about the Apple Tree, and I will share these words here:

"Have a look at the apple tree in your yard. Look at it with complete attention. It is truly a miracle. If you notice the apple tree, you will take good care of it and you, too, will be part of its miraculousness. Even after caring for it for only a week, its leaves are already greener and shinier.

"It is exactly the same with the people who are around you. Under the influence of awareness, you become more attentive, understanding, and loving, and your presence not only nourishes you and makes you lovelier, it enhances them as well. Our entire society can be changed by one person's peaceful presence."

What this message tells me is that when we stay aware and open to everything around us—trees, plants, pets, children, other people—we see their growth and development. We see the miracle that they are, and that we all are. If we take good care of these people and things, and of ourselves, our very presence will be nurturing, and society at large will benefit.

With just one person's loving presence making a difference in our world, imagine what the world would be like if everyone lived peacefully, calmly, and lovingly. If every growing thing and every developing person was allowed to unfold at a natural, God-given pace without being poisoned or infected by blight, bugs, or damaging thoughts and ideas, our world would be an entirely different place.

When apple trees, and human beings, are noticed and brought into our awareness, the shared attention shows them to be a miracle. When apple trees, plants, and human beings are well-placed, well-tended, well-fed, and well-loved they miraculously thrive. As this wise teacher said, "Our entire society can be changed by one person's peaceful presence." Each of us has the ability to be that one person.

YOU'RE NOT INFERIOR

Many people feel a lack of worth or experience feelings of being inferior. They think they are no more important to this world than a grain of sand, that their one human life doesn't have much meaning. This is the kind of inferiority complex that too many people suffer from in today's world. When we look at reality only in terms of the historical dimension, or what has been accomplished throughout time, the world we see might seem like there is little that one single human can do to make this world a better place. But if we can get in touch with the ultimate dimension of reality—the whole picture—we are able to see beyond the limitations of perceived time and space and beyond our own notions of inferiority and powerlessness. We all have great stores of knowledge, spiritual energy, and love to share with the world, and each single life has great meaning.

The ultimate goal of every human being is to live peacefully and happily, but it's hard to find that peace when we don't feel good about ourselves. This, unfortunately, is particularly true with children. The good news is that any person who feels inferior can be helped by another who is confident and has healthy self-esteem.

Confident people can help by showing appreciation, demonstrating approval, and congratulating every good thing less confident people say or do—especially children—in order to help them develop self-confidence with a healthy feeling of self-worth. Confident people can take notice of any talent or positive quality and show admiration.

When someone who feels inferior finds that someone else notices and admires something about them that they might not be aware of themselves, their acceptance of themselves begins to develop, and with continued encouragement, their self-esteem and confidence will begin to grow. Every one of us has the God-given capacity to be the best we can be, and it's not prideful or egotistical to admit this.

If you are feeling inferior or less-than, try to surround yourself with loving people who can see through the dark cloud you've locked yourself under, and believe in the good that others see in you. Fyodor Dostoevsky observed, "Only by self-respect will you compel others to respect you."

As a confident person, if you know someone who feels inferior, lift their spirits with positive observations and let them know you see the truth in them. When everyone understands their own worth, then every one of us can make an important contribution to the world, and life will become simpler for all.

IN THE DEPTH

Eli Stanley Jones was a 20th century author and Christian missionary in Southeast Asia. He tells of natives in Malaya sitting in rice paddies fishing in one foot of water just steps away from an ocean teaming with an abundant supply of fish. These people were limited thinkers. The fish they needed were readily available to them, but they remained in the shallows, hoping to make a catch.

Too many people remain in the shallows of thinking and living and miss out on doing much of what they dream of doing. On the wall of the National Library in Washington, D.C., is the inscription: *For a web begun, God sends the thread.* There is a limitless potential of wisdom inside that library, and there is a limitless potential of wisdom, strength, and substance within *you*. When you take the thread offered by God, potential begins to build a web.

How many of us carry hopes and dreams that are buried within us by indecision, lack of motivation, and limited thoughts, even though we have the inborn possibility of limitless life? When we get out of the shallows and dive into the depths of true limitlessness, some would say we've "gone off the deep end." But stepping into the depths is the first step in the direction of our dreams. God sends the thread, the guidance, the creative ideas, and sometimes, even the money to manifest our dreams. Then it's up to us to take action, knowing we can do whatever we set out to do.

When Jesus stepped onto Simon's boat in the Sea of Galilee, he told Simon to *Put out into the deep and let down your nets for a catch.* (Luke 5:4) Simon objected, saying they'd fished all night and had caught nothing. But he finally did as Jesus directed, and his nets hauled in so many fish he had to call for help to land them all.

As students of Truth, most of us are "over-read and under-done." We keep accumulating knowledge without taking action. It's like the old farmer who said, "I ain't farmin' half as good as I know how to." He had full knowledge of *how* to farm but wasn't fully acting on that knowledge.

Let your dreams challenge you, let them set fires under you, let them release your inner power. Awaken your potential for a limitless life that has been lying dormant. Go off the deep end and explore the real depths of your life.

BE NICE TO YOURSELF

The ability to see life as a classroom can turn obstacles or setbacks into opportunities to grow and feel confident," say Elisha and Stephanie Goldstein, co-authors of *99 Ways to Live a Mindful Life.*

When a self-limiting belief comes to mind, simply notice it, then try responding with something like *This might have been hard for me before, but this is a new moment, and maybe I can learn from it.* A mind focused on learning isn't just about achieving something, it's about constantly getting better.

If a circumstance comes along that shakes your confidence and you feel you *can't,* simply open your mind and be curious, and you might just find that you *can.* When you counter self-doubt with gentleness, understanding, and self-acceptance you'll feel your confidence growing by leaps and bounds. When you make friends with yourself and embrace every part of yourself, you will feel an expansive sense of welcoming kindness and compassion not only for yourself but for everyone else. When you can see the best in yourself, it follows that you will see the best in others. When you have compassion for yourself—when you can forgive your perceived mistakes and shortcomings—you can also forgive the mistakes and shortcomings of others. In this classroom of life, if we keep our mind and heart open to turning obstacles and setbacks into experiences for growth, we will never stop learning.

Prejudice, social inequality, and bullying are a means of trying to raise one's own self-esteem at the expense of another. Basing our own self-worth on constant comparison to others is impossible to maintain for very long. Real self-compassion emphasizes the connection of everyone rather than the belief in separation. As a bonus, real compassion for ourselves also offers us emotional stability because it's always there, whether we're feeling on top of the world or falling flat on our face. In my yoga classes, I tell my students that they are doing yoga for themselves alone, and not to compare what they can or cannot do with what anyone else can or cannot do. Life is not a competition.

Remember who you are, recognize your worth, give yourself kindness and understanding. Don't compare yourself to anyone else, and don't look for faults in another. Remind yourself that a certain amount of discomfort is part of the human experience, and if you remain in a state of kindness to yourself and to others, this, alone, is worthy of your self-love and self-confidence.

ATTITUDE

Life is constantly handing us new opportunities as well as new challenges. Sometimes they encourage us, and sometimes they bury us in the depths of depression. How we see these opportunities and challenges depends on our underlying attitude.

When things go wrong or we come up against difficult situations, we tend to think of the situation *itself* as the problem, but in reality, whatever problems we experience come from inside our mind. When we keep a positive attitude about things and respond to difficulties with a positive and peaceful mind, they cease to be problems for us. We may even come to regard any challenges as opportunities for growth and development. Problems are only problems if we look at them with a negative state of mind. To be free of problems, we simply need to transform our mind and to change our attitude.

Some people have such a negative attitude that they fail to see the good in anything. They just grouse and complain and remain unhappy with themselves and everything around them. Some teenagers seem to *cop an attitude* and think their parents have lost their minds and that *responsibility* is a made-up word. Still others hold an attitude of gratitude. These people are grateful for their good and understand that they have the tools to overcome the not-so-good. They are able to maintain an up-beat attitude.

Barbara Johnson, best-selling author of books with titles like: *Plant a Geranium in Your Cranium* and *Every Time I Get My Act Together the Curtain Comes Down,* remarked, "Attitude is the mind's paintbrush; it can color anything, so always keep it fragrant with positive and loving thoughts."

This quote has become a mantra for me. When things aren't going the way I think they should and I start to see them as negative, I call her words to mind and change my attitude. I look at things differently and see the positive outcomes that can come from temporary negatives.

Attitude influences our choice of action and our responses to challenges, incentives, and rewards. It affects not only actions, but our thoughts, emotions, opinions, and behavior. A positive attitude is a little thing that can make a big difference. Remember this: A bad attitude is like a flat tire. You can't go anywhere until you change it.

YOUR THREE BODIES

I knew a woman who had triplets. She said that having three babies and only two hands became a balancing act. She would take turns holding and nurturing these babies, making sure that no one of them got any more attention that the others. Even as the triplets grew older, when they went out, she would hold one hand in each of her own and make sure one of the children was holding the hand of the third, and off she would go with her chain of children.

This got me to thinking about our own three bodies: our physical, mental, and emotional bodies. If we give attention to one of these bodies more than the others, we become unbalanced. When we spend hours every day at the gym to develop our physical body, our mental and emotional bodies might suffer. If we spend all our time alone at the computer developing our mental body to the exclusion of enjoying the stimulation of developing relationships, our emotional body is left lacking. If we live strictly by letting our emotions take over, our mental and physical bodies don't develop.

It's good to do what we enjoy, but to maintain balance, we must take care of all three of our bodies. Our mental body stays alert by the stimulation of projects, ideas, and deep thinking. Our emotional body is nourished with music, the arts, and by love given and received. Our physical body needs exercise, proper nourishment, and adequate rest. Healthy, successful, peaceful living is not a mystery; it's simply a balancing act.

Do you know someone with a perfectly developed body, one who is toned and has close to zero body fat but who can't carry on a meaningful conversation? Do you know someone who could be called a "geek" because they are so mentally developed that if you ask them what time it is they'll tell you how to make a watch, but whose physical and social skills are lacking? Do you know someone who is deeply emotional, feeling not only their own pain, but everyone else's as well, but who is unable to give words to what they feel, and doesn't have the physical energy to walk around the block? If you fall into one of these categories, you will do well to shift focus on developing all three of your bodies. When you are physically strong, mentally sharp, and emotionally loving, your triplets will grow and prosper, and you'll find that your life will be simpler.

HOW WE LEARN

We sometimes wonder why our education system leaves some children behind, but with our elementary schools packing 30-plus little bodies into a classroom, it's really no wonder. Different people learn in different ways, and when our schools accommodate all learning styles, learning can become a more pleasant experience for the child.

Logical learners use reasoning and logic to understand concepts. Visual learners do best using pictures, diagrams, and colors. Physical learners use their bodies to assist in their learning. Aural learners like using sound, rhymes, and music to enhance their experience. Verbal learners do very well listening to concepts being explained verbally and writing about those concepts. Because curriculums in our public schools are determined mostly by our government, verbal teaching methods are emphasized, which leaves some types of learners in the dust. We all use a bit of all these learning techniques, but most people—not just children—lean toward a single approach.

One of my grandsons is a physical, or kinesthetic, learner. Studying spelling words sitting at a table was a futile exercise. But when he could ride his bike in circles in the driveway as I recited his spelling words, he learned to spell each word correctly, and earned 100% on his spelling tests. He learned best when his body was in constant motion. This was a kid who incited ire in his teachers by fidgeting and tapping his pencil on his desk while doing assignments in class. He needed to be moving to be learning.

In first grade, this same grandson's teacher turned his desk to face the wall, thinking he'd stop his fidgeting. His second-grade teacher had a different approach. If he was quiet in class and didn't disturb the other students, he could have five minutes before the lunch bell every day to tell jokes or stories or do whatever "entertainment" he chose. She called it "Thomas Time." He was then able to sit still, knowing his time would come, and he did very well scholastically. It's the wise teacher who can recognize the learning style of a child and build on it.

The word *education* comes from the Latin *educare* which means to draw forth from within, but the traditional manner of teaching is more like pound-in-from-without. It works for some, but not for all. Our mutual goal in educating our children is to allow them to bring forth their inner greatness. It's in there because we were all meant to be great!

REVENGE

When you are wronged or treated unfairly, is your first instinct to forgive, or to seek revenge? It's human nature to seek revenge, but will getting even really make you feel better in the long run?

People are motivated to take revenge, to get even, to harm someone who has harmed them when they feel attacked, mistreated, or socially rejected. Getting an eye for an eye, Old-Testament style, is thought to bring a sense of catharsis and closure, but there is a growing body of research that suggests it may have the opposite effect. While most of us wouldn't engage in the kind of vengeance that makes the nightly news, or warrants prison time, our everyday lives often include small acts of retaliation, like giving a bad review on Yelp after poor customer service, or spreading rumors about someone who snubbed us, or engaging in endless social media tit for tat.

In ancient times, before laws and prisons, our ancestors relied on the fear of retaliation to keep the peace. Acts of revenge were thought to deter a second harmful wrongdoing, and they also acted as insurance against other future wrongdoings. Revenge served as a warning that they were someone who would not tolerate mistreatment.

"Revenge is sweet," you may think, but studies have shown that although revenge may provide a lift in the moment, any positive effects are short-lived. Getting revenge can make us feel good at first, but when followed up 45, 30, 15, or even just 10 minutes later, subjects in the studies reported actually feeling worse than they did before they carried out these vengeful acts.

Stewing over what someone did to us and thinking about what we would like to do to them in return interferes with our day-to-day well-being and happiness. Feelings of revenge also take up important cognitive resources. They deplete us of time and energy that could be better spent on healthier, more constructive ways of dealing with anger. We can learn to accept any injustice and acknowledge that we, too, may have hurt someone in similar ways. Research suggests that when it comes to valuable relationships, what the "angry mind" really wants is a change of heart. When a victim receives an explanation or an apology, the desire for revenge weakens. This is not to say we should give our wrongdoer a free pass, but staying open to an apology and a chance for the offender to make it up to us, will reap dividends over a lifetime, and that lifetime will become simpler.

LOVE AND JUSTICE

I ran across an article in *Mindful* magazine that I would like to share. It was an interview with Omid Safi, the director of Islamic studies at Duke University. What impressed me was that his thinking about staying in a positive frame of mind and finding peace was no different than any Christian, Jewish, Buddhist, or New Thought teacher. It's about linking love and justice.

He talked about rediscovering the mystery of breath. Creation is not something that took place in some mythical past; creation is a continuing occurrence. We are reborn with every breath we take. The you that exists in this breath—the one you're taking now—has never been before and will never be again. As you breathe, you return to your center, your core. You move from a state of agitation toward a place of peacefulness.

As a progressive Muslim, Safi states that his people are concerned about their fellow brothers and sisters, about all creatures, and about the planet. He points out that there are people in a position of power who thrive on fear-mongering and targeting the most vulnerable in society, and for us to be angry is understandable. But we can't rely on anger to drive the engine of transformation. Anger, by itself, never transforms anything into something more beautiful. When we come back to love, there is a shared commitment about the welfare and well-being of all. Love is not a private thing, love is something we *do*. Love is something we *are*.

Prayer has been ingrained in Safi since childhood. It is to be repeated no fewer than five times a day. He's found prayer to be much more than a mechanical repetition of ritual; it is ultimately a process of one's heart and awareness, of body and breath becoming one, instilling tranquility. Prayer can be a sense of healing not only for the one prayed for, but for the one praying. Even the roses and jasmine in his garden, Safi says, are beneficiaries of sacred presence and attention.

In today's world, with people in power openly exhibiting biases against certain groups based on their religious beliefs, it was encouraging to me to read about the thoughts and ideals of this well-educated, peace-loving Muslim man whose greatest joy is hugging his children, looking deep into their eyes, making sure they know they are loved, and working toward a peaceful world in which to grow.

BOMBS

When we fly on a commercial airline, we are asked if we are carrying anything given to us by a stranger. The airline agent is, of course, making sure no one is inadvertently carrying something dangerous onto the plane. But this same cautionary question is one we can ask ourselves. Are we carrying anything harmful that was given to us by someone else?

We often carry with us thoughts we have adopted from others: beliefs, judgments, opinions, moral values, and even political views. While we can benefit from learning from others, when what we've been taught feels uncomfortable and isn't serving to improve our life, we don't have to keep carrying it with us.

When we feel conflicted, we might want to consider how we're looking at life and at the world. A parent, teacher, minister, or anyone we looked up to and trusted throughout our life may have given us valuable life lessons, but they might also have planted seeds of fear and prejudice. Learning from others is natural, but unless those lessons serve us, they can be harmful, causing us disfunction in relating to others, in financial matters, or in our employment. These misplaced values could be like a bomb a stranger has placed in our luggage.

When we become aware of the damage that can be done by accepting—and carrying with us—thought patterns fraught with unease, we can lay aside those thought patterns and accept that we have the wisdom and the strength to let them go and to change our thinking.

Because my parents and my grandmothers described our family as "private people," feelings weren't discussed and thoughts that might not correspond to someone else's opinions were not expressed. Their reasoning was that by not disclosing anything remotely personal, they were avoiding any possibility of conflict or judgment. For a long time, it was hard for me to express myself because I was continuing to carry those thought patterns. When I recognized my own strength, my own self-worth, and had the confidence to be my authentic self, I was able to leave this "bomb" behind and communicate freely and openly without fear of being misunderstood or judged unfairly.

When we stop carrying "explosives" given us by someone else and feel comfortable with the values we've come to embrace on our own, and can express those values without fear, our life will be simpler.

CHANGELESS TRUTH

Truth is infinite and immeasurable. The allness of Truth, in its absolute sense, cannot be defined in words. Truth is the underlying, changeless reality of the universe. There is an outer side (what we see and interpret), and there is an inner side (what we know in our heart and soul) to everything, and Truth is the key to the inner side. Truth *is* the inner side. On the inner side, no matter what the outer side appears to be, we find God, we find good.

God is the changeless reality, the changeless essence of all that is. It sometimes appears that, through prayer, God becomes more responsive to us, but actually, in a prayerful state ourselves, we become more accepting of what is. Prayer simply sets our own mind at ease. Prayer changes *us*, it doesn't change God. God is changeless.

In this changeable world, we see in people what we determine to be good and what we see as bad, but no person is inherently bad. Some simply act in unacceptable ways. Someone who robs a bank is not an evil person, he is simply a person who did an illegal deed and must pay the consequences. A child who plays in the mud and is dirty from head to toe is not a dirty child, he is simply a child who got dirty and needs a bath. This is a vital realization. Even when people act in what are considered "bad" ways, they can change because they are naturally, innately, a good human being who may be concealing that goodness by doing bad things. There is a changeless reality of God and good at the heart of every person.

God is not an entity that must be flattered or coaxed to come to us. As Alfred, Lord Tennyson put it, "God is closer than breathing and nearer than hands and feet." God is personal and always available. This is the changeless Truth. God is never depleted or overburdened. It takes no more effort for God to animate every person in the world than it does to give life to one newborn baby.

God is Truth, and Truth is God. It's as easy to understand as simple arithmetic. Two plus two will always equal four; that never changes. When an acorn breaks loose from a giant oak, the law of gravity will always allow it to fall to the ground. Gravity is true and unchanging. Truth is always true, whether we believe it or not. The Truth of us is that we cannot exhaust life by living it, consume substance by spending, dissipate ideas by putting them into action, or keep life from being simple by not believing it is possible.

When we understand the changeless truth of God and of our goodness, and the goodness of others, our life will be simpler.

DOGGONE IT

I often look at my cat and think about all the cats and dogs I've had throughout my life—animals eating, sleeping, wandering around my house, trusting me, and in their own way, communicating with me. And I think how strange it is to have "wild" animals living with people.

Dogs are perhaps the first animal to be domesticated, starting with the taming of wolves in Europe and Asia about 15,000 years ago. It has now become customary to have dogs as pets, inviting them to live with us. These domestic dogs have been bred, inner-bred, and cross-bred until, at this time, there are about 340 breeds of dogs, with new breeds recognized every year at dog shows. These dogs vary in size from the Chihuahua (the smallest being Miracle Milly, standing only three and a half inches high and weighing roughly one pound) to the Great Dane (the tallest, Giant George, measuring nearly four feet from paw to shoulder and standing seven feet three inches when up on his hind legs).

Many dogs are soldiers—more than 100,000 have served in the U.S. Military. Police dogs, search and rescue dogs, and service dogs assist their masters, and we all know the spotted Dalmatian on the fire engine.

The Canary Islands were named for dogs, not for birds. Large dogs lived there in ancient times, and the islands got their name from the Latin *Incula Canaria*, which means "Island of the Dogs." The expression "Three Dog Night" came from an Eskimo saying, meaning it is so cold that you have to huddle with three dogs in order to stay warm. The Romans believed that Sirius—the Dog Star—added to the heat of the sun during July and August, creating the *Dies Caniculares*, or the "Dog Days of Summer."

Now that you've learned all these random facts, give your dog a hug! Many health benefits are derived from being a pet owner. Pets, dogs especially, keep us active by playing and walking with them. Pets help us beat the blues . . . who can resist a purring cat or a wagging tail? Cuddling with a pet makes us happy, and feeling the heart-beat of a pet makes our own heart stay healthy. Pets are a social ice-breaker; pet owners like to meet other pet owners. Being responsible for a pet helps bring focus and routine to our life and gives us a sense of purpose. Pets reduce loneliness, which can reduce anxiety and lower blood pressure. Having a pet is *good for you.* These "wild" animals help us to stay healthy and to keep life simple.

THE SECRET OF LIFE

Life is in constant motion. Laws of gravity, cause and effect, and momentum are always at work in our life. Things that we consider blessings happen, and things that leave us feeling sad, frustrated, fearful, or angry also happen. But everything that happens in life offers us an opportunity for learning, healing, growing, and forgiving. When we respond from our heart to the good, or to the not-so-good, we will expand to a greater awareness, and come to realize that the secret of life is to *Live.*

When we live life to the fullest and look at each new day as an opportunity to be creative and expansive and loving, we find our life filled with endless possibilities. The goodness that surrounds us is often so simple that we may overlook it, but if we stay awake and aware, we *will* find it. Sometimes we may be in a funk. It might feel good to wallow in it for a while, but when we remember our reason for living is to *live*, we will come alive, feeling amazingly free, and we will find that there's no way we can stay in a bad frame of mind very long.

Living life is different for each individual person. It is beauty, laughter, and love for some people. For others it may be more complex, or it might appear to be more interesting. For some, life is smooth; for others, life can be bumpy. Whatever path life leads us down, the most important element is that we be authentic—that we be true to ourselves. When we are authentic, we are living the life we were meant to live. If we look at someone else's life, and it seems better than ours, we might want to try to copy it, but it would be just that, a copy, not an original. It would be inauthentic. Only *you* can be the real, authentic *you.*

To be authentic, let your passion for what you love be your guide: Follow your bliss, your heart's desire, and create your unique life as an original. Become aware of the presence of God moving within you, guiding you, and be grateful for this awareness. Celebrate life. Feel its good coursing through your veins. Grow, heal, love, develop, and experience life in every way, every day.

The secret of life is to *live*, so live life! Make your life an original masterpiece. Fulfill your life purpose as you live authentically, and know you have everything you need. You are unique, you are enough, and you deserve to live life with happiness, fulfillment, and simplicity.

DETERMINATION

Things most people view as bad happen all the time to people who are good, and we wonder why. But there is a lesson in everything, and what we learn from those lessons is what matters. With determination, dedication, and a strong will, we can overcome what we perceive as bad.

Denise DeSimone wrote a book called, *From Stage IV to Center Stage.* Denise was a singer and inspirational speaker until a diagnosis of stage IV throat and neck cancer knocked her for a loop. She was given three months to live if aggressive steps weren't taken immediately, and she was told she might never talk or sing again. Her book chronicles her journey through shock, fears, emotions, surgeries, and a hard recovery, but it's mostly about her determination to not allow the diagnosis stop her. She chose not to battle cancer, but to embrace it and allow it to become her teacher. She learned that self-love is the all-time greatest healer. Three years after her diagnosis, Denise was standing on home plate at Fenway Park in Boston, singing the National Anthem before 35,000 Red Sox fans.

Keith, a neighbor of mine, was a strong and very active young man. He somehow developed a brain aneurism, and a mis-diagnosis caused him to have a stroke. As a result, he had no use of one arm and hand, and he couldn't walk. Like Denise, his determination to move on was stronger than any disability or anything else that would hold him back. He gradually learned to walk, though he dragged one foot, and he was able to use the good arm and hand to lift up the bad one. Keith never stopped working to get his strength and his physical ability back, undaunted by anything anyone told him he couldn't do. Now, within just a few years, he has almost full use of his hand and arm, and he walks with an almost undiscernible limp. He's still a young man, with a lot of life in front of him, and he's unstoppable.

Tommy Lasorda, long-time manager of the Los Angeles Dodgers baseball team, said, "The difference between the impossible and the possible lies in a man's determination." Almost anything worth achieving in life will be beset with obstacles, but if we have the drive and determination to overcome those obstacles, we will accomplish our goals. Too many people give up just before they're about to make it. We never know when that next obstacle is going to be the last one before we are able to overcome our challenges.

HOME

I live in a big, old house, too big, really, for one person, or even two, and too old to stay in tip-top shape. I feel a great affection for my house, and my house trusts me to take care of the "big stuff." When things break, I fix them—or hire someone to do it. I replace windows and locks and roofing tiles when they break. I keep the weeds pulled and the grass and plants watered and healthy. I have tree-trimmers thin out the many huge trees when they need it. But I don't "pamper" my house. I do my best to keep it clean, and I rationalize that because it's old, a little dust just adds to its charm. I don't try to keep up with every new trend in *House Beautiful* or *Architectural Digest*. My house is well-decorated, cozy, and comfortable, just as it is.

My house—my home—is my sanctuary for curling up with a good book or spending time writing. It's also an entertainment center for enjoying my visiting family, friends, and especially, my grandchildren and great-grandchildren. There is a swing in the back yard that is tied to a tree limb about 50 feet above the ground. The kids love that swing. They take turns pushing each other, trying to get high enough to reach branches of the nearby redwood tree with their feet. And the grown-ups do the same; a swing brings out the kid in everyone. And, *I* like that swing. Gently gliding back and forth on a balmy evening brings me a profound peace, and any perceived troubles just float away.

There's a "spirit" that lives in my house. I felt it the first time I climbed the stairs. It's a friendly spirit, and it lives on the landing where the stairs turn. A lot has happened in that house since it was built 90-plus years ago, and it holds many secrets. The spirit knows those secrets. There are years of love in my house and that love enfolds me. I love my home and it loves me back.

It's said that home is where the heart is. If traveling is what you love, the home in your heart might be on the road to somewhere. If your heart is in your work, you may feel at home in your office or classroom or factory. Wherever you feel at home, remember to appreciate the gift of that special place. Take time to discover and to celebrate wherever your heart is most at home. My heart's home is my big old house, because life is simple there.

DISCIPLINE

Tantrums are acceptable at age two, but not so much at forty-two. We all have desires—things we want that may not be good for us—and we let it be known that we want them. As adults, we have to know how to control those desires because sometimes they can lead us down a wrong path. You might tell yourself that a second piece of pie won't matter, but the scale might tell you differently. Telling the boss off might make you feel better in the moment, but think how you'll feel when you're out of a job.

Sometimes the flesh—or the ego—tells us one thing, but reason—spirit—tells us another. Flesh and Spirit are often at odds. But there is a still small voice within, guiding us, and it comes down to discipline. If we can maintain discipline, Spirit will win.

My friend, Wally, an avid golfer, came across the set of Callaway irons he'd been yearning for on sale at his local sporting goods store. He was very tempted, but even at the sale price, the clubs were as much as his mortgage payment. Desire and discipline had a little fight, but discipline won out. He couldn't, in good conscience, put his family in jeopardy by spending the money on the clubs and getting behind on his mortgage. Sometimes when desire is so strong that we are tempted to react, and to throw a little tantrum, we can just say to temptation, "You are not the boss of me" and take the high-road to discipline.

God made us emotional beings, but just because we feel something, doesn't mean we have to act on it. It's okay to feel anger sometimes; just don't fly off the handle and do something rash. When we feel hurt; we don't have to hurt back. When someone makes us angry or offends us, we don't have to respond in kind; we don't need to defend ourselves. It's better to reach a reasonable compromise. Remember, when people are angry or offensive toward us, it's more about them than it is about us. If we have to disappoint ourself by not getting something we really want, we can remember that something better might be in store for us. Even the two-year-old's tantrum can be abated with a calm offer of a substitute, as long as the parent is disciplined in his or her reaction.

We can take ego off the throne and let the still, small voice be our teacher. We need to be consistent. This is not something we do one time, then we're done; it's an on-going discipline, and a disciplined life is a simpler life.

WHAT IS LOVE?

In a *Peanuts* comic strip by Charles Schulz, Peppermint Patty says to Charlie Brown, "Tell me what love is, Chuck." Charlie says, "Well, years ago my dad owned a black 1934 two-door sedan and, this is what he told me . . . There was this real cute girl, see. She used to go for rides with him in his car, and whenever he called for her, he would always hold open the car door for her. After she got in and he had closed the door, he'd walk around the back of the car to the driver's side, but before he could get there, she would reach over and press down the button, locking him out. Then she'd just sit there and wrinkle her nose and grin at him. That's what I think love is." Patty, shaking her head, responds, "Sometimes I wonder about you, Chuck."

I have to wonder about Chuck, too. With her grin and wrinkled nose, the girl might have been flirting to show affection, but in that scenario, if Charlie had said the girl reached over and pulled *up* the button on the driver's door so he could get in, that would be what love is. Love is consideration, kindness, giving, respect, trust, compassion, appreciation, acceptance, intimacy, and comfort.

The physical senses can't perceive love; it isn't seen with the body's eyes or heard with the body's ears. Love is the intuitive knowledge of our hearts. Love is being aware of the needs of another and of reaching out with actions that are helpful. Love isn't the value that we attach to things like money, cars, houses, or prestige. These material things mean nothing, and love for them is loving things that can't love us back. There's a song that goes: *Love isn't love until you give it away*. And when you give love away you receive love in return.

God is love. God has always been the energy and the thought of unconditional love. Love is all around us, but because our world hasn't fulfilled its potential to love, we don't always feel it. In fact, it's hard to imagine a world filled with love. But if everyone really knew love, felt it in their hearts and passed it on to each other, there would no longer be wars, there would be no hunger, there would be no environmental breakdown. There would be no prejudice, oppression, or violence. There would be only peace.

According to *A Course in Miracles, We seek not to find love, but merely to find the barriers we've built against it.* Let's break down those barriers to love. Let's pull up the button on the car door. Let's show someone who gives us love that it is appreciated. In short, let's Be Love, When the barriers to love in our own life are down, perhaps our little part of the world will follow.

ASSERT YOURSELF

We live in a world where just about everyone wants their opinion known. This is usually beneficial to society because without differing points of view and original ideas, nothing new would ever come about. There are different ways, though, for people to voice their opinions. They can be aggressive or they can be assertive, and there's a big difference between the two.

Aggressive people attack the opinions of others, or ignore them altogether, in favor of their own. They tend to interrupt and talk-over others, and they speak loudly, often getting off-message. They intimidate by glaring, standing or sitting rigidly with arms crossed, and they invade others' personal space by pointing or shaking fingers. Aggressive people tend to dominate groups, not considering the feelings of others, and they sometimes hurt another to avoid being hurt themselves. They use exaggeration to make their point, and although they often get their way, they are seen as rude or unkind.

Assertive people, on the other hand, will state their opinions while being respectful of the opinions of others. They tend to speak more softly, using a conversational tone, make eye-contact while speaking, stay on message, and show expressions that match that message. An assertive person is a participant in group discussions, letting others be heard, reaching goals without hurting others in the process.

It's sometimes hard to assert ourselves in the face of an overtly aggressive person, but it's something we can all learn to do. We can speak up confidently when we have an idea or an opinion, simply ignoring the glares of the aggressor. We can stick to our opinions without being influenced by someone who wants to change our thinking. If an aggressive person makes a demand that makes us uncomfortable, that we don't have time or resources to fulfill, or if we simply don't want to comply, we can assertively turn them down by saying something like, "That just doesn't work for me." Assertive people can, diplomatically and kindly, insist that their rights be respected. An assertive person can say, "I disagree" rather than, "You're wrong." Assertive people can impress by respecting ideas and opinions of others and by being grateful for positive, helpful input and criticism.

Both aggression and assertiveness can get us what we want, but we'll be much happier when we get it with calmness, composure, and evenness of temper.

THE HERO

As we move through life, we seek support for a number of things. We might be moving through an illness, changing careers, or stepping into a new phase of living: getting married, becoming a parent, getting divorced, or aging, and we want a deeper relationship with our authentic self.

At some point we realize we might be making life harder than it needs to be. We begin to notice increased frustrations, resentments, or disappointments. Or we feel as though we lack the time, money, or creativity to turn our dreams into reality or to change our situation and make our life better and more rewarding.

This is where our Hero steps in. The Hero, a term used by teacher and philosopher Joseph Campbell, is an architype of what keeps us moving forward through life. Our Hero is that part of us that remains constant and courageous no matter what is happening around us. Our Hero is our authentic self.

When you get bogged down with worry, frustration, or feelings of lack, and life seems to be too difficult, you can rediscover The Hero within you. Simply ask yourself: *Would it be okay if my life got easier?* Just asking this question connects you to the divine in you, the guidance that is always available. Then ask yourself; *Am I willing to be authentic?*

Being authentic is the quality of being real and genuine. If we are willing to be authentic, we will find, and focus on, the qualities that make us who we are, and we can affirm their importance in our life. To understand what being authentic means, we can tell ourselves, *I am willing to be courageous, loving, creative, and kind when I interact with people today.* We can start with today. New habits and beliefs about ourselves are built one day at a time.

We build on habits and beliefs by *observing* rather than *analyzing* our life. When we analyze, we stay engaged in the same self-talk that has stopped us from moving forward up to now. But when we *observe*, we give ourselves space to figure out what's happening and then act with wisdom. If we're willing to say *yes* to what is, even in situations that are causing discomfort, we are accepting the facts of the situation but not their power over us. *Yes* changes the energy in our body, and our courageous heart opens up. *Yes* lets The Hero take charge, and lets acceptance open us up to new possibilities, then we clearly see the choices that are before us.

SAMSUTA

The Buddha spoke about the practice of *Samsuta,* which is the recognition that we have enough to be happy right here, right now, no matter how much we have or what we think we lack.

Whatever we are, whatever we have, it is enough. Happiness isn't determined by how much we have; happiness is realizing that we can be satisfied with a little or with a lot. It makes no difference. When we view all the conditions of enjoyment that we already have in our life, we will find they are more than enough for us to be happy right now.

We keep running after things that we think we need to fill some void, but even if we get the object of our desire, we find we still aren't completely content, and we run after another desire. This is because it's not *things* that make us happy, it's *thinking.* Happiness is a choice, and when we sincerely choose happiness, fully feeling it in our heart and in our mind, we find it.

You may have planned some activity or attended an event that you just *had* to do in order to be happy, then found some disappointment in the actual activity or event because you'd held your expectations so high that nothing could have satisfied your anticipation. When you can learn to take life as it comes and allow what comes to bring you happiness, you will find that even a blooming flower, the soft fur of your cat, a cleansing rain, or just finishing a chore can bring you happiness and peace of mind. But when you never stop striving for something more and something better, you will never find true, fulfilling, gratifying, comforting happiness.

God's will for us is perfect happiness, and God wants us to be happy so that the world can see His love through us. Living the practice of *Samsuta*—reflecting that we all have enough to make us happy here and now—is one of the greatest gifts we can give to those around us.

GET MAD OR GET EVEN

When someone does something that you don't like or that makes you feel bad, is your first impulse to get mad, or do you want to get even? Do you want to get back at them in some way?

When you get angry, your anger doesn't really hurt anyone but yourself. Anger is a corrosive emotion that can affect your mental and physical health, and the person you're angry with doesn't really care. When the person who hurt or angered you did whatever it was that set you off, he wasn't thinking of consequences, or he wouldn't have done it in the first place. Thinking you'll get back at this person by hurting or getting even are retaliatory thoughts; acting on them will hurt you more than it will hurt that individual. Plus, planning or carrying out revenge can be exhausting.

There is another way to respond to bad treatment, and that is to change our mind, to rise above thoughts of anger or revenge. We can't always know why people act the way they do, and if we get mad or try to get even every time we are wronged, we are simply exacerbating the situation. If we can look at an uncomfortable circumstance with an open heart and an open mind, we might be able to see beyond the perceived provocation, the hurt, or the threat, to the pain in the person who has hurt us. Otherwise, we will be hurting someone intentionally and keeping everyone concerned in an unhealthy frame of mind.

Anger can actually be handled productively. When we stay calm and work on understanding our anger or our desire to get even, then we can communicate our feelings in a constructive, assertive manner that will be less likely to hurt anyone.

It's natural to feel anger at times, but we can't allow it to take over our life or even to ruin our day. Keeping our cool, looking at upsets from a different perspective will teach others how to behave well. When we show anger, anger grows in the other person, and no one wins. If we "get even" by retaliating in a negative way, we are inviting more bad treatment.

Getting mad or getting even can interfere with your job, your relationships, and your social life. Sometimes it's best to just consider the source and walk away.

DID I DO THAT?

I'm pretty sure that at some time in your life your parents, teachers, or others in authority have said to you, "You should be ashamed of yourself" when you did something amiss. But that kind of shaming sinks deeply into a child's psyche and can color their long-term view of themselves, leaving a permanent mark on their character.

For you, in adulthood, feeling shame doesn't have to be a life sentence. When you do something or say something out of place, thereby hurting another, the shame of this can usually be overcome with a sincere apology. The replacement of something that was broken, or payment of a long over-due debt, can wash away shame.

Embarrassment, more than shame, is what we experience in our lives. For example, if we've ever tried to sneak into a meeting or class late and tripped or dropped something, causing a noisy disturbance, we feel so embarrassed that we want to fall through the floor. After going about our business all day, we discover we have something green in our teeth from lunch, we re-live the afternoon to determine just who we feel the most embarrassed about having seen this. How many times have we been introducing someone we know well to another person, hoping they will say their own name because we've momentarily forgotten it?

Embarrassment arises from different scenarios, but there's always a common thread of blundering in front of others and, in that moment, fearing it makes us look bad. But embarrassment is a fleeting thing. In fact, we can often find humor in the whole mishap. We might be embarrassed by having been socially out of step, but it doesn't mean we were morally so.

Maybe a better way to admonish a child—or anyone, for that matter—would be to ask, "Are you embarrassed by doing that?" Embarrassment comes and goes, but deeply ingrained shame can affect a lifetime.

When a child begins life without having had negative thoughts drilled into him, and, instead, gets positive how-could-you-have-done-this-differently feedback, that child's life will be simpler. And if everyone kept in mind affirmative thoughts rather than contrary ones, *everyone's* life would be simpler.

THE COMPLETE PERSON

Everyone has a story. We may think we know someone well—a friend, family member, or work associate—but behind the exterior, the obvious, there is an underlying story that contributes to the part of the person that we don't see. Some stories portray positivity and creativity, while others show someone as limited and self-defeating. We all seem to be in such a hurry that we don't take time to tune-in to our friends and colleagues and to get to know them on a deeper level . . . to know their story.

There may be someone we know who is positive and up-beat, exhibiting the potential for abundance, but underneath this façade is a person who has fought the dragons of an abusive or neglected childhood, and has slain those dragons. If we can take the time to hear this person's story, we will gain an even greater respect for them. There might be another person who appears to feel limited, to have low self-esteem and sees his or herself as a victim, but who, in reality, has the same underlying potential for greatness. Rather than dismissing this person as a loser, we will gain a better understanding of them if we take the time to listen to, and hear, their story. We might even be able to build their self-confidence by offering our loving support.

We see each other through filters and lenses. We get an initial impression of someone when we first meet them, and what we see, with no more information than what comes through our filters, is what we believe about them. We rarely step back and ask whether what we learn from that initial impression is supportive or destructive. But when we open our minds to learning their story, seeing more than we thought was there, the impression changes because the lens clears up. Getting to know someone's story is like meeting them again for the first time.

You, too, have a story. Don't be afraid to open yourself up to sharing your own story. Orson Wells said, "If you want a happy ending, that depends upon where you stop your story." Sharing stories that have shaped our lives doesn't make us weak, it makes us human. When we share stories of defining experiences, we connect with others on a deeper level, beyond the roles we play.

Sharing stories means revealing our own vulnerabilities and helps others to reveal theirs. Disclosing stories, sharing life-altering moments, helps us get to know the complete person and lets them get to know the whole of us.

LET ME HELP YOU

In a dream, I was working for a company that hired contractors to rebuild houses which were destroyed in the wildfires in northern California. Each contractor submitted a normal bid, and after reviewing the bids, the company narrowed the field down to five, then interviewed each of them, asking questions that had nothing to do with construction. They were "feeling" questions to determine whether the contractor was bidding the job simply for the almighty dollar, or because he felt the desire—and the need—to help those who had been displaced. The vivid memory I have of the dream is the face of one of the contractors. It was a ruddy, well-worn face, obviously someone who was used to hard work. The eyes in this face were full of love, and the mouth formed a smile that went straight to the heart. That's all I remember of the dream, but that face has stayed with me.

This dream made me think more about how tragedy brings all manner of people together. A man I know, who has lived a sketchy life, in and out of jail, loaded his trailer with bottled water, non-perishable foods, and personal items like toothpaste and soap, and delivered them to still-full evacuation centers two weeks after fires had destroyed homes near where he lives. He even put bales of hay on the trailer to help feed livestock that had been taken to safety.

Area churches came together, preparing and serving food to the evacuees. Children set up stands to sell cookies and lemonade, donating the money they made to relief efforts.

This is just a smattering of many stories of strangers helping strangers. These stories of kindness and compassion remind us that we are all connected. The face of that contractor in my dream showed the kind of love that lives in all of us. Love for our fellow man. Love to offer to those in need. Love that we all have in our hearts but too often keep hidden. And I wonder why it takes a tragedy to bring people together to demonstrate that kind of love and caring

Coping with the challenges people face after a great loss becomes more bearable when they can rest assured that there is someone out there showing solidarity and kindness. When we can be open to helping each other, together we can ease the trauma and allow the stress to dissipate with the smoke. If we all do our part to build a selfless society where the needs of others are as important to us as our own, where we can maximize kindness, helpfulness, and gentle generosity, this world can become a better, more peaceful, kinder place, and everyone's life can become simpler.

UNITY DAY

Today is National Unity Day. This designation came about in 2011, and is the signature event of National Bullying Prevention Month. Individuals, schools, communities, and businesses are encouraged to wear or display orange on this day to show support for students who have been, or are being, bullied.

I am encouraged by our country's recognition of the proliferation of bullying, especially in our schools, and that we're standing up for reform. Whatever it takes to unify the people of the world and to make life simpler for all of us is to be celebrated.

In the comics today, *Zits* by Scott and Borgman, showed a great demonstration of Unity Day. Jeremy, Hector, and Pierce are in the cafeteria carrying their food trays, trying to figure out where they want to sit. Hector says, "What about that table?" and Pierce answers with, "Dude, Andy's sitting there. He's super-awkward and unpopular. Nobody sits with Andy." In the final frame, the three boys are approaching the table where Andy is sitting. Hector says, "Hi Andy." Pierce says, "Sup?" and Jeremy asks, "Mind if we join you?" That was Unity Day in action. When we make friends with the underdog, his self-esteem grows, and the bullies may not see him a target anymore.

It's easy for an adult to tell a youngster who reports bullying, to neutralize the situation by simply not engaging, but it's not always that easy for the young person. The hurtful comments, and sometimes physical harm, stay with the child and can affect them for the rest of their lives.

Children are not the only ones who are bullied. Some adults are also treated badly. If we could all adopt an attitude of joining with someone who might not have the self-confidence we have, and who's life could be changed by being accepted, the bullies of the world might take notice and stop treating people they feel they can overpower with cruelty.

Let's celebrate Unity Day, acknowledging that we are all children of God, each with the gift of our own unique talents and capabilities. Let's celebrate the ways in which we are alike and the ways in which we are different. Let's be blind today; blind to skin color, sexual orientation, religious beliefs that differ from our own, and anything else that we think makes another unlike ourselves. Let's treat each other with kindness, acceptance, and inclusion. Let's let the bullies know they are not in charge. Let's make life simple with random acts of kindness. Let's accept and include those who may be hurting. Let's let love have all the power today and every day.

G.I.F.

There is a whole new language afoot. Recent studies show that up to 93% of communication is now non-verbal, that we relate to others with more than just spoken words. And there are actually some advantages to this.

One reason for the preference of writing vs speaking is that we can massage the message. When speaking to another, we might inadvertently blurt out something that hasn't been thought through, causing the message to be interpreted in a different way than it was intended, and it's impossible to un-say something once it's out. Written missives like e-mail and texts allow us to read over our message and to change it as needed before clicking *send*. We can also add emotion to the message by using pictures.

For a while, to soften or emphasize a statement, we added a colon, a hyphen, and one parenthesis to create a happy face or its opposite, a frowny face. But things have advanced past this, and now emoji—little round faces with myriad expressions—are available on almost all cell phones, tablets, and computers. To soften or strengthen a message we can add the expression that corresponds with the feeling we have when writing it.

Emoji originated in Japan but weren't popularized here until 2007, and the choices of expressions are expanding every day. Plus, we have hearts, birthday cakes, firecrackers, food, animals, and a ton more choices to add emphasis or clarity to our written text.

Just as we thought we had the whole non-verbal messaging thing figured out, though, along comes G.I.F. (Graphics Interchange Format). These GIFs are much flashier than emoji, and that's where the appeal lies. They are split-second pictures or film bites that replay again and again. GIFs are heavily pop-culture oriented and can add excitement to a message. But, hang on! I've got about as much excitement in my life as I can handle, so I haven't delved into the world of "giffies" yet. Life, to me, is keeping things simple, and I can do that with verbal interaction, with emails and texts, and with emoji in electronic messages, and that's all I need for now.

I know I'm behind the times when it comes to technology. I didn't grow up with it, and I get frustrated by so much new stuff. But my frustration vanishes when I remember that I am perfect just the way I am, with what I know, and with what I can do, and my life is simple.

BEATITUDES

It seems everyone these days wants a better life and is looking for a way to get it. That's why the shelves in book stores are packed with self-help books; we want to learn how to fix all our problems. That's why I've written these pages: to help and to guide people in achieving their goal of a happy, simple life.

The answer to attaining a happy, peaceful life has been available to us for centuries; it's in the Bible—the Beatitudes from the Sermon on the Mount (Matt.5:3-11).

Blessed are the poor in spirit, for theirs is the Kingdom of Heaven. Being poor in spirit means to be humble, and humility makes us teachable.

Blessed are they that mourn, for they shall be comforted. We all endure some kind of sadness in our lives, and if we never knew suffering, it would be impossible to know strength and compassion.

Blessed are the meek, for they shall inherit the Earth. The meek that Jesus speaks of are those who are gentle, kind, patient, and tolerant, not proud, mighty, or self-absorbed.

Blessed are they which hunger and thirst after righteousness, for they shall be filled. When we show our love for God and for our fellowman, we will find contentment.

Blessed are the merciful, for they shall obtain mercy. There is no better exercise for the heart than to reach out to help another.

Blessed are the pure in heart, for they shall see God. When we strive to live the life God sees for us, our motives and actions will be honorable and our hearts will be pure.

Blessed are the peacemakers, for they shall be called the children of God. When we keep ourselves and those around us from friction and discord, and when we work to understand each other so we can live together in peace, we are living in God.

Blessed are they which are persecuted for righteousness' sake for theirs is the Kingdom of Heaven. We may feel pressure from society about the way we live and the things we believe in, but if we are proud to stand up for our principles and are the best we can be, we will find happiness

Jesus taught these principles centuries ago but they are just as true—and attainable—today as they were when he spoke them. When we are rich in love and kindness, with a caring heart, we have all the riches we need. If we remember these words, and live by them, we'll find that life will be simpler.

NEW GROWTH

Several years back, I wrote a poem about new growth, and how tragedy can become a blessing. I sent a copy of it to a good friend when she was going through a tough time. Several years later, when I was dealing with a loss, she sent it back to me with a note saying a friend had given the poem to her and it meant so much that she felt I might need reminding. Here's the poem:

It's late October
in the middle part of California.
Green is beginning
to peek out on the brown hillsides,
showing first in the areas
blackened during August's raging heat
and torrid winds
fanning quickly-moving fires.

Changes in nature make me think
of changes in my own life.
New growth . . . fed by fires of before.

My life has been altered . . . and matured
by experiences, like fire,
tragic at the time.

But, just as fire is nature's way
of fertilizing her land,
so, experiences work to promote
new growth in me.

It's really true that no matter how hard it is to go through tough times, there really is light at the end of the tunnel. If we can keep our heads when things go wrong, we will find something better—new growth— at the other end.

MIND OR BRAIN

A Course in Miracles tells us *Fear binds the world; Forgiveness sets it free.* Whenever we hold on to perceived injustices, we're living in a kind of fear, and our ego (the belief in separation) is telling us that we need to "fight back." But since, in reality, we are all one in God, who are we fighting? Ourselves? The workbook of the *Course* contains exercises designed to bring about the experience of love, forgiveness, and oneness, not just "book learning" that tells us what to believe. The real answers to the world's problems are not found in the intellect (the brain), they are found in the mind, in the heart, in the choices we make every moment of every day, in the shift from a state of conflict to one of peace.

We've always assumed that our eyes see the world, our bodies feel what we see, and our brains interpret it and determine our actions. But, it's not what our eyes see that creates our life experiences; it's our *mind* that's telling our eyes what we're seeing and how to interpret it

There is a difference between the brain and the mind. The brain's function is to *think*, to pack information in and figure things out, while the mind *feels*. The mind is the feeling center of our body that creates the experiences we learn through. Both are needed to make wise decisions. The brain gets the necessary information, and the mind determines the most beneficial way to continue.

Using the brain, human beings tend to blame each other for their lot in life, and this results in the loss of peace that, in time, will feel like a permanent fixture of their existence. Someone or something can always be found to be the cause of our problems (except for those tortured souls who blame themselves for their own unfortunate circumstances). But whether blaming ourselves or someone else, we're still blaming a body, and it isn't bodies that hurt one another, it's brains. Even bullies in school are, in effect, saying, "We're cool, you're not." Extreme religious sects are proselytizing, "We're going to Heaven and you're going to fire." When this false sense of guilt is raised to the surface, fear is the result.

When we are ruled by our *mind*—the activating agent of spirit which supplies creative energy—we live in a state of forgiveness. Our body's eyes see what our minds direct, and if we keep our minds in a state of peace, we will experience peace at all time. We will be free, and life will be simple.

LINDA

When I lost my sister, a piece of my heart flew out of my chest. She had a ruptured aorta and died very soon after reaching the hospital. It was so sudden that there was no time to say goodbye. I felt so many emotions all at once: shock, sadness, anger. I thought, if this was *Grey's Anatomy*, they would have taken her right into surgery and saved her. But that's a television show, and this was real life. I miss her every day.

When we lose someone we love, it makes us think about our own mortality and brings up things that are really important in life. Each of us was put here on Earth to learn, to love, to appreciate who we are and to share all this with others. None of us knows when this experience we're having will end. It could be taken away at any moment. Maybe this is God's way of telling us to make the most of every single minute we have.

To really appreciate life, we need to take time to notice something beautiful as often as we can. There is beauty all around us; beauty that goes unnoticed until we make ourselves aware of it. We can notice the way the sun casts shadows of ordinary things. We can stop to enjoy the fiery sky of a sunset. We can take a look around our home and take notice of things that give us pleasure. The beauty around us isn't always something we can see, though; it could be the smell of a flower, or newly mown grass, or bread baking in the oven. It could be the sound of the breeze through the branches of a tree, a bird singing, the crunch of fall leaves under our feet, or the laughter of children at play.

Let's take time to notice the beauty of this world and to cherish it. This is the real "stuff" of life. It's the little things that are here to enjoy. It's the things we so often take for granted. Let's let the people we love know that we love them. As we get older, it's not the things we did that we often regret, it's more the things we didn't do.

In the words of Phillip James Bailey, "We live in deeds, not in years; in thoughts, not breaths; in feelings, not in figures on a dial. We should count time by heart-throbs."

Let's remember to love and help each other. Let's go barefoot in the grass. Let's get a double-dip ice cream cone. Let's do whatever warms our heart. Let's enjoy every moment, and let's live life simply.

Today is my sister's birthday. Happy Birthday, Linda.

THE PAST

The only thing we really know for sure in life is what has already happened . . . the past. We have many good memories of the past, but, for some, the past is full of fear, and those memories of fear are carried into the present. Memories of the past, though, are not always accurate. We remember wrongs done to us and wrongs we have done, but with a shift in perception, looking at things more clearly, we can see the past and everything in it differently.

It's only the past that makes us fearful in the present. Young children don't hold memories of past events that give rise to fear in the present. That's why they so often seem lacking in fear and take chances that we grown-ups would be afraid to.

The past is gone; nothing is left except a memory, and memories are nothing but the play of thoughts in our mind. Consider an ocean wave. We see a wave building and crashing onto the shore, then it's gone, all its energy dissipated. With no sign of the wave left, we may wonder if it really happened at all. A wave is nothing more than physical energy in water—here one moment, then gone the next. It's like that with the past—here one moment and gone the next. That wave has not affected the ocean, just as events of the past need not affect us in the present or change the way we view the future.

We may assume that our distorted memory of the past is telling us something about how we should be viewing our present life when, in fact, it is simply telling us about our state of mind. Our perceived fears are only reflections within our own mind. When we bring our mind to peace, knowing that events of the past are distant mental energy and have no power over our present or our future, we see clearly through the veneer of fear we have placed over reality. Any fearful memories now lie placid and calm on the shore, their energy completely gone.

A big part of leaving the past behind lies with forgiveness. When we forgive those who have wronged us and forgive ourselves for holding those wrongs in our mind, it's like the wave dissipating and becoming simply foam on the shore. Paul Boese said, "Forgiveness doesn't change the past, but it does enlarge the future." Letting go of bad memories of the past will make our future much brighter, and life will be simpler.

DON'T THINK ABOUT IT

On this Halloween Day, our thoughts turn to spooks. One of my favorite comic strips is *For Better or Worse* by Lynn Johnston. In a recent strip, little Lizzie is in bed holding the covers under her chin and clearly afraid. She asks big brother, Michael, "Do you think there's any spooks in my room?" Michael answers, "Of course there's spooks in here! They're in your closet, they're under your bed, they're lurking in the shadows . . . watching . . . waiting." Then he starts to leave the room, when Lizzie cries out, "Wait! How do I keep them from coming to GET me?" Michael says, "Easy. Don't think about them." Not thinking about spooks might have been hard for little Lizzie, but Michael was right; thinking about things is often scarier than the things themselves.

How many times have you felt anxiety or even fear about something and driven yourself crazy by thinking about what you're fearing? First day of school or first day on a new job can bring up fears: What if they don't like me? What if I mess up? But, when you stop obsessing about what could go wrong, you usually find that things actually go very well. Whatever thoughts you *feed* are the ones that will win and rule your life. When you give in to thoughts of fear, you will remain fearful and afraid. When you hold thoughts of love and peace, confidence and self-worth, happiness and fulfillment, that is what will win and guide you in being your true self.

It's not that hard to do. When we start a project, or a new job, or even a new relationship, we can step into it with full confidence that it will work out well for us. We can push away any thoughts of failure that might sneak in, and live with that confidence.

I quit using the word *can't* a long time ago because if I think I can't, I won't. Henry Ford said, "Think you can, think you can't; either way you'll be right." So, think yourself safe from the spooks that you've imagined are lurking in the shadows; think yourself healthy, happy, and successful, and that's what your life will be.

(And welcome the happy little spooks that come to your door tonight.)

MINISTRY

I attended a workshop at which the featured speaker was a retired Protestant Minister. What she had to say, of course, held to her religious belief and training, and she was eloquent. In conversation following her presentation, one of the attendees remarked that she *was* a great minister, but that we are *all* ministers. And she was right . . . we *are* all ministers, not schooled in theology perhaps, and not an ordained member of clergy, but ministers all the same, ministering through love, caring, and kindness.

To minister is to attend to the needs of others. Doctors are ministers, giving curative care to the sick and injured. Social workers are ministers, seeking and finding much needed assistance for those in need. Educators minister as they train or mold students, drawing out newly discovered or deeply hidden information and concepts. There are cabinet members in government who are ministers and work in specific areas of politics. In Europe, whole governments are led by Prime Ministers. And, of course, one of the greatest ministers of all was Jesus, who walked among the people of Biblical days, spreading the good word, performing miracles, and teaching, by his own actions, how to live and how to love.

When we give a hand to our fellow man, we are ministering. When we offer kind words of praise, appreciation, and approval, we are ministering. Many famous authors minister through their writing. I am ministering as I teach my yoga classes. Sharing gifts of time, talent, and knowledge is ministering. We all minister when we offer a smile or a friendly hello to the people we encounter.

Even as we raise our children, keeping them safe, clean, and well fed, we are ministering. When we teach our children right from wrong and demonstrate kindness, love, and forgiveness, they learn to be kind, loving, and forgiving. Even in teaching children how to swim, or ride a bike, or to drive, we are ministering.

We can also become ministers to ourselves by staying strong, remembering our worth, holding a positive attitude, and not being led down a rocky path or accepting less than we deserve as beloved children of God.

Be a minister of what you are . . . You are love!

UNCERTAINTY

We think certainty, knowing what the future will bring, is what makes life simple, but it's *not*. The only things certain, as they say, are death and taxes. But the good news is, there is a certain excitement to uncertainty, an invisible reality that can make life more interesting.

When we think happiness depends on something expected in the future, we are chasing rainbows. Life is ever-changing, and the only way to make sense of change is to plunge into it and move with it. Trying to live in absolute certainty is like trying to pack water into a paper bag or put wind in a box. Nothing is certain, and if we learn to live with this knowledge, life *will* be simpler.

Not knowing outcomes creates a sense of uncertainty. For instance, when we enter into a new relationship, there is mystery and some mystique that holds our interest and keeps us coming back, even though we don't know the outcome. When we start a new job, there are things to learn that are new to us, and we feel some uncertainty. When we try a new restaurant, we are never certain which entrée will please us the most. Even when we prepare dinner from a new recipe, we can't be certain it will look like the picture in the cook book.

There is uncertainty in almost every undertaking, and if things don't go as we'd planned, we can see it as a learning experience. We can learn to accept failure or defeat with our head held high and our eyes looking forward with confidence instead of self-recrimination. Sometimes defeat is a gift, it frees us to try something else.

Uncertainty can make life exciting. As we go through each day, we come to learn to live in the wisdom of uncertainty because tomorrow is often too iffy to make plans.

Go ahead and plant your garden, but don't feel defeated if your tomatoes aren't plump or your flowers don't bloom as profusely as you'd hoped. The only thing that is certain is your strength to handle anything that comes along, that you can accept disappointments and come away from them stronger, and that you are secure enough in your own worth to learn to live in the wisdom of uncertainty, staying open to all possibilities.

HAVE A GOOD CRY

Are you sad, disappointed, angry, frustrated, lonely, or stressed in any way? Do you feel like having a good cry? Go ahead. Bring on the tears. Crying is good for you. It releases toxins and relieves stress in your body. There's a physiological element to crying. When we're stressed, certain hormones and other chemicals are activated, and crying reduces the levels of these chemicals, which reduces stress. Experts have theorized that crying may be a way of excreting chemical byproducts of stress, thus helping restore the body's chemical balance, reducing the effects of stress.

There's a difference between chemical tears and the tears shed while slicing an onion. Studies have shown that emotional tears contain protein, and that certain key neurotransmitters in the brain associated with stress are present in the tear glands and trigger tears in times of stress. Crying helps release tension and pent-up emotions and we feel refreshed and better able to cope after a good cry.

Many people, especially men, feel that crying is a sign of weakness, and they hold the emotions inside. This is not surprising because these same studies found men are far less likely than women to openly cry, and a smaller percentage of men said they felt better after a cry than did women. Holding on to emotions, not releasing them, can have an adverse effect on the heart and other organs. And releasing emotions through crying is far safer than lashing out in anger. So, let the tears roll.

It's comforting to know that there are many benefits to crying. It helps relieve pain; children cry when they get an "owie" and get past the pain more quickly if they can cry into mommy's shoulder. Crying activates the parasympathetic nervous system, which helps people relax. That's why babies tend to sleep better after crying. Tears fight bacteria and improve vision by washing out the eyes and keeping them moist. After a good cry, we usually feel better and less stressed, and that alone should be reason enough to turn on the waterworks.

And there are happy tears. I can't watch a bride walk down the aisle without crying. Newborn babies make me cry. I get choked up looking at a beautiful sunset and when hearing *The Star-Spangled Banner*. I've always said that when I cry, it's emotion coming out of my eyes, and after seeing these studies, I think that's true.

EXCUSES

Along with dozens of quotes, jokes, wise advice, and positive thoughts I have taped to the wall over my computer is one that says, "A man who is good at making excuses is rarely good at anything else." Having this in front of my face every day reminds me to take responsibility for my thoughts and my actions, and stops me from making excuses about anything.

Jon Tapper, in his book *Don't Bull***t Yourself,* points out that "Excuses are the common denominator of failure; they paralyze us." When dealing with having to face up to mistakes or wrong doings, our first impulse is to create an excuse. By doing this, we are rationalizing those mistakes or wrong doings and trying to make them okay. If we hadn't done something we shouldn't have done or if we didn't do something we should have done, we wouldn't need an excuse. Making excuses is actually a way of acknowledging our mistakes.

We make excuses for a variety of reasons, the biggest one being fear. When we told our teacher that the dog ate our homework, we did it because we feared reprisal for not doing our homework. Another reason we make up excuses is to intimidate others. With our well-crafted excuses we give the impression that we think we know more than the other guy, and he believes us. He might even become convinced he caused our problem. We also make up excuses in certain circumstances to cover our own bad choices. Excuses replace action. If we can get by with a good excuse, we don't have to take responsibility for inaction. And when we don't step up to self-accountability, we can blame our shortcomings on someone else with excuses.

Life really is simpler when we just fess-up to the truth, do whatever we can to right a wrong, and stop making excuses. Even the best excuse-makers can change this habit by recognizing excuses as thoughts, and knowing that thoughts can be changed. Every time we start to make an excuse, we can simply stop ourselves and start over with the truth. Making excuses is a waste of time. To become results-oriented, we need to consider how we can do the right thing rather than creating a reason for why we can't. We can find answers, not excuses.

We don't want to accept excuses from others, either. Excuses are usually easily recognized as just that, and by blindly accepting them we are crippling the excuse-makers and enabling them by not making them accountable. Tapper says, "Excuses are poison—don't let them come into your mouth."

BABY STEPS

Swedish Missionary Jonatan Mårtenssen said, "Success will never be a big step in the future; success is a small step taken now." We may have a project in mind and have a vision of what the final product will look like. It's too bad we can't just propel ourselves to the end, but we know we can't. We have to take the first step first.

Watch a baby learning to walk. He doesn't one day just pop up off the floor and start walking; he gets onto his feet, puts one foot out, then falls over. He gets back up, this time putting one foot out and then the other before he falls. In a few days, this baby can take a few more steps, and within weeks he's walking unaided.

While our vision may certainly be worth pursuing, when we get down to actually making that vision a reality, we have to do it one step at a time. Someone may tell us it's an impossible task, and we may even tell ourselves that, but if we keep going, taking lots of baby steps, it will come to fruition, and we will have a sense of job well done.

When I decided to write my book *For the Love of Yoga*, I had a vision, but not much more. I began writing on January first, and really thought the book would be published by the end of that year. Boy, was I wrong! I guess I thought I could walk before taking the necessary baby steps. Since it's an instructional book, I *had* to get it right, and it took four years of research, writing, formatting, photographing, recording the CD, and finding a printer to produce the book with the spiral binding I needed. But it happened, one step at a time. The book's final manifestation matched my vision perfectly. Today, that book is helping those who are purchasing it by changing bodies, attitudes, and lives, and that's my reward. If I had rushed through the process, the outcome wouldn't have been as satisfying. The book wasn't one big step, it was countless baby steps.

If you have a vision, don't try to rush it. It will take baby steps to accomplish your goal, but it will be worth it. Above all, don't let anyone stand between you and your dream. It may not seem important to someone else, but it is precious to you. If you should stall along the way, don't get discouraged. Keep taking those baby steps, and eventually you will walk the world of your vision.

PEACE

A Course in Miracles tells us *There is no peace except the Peace of God.* You've felt moments of pure peace throughout your life, I'm sure, and you might think they come from a happy relationship, a successful job, or a noble purpose you've worked for. But when you've pinned your hope for permanent happiness on these things, you find they are all of the world and can have an ending, making them a temporary peace. Everything in this world ends. No matter what course we follow, no matter how hard we strive, we end up losing everything in the end and find that we have been seeking happiness where there is none. When we give up the futile search for happiness and peace through our bodies and the world, we will relax into the peace of God. We are all children of God, and God's will for each of us is perfect peace and happiness.

The peace we're seeking begins with a new perception of the world, seeing the world as a classroom, not as the end all, be all. Peace is letting go of what we think the world is for and allowing ourselves to recognize its true purpose. We're here in a body, and bodies were made for communication and nothing more. Peace isn't found in bodies; peace is found in the mind. When we are in nature, it's not surprising to feel a deep peace in its beauty. We feel this peace in our body through relaxation, but the real peace is in our mind, and it is our mind that communicates to our body how to feel. When our mind feels peace, it tells our body to feel peaceful and our body responds, but that peace can be lost again when another stressor comes along.

When we change our minds about the purpose of the world, leaving behind conflicting goals and meaningless pursuits, and lay aside all hope of finding happiness where there is none, we will find the peace of God. We will even see peace in chaos and joy in misery.

We already have the peace that comes from God within us. It's part of our created being; it's real and it's eternal. It's a simple way to leave the world of ambiguity and replace shifting goals. We can find it through forgiveness and by giving up the futile search for happiness through our body and relax into the peace that our mind holds for us. I find personal peace through these words from the *Course:*

> *There is no peace except the peace of God,*
> *And I am glad and thankful for this.*

THINKING MAKES IT SO

One thing I know for sure is that if you want change in your life, you simply need to change your mind. It was Wayne Dyer who wrote, "Change Your Thoughts—Change Your Life."

When I was diagnosed with breast cancer, I had a choice; I could either cry and carry on, asking, "Why me?" Or I could accept it as a fact, take whatever steps necessary to get through the experience, and come out wiser in the end. I went through the excruciating pain of biopsies, three separate surgeries, and many months of radiation that caused the most profound fatigue imaginable. But I did come through it.

I could have chosen to let this experience define me, but it's all in the past now. I don't think about it, I don't talk about it, and I'll never call myself a cancer survivor. I didn't "survive" anything, I simply did what I had to do and followed instructions. Others might have a different experience when faced with an unwanted or uninvited circumstance, be it an illness, an injury, the death of a loved one, or even a job loss, because they don't know the truth that no matter how bad they feel, they have it within themselves to overcome and to see the situation differently. Some pain is inevitable in life, but suffering is optional.

We all came into this life to learn lessons, and if we regard hard lessons as "disasters" and slip into a poor-me mentality, those disasters will come to define us, and we will entertain ourselves with an on-going pity-party. When we recognize them as lessons, however, we can rise above our self-pity, correct what needs to be corrected and move on to helping others who are having a hard time.

When something in my life doesn't feel right to me, I stop, think, and maybe meditate on the feeling. Then I can discover what the lesson is. My most recent lesson was to stop stressing about my yard. We've undertaken a large landscaping project, and now the rains have begun, putting any work on hold. The truth in this scenario is that I can't change the weather, nor can I continue with the work in the rain. I know this is true, even though it's a bit distressing, so I can rest into it, knowing the job will be completed in its own time. I can change my thoughts.

Even when you don't feel at peace, you can *think yourself happy*. It's simply a matter of choice.

LIFE-TEAM

When my sons were young, they both played on city sports leagues—football, basketball, and baseball. Mike's team was clearly champion, winning almost every game they played, and Steve's team had about a 50/50 winning record. (Although Steve was probably the best first baseman in the whole league.) What was good about both these teams was that their coaches were positive and supportive of the boys, win or lose. When they won a game, they celebrated together, acknowledging it had been a team effort and that they'd all played a part. When a game was lost, the coaches told them not what they did wrong, but what they did right. It was a *you gave it your all, I'm proud of you, and you should be proud of yourselves* kind of encouragement.

As we travel on this rocky road called life, there is a baffling blend of win and lose, happy and sad, conflict and peace. It's never just one or the other; it's always some of both. And when we can embrace conflicting emotions with peace, grace, and honesty, we know what it is to be truly alive.

We're all on this journey together. We need to care for each other, teach, protect, and encourage each other. We must be able to rely on each other. We are a kind of life-team, and when we keep the needs of each team member in mind, we will win more than we lose. It's a matter of faith, a belief in humanity, and being practical, to make sure we all survive. When we work as a team, every team member is responsible for all the others. When one wins, we all win.

Even though peace is our natural state, there will be some conflict from time to time. We don't have to search for it, because it has a way of finding us. In order to resolve conflict, we need to do our best to understand it. Then we can figure out a way to work through it. And the best way to resolution is to find peace within ourselves and offer that peace to those around us.

Some things that the coaches drilled into the boys were: Stop shouting and listen. Don't name-call; instead, say what you have to say with respect. When a conflict arises, use your words to resolve it, not your fists. When you ask questions, wait to hear the answers. First try to understand before trying to be understood. Be polite but persistent when you know what you need or have a good suggestion. Do your best in every game, and in the game of life. Be proud of your efforts and those of your teammates. Finally, always show up for practice. When we show up and practice peace, our life will be simpler.

MISPERCEPTION

Perception is a funny thing. Two people can see the exact same thing, but each will perceive it differently. I might see a rose as a beautiful, fragrant flower, while someone else might see it as a thorny plant, always in need of pruning. It's all in perception.

We also see other people, and even ourselves, from differing perceptions. Perception is a dualistic form of knowing, requiring a seer separate from what's being seen. Therefore, what we are seeing is always a symbol, an imperfect representation, and for this reason, perception is often misperception.

Guilt and innocence in ourselves and others are almost always misperceived. If I see guilt in myself, I don't like what I see, so I try to get rid of it by projecting it onto another. I then see that person as guilty because I *want* to, and I think seeing the guilt in others will get rid of it in me. If you think this sounds a little insane, you're right, but that's the way our less-than-peaceful brain works. To correct misperception, we must recognize when we're not at peace, when our life doesn't feel simple, and realize we've decided wrongly. We can *decide* to see others as innocent, and when we've truly made that choice, we will see their innocence as well as our own.

We see what we believe is there, and we believe it's there because we *want* it there. Whatever we see in anything, a person, a situation, or a rose, stands for what we want to be the truth. We see results from choices we've made about what we *want* to see, and we respond to what we *think* we see. This is obviously not always how it seems to us because we are convinced we are seeing what we are seeing and that's the way it is. But no matter how much it seems that way to us, we are misperceiving; we are responding *only* to what we *want* to see, not what is really there.

Then what is real? Love is real. Love is the only reality, and when you see everything with love, love is all you will see. When you perceive things—even tragedy, upheaval, and wars—from love, you will find only love and forgiveness. You will accept that everyone doesn't see everything in the same way you do. They may not have discovered how to let life be simple.

Life is simple when it is seen through the eyes of love. When you don't like what you see, it may be a misperception, but when you keep love in your heart, what you perceive will be seen with love.

AGING

Aging is a given. It's been happening longer than any of us have been around, so you'd think we'd have accepted it by now, but many of us are still fighting.

Through my life, I watched my grandmothers age. I saw hair turn white, faces wrinkle, and I had to talk a bit louder. My grandmothers were beautiful to me at every age, and with evidence of aging came increased wisdom, so I never stopped learning from them. But lately, a booming "anti-aging" industry has emerged. We're told if we purchase special vitamins, herbs, creams, hair coloring, and other youth-enhancing chemicals, we will promote longevity. There are even "anti-aging" clinics where, for a few bucks, we can freeze off fat or have a nip here and a tuck there to keep us looking young forever.

Being aware of aging and taking steps to keep our body healthy and fit and our mind sharp, does make sense. Why not stay vital and healthy as long as possible? But there is a glitch in our design, and as much as we try to avoid accepting it, knees, hips, hearts, and other body parts weaken. We can't do the physical activities we used to do, and when we look in the mirror expecting to see our 20-year-old selves looking back at us, we see a spot here and a sag there and little lines everywhere.

But, what if wisdom, connection, depth, and richness of spirit come with age? What if, in aging, we grow closer to our Creator? What if, with the busy days of earning a living, raising a family, and a whole lot of heavy responsibility behind us, all we have to do to stay present is to forgive whatever may be keeping us chained and advance into the best part of our life? Realizing that we are older today than we were yesterday is part of being alive.

Older people have a happier outlook and better coping skills when faced with hardships or negative circumstances. Older people don't have to "impress" anyone, so they are more comfortable just being who they are. They also have more time to pursue long-held dreams and passions they may have put on hold. Older people have decades of experience, the gift of time, and a wiser perspective to pass along to younger generations. And, let's not forget benefits like senior discounts for dining, entertainment, and travel.

Aging is easier if you start when you're younger. Treat your body like you'll need it for 100 years. Never stop learning and growing because idle minds atrophy. And, don't forget, age is just a number; you are only as old as you feel.

THANK A VETERAN

Major hostilities of WWI were formally ended at the 11th hour on the 11th day of the 11th month in 1918 when the Armistice with Germany went into effect. The U.S. first observed this day as Armistice Day, but it was renamed Veterans Day in 1954 to encompass all military service members. Veterans Day is a time to reflect on the brave men and women who boldly step up to defend our country's freedoms. It is a day set aside to honor members of our armed forces, past and present, and to show gratitude for their service.

Most non-military people tend to take for granted that there will be those who valiantly enlist in the armed forces and who, as a group, will keep us safe in our homes, on our streets, and in our country. But for those who are serving or have served, or those of us who have close family members who have served or are serving, the day has a special meaning.

There will be parades today with heroes marching, but as Roy Rogers said, "We can't all be heroes; someone has to sit on the curb and clap as they go by." Veterans Day is a great day to do just that, to show our appreciation from curbside. We can fly the flag today to show our support, and when we see someone in uniform, we can thank them personally. If they feel like talking about their service, we can honor them by giving them our full attention. They deserve it. We can also volunteer at a VA hospital. Even if we don't actually interact with a veteran, it's a good way to give back.

Don't confuse Veterans Day with Memorial Day; to do so diminishes the importance of both. Veterans Day is a time to thank and show support to those who are currently serving, or have served, and are still with us. Memorial Day, in March, is a day to reflect and remember those who made the ultimate sacrifice for their country—losing their lives.

As we live our individual lives, we have a way of thinking of Veterans Day as just another day off work, a day to have a picnic or to watch a football game. We overlook the important meaning of the day. So today, and maybe even every day, make it a point to thank a Veteran.

COMMUNICATION

Getting our message across to another can sometimes be as confusing as this explanation of communication:

Communication is the consideration and action of impelling an impulse, idea, or thought from Source point across a distance to Receipt point with the intention of bringing into being at Receipt point an exact duplication with understanding of that which emanated from Source point. Huh?

We intend to have what we say understood by another, but what we say isn't always what is heard because it's received through the filter of another mind. This leaves us thinking: Hmmmm. I know you think you understand what you thought I said, but I'm not sure that what you heard is what I actually meant. It's like the child's game of telephone with the message changing as it's whispered from child to child.

A single word can alter even the most important message. Mark Twain said, "The difference between the right word and the *almost* right word is the difference between lightning and a lightning bug." Sometimes the most important things we need to communicate to another are the hardest because thoughts are greater than words.

Unless we all had ESP, we can only project a thought with words, and words can diminish the thought. If you doubt this, try describing *love* in words, or *God*, or *elation*, or *deep sadness*. All too often, when we communicate with words, the recipient isn't listening, so no matter how well we express ourselves, our message falls on deaf ears and is lost.

Walt Disney had it right when he said, "Of all our inventions for mass communication, pictures still speak the most universally understood language." That's why we seem to remember television shows and movies better than if someone simply told us the stories with words. For this reason, Skype and Facetime have made communicating more effective than simply talking on the phone. I tend to talk with my hands and find myself gesturing when I'm on the phone which, of course, means nothing to the person I'm talking with.

Communication can also become confusing when we talk too much. Too much talk tends to turn off listening ears. Let's take the hint from Plato's words, "Wise men speak because they have something to say; Fools because they have to say something."

PAUSE

We live in an age of speed and accomplishment. We go more places and do more things than there is time for. Industry, ingenuity, and technology have made our country great and have also made our lives easier, but it may be time for us to decide whether we're going to let machines and high-technology master us, or if we are going to master them and keep ourselves in rhythm with the universe.

When we find ourselves with so much to do and wonder how we can get it all done, it might be time to pause and take a break. Whenever we're rushed, we're out of tune with the universe, and hurry won't get us back in tune any more than racing the engine of our car with the gearshift in neutral will get us where we need to go. Only when we pause and release thoughts of hurry can we find the stillness and peace that will revitalize us.

Quietness seems to suggest something soft and easy, but it isn't. Quietness is strength. Only the very strong person can be quiet, and only the quiet person can be strong. It takes strength to discipline ourselves to stop every now and then, to pause and take a breath.

One of the big problems of the industrious get-it-done-now person is cramming life full of every conceivable activity and taking pride in never having an idle moment. But what we need in order to keep from burning out is to discover the pleasure of pausing. Sometimes we're in such a hurry that we can't tell if we rush because we feel things are urgent, or if the habit of rushing makes things appear urgent. Sometimes when it seems that we must *do it now*, it might be better to do it tomorrow instead, to save our sanity.

To keep life simple, we all need to learn the art of pausing. We need to put off the thing that is causing us tension and take time to let the subconscious mind help organize ideas and solve problems. We need to let our souls catch up with our bodies and get back into tune, to dance with life, stretching and resting in rhythm with the universe.

We can give thanks for this realization: *For everything there is a season, and a time for every matter under heaven.* (Eccles.3:1) We can resolve that we won't be rushed, and that we don't necessarily have to "do it now." That will make life simpler.

WISH VS ACTION

Beyond the news of the day, local sports, and the comics in the hometown newspaper I read daily, I like to read the advice columns. There was a woman who wrote in saying her husband always celebrates his own birthday with cake and company, but he never makes plans to celebrate her birthday and to make her day special. She said she can't seem to get her husband to see how hurt she feels by this oversight. When I read this, I said, "So, tell him how you feel." And the columnist's response was, "Have you tried telling your husband how you feel?" (Maybe I should be an advice columnist.)

The point here is that we can't just *hope* someone will get it—whatever "it" is—by wishing it so. Dropping hints doesn't work because too many people don't pick up dropped hints. Besides, sometimes these hints are misunderstood and we end up with something other than what we think we're asking for. When we want something from another, we need to be specific. We need to *say* what we need. We need to be clear and direct.

Husbands, wives, other family members, friends, bosses, even the butcher and the hair stylist aren't mind-readers. We have to give them something to *read*. Stating directly what we want is our best chance of getting it.

How much of your time is spent *wishing*? How much is spent *acting*? If you wish you could dance. Take action. Take dance lessons. If you wish you could take a vacation trip. Take action. Plan a get-away. If you wish your lawn was mowed, or your house was painted, or your kitchen faucet didn't drip. Take action. Mow, paint, or fix. If it's beyond what you can do yourself, find someone to do it for you, and make sure to explain exactly what you want. Taking action is the only way to turn your wishes into reality.

The letter-writing woman could, after telling her husband how she feels, ask him to help plan a birthday celebration for her, inviting friends, making dinner reservations at her favorite restaurant, and asking hubby directly, not subtly, to get a cake. In time, if her action is clear enough, and he's willing to listen, he'll get the message.

Life really is simpler when you stop wishing and communicate your wants and needs rather than hoping someone will figure it out on their own. You can't read another's mind, so it follows that you shouldn't expect anyone else to read yours. Make life simple—wish for what you want, then take action.

GIRL POWER

Even with an increasing interest in gender equality, our country hasn't quite caught up. There is a glass ceiling that is yet unbroken. People in power—especially women in power—are working hard to bring about this equality, and they're winning, just as the brave suffragettes won the battle for a woman's right to vote back in 1920.

A personal experience with gender discrimination occurred in my journalism class in high school. The class members nominated two students to be elected editor of the school paper. I was one of those nominees. The other was Dick Shockley. (Yes, I still remember his name.) When the votes were counted, there were an equal number for each of us, so the instructor voted to break the tie. She voted for Dick because, she declared, he was a *boy*, and editors of newspapers were *men*. Talent and ability didn't come into play in her decision; it was simply a boy vs girl issue. Girls and women have come a long way since my high school days, and we're still fighting.

For many years, women were considered the weaker sex and were taught to be subservient to men. In fact, in some religious sects and even in areas of our own country, this kind of thinking is still in place. But girls and women are standing up to outmoded ideas more and more today and demanding their rights. Women, as a whole, are becoming stronger. We're teaching our daughters to speak up and ask for what they want and need, and women all over the country are helping and supporting other women. We're celebrating women's accomplishments, and we're speaking up when we see women disrespected.

Unfortunately, old thinking plays a big part in holding women back. If all people were self-assured enough, if they fully understood and acted on their own strengths, they could see these strengths in all people, and they could successfully work alongside anyone rather than feeling that men have to have the upper hand. What might be called assertive, stern, or commanding in a man is often called aggressive, bossy, or pushy in a woman, and this is unfair.

People must overcome feelings of insecurity and look at others as their equals rather than as objects. We can be advocates for all women and any other disrespected human being. Men and women are equally effective leaders, working side by side to make homes, businesses, and our country, work more successfully. With a release of discrimination, life can be simpler, not just for women, but for all.

MIRRORS

There's a Bo Diddley song that says: "You can't judge an apple by looking at a tree. / You can't judge honey by looking at a bee. / You can't judge a daughter by looking at her mother. / And you can't judge a book by looking at its cover."

It's easy to look at someone's outer appearance and make initial judgements about them, but these judgments can be skewed. Everybody seems to have a pre-conceived idea of how others should look, act, and think, and when someone doesn't live up to those ideas, we often judge them unfairly.

If you meet someone new do you immediately impose certain expectations? Are they physically attractive? Do they seem to be intelligent? Is there something about them that attracts you or something that you find offensive? Or do you take them at face-value, accept them just as they are, and try to learn as much about them as you can before forming any opinions?

What you may not realize is that we are all mirrors to one another. This is a hard concept for some to accept, but traits that you see in another are also traits that you have in yourself. When you judge others and see a trait you dislike, it's very likely you have that same trait, and you don't like it. It's also likely that when you see something you admire about another, you also admire that same trait in yourself.

Just as we can't judge the content or value of a book by looking only at its cover, we can't make good assessments of people based on what they look like on the outside. We have to look inside to learn the value of a book, and we also have to look inside a person to learn who they really are and to recognize their value.

We don't want to be in a hurry to judge people by first impressions. As we get to know them, we will decide if they are someone we'd like to get closer to or not, but at least we've given them a chance.

When we see an attribute in someone else, remember, *we're looking in a mirror*. Before judging, we need to take a good look at ourselves. First impressions of others can be first realizations of our own characteristics—sometimes good, sometimes not-so-good. We can't change someone else, but if we see something in ourselves that we don't like, we have the power to change any feature, quality, or habit we don't like, and enlarge upon the qualities, mannerisms, and quirks that we do like. Recognizing that we see a little bit of ourselves in everyone we meet, we can accept it or change it, and life will be simpler.

SURVIVE OR SERVE

Not all lives run smoothly. Many of us have faced hardships, losses, illnesses, painful situations, even abuse, and we've somehow survived. Some of us try to simply put these experiences out of our minds and move on, but sadly, the memories of those times lay dormant in the subconscious and continue to affect our lives.

Sometimes when we've lived through a lot of unwelcome experiences, even surviving can lead to "catastrophic thinking"—continuing to live in fear that the worst will happen no matter what. The best way to get past that kind of fear is to embrace what we've survived, to lean into the pain, loss, unhappiness, or danger. As Robert Frost so wisely put it, "The best way *out*, is *through*." We have to go through the feelings and emotions rather than trying to avoid them in order to get past them. This is not always easy, but it is the most effective way to get our *self* back.

On the other side of darkness is light, and to make our way through the shadows—the fears, sadness, and lack of confidence— to find the bright side is to accept what we've come through and to know it's behind us. It happened, but it's not happening now, and then we can leave it behind, recognizing and believing, that we are deserving of all the good that is waiting for us.

When we find the bright side we can say, "Ok, I'm here. Now what am I going to do?" When we're free of the pain, sadness, and fear of the past, we will start on a new journey. We may not know where we're going to end up, but if we keep our mind open and value our ability to feel, connect, and trust that we can handle whatever comes along, we'll know we will be okay, that we will survive.

A survivor is a person who continues to function and prosper in spite of op-position, hardships, or setbacks. On the other hand, people who continually talk of their troubles aren't listening to themselves, let alone looking for a way out. Such an individual could be called a "servant," a servant to the desire to keep running away instead of going through. This is *serving* his problems rather than *solving* them.

Be a survivor, not a servant. You can find your way *out* by making your way t*hrough*. When you've tried this and know it to be true—and you can live it—life will become much simpler.

ATTITUDINAL HEALING

At a seminar led by Gerald Jampolski that I attended years ago, Attitudinal Healing concepts were discussed. Dr. Jampolsky taught that love is total acceptance and total giving, with no boundaries and no exceptions. Attitudinal Healing is learning to look at life in a way that makes it possible for us to walk through this world in love, at peace, and without fear. It requires no external battles, only that we heal ourselves.

As an exercise, a woman who had been experiencing pain for a long time, was asked to stand before the group and to hold love for everyone in the group as everyone in the group held love for her. This transfer of love—this accepting and giving—lasted about ten minutes. There was no expectation of hearing how the exercise affected the woman because that would have been to put judgments or presumptions on the experience. But I felt such a strong, powerful sense of healing through all this love that I wanted to learn how to do it for myself.

This kind of group experience is indeed powerful, but you *can* also do it for yourself. It's not just physical pain that can be alleviated through this exercise, it's also negative beliefs about self-image, self-worth, self-confidence, and all the things that hold you back from loving yourself freely and totally. It isn't done with the intellect, which is how most of us feel we need to learn new things; it is done experientially.

Dr. Jampolsky believes that Attitudinal Healing, when practiced properly, will allow anyone, regardless of their circumstances, to begin to experience the joy and harmony that each moment holds. The mind can be retrained when we begin by holding strong, genuine, powerful love *for ourselves* for just two to three seconds. As we gradually add seconds, then minutes, then hours, eventually the experience of love and peace will extend throughout a whole day. As day follows day, this self-acceptance, this self-love becomes what we believe and what we live.

Although it wasn't expected of her, by the end of the seminar, the woman who'd been the focus of this powerful love felt she needed to express that she felt free of pain for the first time in many months. The powerful exchange of love, both giving and accepting, had left her with a deep feeling of love for herself. When you feel a strong love for another, it's hard to escape feeling love for yourself.

JOY IN THE JOURNEY

There are so many high, remote, hard-to-reach places on our planet that are accessible only to the most hardy, athletic dare-devils that we "town-folk" will never see except in National Geographic or on the Discovery Channel. But in a *Wumo* cartoon, writers Wulff & Morgenthaler had a good idea. A couple of guys in full climbing gear are part-way up a mountain when they look to the side and see an elevator full of people relaxing and drinking wine on their way up the mountain. The caption reads: "On their fourth climb, Thomas and Willy discover another route up Kilimanjaro."

Through our lives, we face many "mountains." There are obstacles, hurdles, draw-backs, and problems that we encounter, and we often have a hard time getting up and over them. When we remember, though, that we are not defined by our difficulties, but how we respond to those difficulties, we can stay positive, and our lives become simpler.

I've always loved a challenge—not Kilimanjaro—but every-day challenges that frame and change my life. I've found that when I'm more interested in reaching a destination than in the journey that gets me there, I often hit snags and setbacks. So, to reach the destination without stress, I choose to relax and find joy in the journey.

Life *is* simple if you will let it be. It may not be as simple as an elevator ride up a mountain, but if your purpose in life is to simply advance from point A to point B, you will miss a lot along the way. When you can relax and reach your destination slowly, forging your own path without footprints to follow, you will enjoy the journey more.

Challenges should not make us bitter, they should make us better. There is wisdom to be found in challenges, and they can make us or break us, it all depends on how we respond to them. If we welcome challenges and see them as opportunities for growth, they won't stop us on our journey, and we won't become stuck by identifying with them. We don't grow when things are easy, we grow when we are challenged. If we are never challenged, we will never realize what we can become.

Although an elevator up a mountain seems like a good idea, those riders won't experience the feeling of accomplishment that they'd get from actually challenging that mountain and coming out on top. Whatever our challenge, we can choose to find joy in the journey.

LIVE YOUR STRENGTH

I had a very weird dream one night. I was in a rather large house with people that I didn't know. The people were equally divided between men and women. In the house were little shut-off rooms, like cells, into which the men locked up the women. I kept releasing the women from these cells, encouraging them to flee the house, but none did. In the dream I was so focused on getting those women out of a bad situation that I became imprisoned myself. All I really had to do was to leave and take with me any women who wanted to go.

I felt frustrated when I woke up because I'd wanted to *fix* the women's predicament. But we can't fix other people's problems. We can offer suggestions, advice, and appropriate aid when asked, but then we have to allow them to work through their own hard times in their own way.

This dream made me think about the many women—too many women—who feel they must stay in abusive situations for financial, emotional, or other complex reasons. Abusers often convince them to stay by saying they're sorry, that they love them, and that it won't happen again. The same thing happens with women abusing men, although we just don't hear about that as much.

We were never meant to be mistreated. None of us! We are all valuable human beings. We are children of God, created for happiness. But we have to *believe* this about ourselves. We have to learn to recognize our good. We have to remind ourselves every day that we are whole, healed, and worthy of the best in life. We have to find the strength—and we do have that strength within us—to remove ourselves from any situation we find uncomfortable. No one needs love from an abuser. Loving ourselves and having enough respect for ourselves to know that abuse is not normal, it's never acceptable, and it's never connected to love, will help us find the strength to take care of ourselves

Don't be one of the women in my dream. You don't have to look for or find strength, because you already have it within you. You simply need to bring it to your consciousness and *live* that strength.

DISTRACTIONS

As we work on an assignment, project, or any task—whether at our employment, a household chore, a hobby, or whatever holds our attention—there will always be a certain amount of interference or distraction. This distraction is often the compulsive need to check our cellphone for Facebook, twitter, or text messages every five minutes or so. This switching of focus, taking our attention away from a task-at-hand, impedes the achievement of our goals and makes us less effective.

Constant competition from all the goodies on our phone and other screens means we engage in what Microsoft scientists call "continuous partial attention." We don't get our minds deeply into any task or topic because that distraction is there to tempt us.

Before the lure of the phone sitting next to us, distractions took effort—like getting up to make a sandwich. Now, because they're right there beside us, it takes considerable effort and mental resources to *ignore* distractions.

Signals from the prefrontal cortex in our brain run down to the visual cortex, suppressing neurological activity, thereby filtering what the brain's higher-order of cognitive regions have deemed irrelevant. If all this brain activity is working properly, distractions won't take our attention away from what we're doing; the distractions will be unimportant so they can be ignored. The problem is, according to neuroscientist Adam Gazzaley of the University of California at San Francisco, that the same prefrontal regions are also required for judgment, attention, problem-solving, weighing options, and working memory, all of which are required to accomplish a goal. If the brain is working overtime to resist distractions, it still isn't fully functioning to finish that term-paper, monthly report, sales projection, or other goal that it's supposed to be working toward.

What's the answer? To make life simple, we can simply leave our distracting devices in another room while we keep our attention on our task-at-hand. Those Facebook, twitter, and text messages will wait for us. We won't be missing anything except the distraction, and our goals will be accomplished with less stress, in less time, with less risk of error . . . and life will be simpler.

CAN WE TALK?

With the holidays approaching, you will likely be attending a number of parties with family, friends, and co-workers. Most people in these gatherings are smart enough to know that it's best not to bring up touchy subjects like politics, religion, and other topics that can carry widely divergent opinions. But there is often one person who's looking for an argument. When this happens, you can handle it in one of three ways: 1) you can simply walk away; 2) you can take the bait and fight to be right; or 3) you can be a respectful adult and listen but not challenge.

No real good can come from getting into an argument. When someone challenges our perspective, we can show that we are listening, but that we are not someone who blindly follows the views of another. Thoughtful people show respect for other thoughtful people, even if they don't agree. This may come as a surprise to some, but it *is* possible to disagree and not call names or raise voices. When we are respectful, we might find that through these conversations we can learn something or be able to see things from a different perspective.

Humans are social animals. We all have different lives and experiences, which ensures that we all have different views. It's good to share these views without needing another person to fully agree with them. We learn from each other, and it's healthy to have positive exchanges as long as everyone keeps their cool and conversations don't devolve into heated tirades.

When we know our audience, when we can feel comfortable that a word of disagreement won't set somebody off on a tangent, we can simply listen and really hear what the other person is saying. We can usually find some common ground and come away feeling good about the other person and about ourselves. Differing opinions or the need to prove someone else wrong so we can be right, is not worth losing our peace over. Righteousness feels good; peace feels better.

FAMILY TIES

We all have families. There are mothers and fathers, brothers and sisters, aunts and uncles, and cousins. There are also husbands and wives and *their* fathers and mothers and other family members. We create new families when we have children. Webster defines "family" as *a social unit consisting of a group of persons closely related by blood.* But as we go through life we also connect with people outside our blood-line who become like family

Family, to me, are people who understand you, who "get" you, people who know exactly who you are and stand by you, people who see what you need and are there to help and support you, and people you feel the same way about. We say we love our families, but love is not just a word, it is a *feeling*. We have a family of origin toward whom we may or may not feel loving.

In the families we're born into, there may be friction, and there may even be abuse. The children in these families may strike out and find a new family, a tribe of people who think like they do. Sometimes this is a good thing, sometimes it isn't. But however we relate to our family of origin, even if it's uncomfortable, there's an emotional tie, an almost inexplicable feeling of loyalty that can sometimes feel confusing. We can't blindly expect someone to treat us a certain way just because they're family, and this is where our family of friends can help. Their presence, love, and support can help us understand that we can't always fix family relationships, but we can give thanks for the ones that work. And we can cleave to our family of friends.

We hear about families that are abusive or filled with friction. My family of origin was very different. There was no friction, no disagreement, no waves on my pond. I didn't know about these possibilities until I married and my new life was no longer friction-free. I hadn't learned to handle differing ideas and opinions, and I reverted back to my family of origin for their quiet comfort. This had a negative impact on my marriage that took some work to get past.

Most families are full of love, even during frustrating times. At this season of Thanksgiving, consider reaching out to family members, and to your family of friends, not by social media, but with a phone call or a visit if possible. Give thanks for your family, your friends, your tribe; *feel* your love for them, and feel their love coming back. Family, whatever its makeup, is truly the tie that binds.

BLAME

We've all played the blame game. It's a common reaction to want to blame someone else when things go wrong. In a *Pickles* comic strip by Brian Crane, Grandma, while walking with Grandpa, exclaims, "OW!!!" Grandpa asks what's wrong, and Grandma, bending to rub her foot, says, "I stubbed my toe. Darn YOU!" To which Grandpa responds, "Me? What did I do?" and Grandma replies, "Nothing. Whenever I stub my toe, I automatically blame whoever's nearest to me at the time." This, being a comic strip, is funny, but the sad thing is, it's all too true. It's human nature to want to lay blame on another when something hurtful happens to us.

Joe Martin gives another twist on the blame game in a *Mister Boffo* cartoon with legislators at a table and the capitol building in the background. The man at the head of the table is saying, "Let us not look for someone to blame. Let us search, instead, for someone to accept accountability." Again, humorous, but too true. Politicians are skilled at deflecting blame because they don't want to be seen by their constituents as coming up short.

The antithesis to blaming is to recognize, and to admit, responsibility in ourselves. Blaming is an unconscious self-defense mechanism. It's a form of delusion or denial, projecting feelings or emotions onto someone else rather than admitting or dealing with these unwanted feelings one's self. Wise words from the *Tao-te-Ching* tell us: "Failure is an opportunity. If you blame some-one else, there is no end to the blame. Therefore, the Master fulfills her own obligations and corrects her own mistakes. She does what she needs to do and demands nothing of others."

Confucius also had wise words to impart about blame: "In the archer there is resemblance to the mature person. When he misses the mark, he turns and seeks the reason for his failure in himself."

This isn't to say that we must take responsibility for everything that goes wrong in our life. Sometimes it *is* the fault of someone else, but we need to be conscious of what happens and the how and why of these happenings. More important than laying, or even taking, blame, is to look at how a circumstance can be corrected and take steps to make things better. Grandma could have simply commented that she stubbed her toe then soaked her foot in Epsom salts when she got home. Blaming others causes hard feelings, and it's difficult to let life be simple when there are unresolved feelings.

BEST FRIEND

I don't want to creep you out, but if you have a dog, your every move is being watched. There is nothing you can do that your dog is not aware of. Your dog is learning something new from you, and about you, every day.

Your dog knows that any time the doorbell rings there's someone on the other side of that door, and it becomes either an exciting event or an opportunity to protect you. Your dog waits outside the bathroom door while you're showering, and he's as happy to see you when you come out as he would be if you'd been gone for days. He also knows that when you put on your walking shoes and get the leash out, you're about to take a walk together. Just the sound of the dog food container being opened makes him salivate. Your dog learns what's acceptable and what's not from the tone of your voice and the subtle movement of your hand.

Your dog learns from you, but you can also learn from your dog. The number one thing your dog knows that you might not, is how to live in the moment—to feel the moment, to embrace the moment, and to become every moment. Your dog uses all his senses in the world around him; he sniffs it, feels it, hears it, and engages in it. Your dog is fully forgiving, and his love is truly unconditional. When you've had a bad day and take your frustrations out on your dog with impatience and harsh words, his love for you won't be affected or diminished. He accepts you with peace and grace, no matter what.

You can talk to your dog without fear of being judged. He will listen without comment, allowing you to vent. Your dog will always be joyful. Happiness, for him, is just a ball-toss away, and there is always a sloppy dog-kiss to let you know things will be okay.

Dogs trust that most people are innately good, and that if you greet them happily and treat them with respect, your interactions with them will be comfortable. Your dog can also teach you to stand your ground. He will growl or bark when he feels threatened, and this lets you know that you, too, don't have to take guff from anyone and that no one can make you feel threatened unless you allow it.

Your dog can teach you that there is great beauty in quiet stillness. He can fall asleep just about anywhere, and he doesn't waste time worrying that he might be doing something in the wrong way or at the wrong time. He takes life as it comes, greets every moment with enthusiasm, and is truly a loyal best friend.

MOCHA FRAPPUCCINO

Some people can work or study in the corner of a coffee shop with the constant movement of people, cappuccino machines roaring five feet away, and an angry toddler throwing a biscotti at her father at the next table. These people are busy writing their Great American Novel, or a paper for class, or reading a textbook. I even know a minister who writes his best sermons at Starbucks. I admire these people who seem to have the capacity to shut out extraneous noises and concentrate on the task before them, but I'm not one of those people.

To do a task that requires concentration—like writing, reading or studying—I need to have quiet, uninterrupted time alone. I do my best writing first thing in the morning before I get out of bed, even before the sun comes up. I prop myself up with pillows, grab my writing pad or laptop and delve into the job. My mind works better when my world is peaceful; the writing comes easier and makes more sense, and I find it easier to read and retain information without other external noises.

I've always been this way. I remember that in grammar school I was easily distracted by the rowdy boys in class when doing reading or writing assignments. My teachers told me I'd have to get used to working with distractions and figure out how to live with the noise. I learned that the world *is* loud and messy, and that I needed to adapt. Gradually, I did, but I still try to find quiet places to work when I can.

Virginia Woolf famously wrote, "In order to write, a woman must have a room of her own." Some people need a well-organized, clean workspace to get things going, but all I need is a quiet place with the phone on silence, no one coming to the door, and the dog asleep.

Whether you prefer a clear space, all alone, or the hurry-scurry of a public place, it still takes a clear mind to work successfully. Your mind is what gives you the inspiration you need—whatever you're doing—and if you can maintain a clear mind in a chaotic setting, good for you. So, I'll see you at the coffee shop, only I won't be working, reading, or studying; I'll be enjoying the company of friends and a nice Triple Mocha Frappuccino.

MATHEMATICS

When you think you need to add something to your life to make it better, or even to subtract something to be happier, it can happen, or not, depending on what you are adding and subtracting. We make changes all the time, every day, sometimes by the minute. But are these changes always beneficial?

I saw a *Peanuts* cartoon by Charles Schulz in which Lucy had her *Psychiatric Help 5¢* stand set up. Charlie Brown comes to Lucy and expounds on how he feels like nothing because he can't approach the little red-haired girl, that someone who is *nothing* can't just go right up to someone who is *something* and talk to them.

Lucy tells Charlie that she thinks his problem is mathematical and asks, "If you add nothing and something, what do you get?" Charlie says, "Something, I guess." Then Lucy says, "Right. Now, if you subtract nothing from something, what do you get?" To which Charlie answers, "Something." Then Lucy says, "Very good. Now, if you multiply something by nothing, what do you get?" Charlie, looking dejected, says, "Nothing." Then Lucy asks for her 5 cents.

The message here is that even when we think we don't have what we want, if we can *add* something, we will *have* something. And that's right, as long as the something we add increases the good in our life. The sum of nothing plus something will always be something. The good is always available to us.

If we shut something that is bothersome out of our life, if we subtract just one thing, we still have something left. We haven't lost everything. Eliminating just one thing doesn't take away the good of something. The difference of something minus nothing is still something.

But if we multiply what we feel is nothing—thoughts or behaviors that don't support our good—by nothing, we will get more of the same. The product of something multiplied by nothing is still nothing. If we continue the same self-defeating behaviors, and keep up the same self-disparaging thoughts, we won't grow, we won't achieve the goals we set, and we won't gain the confidence to be our best. But if we work to multiply the good that we have in our life, that good will grow into something better, and we will be successful.

We spend our life adding, subtracting, and multiplying things, and when we know what we want, we can get it with simple mathematics.

KALEIDOSCOPE

People, experiences, and preferences come into our lives, usually for a particular purpose. Then, after we've learned what they've come to teach us, they are gone. Changes are constantly coming and going. In fact, you could compare life to a kaleidoscope. Just a small movement is enough to make something different appear. Different shapes and different colors are manifested with every small turn of the kaleidoscope, and we never get the exact tableau of colors and forms again.

When we look at life as an ever-changing tableau, we can never be disappointed when things change. Life is no more static than a flower which manifests as a lovely blossom, then fades and disappears. When we look deeply at things in our life, we will see this reality. We manifest, then disappear. This is the kaleidoscope of life.

Some people adapt to change gracefully, while others fight it all the way. When we get too comfortable in our circumstances, it can be jarring when a change comes, but when we are aware that change is a part of life, we can go with the flow.

My long-time friend, Doris, was an Army wife, and along with her husband and three small children, moved from post to post so many times she lost count. When the Viet Nam war started, her high-ranking husband was sent there, not to engage in combat, but to be an advisor to both American troops and Vietnamese citizens. Of course, Doris and the children couldn't go with him on that tour of duty and, even though she missed him and now had full responsibility of the children, she was relieved. After all the changes, her life felt easier, calmer, and simpler because she wasn't someone who adapted to change gracefully.

Another friend, Amy, whose husband was also a military officer who was reassigned often, and who also had three children, found the best in every move. She learned new things about places all over the world, and even got pretty good at new languages. The kaleidoscope of her life brought welcome and enjoyable changes, and she adapted easily.

Both these friends are now widowed. One of them is settled into routine, the other still looks forward to interesting changes. Change is good, change is growth, and accepting inevitable, unavoidable change is part of living simply.

THE POWER OF LOVE

There have been millions of discoveries over several millennia in our world, some of which have dramatically changed the way we live and the way we think. One of these discoveries is fire. Before fire, homo sapiens were completely at the mercy of the environment, but when we began to manipulate fire, a number of luxuries became available. Fire provided a source of warmth, controlled fire gave us the ability to cook our food, and fire protected us from predators. Widespread fires helped the fertility of the land where crops were grown, and campfires introduced a social aspect to life, prompting the development of language. Today, the power of fire is used in our factories, in our cars, and in our homes. Without the power of fire, we would be living in a very different world.

Another powerful discovery was the wheel. Its power has been utilized in countless ways, from making pottery and spinning fabric to an easy way to move things around.

But there is another, most important power that has been alive since the advent of man: the power of love. Love can make as much a difference in our life as fire and the wheel, and it is available to everyone, everywhere, all the time. But like fire and the wheel, love is worthless unless we use its power. When love becomes the basis of how we live—the power we live by—the world will become a sanctuary; no child will ever go hungry, there will be no judgment, bigotry, or discrimination, no social or economic biases, no wars. When the full power of love is unleashed, fear will not exist, hate will be no more, and we won't need courts and judges. When love becomes the way, there will be room for all of God's children to live together in peace and harmony. There is unlimited power in love.

Many have expounded on the power of love. Martin Luther King, Jr. said, "We must discover the redemptive power of love." Episcopalian Bishop Michael Curry said, "There's power in love to lift up and liberate when nothing else will." And in the Bible, the Song of Solomon says, "Many waters cannot quench love, neither can floods drown it."

When we can capture the energy and the power of love the way we captured the energy and power of fire and the wheel, we will see a whole new world. Love IS the power. Love IS the way.

FRIENDLINESS

Being friendly can make us happier and healthier. Humans are like pack-animals; we get pleasure and feel safety by social interaction with others. When we smile at each other, we release natural pain-killers, boost our immune system, and lower our blood pressure, but when we simply ignore those around us, our nervous system is affected, which can lead to disease or depression.

There are times when, living and working alone, I begin to feel pain in my body and my mood gets kind of gray, but if I get out and interact with people— my pack—my mood lightens and the pain goes away. This is a demonstration of how friendliness is actually healing.

A good example of how friendliness works is to watch people at a sporting event. It's amazing how people of all backgrounds, political views, economic status, ages, and interests can bond together to root for and cheer on the same team. They have a common interest and a common goal that binds them together.

For a person who is more introverted, being friendly can be pretty scary. What if I smile at someone and they don't smile back? What if I strike up a conversation and the other person isn't responsive? What if I just feel too insecure to interact with someone I don't know? Granted, it will take courage, but when we can simply step forward, take a chance, and courageously cultivate friendliness, we discover that friendliness is its own reward, no matter what comes back, because it makes *us* feel better.

Every time we try, it becomes a little easier and, in time, friendliness becomes a habit. If we're on the watch for positive, warm, or even neutral moments, taking time to register that things—and other people—are okay, we will find this has a tremendous impact on our psyche and our self-confidence. If we can build the habit of seeing the good in others, and of approaching people with warmth and openness, over time our whole outlook can change.

And don't forget to be friendly with yourself. Look for, and find, your positive aspects and attributes. Cultivate those attributes by stepping out and allowing others to see them in you. Praise yourself when friendliness to others carries you past any doubt, and your circle of friends—your pack—starts to grow.

THE GOLDEN KEY

New Thought teacher Emmet Fox produced a pamphlet in 1944 about overcoming difficulties. He called it *The Golden Key*. It was not intended to be an instructional treatise but a practical guide for getting out of trouble. It worked way back then, and it works today. The Golden Key is *scientific prayer,* and can get you, or anyone else, out of any difficulty. It's the key to harmony and happiness. If you are open to The Golden Key and have faith enough to try it, you will find it works because, in scientific prayer, it is God who does the work, not you. Your mind-set is limited, while God's is not.

There's just one rule to making The Golden Key work. All we have to do is this: *Stop thinking about the difficultly, whatever it is, and think about God instead.* That's all. That's the complete rule. If we do this, the difficulty will disappear. It might be a big thing or a little thing; it might concern a health issue, a lawsuit, or any difficulty we face in our life, but whatever it is, *stop thinking about it and think about God instead.* What could be simpler? God makes it simple, and it never fails to work when seriously given a fair trial.

Fox cautions us not to form a mental picture of God, because God is formless and cannot be pictured. God is wisdom, truth, and inconceivable love. God is present everywhere, has infinite power, and knows everything. God heals when held in mind. If we continue to think about our difficulty, or try to figure out a solution for ourselves, then we are not thinking about God.

When using The Golden Key, the object is to drive our difficulty out of our consciousness by substituting it with thoughts of God and nothing else. To use The Golden Key, we can repeat statements like: "There is no power but God." "I AM a child of God, filled and surrounded by perfect peace." "God is guiding me now." or simply, "God is with me." When we do this quietly but insistently, in time, we will stop thinking about any difficulty, think only of God, and leave the ways and means of solutions up to God.

After we find how well The Golden Key works for us in our own life, we can "Golden Key" others. If someone we know is going through a difficult time we can *stop thinking about his problem, and think about God instead.* We can see God making this person healthier, calmer, or out of danger. The Golden Key is a simple tool to get out of our own way and let God do His work.

I FEEL PRETTY

I just watched the movie *I Feel Pretty* with Amy Schumer, again. It's an enjoyable, funny movie that carries a great message. Amy's character has an accident resulting in a bump on the head that affects her brain and makes her see herself differently. She had always seen herself as timid, unattractive, and not good enough for a job better than the mundane one she had. After the accident, she saw herself as beautiful, confident, and capable, and believed that others saw her this way as well. With her new-found confidence, she got a glamourous job with great responsibilities—which she handled well—and even found that men were attracted to her.

After another accident, and another bump on the head, she again saw herself as she did before, and all the positive beliefs she had about herself vanished. When she discovered that the old self and the new self looked exactly the same, however, she woke up to the fact that she really was that confident, capable, lovable person. She just hadn't believed it about herself before.

The movie pointed out that we are indeed what we believe about ourselves. We tend to judge ourselves by what we look like on the outside, and if we don't like what we see, it's hard to feel beautiful and confident and lovable. But it's really what's on the inside that matters. How we *feel* matters far more than how we *look*.

It's not the beauty products that cosmetic companies make billions of dollars selling with a promise of changing our life for the better; it's what's behind all that artificial stuff that determines who we really are. It's what inside our mind. It's what's in our heart. It's what we believe about our abilities, our talents, and our potential that can change our life for the better. We can be just as beautiful in jeans and a tee shirt as we can in a Gucci gown. And men can be just as handsome and alluring in their old favorite flannel shirt and flip-flops. They don't need a tuxedo to be a heart-throb.

When you like who you are, when you have a strong sense of self-worth and confidence and see yourself as beautiful and capable and loveable, your real beauty will shine through. On some level, you already know all this, but you can't be reminded too often to remember the beautiful, competent, gifted, talented, lovable person you are. By not obsessing about what you *look* like, and letting your authentic self show through, you will find your life to be much simpler.

BLUEPRINT FOR LIFE

A life well-lived follows a pretty standard pattern for most people. We grow physically, mentally, emotionally, and spiritually, and we learn important life lessons along the way.

It all starts at birth when we leave the warm, safe environment of the womb and come into a cold, noisy, rather frightening world, fully dependent on someone to care for us and keep us safe. But as the years go by, things change.

By the time we were a year old, we've started to walk and talk and to demonstrate that we want what we want, and we want it *now*. However, there is still no one more important to us than mommy and daddy. At age five we begin to make friends outside our family to share the joys of play, and by age ten we've learned responsibility and how to peacefully interact with others.

By 16, we learn that crime doesn't pay, and neither does trying to fool our parents. By age 20, we begin to realize that father—and mother—actually do know best. By 30 we've learned that having a new baby drastically changes our life and our sleep patterns. By 35 we know that the future is not what we inherit, it's what we create, and by 40, we know that the secret to a happy, successful life is not necessarily doing what we like, but liking what we do.

At age 50 we realize our children aren't children anymore; they've grown up and learned how to live on their own. When we reach 55, we know that little decisions should be made with the head and big decisions with the heart, and we've learned that a dog is man's best friend and that dogma can be a man's worst enemy. At age 60, we've found that we can give without loving, but we can never love without giving. And by 65 we can enjoy life to the fullest; we can eat whatever we want after we've eaten what we should. By age 70, life is not about holding the good cards but more about playing the hand we've been dealt well.

By the time we reach 80, we've come to know that to love is to be loved, and that loving is the greatest joy in the world. And as we continue to age we may, again, become fully dependent on someone else to care for us and keep us safe. When we've finally come full circle, we can look back with pride, knowing we've had a life well lived.

WHO'S YOUR FRIEND?

A friend is someone who knows everything about us and stays true to us anyway. A friend sees the best in us because they love us. A real friend is there for us even when they'd rather be someplace else.

A friend is someone we can trust to hold our car keys and our wallet. A friend is someone who will listen when we have the hard conversations. A friend is someone we can confide in and know our confidence won't be broken.

A friend is someone we can play with, work with, and above all, be our self with. A real friend has our highest good at heart. A true friend is loyal, strictly honest with us, and we are the same with them.

A real friend is one who listens and doesn't judge. A real friend is someone we can get mad at but know they'll still be there when we've gotten over whatever made us mad.

A friend who is helpful, good-hearted, sympathetic, and stands up for us—and we do the same for him—is truly a friend to be cherished.

Friends are like stars; we may not see them all the time but we know they're always there. Friends are God's way of taking care of us.

We often call acquaintances friends. Real friendship, however, goes deeper than simply being acquainted with someone. In the context of social media, the term *friend* is used to describe *contacts* rather than *relationships*. We can "friend" people on social media, send messages to them and read messages they send to us, but this is not the same as having a personal relationship with a person. People brag about how many hundreds of friends they have on twitter, Instagram, or Facebook. But how many of these *friends* will come running if we have a need? How many will bring us chicken soup when we're sick? How many will loan us a few bucks to tide us over until payday? How many will bring jumper cables when our car battery dies?

Friendship isn't just one big thing, it's a whole lot of little things. Friendships are one of life's greatest blessings. A true friend can make our life easier to bear, and much simpler.

WHAT'S YOUR TAFFY?

I'm reminded of a cartoon showing a couple opening a Christmas gift and the husband saying, "It's from our dentist. He sure knows how to keep his patients coming back!" The gift was a box of salt water taffy.

What does keep people coming back? Coming back for good experiences is easy, and for the most part, enjoyable. I have a friend who purchases season passes to Disneyland every year for the entire family. They come back to the park five or six times a year and totally enjoy themselves. Fun in the "Happiest place on Earth" creates a family bond, and cares of the world are forgotten.

One motto of twelve-step programs is, "Keep coming back." When the addicts keep coming back to meetings, they usually find that the sharing, the interaction, and learning how others have overcome, help to make their lives simpler and more enjoyable.

We also hear about animals that get lost and show up months or even years later, instinctively drawn to come back to the family they love.

There are triggers that keep us coming back. Some, however, are triggers we should learn to recognize and not surrender to. Consider the naïve person who is trusting of everyone and everything. Their unsuspecting nature keeps them coming back to be repeatedly cheated by unscrupulous salespeople and scams.

Taffy is the trigger for cavities. We need know our triggers, to know our taffy, because when we are aware of the things that cause strife, sadness, or pain in our lives, we can learn to recognize what triggers them so we won't keep repeating those patterns. We need to remember the old idiom, "Once bitten, twice shy." Coming back to that dentist may be good for his business, but it doesn't serve us well.

In life, we have unlimited choices. When something unpleasant or harmful is triggered, and we recognize those triggers, we can choose, instead, to acknowledge our own goodness and honor our right to be treated with respect and to live in peace and happiness. Taffy is tempting, but peace and happiness is what makes life simple.

F—WORDS

No, I'm not going to write about the F-word you're thinking of. These pages are meant to be inspirational! Not X-rated. There are other F-words, however, that *do* have a place in our life and can help us live more simply and feel more contented. Here they are:

Fun: We need to keep fun in our lives and on our agenda. Laughing—from a little titter to an all-out guffaw—releases natural "feel-good" hormones which combat stress and are therefore good for us and for everyone around us.

Fitness: Keeping the body fit is a very important part of life. Sitting at a computer or watching TV hour upon hour doesn't allow the heart and other muscles to work the way they were designed to. It's a good idea to step away every 30 minutes or so and walk through our house for a while. Walking a couple of blocks down our street and back is even better. If we can carve out time to go to the gym, we'll get an even better workout. That's why I practice yoga. It not only keeps my body moving, stretched, and balanced, it lifts my spirits and keeps me calm.

Finances: No matter if we're making a lot of money at our job or from investments, or if we're living on a meager income, keeping a sharp eye on spending is important. I'm retired, but I have enough income for what I need. I don't need the latest technology, the hottest car, or new clothes for every season. The money I spend on the people I love is what holds the most meaning for me.

Family: The people I hold closest and dearest are those who are related to me by blood or by marriage, but family can also consist of friends, people we work with, worship with, or work out at the gym with. People in civic clubs or other organizations can also be classified as family. The word "family" has many meanings.

Faith: Faith is something that embraces us and keeps us from falling. It's an authority that knows its way through darkness because it comes from the light. Faith sees us through hard times letting us know that all is well and that we are not alone.

Failure: We can try new things, and if they don't work, we might think we've failed. But failure can be a stepping stone to success.

When we keep these six F-words in mind, we will discover the best F-words of all: *Feeling Fine*.

LAYERS

In a *Baldo* cartoon by Cantŭ and Castellanos, Baldo and his father are working on their car, and the father says, "Don't ever sell yourself short, Baldo. Deep inside you is the creativity of Salvador Dali . . . the athletic ability of Roberto Clemente . . . and the wisdom of Sonia Sotomayor." To which Baldo replies, "I know. But they're all covered up with layers of Baldo."

Baldo hasn't yet become fully aware of his potential. He's still living under layers of the kick-back, kind of lazy teenager. Many young people have this same affliction, not giving thought to where they want to be in the world, and, unfortunately, many schools don't have the budget for counselors to help guide our youth.

My 18-year-old grandson was given a full college scholarship as a surviving dependent when his father lost his life in Iraq. He just graduated high school and hasn't yet found a path, nor does he seem interested in finding one, and he doesn't have much interest in college at this point, either. I have, like Baldo's father, tried to impress upon him how smart, talented, and capable he is, and that his potential is limitless. But so far, he's living under layers of "It doesn't really matter" and goes back to video games. He's had jobs at fast-food places, but that doesn't seem like a career.

Which makes me wonder just how important is a *career*? I've gone down several career paths in my own life, never landing on one specific path, and I've done okay. I don't have the benefit of a retirement plan, but I've managed to save enough to get by. I guess I've had layers of Judy—many wanderlust layers—all my life. I've learned a lot because I've done a lot, and I'm still learning.

I'm not an artist, athlete, or Supreme Court justice, but I've been a deputy city clerk, successful in sales, did well as a newspaper columnist, was a good Realtor, and managed a small airport for many years. I had great fun as an interior decorator, and I'm still doing okay with property management. And I've been happy.

I'm not suggesting people be blasé about their life's work, and college *is* important, but I do think we sometimes get too hung up on one thing when there are new and different avenues to explore. I have a T-shirt with the words *Not All Who Wander Are Lost* on the front. That shirt reflects the story of my life. I've done a lot of wandering, but I've never felt lost. Baldo will probably succeed in life, even with layers of Baldo.

EQUALITY

Whether you believe there is a Divine Being creating everything, or that it's forces of nature, it is clearly a myth that all humans are created equal. In fact, the opposite is true. We are all unique individuals.

Granted, we all have equal *rights* under the Declaration of Independence of our great nation: the right to Life, Liberty, and the Pursuit of Happiness. But, let's face it, even though people have equal rights, they are not equally alike. There are tall people and there are short people, and there are millions more somewhere in between. There are people with different shades of skin, color of hair, and shapes of eyes. There are physically strong people, and there are those who have a hard time opening a jelly jar. Humans differ in intelligence, cultural backgrounds, language skills, and just about everything else, except the fundamental equality of their right to full membership in humanity. No two people are exactly the same. We are all unique in our own way. That uniqueness is what keeps this country interesting.

Unfortunately, the American Dream of equal rights for all people is not yet a reality; it remains a dream in process. Women are fighting for equal pay for equal work, not because they're women, but because they're human. There are still not enough neighborhoods sharing openly and easily the diversity of different cultures, with people who look, think, dress, and pray differently. We *are* getting better at it, though, and younger people are way ahead of most older folks.

There is a vast difference between simply putting up with people somewhat unlike ourselves and enjoying the benefits of learning from them. When we are accepting of differences, we find that unfamiliar groups offer a diverse, enriching viewpoint, and they can be unique inspiration to a mix of caring people who enjoy living together in civilized prosperity. With a change of viewpoint, this can happen sooner than we hope. Celebrating diversity isn't always easy, but nothing worthwhile ever is.

The next time a discussion comes up about everyone being equal, please remember how *unequal* people must strive to *feel* equal, to feel what it is to have the right to live freely and safely and to pursue happiness. Share with them the freedom of ever-growing equality. Being different doesn't equal being less. When you meet any unique individual, and you treat them with love and respect, everyone's life becomes simpler. Whether through divinity or nature, simple living is what we were created for.

MATURITY

As we age, we gain wisdom, and we also gain the maturity to listen to that wisdom. We may consider ourselves mature when we've reached adulthood, but we're not really mature until we've developed a healthy emotional maturity.

An emotionally mature person knows how to settle differences without anger or violence. As we mature, we develop the perseverance to stick to what we know is right in spite of heavy opposition and discouraging setbacks.

With maturity, we have the capacity to face unpleasantness, frustration, discomfort, and defeat without complaint or collapse. A mature person has learned patience and is willing to pass up immediate pleasure in favor of long-term gain.

Maturity is being big enough to say, "I was wrong" when we've been incorrect or mistaken. When right, maturity is the ability to refrain from needing the satisfaction of saying, "I told you so."

Maturity is the ability to make a decision, stand by that decision and take action. Maturity means dependability, keeping our word and coming through in a crisis, rather than being a master of alibis, blame, and good intentions that somehow never materialize.

Mature people are cool and collected in difficult moments, and they know where to go for help when it's needed. An emotionally mature person can maintain poise in all circumstances and knows how to act appropriately.

Maturity is the ability to think, speak, and act our feelings within the bounds of dignity. Maturity is knowing the right thing to say at the right time, knowing when not to say anything, and recognizing how many things don't need our comment.

Maturity is the art of living in peace and teaching our children not by words, but by actions. Maturity doesn't mean age, it means sensitivity, manners, and how we react to the world.

There's a confidence that comes with maturity, and being accepting of our self is a sure sign of maturity.

Our life experiences, good and bad, make us who we are. By learning to overcome difficulties, we gain the comfortable strength of maturity and life becomes simpler.

SACRIFICE NOTHING

People tend to think that if someone has gained, another has lost. This is not true. What we give to another, we also give to our self. *A Course in Miracles* tells us that we are all one; what we gain, others gain also, and there is no loss.

Medical practitioners, social workers, ministers, and others in healing or teaching professions often report feeling burned-out, becoming stressed or ill and less effective in their work because their energy is depleted. They use it up, and have no more to give. This need not be. The good work these people are doing is inviting the patient, client, or student to rise to a higher consciousness, a greater awareness of healing or learning. No loss is required of them in order for others to benefit. The more positive these professionals can stay, the more favorable the environment for healing, learning, or helping themselves while they're helping another.

People often come to me with their problems, expecting me to fix them. But I've learned that I can't do that. To try to fix another's problem would be taking on an unreasonable responsibility. I can hold a high vision for these people, seeing their problems as resolved, but I can't lose *my* peace by trying to help others find theirs. I can't let my own energy be depleted because, if I did, then I wouldn't be good for myself, let alone good for anyone else.

To be a "fixer," the true healer simply recognizes the power and presence of wellness, knowledge, and self-confidence in those who come to them for help. The spirit within them is awakened, requiring no sacrifice from the healer.

I've talked with massage therapists who feel spent and sick at the end of the day, feeling they've taken on the discomforts of their clients in order to make them feel better. But this experience is unnecessary. These therapists can be using their own energy to lift others to their level, not the other way around.

The *Course* says, *He who understands what giving means must laugh at the idea of sacrifice.* This simply means that we never have to sacrifice anything in order to give to another.

It's okay to use our energy to help another, but remember, what we give, we also gain. As we give energy or healing to another, we are gaining energy and healing for our self.

JOY TO THE WORLD

It is within our power to bring a little joy to everyone we encounter. We can do it with a friendly greeting, a word of well-wishing, or simply with a smile. This Christmas season is a good time to start, or to renew that commitment.

I facilitate a study group in *A Course in Miracles*. This is not a course to be learned academically but rather experientially. One time I gave the group "homework." I suggested that when they are shopping at the market, in line at the bank, or even the DMV, that they spread some joy and see what kind of response they get. The joy could be smiling at a stranger, a sincere compliment, striking up a conversation, or some small act of kindness. There were some great stories that came back as a result of this homework. There were returned smiles and friendly responses, even stories of people who thanked them for their kindness. The most fun responses were from children whose faces brightened when spoken to.

If we stay open to people we come in contact with in our everyday life, we can never know how our smile or kind word may affect them. There might be someone who is experiencing a rough patch, even considering a disastrous act, and our smile and cheery hello could lift their spirits enough to bring them back to believing in themselves.

One of my houses came up for rent a while back. I advertised the house, got several responses, and took applications. Because of some bad experiences with tenants in the past, I wanted to carefully review the applicants to make sure I chose someone responsible and who really wanted to live in the house. When I had made my decision, I called the couple to tell them they were the ones I'd chosen. The wife shrieked with joy when I told her and called out to her husband, "We got the house! We got the house!" She was overcome with joy, and I knew I'd chosen wisely.

Never underestimate the power of kindness and trust. I didn't think of making my selection of a tenant as an act of kindness, but it did entail some trust, and the result was pure joy. When we bring joy to another, we feel warmth in our soul, knowing we've brightened someone's day.

We can choose never to waste a chance to bring a little joy into the life of another. Our own life is simpler and enriched when we share our joy.

CHANGING TIMES

We think we live in a free country, but are we really free? Are kids today free to do what we did when we were kids? Much of what was natural for us is strictly taboo for kids today, partly because we've become more protective, and partly because there are additional dangers out there. Dangers might have been just as prevalent when we were young, but before instant news and far-reaching reports from across the country and around the world, we didn't hear about them and were, therefore, not as afraid of them happening.

When I was a child, we played outside until dark, and we rode our bikes anywhere we wanted as long as we were home by dinnertime. We climbed trees, and we walked on the top of fences.

When I was young, we swam in the creek and played in the orchard. We drank from the garden hose, we didn't have bike helmets, we didn't have seat belts, we walked to and from school every day, and there was lead paint in our houses. And we didn't have car seats. Even when my babies were born and ready to leave the hospital, they were wrapped up and handed to me to carry for the ride home. There were no regulation car seats, in fact, until my children were old enough to behave themselves in the back seat, their car seat was a simple little canvas thing with handles that hooked over the back of the front seat. The only real purpose it served was to keep the child in one place.

When I was a child, imagination was my favorite toy. Any piece of furniture could be a house for my paper dolls, and by putting my little feet into my mom's too-big shoes and draping a towel over my shoulders, I became a princess. By holding my arm out the car window, I was flying. I wasn't afraid of mud, I happily ate left-overs, I licked postage stamps, swallowed chewing gum, and dogs ran free in my neighborhood

When I was young, my mother wore dresses, even to clean house, and I wrote thank-you notes when I got presents. Good manners, values, and morals were drilled into me.

But times have changed. Life was simpler when I was a child and I sometimes wish it could be equally simple for my young great-grandchildren. Young people do mature faster today, and, hopefully, as they gain strength, awareness, and resilience, they will help to create a simpler life for everyone.

HAPPY BIRTHDAY

Every day of the year, the world is changed because new lives are added. On this day, many years ago, I was born and added another life to live, love, learn, and laugh. The baby that was me was like no other before me or any that has come after me. The day you were born also changed the world. You added a soul and a spirit with new thoughts, new ideas, and new ways of doing things. You brought new talents and new visions. You brought a new light, and the world became a better place.

Each of us is born with a pure innocence and wonder, and we have enthusiasm for everything because it's all new to us. As we take on challenges throughout our lives, facing fears and difficulties, working through them and coming out stronger, the world is enriched.

Every year, on our birthday, we can take time to count our blessings. We can consider the people we love, those who support us and always have our back. We can be grateful for the beauty we've seen, the wisdom we've gained, and the strength we've built. We can take stock of the ideas we've had that we've brought to fruition. We can be grateful for our health, our creativity, our uniqueness, and especially for our laughter. What seems, at times, like foolishness can actually be wisdom, and if we don't take everything too seriously, doors can open for us that might remain closed if we were to attempt to push through them with intellectual manipulation. We must never forget that our life is a gift to be celebrated, not a problem to be solved.

Through the years, I may have let things bother me too much, but today I can let those worries go. I can't change outcomes, but I can change my mind. Today, I choose to be free to let life be simple. I will celebrate that freedom in a way that pleases me. I will take time for reflection to remember what brings me joy and delight and will celebrate that joy. I will remember the wondrous gift I've been given, and I will be happy because I deserve to be happy. We all deserve to be happy, not just on our birthday, but every day of the year.

There's a Shaker song that says, "Tis a gift to be simple, tis a gift to be free." Every year, on your birthday, sing that song. Return to the innocence of childlike wonder. See the beauty that surrounds you. See the magnificence of the life that has been created for you. Be grateful, joyful, and free to let your life be simple.

GRACE

Grace is one of the hardest words—or concepts—to understand. The dictionary defines *Grace* as: "The free and unmerited favor of God . . . the bestowal of blessings." We are all favored children of God because we are God expressing as *our unique self.* We are favored and blessed by the grace of God.

God's will for all of us is perfect peace and happiness, and this is given to us by grace. The will of God is so great that it even seeps through negative thinking about ourselves. When we slip into a negative state of mind, feeling a lack of self-worth, self-confidence, or self-love, we can be comforted by remembering that God's Grace and Love are still a part of who we are.

Eric Butterworth, in his book *Celebrate Yourself* explains grace as, "God's desire to express completely through you. It is so great that you never completely reap the harvest of error, and you always reap more good than you sow."

"You are not a helpless creature bobbing about like a cork on the sea of life." continues Butterworth. "You are the very self-livingness of God." When we strive for spiritual growth, advancement in our work or a more satisfying lifestyle, it is God's desire and urging that spurs us on, even if we aren't consciously aware of it. We are the activity of God in expression. We are bestowed with an everlasting love. This is grace.

We don't have to do anything to earn grace. Grace doesn't come only to the good and the obedient. It comes to everyone because we are all expressions of God. By the Grace of God, a hardened criminal and a devout follower are loved equally.

Grace is an explanation of a wonderful facet of the activity of God in us. It's not something we work to develop; it simply is. Grace is an assurance of why things are never quite hopeless. When we hear the words, "He was healed by the Grace of God," don't forget it's not just a special act for one person; it's a demonstration of God's good pleasure for every person. It is the unmerited, unasked for favor of God, and it's ours, even when we don't ask for it, or even if we don't believe it. It's grace that makes our life simpler.

THOUGHT

Never underestimate the power of thought. The thoughts we think are as powerful as the words we speak. Thoughts of peace make us feel peaceful. Gentle thoughts make us feel gentle. Fearful thoughts make us afraid. Judgmental thoughts cause us to judge others. When we take notice of what makes us happy, and we think about those things, we are happy. The same is true with what makes us unhappy; our mind makes the necessary adjustments.

Gerald Jampolski, in his book *Teach Only Love*, cites his experience of taking the oral testing for the boards in psychiatry and neurology. He had studied hard, had the necessary knowledge, and decided he would be the calmest, coolest person ever to take the exams. He put on a mask of composure and all his energy went into pretending to be in control, thinking, "This is a cinch." But because his thoughts were focused on being so cool, rather than on his knowledge, he failed the exam. Later, at a second attempt in which he felt some trepidation, he sailed through the test.

When our thoughts are of fear of failing, we tend to fail. But when our thoughts remain positive, the result is usually positive. This doesn't mean we don't have to bother studying and learning what we need to know to pass an exam, use a computer, or change a tire, it just means that thoughts in mind always produce in kind. Because Dr. Jampolski was so focused on appearing cool and collected, his ego thoughts were stronger that his truth.

Thoughts are energy. When we are in a situation that makes us feel uncomfortable and we act like it's okay, those around us are aware of our discomfort because of the energy we exude. The best way to approach any situation is to express our thoughts honestly. The experience of love and peace is the only thing of importance that is communicated between people. It's the attitude of the heart, the thoughts we think, and not what is said that links people together.

If we keep our thinking pure, clear, and true, our verbal messages will be pure, clear, and true. If we hold thoughts of love, love is what those around us will see. In seeing that love, another's thoughts can be transformed to thoughts of love. Remember, what isn't said is equally as important as what is verbalized. If we keep our thoughts pure, we can truly build a world of beauty with those thoughts.

NAME THAT FLOWER

In many ways, I'm very much like my mother, but there are some things about her that I never thought I'd emulate. My mother was an avid gardener, and our yard was always abloom. When people came to visit, she would take them into the yard so they could enjoy its beauty, and they did enjoy it. They also enjoyed the cuttings she would give them so they could grow the same plants in their own yards. I have vivid memories of my mother proudly pointing out the campsis, the potassium umbellatum, catharanthus, and the strelitzia. I never knew, or even cared, which was what. All I knew was that the flowers were pretty—especially the poinsettias at Christmas time.

One day last spring, when my yard was looking particularly nice, a friend came by and, looking out the window, commented on the flowers. We went into the yard, and I found myself pointing out the Peruvian lily, the day lilies, the Shasta daisies, and the vividly blooming geraniums. There is another plant with pretty purple flowers and my friend asked the name of it. I answered, "Um . . . something with pretty purple flowers." I don't even know the common names of all the plants, let alone their botanical names, but my mother was a walking garden encyclopedia, she knew them all. My mother really loved and took pride in her garden, and she scolded me continually for popping the 6-inch long buds on the trumpet vine when I walked past it to take out the garbage.

My mother also had a knack for arranging the flowers she grew. Several arrangements were entered in county fairs and won blue ribbons. I still have a few of her vases, and there's one little pewter one that I can't look at without seeing the smiling faces of pansies.

I had to laugh at myself, though, as my friend and I toured my yard, it took me right back in memory to the pleasure my mother got from sharing her garden with friends. As I get older, I guess I'm like my mother in more ways than I thought.

I find it's okay to be like my mother. She was a beautiful, powerful, loving woman, and I miss her. During the holiday season, seeing all the poinsettias everywhere, I miss her the most.

To make our life simple and more beautiful, we can all have something we love and get pleasure from sharing, the way my mother loved and got pleasure from sharing her garden. Love and pleasure are what makes this life worth living.

RUNNING ON EMPTY

We all have energy-zappers in our lives, but when we learn to control them, to turn them into positive action, life becomes simpler.

Feeling a need to control is a huge energy-zapper. The compulsive need or desire to know everything and to control outcomes takes up so much energy that there's none left to enjoy the unexpected and spontaneous things that bring joy into our life.

Perfection can also steal our energy. If we believe there's no room for mistakes, and that even our best is not enough, it can be demoralizing and we might limit what we do for fear of doing it wrong. No one is perfect, and mistakes are a part of life, so if we can accept nothing less that perfection in all things, we are depleting the energy we could be using for things that matter.

Too much drama in our life is a sure way to zap energy. We can be attracted to it or we might even create it. It's common for people to invent stories taking bits of information and creating a storyline that is overly dramatic. If we find ourselves doing this and recognize the story as drama, we can eliminate the exaggeration by asking ourselves, "Is this true, and is it kind?" If the answer is *no*, we can put a stop to the downward spiral of drama, dismiss it from our mind, and remain in a place of peaceful energy.

We are all aware of the concept of the glass half-empty or half-full. A half-empty outlook focuses on what's going wrong, which can be exhausting. Instead, we can turn to the half-full mind-set, recognizing and celebrating what *is* working and turn our positive energies there. This doesn't mean avoiding or denying issues and challenges, it simply means to start with the positive—the win—first.

Not having boundaries about what is comfortable and acceptable can drain energy. There is always going to be a certain amount of confusion in our life, but when we can set and communicate boundaries—for ourselves and for others—everyone will know what is expected and accepted, and this will keep our energy flowing in a positive direction.

Life is simple when our energy reserve isn't running on empty. Releasing control, allowing some imperfection to be okay, avoiding drama, looking at the positives in life, and setting and sticking to boundaries, leaves us open to seeing things from many points of view. We might come to see that almost everyone means well and is acting with the best of intentions.

SACREDNESS

People tend to give a religious connotation or assume connection to a deity with the word *sacred*. But we all have tangible things in our lives that we also hold sacred—a person, a purpose, or an object, things we regard with reverence and are connected to by love.

No one wants to have to choose what they would save in the event their home was in danger of being destroyed, but every day in the news, we see reports of devastating fires and floods, in which people lose everything. These reports make us think about what we would save—what we would consider sacred—if we had to evacuate.

Most people would first rescue the four P's: people, pets, pictures, and papers, but what else do you hold sacred? In today's world, with so much stored on our phones or notebooks, on flash-drives and in the cloud, carrying out photos and important documents is pretty simple. But what about the bedspread your paternal grandmother painstakingly crocheted over 80 years ago? What about the steamer trunk with which she sailed over from Norway when she was fourteen? What about the quilt your mother hand-quilted especially for you? What about all the old photo albums that never made it into the digital world? What about the Bible your maternal grandmother gave you when you were ten? If you were to take a mental journey through your home, you would be sure to discover many things that aren't especially monetarily valuable but are sacred to you.

When I take my mental journey, I see paintings and sculptures done by people I have loved or admired, and some painted or sculpted by me. I see my grandmother's china in the cabinet in my dining room, and my little blue dishes from childhood tea parties. These are things that are sacred to me, that no monetary value can be placed on, and that are truly irreplaceable. What is sacred about these things is the effort and creativity that went into them, and the loving memories they hold.

Sacredness isn't limited to religion. Sacredness lives in everyday spaces in our everyday life and in things we allow God's love to permeate. Computers, TVs, furniture and clothes are replaceable, or covered by insurance, but there is no way to insure your heart or your love for personally sacred things.

Take a minute to look at your life and your surroundings. Think about all you hold sacred, and take comfort in those things. These cherished objects remind us of what matters most.

TREE BATH

In Japan there is a practice they call "forest-bathing," which they claim is good for both the body and the mind. It simply means sitting quietly, surrounded by trees, and letting go of whatever is bothering you. Researchers conducted an eight-year study of this forest-bathing and found scientific backing for the practice. They studied the psychological and physiological effects of spending time among trees and found significantly improved immune function, lower stress levels, reduced depression, and decreased feelings of hostility or anger. Based on these findings, maybe we should all take an occasional tree-bath to make life simpler.

When I bought my current house, I wanted to create a little meditation garden. The back yard is very large and has several big, old trees. I spent some time feeling the energy in every part of the yard to find the most peaceful place that would be most conducive to quiet meditation. I felt the most serenity under the three 90-plus year-old redwoods. I hired a friend to build a waterfall, planted gracefully trailing vines on top of the waterfall, placed paving stones on the ground, and I had my beautiful meditation garden. But even without the waterfall, the trees alone inspire an inner peace.

I've found that tree-baths do all those things the scientists discovered. My son, Steve, has found it, too. He takes at least one hunting trip every year and loves being in the mountains. He's found that being in the open among the trees has a profound effect on his psyche—and he doesn't have to turn off his cell phone because it doesn't work in the wilderness, anyway.

If you don't have nice, big trees in your own yard, you can go to a park, or to any grove of trees, turn off your phone, take a tree-bath, and feel stress, sadness, and negative thoughts or emotions wash away. You will come away feeling cleansed by the therapeutic landscape and ready to look at whatever is bothering you with fresh eyes and a new outlook.

I think you'll find tree-bathing can be time well-spent, and the inner peace you gain from it will simplify your life.

SIMPLICITY

Increasing the complexity of life doesn't necessarily deepen its quality. In a survey taken in the 1950s, about 60 percent of people interviewed described themselves as *happy*. When another similar poll was taken in the mid-1990s, about that same percentage reported being *relatively happy*. During the 40 years between these two studies, technology had advanced tremendously, supposedly to make life simpler, but it wasn't making people any happier. In fact, it seems people were less happy after those 40 years, even after they'd advanced technically, intellectually, and socially. It would be interesting to take that same poll today to see if that trend has continued. Have more complicated intricacies made people any happier?

Technology was meant to make life easier, but it also makes it more complex, and when life becomes complicated, we lose the simplicity we once felt. This is because happiness comes from the inside—from our heart—and not from the discovery of outside "improvements."

I have a friend who is an accomplished percussionist and who can make music with pretty much anything. He has thousands of dollars' worth of sophisticated drum equipment but can make drumsticks on a plastic bucket or brushes on an old thick phonebook sing with a sound as good as anything he can do with his expensive equipment.

Think of the simplicity that surrounds us—the sound of the ocean, wind through tree branches, rain on the roof, children playing, and the universal sound of laughter—and know that the universe provides all our needs if we trust it. We can find beauty in even the simplest things if we are open to it. There is beauty, talent, wisdom, and even music in each of us. We don't have to go through a complicated learning process to learn to let life be simple because it's already there within us.

We can approach every day effortlessly, letting our contentment determine our quality of life. Neither worry nor stress has ever solved any problem. A simple life is a choice; we can elect to make life complicated or we can remain tranquil, taking things as they come, solving every problem with a relaxed attitude. We can make music with expensive equipment, or with a bucket or a phonebook. Quality of life isn't based on how hard we toil, it's based on how we look at it, and the choices we make.

GOOD OR BAD

He sees you when you're sleeping, he knows when you're awake, he knows when you've been bad or good, so be good for goodness sake. Yes, Santa is getting ready to make his annual rounds, he's making his list and checking it twice, and every child is trying hard to be good so they won't get a lump of coal in their Christmas stocking.

But what is good, and what is bad? What is naughty, and what is nice? Shakespeare's Hamlet said, "There is nothing either good or bad, but thinking makes it so." And Oscar Wilde said, "It is absurd to divide people into good and bad; people are either charming or tedious." From this we could deduce that good, bad, naughty, and nice are in the eyes of the beholder. *A Course in Miracles* tells us *Nothing, in and of itself, is either good or bad; it's the meaning we put on something that makes it so.*

For children, simply keeping their rooms tidy, eating their vegetables, and brushing their teeth is good enough to keep them in Santa's good graces. Being kind also helps, as does forgiving the misdeeds of others, helping someone in need when given the opportunity, and not speaking badly of another. Ideas about good and bad are subjective. Someone might feel it's perfectly fine to ridicule others because they're different. Another might believe it's okay to cheat others or steal from them. But the majority of us go through life doing the best we can to be *good* and feel that those who are *bad* will get the punishment they deserve.

It isn't just children looking for Santa's approval who try to be good; it's the grown-up children as well. We don't do it for Santa anymore; we are good and charming and kind and helpful because it *feels good.* How it *feels* to be naughty or nice is what actually makes it good or bad in our own eyes and in the eyes of others.

Every day, but especially during this holiday season, give thought to how you perceive things and try to see the good in everything, knowing that your reward is peace and happiness. For a child, it's the presents under the tree that is the indicator of having been good, but for the rest of us, it's the giving and receiving of love and respect for each other that lets us know if we're good or bad, naughty or nice. Sometimes it might be kind of fun to be just a little bit naughty, but being nice will keep us on the good list, and life will be simpler.

ENJOY THE RIDE

It's winter, and it's cold. There's no snow where I live in the middle of California, but people in other parts of the country are enjoying falling snow, playing in snowbanks, skating on frozen lakes, building snow men and making snow angels in their yards. Young athletes are working hard to perfect their sport in the hope of someday competing in an upcoming winter Olympics.

I ran across an old *Frank and Ernest* cartoon by Bob Thaves, that appeared in the paper during the winter Olympics, showing them bobsledding. They were comparing bobsledding to life. Ernest says, "Frank, a bobsled run is a lot like life. We start out with youthful energy, running as fast as we can. Later, we have to steer through curves that come at us. Then, if fortunate, we slow down in a smooth, controlled way, and enjoy the golden days." In the last frame of the cartoon strip, Frank and Ernest are out of the bobsled and Ernest says, "But I think bobsledding is most like life in that, with both, we should never forget to simply enjoy the ride."

This cartoon is a metaphor for life. In our youth, we work like mad to get ahead, setting up our place in life. Then, as we encounter snags or detours along the way, we have to concentrate on steering through those sidetracks—or curves—until, if we're lucky, we can slow down to a steady, peaceful pace. When we look back, we can appreciate the hard work, the smooth road, the challenges, and the restful times it took to get us to where we are.

Wherever you are in life, remember this: It's not the destination that matters, it's the journey. If you stay in the mindset of enjoying every part of the journey of life, the destination will take care of itself.

In fact, when we think about it, there really isn't a destination. Life just keeps going on. The show isn't over until the fat lady sings, and right now the fat lady is still putting on her makeup.

Enjoy the ride. Work hard, play hard, love deeply, and laugh often. Make the journey productive and share your good with others. If you relax, and remember that peace feels better than panic, your life will be simpler.

GLAD TIDINGS

So many Christmas and holiday cards relay a message of peace, joy, and glad tidings. What a wonderful gift this is to give your family and friends. This blessing is so profound that it carries over to people of all creeds, religions, beliefs, and even to those who don't adhere to any faith tradition. It simply says, peace and joy to me, peace and joy to my brother, peace and joy to all the world.

We find peace for ourselves by extending it others. Sharing peace with another confirms it in ourselves. There is a place deep within each of us that is at perfect peace always, and in that peace, we find joy.

We don't really have to strive to find peace; we let it find us. When we can simply sit in silence, making our self receptive to that peace, it will appear. In this silent time, if a noise or a disruptive thought comes to our attention, we don't let our mind grab onto it; we simply let it go. In this silence, we have no other purpose than to be still. We have no other goal right now but to say, "Peace be in me." When that peace comes to us, however briefly, we can add, "And peace be to all the world." Gently wish that kind of peace to all people. To feel that peace and to extend it to others is all we're here for. That's all that needs to be done, and it will be enough.

When we receive holiday greeting cards this season, let's not just lay them aside. Let's take the time to really *feel* the message of love, peace, joy, and glad tidings they offer. If we can do this at Christmastime, there's no reason we can't extend it throughout the year. Living these messages all year will make each day more joyful, and life will be simpler

TOUCH

With our five senses we can see, hear, smell, and taste, but there's some magic in the sense of touch. The touch of a hand of someone we love saying, "I'm here for you" or "You are not alone" brings untold comfort and healing. When our children were born, we memorized every part of their newborn anatomy by touching their velvet cheeks, caressing their sweet soft bodies, kissing their fuzzy little heads, and feeling their tiny fingers wrap around our thumb and not letting go.

As our children grow, we pick them up when they fall, pat their backs when they are fussy, feel their foreheads for a fever, and hug them any time we have a chance. The touch of a mother or father signifies security to a child, and it's been shown that preemies develop and grow faster if they are held.

Touching is an essential channel of communication, a brief reminder that we are social animals at our core. Remember the first time your high school crush held your hand and you just kind of melted on the spot? High-fives, fist-bumps, and back-slaps convey messages of friendship or agreement, and there's even a certain degree of intimacy in a handshake. A simple touch conveys so much. We can send and receive emotional signals like joy, love, tenderness, gratitude, or sympathy simply by touching. Touching is good both for the one touched and the one doing the touching. Even self-touching has a calming effect. Rubbing an arm, stroking our hair, and rubbing our hands together somehow makes us feel more comfortable.

Touching the blooms of rosemary or lilac bushes sends forth a wonderful, refreshing aroma that brings us closer to nature. There's nothing like walking barefoot in wet grass to make us feel free. Touch can also make a difference in the clothes we wear. A soft-feeling sweater or a silk blouse can enhance a feeling of self-confidence.

I am a consummate toucher. I touch those I love for no reason except to let them know I see, hear, and appreciate them. When I come across something new to me, touching helps me to understand it.

Even for those with diminished or no sensation of sight, sound, smell or taste, touch can teach them a lot and can make life more fulfilling.

The touch of paintbrushes on canvas brings about fascinating artistic work. The touch of damp clay inspires beautiful sculptures, and the touch of fingers on a piano produces great music. Touching the keys on my computer has made this book a reality.

CHRISTMAS TRUCE

Today is a holy day. It's a day when the world calls a halt to insanity and turns to divinity. The holiday season may have seemed chaotic up to now with all the shopping, decorating, baking, wrapping, partying, cleaning, and cooking, but it's time today to ease up on the chaos and remember the real reason for Christmas. This is the day we celebrate the birth of Jesus, a simple event that divinely changed the world forever.

Another event that changed this holy day during World War I was the so-called Christmas Truce of 1914. It was just five months after the outbreak of war in Europe when this wondrous event took place. Although asked by Pope Benedict XV, the warring countries refused to call a hiatus for the celebration of Christmas. The soldiers in the trenches, however, declared their own unofficial truce.

At first light on Christmas morning, some German soldiers came out of their trenches and called out "Merry Christmas" to Allied troops in their own languages. At first, the Allies suspected it was a trick. Then, seeing that the Germans were unarmed, they climbed out of their own trenches and shook hands with enemy soldiers. German and British troops exchanged presents of cigarettes and plum pudding and sang carols together. There is even documented proof that they joined together in a good-natured game of soccer. For that one day, troops on opposing sides came together, remembering that Christmas is a time of love, a time of joining in a single purpose, a time of celebration. Certainly, soldiers on the Western Front did not expect to celebrate on the battlefield, but even a world war could not destroy the Christmas spirit this day. There were future attempts at holiday cease-fires, but they were quashed by high-ranking officials threatening disciplinary action. This simple act demonstrated that beneath the brutal clash of weapons and the perceived differences in views and objectives, an underlying humanity exists between all people.

That humanity still exists, and we *can* call a halt to the insanity. We can be more like Jesus who lived simply and was gentle in his ways. He didn't need the trappings of kings, nor did he need to destroy those who didn't believe or live as he did. On this Christmas Day, let us live from the simplicity of an open heart, enjoy spending time with family and loved ones, and keep that simple love going after the day is over. Merry Christmas!

YOUR WEEK

The week between Christmas Day and New Year's Day is often as hectic as the days before Christmas. With half-price sales at stores getting rid of old merchandise to make room for new, and everything Christmas-related at 60 to 80 percent discounts, people rush around to load up on what they think they need at the best bargains. I was once one of those people. I bought next-years cards, gift wrappings, and decorations the day after Christmas. Through the years, however, I didn't always use all I had, and ended up with lots of cards, gift wrappings, and decorations left over. When I decided to let life be simple, I stopped doing that and took time to bask in the joy that Christmas Day had been with family, food, and fun. I found that, even without having to push my way through crowded stores, I was never without what I needed for the next Christmas.

I've discovered I can use this week for productive endeavors like purging files in my office, wrapping up loose ends, envisioning direction for the new year, and connecting with friends I haven't seen or talked with for a while.

This is a good time to think of people in our life who have supported us in some way and reaching out to them with a short phone call or an e-mail. Delivering your appreciation, acknowledging them for the good they have given you, even giving a small compliment can bestow happiness to another.

This week is also a good time to acknowledge our own accomplishments and the progress we've made during the year. Maybe we've advanced more than we realize, and we can celebrate that. Some wise person once said, *you are always doing better than you think you are.* This is a good week to recognize that so we can continue to move forward with confidence.

The time after the busyness of Christmas can be a time for reflection. It can be precious and meaningful if we choose. When we focus on the good of the past year, we will attract even more good going into the new one.

MIND POWER

The picturing power of the mind is one of the greatest powers we have. Picturing something we want and seeing it active in our life can actually bring it about. I know a young boy who wanted a motorized go-kart for Christmas. The boy's parents knew they couldn't fit the hefty price of that go-kart into their budget, so they tried to gently let the boy know that he probably wouldn't be getting it. But this didn't stop the boy. He dreamed of that go-kart, he pretended to drive it around the yard, he even cleaned out a space for it in the garage. He *knew* he was going to get that go-kart for Christmas and he never stopped believing that it would be his.

About two weeks before Christmas, when the family was out together, the boy asked to go to the store where they'd seen the go-kart, hoping it might be on sale. It *was* on sale, but the price was still $80 more than the parents had been able to scrape together. As they looked at the go-kart, and the boy sat on it, pretending to drive, another customer approached the parents saying he'd seen this same go-kart on sale at another store for $80 less. The happy ending to this story is that the parents were able to buy the go-kart at the lower price, and the boy found that what he'd set his mind on having was there in front of the small tree on Christmas morning.

This is just one of countless stories proving the power of the mind. When we really want something or some outcome, and we set our mind to it—acting like it's ours already, experiencing the feeling of having it, really knowing it will come to us by the power of attraction—it will be ours.

When I moved back to California from Canada, I needed to buy a house. I figured I'd get one comparable to the one I'd sold before I left, but when I drove around, looking, I found that a house I'd admired for a long time was for sale. I knew it was going to cost a lot more than I'd planned to spend but asked the Realtor to let me see it anyway. When I went inside, I immediately felt at home. I experienced the feeling of living in that house, and I *knew* it was meant to be mine. Not knowing how I'd manage the payments, I bought the house, anyway. Believing in the power of mind over matter, I knew I'd be okay. And I am okay, still living in that house today.

The mind's power goes beyond simply wanting or hoping. *Believing* something with the power of your mind can make it a reality.

THE WHOLE PICTURE

In a strange dream, someone came to me asking for help. In the dream, I just wanted to be left alone to sleep, but I agreed to talk to this person. She brought in a man who was very distressed, and a whole lot of other people came, too. Then she told me that this large group of people was judging the man and causing him pain. I stopped her before she could tell me what they were judging him for because I didn't need to know. I only needed to know that those people couldn't sit in judgment of this poor, distressed man because they didn't know the whole picture. I told them that, and they all left, and that was the end of the dream.

When I woke up, I was reminded of the lesson in *A Course in Miracles* that states, *Today I will judge nothing that occurs.* We can't really judge anything or anyone. We can have opinions based on what we observe, but we can't judge what's right or what's wrong because our observation is limited. We can't see the whole picture.

Letting go of judgment is simply learning to be honest with ourselves, knowing that to judge accurately, we would have to be aware of many things that are beyond our knowledge. We would have to know the *whole picture*, not just what our limited perception is telling us. If we can't do that, any judgment we make is little more than a wild guess. When we hear other people judging a person or situation, we can say, "Thanks for sharing," but we don't need to agree with them because their experience of the person or situation may be very different from our own. We can't judge because we are not "all knowing." Only God has that distinction.

We don't realize how much judging we do every day. When we take a first bite of food, we judge it tasty or not. When we see sunshine, we judge the day as good, and when we see rain, we judge it as miserable weather. But to a farmer, a rainy day can be a good day. We can watch ourselves throughout the day. When we feel judgment about something or someone, we can think again. If we observe someone acting in a way we deem inappropriate, we can remember there is something we don't know about that person. When we're judging, we're putting our own meaning on what we observe, and we aren't seeing the whole picture.

Lack of judgment doesn't mean lack of discernment; we need to keep ourself safe and well. But when we can look at our life, and the people in it, without unnecessary judgment, life does become simpler.

FREE TO BE ME

You, and everyone you know, are free! You are beloved creations of God with the ability to choose your own direction. When you let go of comparing yourself to others and stop trying to be something you are not, you are set free to be exactly as you are.

You may be feeling unsettled, waiting for your life to begin or to meet some worldly standard, but every creature on Earth is beautiful and free just as it is—and so are you! When you know this, and live with that knowledge, your possibilities are endless.

A feeling of freedom expands our appreciation of who we are and the boundless blessings in our life. The Bible describes this freedom well in the Song of Solomon. "For lo, the winter is past, the rain is over and gone. The flowers appear on the earth; the time of singing has come, and the voice of the turtledove is heard in our land." (Song 2:11-12). Just as we can choose the darkness of winter, we can also choose the brightness of spring. The gentle freedom of flowers, joyful singing, and the soothing coo of the dove—what greater feeling of freedom is there than this?

Freedom releases us from any feelings of guilt or shame. As a child of God, we are empowered, we are unlimited. We are free to release attachments to the past and to make new choices in the present. We are free to love ourselves, and to allow ourselves to reach our divine potential. We are free to release outer circumstances or inner desires that are holding us back, and to turn to God as our constant guide and companion.

Freedom is a choice. We are free to be carefree and joyful. We have the power to choose our attitude toward life. We are free to let go of worry and concern and to embrace joy. Regardless of age, we are free to be like a child—adventurous, alive, alert, and passionate about life.

It's said that "If you love something, set it free." If we love ourself enough to set ourself free from any notions that we are not enough, and to step into the uniqueness of who we are, we will find freedom. If we love ourself enough to release anything that is keeping us from being authentic, we will find the peace of freedom, and our life will be simple.

MAKE YOUR DAY

Every day, you wake up and make up your mind to what the day will be like for you. With every contact you make with others throughout the day, you determine the experience of that encounter. *You* are in control, whether you know it or not, whether you want it or not. *You* decide how you will feel and how you will be treated.

When you feel pain or suffering, somewhere in your mind, you think you deserve it. You might say, "What did I do to deserve this?" The answer to that questions is, you *thought* about it. There are people who seem to enjoy their pain, and in some way think suffering is good for them, so they send out invitations to thoughts of suffering and loss, and by golly, they come!

When we make up our minds to have a good, peaceful, productive day, that's what we'll have. Our thoughts have power, and what we *think* will come to us. Ultimately, *we* make up our minds whether to be happy or not. Only *we* have the power to create peace or pain for ourselves. We are in charge. We can make the most of every day and every situation. We *deserve* to be comfortable and at peace every day.

We think we learn through trials, and we do. Sometimes we think if we were to simply be happy, we would miss something. Some of us think that something in our past actions, or even something missing in our personality proves that we don't deserve to be happy. But the truth is, nothing is missing in us. We lack nothing. When we learn—and know—that we are innocent and complete, just as we are, we have no further reason to think such thoughts. We can, instead, sing the song of the joy we feel, of the freedom from pain, grief, and suffering. Our mind has complete power to create the experience of life that we want and that we deserve, and ultimately, we make up our mind whether to be happy or not.

Let's choose to create joy, to invite only goodness into our life. If we feel mistreated or victimized by any person or situation, we can make up our mind to either do what we can to change the circumstances in a kind and loving way, or to simply get away from them.

Pain is sometimes inevitable but can be manageable. Suffering, however, is always optional and lasts as long as we allow it. Pain is not fun. Joy is, so let's be joyful—even in the face of pain.

Today and every day, don't just *have* a good day, *make* a good day. As you embark on the New Year, remember to keep life simple and *make every day a good day*.

MORNING PAGES

I started keeping a daily journal in 1997. This activity was prompted by a workshop I attended using the book *The Artist's Way* by Julia Cameron. The book was written to help people discover artistic creativity with exercises geared toward gaining self-confidence by harnessing creative talents and skills.

One of these exercises was *Morning Pages*. We were to write three pages every day, not as a diary of what was happening, but as a documentation of *feelings* about what was happening. I started out writing about the colors of the sunrise, the way light played on tree leaves and the peaceful feeling that gave me. As time went on, I wrote about my personal journey of discovery, of focusing on the positive, and I've stayed, and grown, on that journey by journaling.

It happens that when I started Morning Pages was the time my parents had come to live with me, and I wrote a lot about frustrations and the hard work of their care, all overshadowed by the deep love I felt for them. I also wrote about the heartache at watching their decline, and the sadness at their passing. The day my mother died, my entire family was at my house. Each grandchild, great-grandchild, and even one great-great-grandchild took their turn telling her goodbye, then were happily at play in the yard as she took her last breath. It was such a beautiful reminder of the cycle of life, hearing the sound of children at play as she set off on her final journey.

I've continued to journal all these years. What journaling has done for me, it can do for you if you care to give it a try. As I write, I find things to be grateful for, and I give thanks. I've kept the journaling positive. Even when things haven't gone well, I've always kept my heart open and looked at situations and circumstances from a positive point of view. I find there is good in everything and that keeping a positive outlook helps to discover that good. Writing about how I feel about things helps me see the good more easily.

At the end of each year, I like to read through the year's pages. When I do, I see that when I've had problems that seemed hard to solve, I've found solutions simply by putting the difficulty down on paper. As I write, answers come.

May the year about to start bring you peace, joy, and happiness. May you find solutions through journaling. May you create a beautiful and simple life. May you have a Happy New Year!

EPILOGUE

I've finished writing pages for this book now, but I haven't stopped internalizing inspiration from things I read, or hear, or see, things I find meaning and wisdom in. I will choose moments of happiness, even in small doses, and enjoy them while they last. I won't worry about whether or not people approve of me; I will just love them. I will *be* love. It's that simple

Letting life be simple is an on-going life experience. When we look for the good, we will find it. When we give love, we will get love in return. When we stay calm, our life will be calm. It all happens in our thinking, in our perceptions, in our responses, and in our choices. It will ultimately determine how we feel about our self and everyone else.

Life *is* simple, if we let it be!

———

Now that you've finished the book, try going back to the beginning and start over. You might get a whole new meaning from the messages because you are now in a more evolved place in consciousness.

CPSIA information can be obtained
at www.ICGtesting.com
Printed in the USA
BVHW081100110220
572026BV00008B/1137

9 780986 211324